THE TRIUMPH
OF FEAR

THE TRIUMPH OF FEAR

Domestic Surveillance and Political Repression from McKinley to Eisenhower

PATRICK G. EDDINGTON

GEORGETOWN UNIVERSITY PRESS / WASHINGTON, DC

© 2025 Georgetown University Press. All rights reserved. No part of this book may be reproduced or utilized in any form or by any means, electronic or mechanical, including photocopying and recording, or by any information storage and retrieval system, without permission in writing from the publisher.

The publisher is not responsible for third-party websites or their content. URL links were active at time of publication.

Library of Congress Cataloging-in-Publication Data

Names: Eddington, Patrick G., author.
Title: The triumph of fear : domestic surveillance and political repression from McKinley to Eisenhower / Patrick G. Eddington.
Description: Washington, DC : Georgetown University Press, 2025. | Includes bibliographical references and index.
Identifiers: LCCN 2024014054 (print) | LCCN 2024014055 (ebook) | ISBN 9781647125448 (hardcover) | ISBN 9781647125455 (paperback) | ISBN 9781647125462 (ebook)
Subjects: LCSH: Espionage—United States—History. | Domestic intelligence—United States—History. | Intelligence service—United States—History. | Political persecution—United States—History. | Internal security—Political aspects—United States.
Classification: LCC JK468.I6 E286 2025 (print) | LCC JK468.I6 (ebook) | DDC 327.1273009—dc23/eng/20241203

LC record available at https://lccn.loc.gov/2024014054
LC ebook record available at https://lccn.loc.gov/2024014055

26 25   9 8 7 6 5 4 3 2   First printing

Cover design by Jim Keller
Interior design by Westchester Publishing Services

To Mr. Charles Beecher Sheeley, Dr. David B. Adams, PhD,
Dr. Meredith L. Adams, PhD, and Dr. David Heinlein, PhD,
for putting me on the path of knowledge, for their endless wisdom,
their intellectual integrity, and above all, their friendship.

CONTENTS

List of Photographs   ix

Acknowledgments   xi

List of Abbreviations and Acronyms   xv

Introduction   xix

1   "With Care, Secrecy, and Dispatch": 1893–1914   1

2   "Disloyal Utterances": 1914–1932   47

3   "The Spirit of the Concentration Camp": 1933–1941   92

4   "We Are Developing a Gestapo in This Country and It Frightens Me": 1941–1945   145

5   "One Nation Divided, with Fear and Insecurity for All": 1945–1952   217

6   "Is This Idolatry of Security?": 1953–1961   285

Conclusion   349

Bibliography   357

Index   363

About the Author   379

PHOTOGRAPHS

1.1 President Theodore Roosevelt 27

1.2 Attorney General Charles Bonaparte 30

2.1 President Woodrow Wilson 67

2.2 J. Edgar Hoover 71

3.1 Lemuel Schofield, Francis Biddle, and Robert Jackson 121

3.2 President Franklin Delano Roosevelt 126

3.3 Attorney General Robert Jackson 127

5.1 Representative John Rankin (D-MS) 226

6.1 President Dwight Eisenhower 287

6.2 Attorney General Herbert Brownell 294

6.3 Senator Harry Cain (R-WA) 314

ACKNOWLEDGMENTS

Despite the somewhat grim subject matter, this project has been the greatest journey of discovery in my life. Along the way, I've benefited from the help and wise counsel of a number of people.

The Cato Institute's vice president for policy, Gene Healy, suggested to me in 2015 that it was time for me to write another book. His encouragement and support made possible the many field research trips to multiple presidential libraries and other archival centers that were crucial to this project. Cato's vice president for criminal justice (and my immediate current boss), Clark Neily, has also been strongly supportive of this project. Gene and another Cato colleague, Aaron Steelman, provided invaluable peer review and editorial recommendations.

Staff at the National Archives (Washington, D.C., and College Park, Maryland) who deserve special recognition are Haley Maynard, Tom McAnear, Eric Van Slander, Alicia Henneberry, Nathaniel Patch, Amanda Weimer, Amy Reytar, Rick Peuser, Adam Berenbak, and Mark Murphy.

William Greene at the National Archives at San Bruno, California, was a life saver in helping me find some key Navy files from World War II.

Franklin D. Roosevelt Library staffers Dara Baker and Pat Fahy pointed me to some specific collections and documents that I might otherwise have missed.

Harry S. Truman Library staffers Randy Sowell, Robert Beebe, and Sam Rushay were invariably helpful, with Randy providing critical background on the Corcoran wiretapping episode.

At the Eisenhower Library, Michelle Kopfer ably helped me navigate the Mandatory Declassification Review submission process.

As I practically lived at the Library of Congress's Madison Building for literally months at a time, I got to know almost the entire Manuscript Reading Room staff. Ryan Reft, Pat Kerwin, Margaret McAleer, Edie Sandler, Loretta Deaver, Lara Szypszak, and Bruce Kirby are among the most knowledgeable and delightful archival specialists in any branch of the federal government.

xii ACKNOWLEDGMENTS

At New York University's Tamiment Library, Danielle Nista, and Allison Chomet ensured I was able to go through the *National Lawyers Guild v. Attorney General* collection.

At the University of Mississippi, Political Papers Archivist and Associate Professor Dr. Leigh McWhite granted me early access to the papers of the late Rep. John Rankin.

My editor, Don Jacobs of Georgetown University Press, has been nothing less than a saint. He patiently put up with my repeated requests for word count increases, and once the COVID pandemic made completing a single book an impossibility in anything like a reasonable time, he agreed to turn it into a two-book project. I will never be able to repay him for his flexibility, patience, and unflagging support for this endeavor.

A number of Cato colleagues provided helpful feedback on the draft manuscript, and I will never be able to thank enough Professor Jack Goldsmith, former head of the Department of Justice's Office of Legal Counsel and Learned Hand Professor of Law at Harvard University, for his invaluable comments and suggestions on the draft.

Journalist Tom Mueller also provided valuable feedback on several chapters.

Finally, the last word of thanks goes to my wife, Robin, who held down the fort during my many out-of-town research trips and tolerated her husband's obsession with working on this book day and night, including weekends, for over five years. I now understand clearly what's meant by the phrase "the better half."

Any errors of fact or omission in this work are mine alone.

Finally, a statement on what I consider to be the completely unconstitutional Supreme Court ruling in *Snepp v. U.S.* (444 U.S. 507 (1980)) that the CIA does, in fact, have the right to review manuscripts of former employees like myself before publication, despite such a prior restraint being clearly contrary to the letter of the First Amendment.

In the *Snepp* case, the CIA argued that former CIA Directorate of Operations officer Frank Snepp had violated his nondisclosure agreement with the agency by publishing a book without allowing the CIA to review it first to determine if it contained classified material. Snepp's book was completely unclassified; he had been careful in writing it to ensure no sensitive sources or methods were compromised. For CIA officials, that was not the point. Snepp had violated his nondisclosure agreement; he was guilty of a breach of contract. The Court did not even bother to hear oral arguments from either side, instead ruling in the agency's favor outright.

ACKNOWLEDGMENTS   xiii

As no challenge to the *Snepp* decision has made it back to the Supreme Court for a reexamination of the constitutionality of the prepublication (read prior restraint) system now employed by the CIA and other national security–related agencies and departments, this author was bound by existing precedent to submit the book you are about to read for said prior restraint review to the CIA. It never has, and does not now, contain any classified information.

ABBREVIATIONS AND ACRONYMS

ACLU	American Civil Liberties Union
ADL	Anti-Defamation League
AFC	America First Committee
AFL	American Federation of Labor
AG	Attorney General
AGLOSO	Attorney General's List of Subversive Organizations
APL	American Protective League
AUAM	American Union Against Militarism
BBB	Better Business Bureau
BEF	Bonus Expeditionary Force or British Expeditionary Force
BOI	Bureau of Investigation
CBP	Charles Bonaparte papers
CF	Confidential file
CI	Counterintelligence
CIA	Central Intelligence Agency
CIO	Congress of Industrial Organizations
COINTELPRO	Counterintelligence Program
COMINFIL	Communist Infiltration
CPI	Committee on Public Information
CSC	Civil Service Commission
CWIRC	Commission on Wartime Relocation and Internment of Civilians
DAR	Daughters of the American Revolution
DDEL	Dwight D. Eisenhower Library
DIO	District Intelligence Officer
DOD	Department of Defense
DOJ	Department of Justice
DOT	Department of the Treasury
EO	Executive Order
FBI	Federal Bureau of Investigation

xvi ABBREVIATIONS AND ACRONYMS

FCA	Food and Fuel Control Act
FCC	Federal Communication Commission
FDRL	Franklin Delano Roosevelt Library
G-2	Army Intelligence element at the division or higher level
GPO	Government Printing Office
HHL	Herbert Hoover Library
HSTL	Harry S. Truman Library
HUAC	House Un-American Activities Committee
HUMINT	Human Intelligence
IIC	Interdepartmental Intelligence Conference
IJN	Imperial Japanese Navy
INS	Immigration and Naturalization Service
IWW	Industrial Workers of the World
JACL	Japanese American Citizens League
JAG	Judge Advocate General
JDP	Josephus Daniels Papers
LOC	Library of Congress
LOCCA	Library of Congress Chronicling America website
MAR	McKinley Assassination Records
MID	Military Intelligence Division
NAACP	National Association for the Advancement of Colored People
NBC	National Broadcasting Company
NCAHUAC	National Committee to Abolish the House Un-American Activities Committee
NCLB	National Civil Liberties Bureau
ND	Naval District
NKVD	Soviet civilian intelligence and espionage service
NNC	National Negro Congress
NSA	National Security Agency
NSC	National Security Council
NSCID	National Security Council Intelligence Directive
NYPD	New York Police Department
OF	Official file
OGPU	Soviet secret police (predecessor to NKVD)
ONI	Office of Naval Intelligence
PPF	President's Personal File
PSF	President's Secretary's File
RG	National Archives Record Group

ABBREVIATIONS AND ACRONYMS   xvii

SACB   Subversive Activities Control Board
SHAMROCK   NSA telegram/cable collection program
SIGINT   Signals intelligence
SISS   Senate Internal Security Subcommittee
SSD   Secret Service Division
SWP   Socialist Workers Party
TRP   Theodore Roosevelt papers
TWEA   Trading with the Enemy Act
UERMW   United Electrical, Radio and Machine Workers
UMW   United Mine Workers
VFW   Veterans of Foreign Wars
WFM   Western Federation of Miners
WHCF   White House Central Files
WILPF   Women's International League for Peace and Freedom
WRA   War Relocation Authority
WTB   War Trade Board
WTI   War Trade Intelligence
WWP   Woodrow Wilson papers

INTRODUCTION

Organized governments have existed for over five millennia, and along with them, some type of surveillance capability to keep an eye out for potential external threats or help achieve victory in war. By the time of Julius Caesar, Rome's military and political intelligence capabilities were well-developed, strongly supported by Romans generally, and frequently very effective.[1] And while rulers in the ancient world through at least the early Middle Ages employed spies domestically against specific enemies or groups, such efforts were generally small and focused on rival religious or political elites viewed as a threat to those holding power, usually hereditary monarchs. Those domestic spying and political infiltration operations generally lacked the kind of centralized control that we see in modern governmental bureaucracies.[2] Even so, the deliberate use of such methods set a precedent, one that was imported from England to its American colonies.

Domestic surveillance and political repression have been a regular feature of American life since shortly after the first British political castoffs arrived in the early seventeenth century. There is a savage irony in the fact that those white English-speaking settlers, many of whom fled Britain because of political and religious surveillance and persecution, would themselves become oppressors. This book is an examination of how their descendants went on to create the modern American surveillance state.

As noted earlier, various types of polities have, over the centuries, developed relatively sophisticated means of foreign intelligence gathering designed to forestall a surprise attack, or failing that, develop the necessary information to see a conflict through to a victorious conclusion. Among modern nation states, such intelligence gathering in peace and war is a well settled and accepted practice. In European democracies and the American republic, however, a legally binding distinction between lawful and unlawful *domestic* surveillance has been drawn.

In the American context, that line has been drawn via the First and Fourth Amendments to the Constitution, along with related federal court decisions that have struck down or otherwise outlawed practices by which the intelligence and law enforcement machinery of the state can be turned

xix

xx INTRODUCTION

inward to track, harass, or even destroy civil society organizations and the lives of those lawfully participating in the political process. Yet as we shall see, those legal safeguards are often no match for the raw political power exercised by government officials, frequently with the acquiescence or outright support of Congress and federal courts in times of war or alleged national emergencies.

The federal government's penchant for surveilling, penetrating, and actively subverting domestic political activities by individuals and groups spans periods of peace and war over more than a century. In contemplating this phenomenon, some obvious questions come to mind: How and why did officials in the executive branch and Congress come to believe that such a system was needed in an ostensibly democratic republic? What factors— internal and external—made possible the growth in size and power of the federal bureaucracy that carries out this surveillance to this day? Why have federal courts too often allowed or even abetted the effective evisceration of American's First and Fourth Amendment rights?

An examination of the existing historical record makes clear that the driving force behind these developments was fear—on the part of executive branch officials, members of Congress, and those on the federal bench—fear that challenges to existing political, economic, or social paradigms would alter the country in ways that would disempower those who benefited from the status quo. And it was a fear that would lead to the employment of extra-constitutional means to try to suppress or otherwise defeat those seeking to reform an American political system that marginalized or excluded whole segments of the population from achieving political, economic, and social parity with those in power.

A common refrain heard from those skeptical of the threat of federal government surveillance and related political repression often goes something like this: *I don't care if the FBI is keeping an eye on me because I have nothing to hide.* As the chapters that follow will show, it has never been a question of what a US citizen does or does not have to hide, but a question of whether federal law enforcement and intelligence agents *believe* you have done or are doing something that is deemed a threat to the prevailing political and economic order, even on the basis of scant, contradictory, or no plausible evidence.

Edward Snowden's explosive revelations of mass, warrantless government electronic surveillance in 2013 were among the most significant in a series of episodes dating back decades. Yet the focus on mass telephone and internet surveillance has obscured the larger issue: the *mentality* behind not only domestic surveillance but also more far-reaching actions designed

INTRODUCTION   xxi

in many cases to actually undermine, if not destroy, domestic civil society groups and movements that very publicly and forcefully challenge the prevailing political paradigm.

Using a classic chronological historical narrative format and drawing on literally hundreds of thousands of pages of declassified federal records, congressional hearings and reports, first-person participant accounts, and relevant secondary sources, this book will attempt answer the questions posed previously. It will also help the reader understand why the creation and rise of the American surveillance state has been and remains a mortal threat to individual liberty and the very foundations of the Republic, including the constitutional rights of you, the reader.

This volume covers in detail, though not exhaustively, events taking place from just after the Spanish-American War to the dawn of the Kennedy era, a more than 60-year time frame in which the laws, organizational structures, and elite attitudes about domestic surveillance and related political repression were formed and made manifest. The result was not distinct episodes of political surveillance and repression but a continuum of such activity stretching over a century. During the period covered by this book, a generally white, Protestant, male political and economic elite, devoted to a particular political and economic vision, controlled the federal government. Any individual or group outside of that elite who sought to challenge that established paradigm was viewed as a mortal threat and almost invariably found themselves targeted for federal government surveillance, and often, related political repression.

Fear of political, economic, or social change that might disrupt or fundamentally alter the long-standing primacy of this elite and the institutions it had created motivated the government's use of illegal surveillance, legal assaults on the press, and covert disruption operations aimed at discrediting, silencing, or even destroying the professional and personal lives of those seeking truly equal rights for racial or religious minorities and women or otherwise seeking to alter federal policies they deemed harmful.

The book you now hold is a historical chronicle of how that reactionary, zero-sum-game mindset has caused real pain, misery, and deprivation of rights for countless Americans through the use of the repressive tools in question, and it all starts with unconstitutional surveillance designed to identify and track those deemed a political, versus criminal, threat to the established order.

For those on the receiving end of this surveillance or political repression, the realization that they were being targeted for activities that were clearly constitutionally protected, or for simply being who they were (e.g., Japanese

Americans), was a faith-shattering experience vis-à-vis the federal government and its claims of "liberty and justice for all" under the Constitution.

Those of us far removed from the times covered in this account can find it difficult to comprehend the sense of dread and terror that a federal employee felt at being targeted for a so-called loyalty investigation, or the fright and constant insecurity that Japanese Americans experienced after being herded into concentration camps, or the stomach-churning panic felt by someone who received a subpoena from the infamous House Un-American Activities Committee after being publicly accused by the same of being a communist. During the period covered by this narrative, that fear-based mentality exhibited by federal officials in all three branches of government was pervasive, toxic, and for its targets, life altering.

Indeed, the mentality that has animated federal surveillance and political repression has deep historical roots that predate the events described in this work.

For Black Africans kidnapped into slavery and transshipped to the American colonies, the loss of their freedom also involved a form of coercive, collective surveillance, rendition, and re-enslavement (for those who managed to escape in the first place) via the infamous "slave patrols."[3] For indigenous people in or near Britain's American colonies, the new arrivals' expansion came at the natives' expense—in lives and territory lost.[4] The eventual creation of Indian reservations by the subsequently independent United States was simply the final step in a form of state-sponsored control and forced assimilation.

Yet in the period between the enslavement of Black Africans by American colonists and the expulsion of the Cherokee from what would become the southeast United States, a new form of organized political repression—one pitting white Americans against each other—emerged.

Just a decade after the ratification of the Constitution, the Federalist-controlled Congress and the Adams administration gave the country the infamous Alien and Sedition Acts. Recent scholarship suggests that the number of Republican newspapers targeted for prosecution under the acts was far larger than previously believed.[5] Much of the Federalist legislative and punitive legal action was explicitly designed by the Federalists to, in Jefferson's words, "shew they mean to pay no respect" to the Constitution.[6] The subsequent reaction against, and repeal or expiration of, the Alien and Sedition Acts during Jefferson's presidency has generally been heralded as a victory for the Bill of Rights. In reality, what it demonstrated was exactly how much damage to individuals and organizations (in this case, opposition

INTRODUCTION   xxiii

news outlets) could be done by the newly created central government of the United States.

This constitutional republic with its far more centralized power structure—including a powerful chief executive via Article II of the Constitution—showed in the Alien and Sedition Act episode that white political factions were capable of using that power against each other in the same way that power had been used against enslaved Blacks and native peoples. An even more consequential political confrontation, again primarily between white political factions, would further alter the course of US history.

The abolitionist movement and the often violent backlash it sparked among supporters of slavery foreshadowed the most destructive domestic use of federal coercive power in the then-short history of the American republic. In 1835, Jackson administration Postmaster General Amos Kendall's proposed federal legislation to ban abolitionist literature (primarily produced by white, northern abolitionists) from the mails after shipments of the material to the South led to white mob violence against some post office locations.[7] Twenty-five years later, the war of words became a civil war on battlefields from Manassas to Vicksburg and almost countless points in between.

Lincoln's suspension of habeas corpus and other draconian measures (including torture, in some cases[8]) during the Civil War were taken, ultimately, in the service of giving an enslaved population its physical freedom. The Lincoln administration's wartime actions were also precedents, ones that would be invoked by his successors in the decades that followed to justify extraordinary measures in the name of securing the nation.[9]

As post-Civil War events showed, freed Black people endured a multigenerational form of political guerilla warfare by a southern white supremacist establishment that used state laws—and the terror of the paramilitary Ku Klux Klan—to deny African Americans genuine *political* freedom. In response, President Grant asked for and got from Congress in April 1871 the Ku Klux Klan Act, which allowed Grant to suspend habeas corpus and employ federal troops to hunt down, arrest, and if necessary kill KKK members. He also employed the relatively new Secret Service to conduct surveillance and disruption operations against the Klan, in some cases leading to acts of torture by Secret Service personnel.[10]

That the Klan was populated with violent, bigoted members who merited arrest and jail time for their crimes is beyond dispute. The collusion between state and local law enforcement officials and Klan elements in several former Confederate states also meant that the beatings and murder of Black

xxiv INTRODUCTION

people—including Black Republicans—ensured the victims never received justice from local or state authorities. For those reasons alone, Grant felt the need to act decisively against the Klan.

But the employment of blanket surveillance, suspension of habeas corpus, torture, and other odious tactics by the federal government against a politically disfavored group was a Rubicon moment, representing the institutionalization of coercive, violent state action against a domestic movement and its adherents. Tactics that were used against Klan members would subsequently be used against others deemed a threat to the prevailing political order. A key factor that would accelerate that process was the rise of pan-national political, economic, and social movements that spread from Europe to America in the decades following the Civil War. Even as the abolitionists were gaining political and social influence in the 1840s and 1850s, aborted political and social revolutions in Europe gave rise to the new political philosophies of anarchism, socialism, and communism. Each represented a direct, and potentially lethal, challenge to the prevailing free-market, private-property-centric political and economic system of the United States.

By the late 1880s, anarchist and socialist clubs, newspapers, and the like could be found in many major American cities. The appeal of socialist and even communist concepts spread among a significant segment of the American labor force, often leading to violence with major businesses, who invariably called up either hired security, local police, or a combination of the two to combat strikes and related labor unrest and violence. The Chicago Haymarket bombing incident in May 1886 was a turning point, leading to executions of alleged anarchist bombers and a crushing national crackdown on socialist or communist-influenced labor groups.[11] Yet no amount of state-sponsored violence could stamp out the radical ideas originating in Europe from finding at least some fertile ground among American workers, public intellectuals, and others.

Just as Enlightenment-era ideas had motivated Jefferson, Washington, and other colonial leaders to start a revolution for independence from the British crown, the ideas of Karl Marx, Friedrich Engels, Mikhail Bakunin, Peter Kropotkin, Errico Malatesta, and John Turner would motivate the likes of Alexander Berkman, Emma Goldman, and other American or American immigrant anarchists, socialists, and communists to seek a radical transformation of American society, economics, and politics.

Prior to the Haymarket incident, federal authorities had treated the growing anarchist and socialist political movements as primarily a state and local problem. No longer.

INTRODUCTION   xxv

By the end of the nineteenth century, the US Secret Service, which heretofore had largely been confined to chasing counterfeiters, became the first federal law enforcement agency to engage in surveillance and political repression targeting anarchists, and later, socialists and communists. And as the first chapter that follows will show, it would, in the hands of a powerful and determined Theodore Roosevelt, set precedents, as well as organizational patterns of behavior, that ushered in an era of sustained surveillance and political repression that has impacted millions of individuals and thousands of domestic civil society organizations—representing multiple ethnicities, religions, genders, and political movements—to this day.

Over the last several decades, a number of authors have looked at slices of this phenomenon.

The late Theodore Kornweibel, Jr. explored federal surveillance and repression against African Americans in the post-World War I period in his excellent *"Seeing Red": Federal Campaigns against Black Militancy, 1919–1925.*[12] Joan Jensen's *Army Surveillance in America, 1775–1980* is required reading for anyone seeking to understand the scope of US Army surveillance and political repression operations from the Revolutionary War through the Vietnam War.[13] The late Athan Theoharis's works on the FBI are too numerous to mention here, but perhaps the most accessible is his *The FBI and American Democracy: A Brief Critical History.*[14] And while there have been many biographies of the late FBI Director J. Edgar Hoover, none can compare to Beverly Gage's amazing *G-Man: J. Edgar Hoover and the Making of the American Century.*[15] For those interested in the development of key electronic surveillance technologies over the last hundred years or so, Brian Hochman's *The Listeners: A History of Wiretapping in the United States* is very much worth your time.[16]

The works listed, and still more too numerous to list here, all represent significant contributions to our understanding of how destructive to individual lives and liberties federal surveillance and political repression have been for most of the existence of the American republic. But as noted previously, they tell only selective parts of the story.

When I embarked on this project, I found only one book written at the scale I had in mind: Robert Justin Goldstein's *Political Repression in Modern America: From 1870 to 1976*, originally published in 1978 and reissued in 2001.[17]

Goldstein's work differs from mine in several important ways: He relied almost exclusively on secondary sources, and his narrative begins 30 years before mine, focused on private security and surveillance operations targeting organized labor. Naturally, Goldstein covers more than industry-labor

xxvi INTRODUCTION

disputes in the book, but those confrontations definitely dominate his work. In contrast, my work covers a far greater range of the targets of federal surveillance power and related political repression, whether by race, gender, or political ideology. I also cover the interactions between the key players—the executive branch, Congress, the federal courts, and civil society organizations—in a more holistic manner than Goldstein. Even so, his book certainly served as the primary inspiration for my own, as I feel that the subject is long overdue for the kind of treatment Goldstein provided decades ago.

Utilizing primary source materials (many not previously examined by or available to other researchers or investigators, including the Church Committee) as well as secondary sources, *The Triumph of Fear* traces the phenomenon of federal surveillance and political repression from its inception in the early twentieth century through the end of the Eisenhower presidency. The book demonstrates how the rise and growth of national or pan-national movements sparked a federal response that led to the creation or expansion of key federal national security institutions and their operating practices against domestic political dissidents and organizations. The role of Congress in enabling the growth of both the mentality of and the legal and technological tools used by federal entities involved in domestic surveillance and political subversion is a key theme woven throughout the narrative. Also integral to the account is an examination of key federal court cases that have enabled executive branch secrecy, surveillance, and political repression. Finally, the book sums up the consequences—human, legal, and political—of the massive expansion of the federal domestic surveillance bureaucracy and offers a preview of the further growth of the surveillance state in response to the tectonic social and political changes that rocked the country from the Kennedy era onward.

One further note. The reader will not generally see references to "a right to privacy" or similar formulations in this manuscript. The reason is that outside of a traditional Fourth Amendment context, the concept of a generalized "right to privacy" did not emerge as a major legal and public policy issue until the mid-1960s, well after the end date of this particular work.

Finally, with respect to the "how" of surveillance and repression during the period covered by this book, where a specific surveillance technique or technology is actually mentioned in the source documents involving a given episode that I describe, I have so named that technique or technology (i.e., dictaphone, microphone, wiretap, etc.). Where the source material is unclear or otherwise vague on the exact means by which information was acquired on a target, I have refrained from speculation on that point unless

I have felt very confident that only one particular technique or technology could have been used to acquire the information in question.

NOTES

1. N. J. E. Austin and N. B. Rankov, *Exploratio: Military and Political Intelligence in the Roman World from the Second Punic War to the Battle of Adrianople* (London: Routledge, 1995).
2. Edward Higgs, *The Information State in England* (New York: Palgrave MacMillan, 2004).
3. Sally E. Hadden, *Slave Patrols: Law and Violence in Virginia and the Carolinas* (Cambridge: Harvard University Press, 2001).
4. Claudio Saunt, *Unworthy Republic: The Dispossession of Native Americans and the Road to Indian Territory* (New York: W.W. Norton & Company, 2020).
5. Wendell Bird, *Criminal Dissent: Prosecutions under the Alien and Sedition Acts* (Cambridge: Harvard University Press, 2020).
6. Bird, *Criminal Dissent*, 4.
7. Devin Leonard, *Neither Snow nor Rain: A History of the United States Postal Service*, Kindle ed. (New York: Grove Press, 2021), location 515.
8. Mark E. Neely, Jr., *The Fate of Liberty: Abraham Lincoln and Civil Liberties* (New York: Oxford University Press, 1991), 109–112.
9. Gene Healy, *The Cult of the Presidency: America's Dangerous Devotion to Executive Power* (Washington, DC: Cato Institute, 2008).
10. For an outstanding account of these events, see Charles Lane, *Freedom's Detective: The Secret Service, the Ku Klux Klan and the Man Who Masterminded America's First War on Terror* (Toronto: Hanover Square Press, 2019).
11. James Green, *Death in the Haymarket: A Story of Chicago, the First Labor Movement, and the Bombing that Divided Gilded Age America* (New York: Anchor Books/Random House, 2006).
12. Theodore Kornweibel Jr., *"Seeing Red": Federal Campaigns against Black Militancy, 1919–1925* (Bloomington: Indiana University Press, 1998).
13. Joan M. Jensen, *Army Surveillance in America, 1775–1980* (New Haven: Yale University Press, 1991).
14. Athan Theoharis, *The FBI and American Democracy: A Brief Critical History* (Lawrence: University Press of Kansas, 2004).
15. Beverly Gage, *G-Man: J. Edgar Hoover and the Making of the American Century* (New York: Viking, 2022).
16. Brian Hochman, *The Listeners: A History of Wiretapping in the United States* (Cambridge: Harvard University Press, 2022).
17. Robert Justin Goldstein, *Political Repression in Modern America: From 1870 to 1976* (Chicago: University of Illinois Press, 2001).

CHAPTER 1

"With Care, Secrecy, and Dispatch"
1893–1914

The first fifteen years of the twentieth century brought enormous economic, social, and political change to America, and with it, associated political unrest and, occasionally, violence. Anarchists, socialists, and communist adherents in the United States were key drivers of protests and strikes targeting some of the biggest corporations in America as well as the federal government itself. Working within the established electoral process, Socialist Party presidential candidate Eugene V. Debs garnered nearly 1 million votes in the hotly contested 1912 election, running on an overtly anticapitalist platform. Multiple labor unions embraced the message of Debs and similar socialist political figures, and multiple anarchists and socialist newspapers helped spread the message of Debs and other political radicals.

The origins and scale of that unrest and antiestablishment political activism triggered the first major expansion of federal domestic surveillance capabilities, human and technological.

At the start of the century, the Secret Service was the dominant federal element involved in domestic surveillance and political repression, targeting first anarchists and later socialists. By 1910, it would be joined in the political countersubversion business by the newly created Bureau of Investigation at the Justice Department. Starting with Theodore Roosevelt in 1901, successive chief executives would use both federal law enforcement agencies to target real or imagined political enemies, from rival politicians in Congress to ordinary individual citizens.

2   CHAPTER 1

Through a key Supreme Court decision in 1914, federal agencies were given a legal way to get otherwise personal or business correspondence sent via telegram when the nation's highest court ruled that such business records fell outside the protections offered by the Fourth Amendment.

And it would be a presidential assassination that would set many of these monumental changes in motion.

A MURDER IN BUFFALO

A beautiful September day greeted the president of the United States and the citizens he'd come to speak to that morning in Buffalo. He was looking forward to spending time with the public. His national security team, however, was on edge.

For several years a radical, international movement had carried out acts of violence outside the United States, but federal officials feared an attack on America was close at hand. Federal agents had been tracking this group and its adherents for several years, both at home and abroad, in full coordination with America's allies and other concerned foreign governments. Only a month earlier American officials received word terrorists intended to strike in North America.[1] However, the lead proved bogus—and the real threat remained undetected.

President William McKinley's speech at the Pan-American Exposition in Buffalo, New York, on September 5, 1901, went off without a hitch, but the next afternoon a recent convert to the pan-national anarchist movement, Leon Czolgosz, took advantage of McKinley's abhorrence of close Secret Service protection to slip into the public receiving line with a revolver concealed within a bandage on one of his hands. He fired two bullets into the president and was immediately tackled and subdued. McKinley held on for eight days but finally succumbed to his wounds in the early hours of September 14.[2]

The public uproar over the attack and subsequent investigations into Czolgosz and the entire American anarchist movement would consume the public, press, and government officials for months. But what the public would never know is that the federal government's first mass surveillance program aimed at a particular group of people, strictly on the basis of their political beliefs, had failed to detect McKinley's assassin in advance. Czolgosz's act of madness triggered a full-scale domestic war on anarchists, but the seeds of that conflict had been sown decades earlier.

A FEAR OF THE "-ISMS"

The social and political revolutions that rocked Europe during the mid-nineteenth century gave rise to new antiestablishment philosophies: socialism, communism, and anarchism. All rejected as illegitimate the prevailing political and economic order, in which power was concentrated largely in the hands of monarchial regimes with close ties to a rising class of industrialists who ruthlessly exploited their workers. Adherents of these philosophies became the targets of the governments they rhetorically (and sometimes physically) attacked. But whereas socialists (and later communists) sought to put the means of production in the hands of a de facto state controlled by the public at large, most anarchists sought to do away with the state altogether, rejecting "the legitimacy of external government and the State"[3] and instead seeking to create "a decentralized and self-regulating society consisting of a federation of voluntary associations of free and equal individuals."[4]

Anarchism and socialism gained political ground in the United States in the wake of the 1873 depression, with pro-labor anarchists forming successful movements in many major American cities, including Chicago. The push by anarchists, socialists, and trade unionists for an eight-hour workday and other labor reforms culminated in the 1886 May Day strike and subsequent "Haymarket Affair"—a labor rights march on May 4, 1886, in Chicago, which became the target of a terrorist bombing that resulted in 11 dead (including four police officers) and dozens wounded.[5]

The anarchist organizers of the demonstration were blamed (likely wrongly) for the bombing and deaths that took place at the event and were subsequently tried and executed.[6] A wave of political repression against anarchists and socialists ensued, and it would take more than a decade before the two movements had recovered enough to begin making a political comeback.

Meanwhile in Europe a violent strain of anarchism emerged. Its practitioners carried out bombings and assassination attempts (several successful) from the 1880s onward, including the assassination of Italy's King Umberto I on July 29, 1900.

Within days of the king's death, American and Italian government authorities had determined that the killer, Italian anarchist Gaetano Bresci, had been living in and planning the king's murder from his home in Patterson, New Jersey—the location of an Italian immigrant anarchist cell since at least 1898.[7] The United States had been used as a staging ground for a terrorist attack against another country.

4   CHAPTER 1

From August 1900 through May 1901, American authorities, at the request of the Italian government, conducted a national search for Italian immigrants with known or suspected connections to the anarchist movement. The Departments of Justice and Treasury, along with the Postal Service, as well as state and local law enforcement organizations, were employed in the effort. The resulting mass surveillance and monitoring of the mail of hundreds of affected individuals was done absent any criminal predicate.[8] By November 1900, the Secret Service had determined that Bresci was likely mentally unstable prior to killing Humberto and that he had acted alone.[9]

The most important consequences of the domestic hunt for Bresci's nonexistent coconspirators were the precedents they set.

First, simply being of the same ethnic or political group of a known terrorist was now enough reason for government authorities to target entire groups for surveillance, including monitoring their mail. Second, the government's reliance on mass surveillance and ethnic or political targeting blinded it to other potential threats from "lone wolf" actors.

By at least as early as 1901, the US Secret Service Division (SSD) of the Department of Treasury was actively monitoring anarchists on a global basis, with the names and known addresses of anarchists maintained in ledger books at SSD headquarters in Washington.[10] The SSD made no distinctions on this list between those who had actually committed a crime and those who had not. Simply being a self-declared anarchist or associating with such persons was enough to get one on the list—and in many cases, to become the target of SSD surveillance.

The name of Leon Czolgosz was not on that list prior to his assassination of President McKinley, but the person who he claimed inspired him was, in red ink, in the SSD anarchist ledger book: Emma Goldman.

Goldman came from a dysfunctional Russian Jewish family—her father beat her regularly—that struggled against societal antisemitism amid the general political repression that was intrinsic to Tsarist Russia. After she threatened to commit suicide at age 16 to escape the daily hell of her existence, Goldman's father let her follow her sister Helena to America in 1885.[11]

Emma was an avid reader of political literature from a young age, and her experience working in textile sweatshops in Rochester, New York, only fueled her belief that the anarchists were right, that only overthrowing the existing political and economic order could end the miserable drudgery, low wages, and abominable working conditions of the working class in America. The Haymarket Massacre was the political tipping point for Goldman. After the anarchist leaders of the Chicago area movement were hanged or

"WITH CARE, SECRECY, AND DISPATCH" 5

imprisoned, Goldman became even more radical in her beliefs—and her willingness to act on them.

The June 1892 strike at the Homestead, Pennsylvania, steel plant owned by Andrew Carnegie evolved over the month into an armed confrontation between the hired guns of the Pinkerton Detective Agency and a group of armed union members. On July 6 a day-long gun battle between the two sides resulted in seven Pinkertons and nine union men dead. Carnegie's plant manager, Henry Frick, refused to budge. The plant remained closed, the workers locked out and on the defensive despite public support.

Goldman and her on-again, off-again lover and ideological comrade, anarchist Alexander "Sasha" Berkman, decided to kill Frick, hoping it would spark the revolution they sought. While Emma helped develop the plot and raise money for its execution, the two decided that Berkman alone would carry out the deed—which he attempted, unsuccessfully, on July 23, 1892.

Berkman would spend more than a decade in prison, while Goldman— effectively an unindicted coconspirator—officially publicly renounced violence but continued to praise and help (financially, morally, and with her pen) anarchists who did commit acts of violence.[12]

Despite the fact that Goldman herself had publicly renounced the use of violence, it was her political activity and pattern of behavior that led federal officials to conclude—wrongly, but perhaps predictably—that Goldman was Czolgosz's coconspirator in the assassination of McKinley.

Goldman was arrested by local police on September 10, 1901, in Chicago and immediately claimed she'd met Czolgosz only once and briefly. She also used her arrest to tell the *New York Times* reporter on the scene that Czolgosz was a "fool" for shooting McKinley, and that

> I do not know surely, but I think Czolgosz was one of those down-trodden men who see all the misery which the rich inflict upon the poor, who think of it, who brood over it, and then, in despair, resolve to strike a great blow, as they think, for the good of their fellow men. But that is not anarchy.[13]

Chicago authorities thought otherwise. They detained, without charge, not only Goldman but several of the people she'd been visiting while in the city.[14]

Indeed, two days after Goldman's arrest, the district attorney in Buffalo admitted that he had no evidence Goldman (or any of her Chicago-area associates) was connected to the McKinley assassination plot and would thus not seek her extradition.[15] Chicago officials were unmoved, and Goldman and other Chicago anarchists would remain behind bars for another

6   CHAPTER 1

two weeks—a flagrant violation of their First, Fourth, and Fifth Amendment rights under the Constitution of the United States.

During this same time, New York City Police Commissioner Michael Murphy launched an all-out war on anarchists:

> I don't propose, if I can help it, to have any Anarchists living in this city. We will enforce the law drastically, and whatever means can be taken to drive them from the city will be taken. When they hold open meetings we can stop them, of course, and we can also keep them under such close watch that they will soon tire of trying to do their work in this community.[16]

Murphy's order to his officers was to "make a police census of all male and female Anarchists residing in the boundaries of your command. This must be done with the greatest caution, so that the names of innocent persons shall not be confused or mixed with those of pronounced Anarchists."[17]

A local American police department was to be used explicitly to surveil and catalogue an entire group of Americans strictly on the basis of their political beliefs. What the Secret Service had started was now being implemented in the country's largest city by America's largest local police force.

Murphy was not alone in his desire to see American anarchists eliminated from the body politic. A few days earlier, former US Attorney S. Taliaferro of the Houston law firm of Taliaferro and Wilson had offered Knox his own proposal. In his September 7, 1901, letter to Knox, after offering condolences on the attack on McKinley and expressing his rage at anarchists, Taliaferro came to the point:

> With the army of Post Office Inspectors, Secret Service Men, Postmasters, Revenue Agents, Marshals, and other forces, it should be a comparatively easy matter to locate every anarchist in the United States and their places of meeting. This being done, it will not be difficult to arrest these persons for violations of some United States Statutes, notably the crime against revenue postage and counterfeiting money laws, committed by such persons, as well as to search their places of meeting and their dwellings for the purpose of discovering a clue to the conspiracy, which I feel confident exists.[18]

Taliaferro went on to state that all anarchist "societies should be fully investigated by the federal government, and it[s] machinery if properly used, is

"WITH CARE, SECRECY, AND DISPATCH" 7

amply sufficient for this purpose."[19] The former US attorney for the Eastern District of Texas summed up his recommended approach and expectations:

> I cannot help feeling that if with care, secrecy, and dispatch, the proper investigations are put on foot, that the government can and will obtain the testimony necessary to bring to the bar of justice a large number of persons equally as guilty as the man who fired the shot and at the same time break up these infernal societies, whose only aim is to dislodge the law from its place in the world and substitute therefor [*sic*] a law of bloodshed and force."[20]

Decades before the term "whole of government approach" would enter the federal national security lexicon, this former federal prosecutor was suggesting to the attorney general of the United States that the full power of the federal government be brought to bear—in open and in secret—to crush an entire political movement because one of its self-proclaimed adherents had killed the nation's chief executive.

Within days of receiving Taliaferro's letter, Knox issued an order to US attorneys around the nation, providing "a list of Italians in your district who are said to be correspondents of the 'Communist' and 'Individualist' groups of so-called anarchists of Paterson, New Jersey." Knox's instructions were specific:

> You will please inquire confidentially as to the antecedents and character of these men, and learn, if possible, whether they are merely subscribers to the publications of the Paterson anarchists, or are correspondents engaged in a common purpose of propagating the tenets of anarchy as an economic doctrine, or in preparing for some concerted action upon these doctrines in opposition to organized society and government.
>
> It is likely that the vague hints and reports of a conspiracy to destroy life and property are greatly exaggerated, but it is important to know whether the bond of union between these people is permissible in the eyes of the law or should be dissolved because the connection in its nature and purposes transcends all civil rights of free speech and action.[21]

The directive targeted nearly 600 alleged or known anarchists living in 33 states or territories. No claim was made by Knox in the letter than any of the individuals listed had committed a federal crime, much less been involved in McKinley's assassination.

8   CHAPTER 1

Acting on his own and without regard to the Constitution's free speech, free association, and due process requirements, Knox unleashed the federal attorneys under his control to conduct a de facto political witch hunt that targeted a group of Americans based not only on their alleged political beliefs but also on their national origin.

ANARCHISM: THE FORBIDDEN IMPORT

Less than a month after McKinley's funeral, his long-time private secretary, George Courtelyou, convened a meeting at his home on October 4, 1901, to ensure his new boss, Theodore Roosevelt, would not meet the same fate as his predecessor.

Joining Courtelyou were Major Richard Sylvester, head of the D.C. Police Department; William Moran, chief clerk of the SSD and deputy to SSD Chief John Wilkie, who was out of town at the time; and W. E. Cochran, chief post office inspector of the Postal Service. Courtelyou made clear that he wanted the organizations represented to "act in perfect concert at all times" to ensure Roosevelt's protection. Sylvester and Moran

> both testified to having pretty thorough records of the criminal and anarchist classes, the Secret Service having in some instances alphabetical lists of all the anarchists known in a city. The national police system of cooperation between cities which is coming into vogue greatly increases the possibility of a full and efficient record of these people.
>
> Secretary Cortelyou said that the State Department would be called upon to give all the assistance it could through the consular services to keep anarchists and people of similar classes located.[22]

Meanwhile, Knox and other administration officials knew they would be on firmer legal ground if new legislation were enacted that would make such surveillance and political repression legal. To that end, during the fall Knox sought the help of the Commission to Revise the Laws of the United States, established by an act of Congress in 1897 to help organize and publish the ever-growing number of federal laws into readily available volumes.[23]

Knox asked the Commission to provide him with a legislative draft, which it did on November 23, 1901. Its key language was as radical as it was sweeping, declaring anarchism "an offense against the United States and the law of nations" as well as criminalizing the teaching of anarchist beliefs or

"WITH CARE, SECRECY, AND DISPATCH"   9

creating anarchist groups or cells. The penalties for violations: a $1,000 fine, up to two years in jail, or both.[24]

The same day that the Commission sent its recommendation to Knox, US Solicitor General J.K. Richards gave a speech in Philadelphia in which he said,

> It is unnecessary to amend the Constitution in order to obtain the power to suppress Anarchism. . . . If Congress [en]trusts to the President the power to exclude alien anarchists and to deport all unnaturalized one[s], I fancy it will not be difficult to put in operation an effective plan of ridding the country of these bloody-minded pests. . . . Anarchists are insurgents against civilization, would-be assassins of society, enemies of the human race. . . . The red flag of Anarchy should be driven from the land as the black flag of piracy has been driven from the sea.[25]

Simply expressing an unpopular political belief and discussing it with others could result in a massive fine and a long prison sentence under the Commission's proposal. The government's chief counsel for arguing cases before the Supreme Court clearly wanted the Commission's approach or something just as sweeping signed into law. Roosevelt made clear his feelings on the matter in a December 3, 1901, message to Congress.

Opening with a tribute to his slain predecessor, Roosevelt said that McKinley "was killed by an utterly depraved criminal belonging to that body of criminals who object to all governments, good and bad alike, who are against any form of popular liberty if it is guaranteed by even the most just and liberal laws, and who are as hostile to the upright exponent of a free people's sober will as to the tyrannical and irresponsible despot."[26] Roosevelt then made his pitch for a legal ban on foreign anarchists entering the United States.

> They and those like them should be kept out of this country, and if found here they should be promptly deported to the country whence they came; and far-reaching provisions should be made for the punishment of those who stay. No matter calls more urgently for the wisest thought of the Congress.[27]

If adopted, the proposals put forward by the Commission, the Solicitor General, and the President would have barred from US entry a class of immigrants based solely on their political beliefs.

And in the age of the telegraph, telephone (becoming increasingly available in America and around the world), wire services and newspapers, the notion that an idea could be banned was as ludicrously impractical as it was constitutionally abhorrent. But facts and reason didn't stop the administration and the Congress from moving forward with the legalization of political repression in the fall of 1901.

For some time, House Judiciary Committee chairman George Ray (R-NY) had been negotiating with Attorney General Knox on language for a bill to make presidential or foreign head-of-state assassination a federal crime and to criminalize anarchism itself. On December 18, 1901, Ray sent Knox his latest version, which made it a federal felony to "advocate, advise, or teach a disbelief in or a disrespect for organized government, and any person who aids, advises, or encourages by his presence, or otherwise, the advocacy, advising, or teaching hereinbefore in this section"—punishable by up to five years in prison. Nothing like it had been seen since the passage of the infamous Alien and Sedition Acts over a century earlier.[28]

Ray was hardly alone in offering radical—and unconstitutional—legislative responses to McKinley's assassination and the rise of the anarchists. During the fall of 1901 and into early 1902, over 30 bills were introduced in Congress in response to the McKinley assassination, some in the form of constitutional amendments to criminalize presidential assassination and anarchism itself.

Several state legislatures also got in on the act. In New York in April 1902, the state legislature passed the Criminal Anarchy Act, which made it a state crime to profess anarchist beliefs.[29] Other states would follow a similar path, but the one provision contained in nearly all of the federal bills that seemed to have universal political support was a ban on "alien anarchists" entering the United States. And it was this language, the ban on anarchists entering America, that would make its way into the Immigration Act of 1903.[30] The bill was the product of a combined executive and legislative branch assault on the core of the Bill of Rights, aided and abetted by the press.

While President Lincoln richly deserves the criticism he received for suspending habeas corpus during the Civil War, as author and constitutional lawyer Geoffrey Stone has noted,

> the nation suffered only a very limited—and largely unsystematic— interference with free expression during the Civil War. The Lincoln administration did not enact a sedition act, it left most dissent undisturbed, and those speakers it did arrest for seditious expression were almost always quickly released.[31]

Roosevelt and the Congress sought to use the power of the federal government to suppress a political idea they loathed and to punish those who advocated it, just as the Federalists had in 1798.

While the bill did not outlaw the advocacy of anarchism by persons born in the United States, the message was clear: if you associated with or assisted non-US citizens who were declared or suspected anarchists, you would be fined and spend time in jail. Anyone who came into contact with the likes of Emma Goldman would now be under immediate suspicion and, based on past Secret Service practice, have their name, address, and other personal information recorded in "The Book of Anarchists" in the Treasury Department headquarters in Washington. Within months, the new law got its first test.

Scottish trade union activist John Turner had first visited the United States on a speaking tour in the late 1890s, during which he made the case to American audiences on why the general strike and union organizing were essential tools in labor's fight against the "Gilded Age" tycoons of the day.[32] By the late summer of 1903, American-born anarchists were busy raising money for another Turner speaking tour, in direct contravention of the Anarchist Exclusion Act.[33]

After Turner arrived in the United States in October 1903, he gave a speech in New York City and was immediately arrested. His hearing before federal immigration authorities went exactly as expected: they declared him an anarchist and ordered his deportation. Turner, with the help of the newly formed Free Speech League, secured the services of legendary defense lawyer Clarence Darrow. Turner lost at the lower court level and appealed to the Supreme Court, which heard his case in April 1904 and rendered its decision the following month.[34]

In delivering the court's verdict, Chief Justice Fuller swept aside the notion that Turner had any free speech rights as an alien in America:

> If the word "anarchists" should be interpreted as including aliens whose anarchistic views are professed as those of political philosophers innocent of evil intent, it would follow that Congress was of opinion that the tendency of the general exploitation of such views is so dangerous to the public weal that aliens who hold and advocate them would be undesirable additions to our population, whether permanently or temporarily, whether many or few, and, in light of previous decisions, the act, even in this aspect, would not be unconstitutional, or as applicable to any alien who is opposed to all organized government.[35]

What Fuller and his colleagues seemed oblivious to was the sweeping nature of the precedent they had just set: antigovernment speech could be made a criminal offense by Congress. If it could be applied to aliens, it could also be applied to those who were friends or colleagues of said aliens with "undesirable" views and who helped said aliens propagate those views to the American public.

As the legislative and legal machinery ground on through the Roosevelt administration, so did the surveillance and repression against known or alleged anarchists. But the federal government's growing penchant to use domestic surveillance soon spread beyond known or alleged political radicals. And the driving force behind such surveillance and political repression was the president of the United States and his most senior advisors, inside and outside the White House. One victim of that surveillance was an American citizen living in the southwestern United States with absolutely no connections to political radicalism or violence.

SEEKING GREENER PASTURES—AND GETTING SURVEILLED FOR IT

Nathan Boyd had a dream. The Mesilla Park, New Mexico, resident and investor wanted to make sure that he and his neighbors had proper access to water in the Rio Grande Valley area in order to ensure a strong farming and ranching economy for his region of the state. To that end, beginning shortly after the turn of the twentieth century, Boyd obtained rights to finance the construction of a dam near Elephant Butte, New Mexico. He was joined in the project by some investors from the United Kingdom.

Just over a year into his project, Boyd learned that the Mexican government had its own dam-related scheme for the area which, if implemented, would preempt his own effort. Boyd also came to believe that Army General Anson Mills, a commissioner on the International Water Boundary Commission, had sought court injunctions to block Boyd's project in favor of a different dam scheme developed by Mills himself. Through a series of letters to Roosevelt commencing in July 1902 and running through at least April 1904, Boyd demanded an investigation of General Mills' conduct, opposed his promotion, and asked for a review of the entire Elephant Butte dam issue.[36]

In an April 1904 letter of over 100 pages, Boyd blasted Mills and provided an excruciatingly detailed account of the Elephant Butte dam saga. Among Boyd's claims was that Mills "associated with the owners of certain lands

"WITH CARE, SECRECY, AND DISPATCH" 13

on the Mexican side of the Rio Grande in the El Paso Valley" and allegedly began "pressing at Washington the alleged claims of Mexico" in opposition to Boyd's project.[37] Mills had, according to Boyd, asserted in testimony to Congress and in court proceedings that the Rio Grande was navigable for hundreds of miles above and below El Paso, Texas, and that the Elephant Butte scheme would thus harm regional commerce.

But the New Mexico Territory Supreme Court, upon hearing Boyd's case, stated that Mill's claims were nothing more than

> the deliberate intention of the Government by its political depart-
> ment to take measures, not for the purpose of improving the navi-
> gability of the river, but of permanently obstructing it at a point far
> below the site of the defendant's works and thus to devote the stream
> to irrigation [around el Paso] instead of navigation.[38]

New Mexico's highest court agreed with Boyd, but because of the federal government's jurisdiction could offer him no actionable relief.

Boyd's letter to Roosevelt repeatedly accused Mills of perjury and other Justice and State officials of incompetence or of not taking his claims seriously. Boyd appealed again to Roosevelt for a truly independent investigation of Mills and the entire federal intervention into his project, and he ended with this offer:

> I beg again to offer to waive, and to forfeit absolutely, if necessary, the
> whole of my personal interest in the Elephant Butte Enterprise, now
> amounting in all to over $300,000, if justice be done to my associate
> investors and to the Territory of New Mexico.[39]

Boyd's letter contained no threats of violence against any federal official. Despite this, in September 1904, SSD Chief John Wilkie dispatched one of his agents from Colorado to New Mexico and placed Boyd under direct investigation and surveillance for almost a month.[40]

Utilizing the local post master as an SSD informant to get information from people who knew Boyd well, SSD Assistant Operative Clarence Park was able to report to Wilkie that Boyd was "an educated man, cultured, of good character and excellent reputation" but that his financial loses in the Elephant Butte dam project had "preyed upon his mind to such an extent, it is believed by some, the subject both excites and irritates him."

Those with whom Park spoke felt the only way Boyd might become violent would be in the context of "a heated discussion upon the subject" but

14   CHAPTER 1

that Boyd had absolutely no prior history of violence. One of Park's interlocutors made clear that he felt Boyd was "a bright, intelligent man, and does not question his sanity."[41] Despite the lack of evidence that Boyd was anything other than an aggrieved citizen petitioning his government for redress, Park closed his report to Wilkie with the recommendation "that should Mr. Boyd visit Washington, D.C., it would be wise to place him under surveillance."[42] Wilkie subsequently took steps to ensure that federal officials in Washington would have advance notice of Boyd's arrival.

On January 14, 1905, and at Wilkie's request, W.H.H. Llewellyn, the district attorney for Dona Ana, Otero, and Lincoln Counties in New Mexico, sent a message to J.R. Lucero, the sheriff of Dona Ana County, asking him to "keep a outlook on the movements of Dr. Nathan Boyd and should he start for the east wire the State Department, Washington, D.C. as follows: 'the Doctor has started for the East.' State his destination if you can find what same is."[43]

State Department officials had previously asked Wilkie to keep them posted as to Boyd's movements, apparently out of concern that if Boyd came to Washington, he might seek to confront Mexican government officials at their embassy over the Elephant Butte dam imbroglio. On January 27, 1905, Wilkie advised Assistant Secretary of State Alvey Adee that "We have made arrangements with the Postmaster at Las Cruces, who is a personal friend of Dr. Boyd, to notify us at any time if the Doctor might start East. Mr. Llewellyn's action in this matter ought to make it certain that we should be doubly advised."[44]

Boyd was no fool. He strongly suspected that federal officials were monitoring him at some level, and in March 1905 he complained to the Las Cruces postmaster, Allen Papen, who subsequently informed Wilkie via letter that Boyd was certain that "his mail has been tampered with, particularly foreign letters and that believes that the Secret Service is doing it on instructions from the State Department."[45]

In his "Personal and Confidential" reply to the Las Cruces postmaster on March 17, 1905, Wilkie stated,

> I am forced to the conclusion that his suspicion has no foundation in fact, chiefly because I know of no reason why there should be any tampering with his mail. Neither the Postoffice establishment, nor this division, has had the slightest interest in his correspondence.[46]

Given the lengths to which Wilkie had gone to employ both Papen and the local district attorney and sheriffs in his surveillance network targeting Boyd, the Secret Service chief's mail tampering denial rings hollow.

"WITH CARE, SECRECY, AND DISPATCH" 15

While Wilkie claimed that the SSD itself was allegedly not opening Boyd's mail, he left unaddressed the question of whether an SSD agent on detail to the State Department was doing the job in Washington, examining letters from Boyd's UK investment partners as they arrived in Washington and before they were forwarded to Boyd in Las Cruces. Boyd's basic instinct was correct about his being under federal government surveillance. What he apparently could never imagine is that his friend, the postmaster, was a key element in the domestic spying operation targeting him.

By December 1905, Boyd had settled his court cases against the federal government over the Elephant Butte dam project.[47] How long the Secret Service conducted its locally outsourced surveillance against Boyd is unknown.

EXECUTIVE BRANCH SURVEILLANCE: PRYING INTO PRIVATE MATTERS

Civil service reform had been an obsession of Theodore Roosevelt's since his days as a civil service commissioner in New York. In picking his cabinet and subcabinet officials, Roosevelt sought out men who shared his view that government employees should be scrupulously honest in the performance of their duties, free of the taint of the kind of corruption that became synonymous with the words "Tammany Hall." But as with any strongly held view taken to an extreme, the quest to determine a particular person's fitness for government service could quickly turn into witch hunt.

Assistant Treasury Secretary Hamilton Fish II was a Roosevelt appointee who shared the president's views on the need for a corruption-free federal workforce. However, as Fish went about the business of filling positions under his purview within the Treasury Department, he went well beyond using an anticorruption standard in his personnel choices, applying his own personal values as a litmus test for the fitness of applicants for federal positions.

In October 1906, Fish needed a superintendent for the Treasury building in New York City. On October 11, 1906, he wrote to Assistant Secretary C. H. Keep about his personnel needs and specifically about one applicant for the position, an engineer by the name of L.E. Bonneaud:

> What I have been able learn about him in this city is by no means satisfactory as to his character. He was in Elmira, N.Y. From March 1901 to May 1903 as Chief Engineer & Electrician, and Inspector of Repairs and Construction, at the New York State Reformatory. I am

given to understand that he is not now living with his wife, she living in Elmira and he is in this city. I am satisfied that he is a competent engineer, but I want more than that: I want a man of the highest personal character, not one of loose morals. I have the honor to ask that you will ascertain through the Secret Service Division all about his career in Elmira and this city. His residence in New York is 122 East 27th Street.[48]

Fish clearly suspected that Bonneaud was an adulterer—a condition which, even if true, was irrelevant to his actual job performance and certainly not a legitimate reason to employ the Secret Service to investigate him. Nevertheless, an SSD agent was assigned to investigate Bonneaud, posing as a shop superintendent from the business of the agent's boyhood friend as a cover in order to inquire about Bonneaud at multiple businesses, organizations, and local governmental entities.[49]

The agent followed Bonneaud to and from his house, place of work, and other locations he frequented over the course of much of October. The agent concluded that Bonneaud was "steady and regular in his habits" and was "morally clean."[50] Whether the agent's report was sufficient to clear Bonneaud for the job, the Treasury Department's files do not reveal.

For years, federal agencies outside of the Treasury Department had used loaned Secret Service agents to investigate legitimate federal crimes—from fraud to murder. With the anarchists, as well as the Boyd and Bonneaud cases, a line had been crossed. No longer would it be necessary for someone to be accused of a federal crime in order to come under federal government surveillance, or worse. And if the federal official who took offense at a publicly voiced opinion was the president of the United States, the full weight of the federal government could potentially be hurled against you.

THE PRESS AND PRESIDENTIAL PIQUE

"This is an infamous article," declared Theodore Roosevelt in a March 19, 1906, note to his attorney general, William Henry Moody. Roosevelt was referring to a piece in the socialist newspaper *Appeal to Reason*, written by his former presidential rival and nationally known socialist political icon Eugene V. Debs. The article attacked the American capitalist system in Debs's usually strong language, specifically condemning officials in Idaho for charging Western Federation of Miners (WFM) president and International Workers of the World (IWW) co-founder William "Big Bill" Haywood

"WITH CARE, SECRECY, AND DISPATCH" 17

and two associates with murdering the former governor of the state, Frank Steunenberg.

In the piece that had agitated Roosevelt, Debs stated that "Capitalist courts never have done, and never will do, anything for the working class . . ." and that if Haywood and his WFM colleagues on trial were executed that "A special revolutionary convention of the proletariat at Chicago, or some other central point, would be in order, and, if extreme measures are required, a general strike could be ordered and industry paralyzed as a preliminary to a general uprising. If the plutocrats begin the program, we will end it."[51]

Roosevelt wanted Attorney General Moody to take direct, forceful action against Debs and the paper, asking, "Is it possible to proceed against Debs and the proprietor of this paper criminally? I haven't another copy of the article, but please notify the post office Department that the paper may not be allowed in the mails, if we can legally keep it out."[52]

Moody dutifully had Justice Department Assistant Attorney General Charles H. Robb examine the Administration's legal options. For Roosevelt, Robb's news was not initially encouraging. "I am sorry to say that notwithstanding the infamous nature of the article, there is no law of which I have knowledge authorizing the exclusion of the paper containing it from the mails, neither is there any statute authorizing the prosecution of Debs for sending such matter through the mails."[53]

While opining that Congress would likely not consider libel legislation for "manifest reasons," Robb went on to say that "there is apparently no reason why it should not be made a crime to use the mails in disseminating a criminal libel as this article undoubtedly is."[54] And Robb went further, stating,

> Moreover, it should be made a criminal offense to disseminate through the medium of the United States mails, seditious or revolutionary matter, whether aimed at the Federal Government, or the Government of any State or subdivision thereof. Such a law would not, in my opinion, conflict with the freedom of the press clause of the Constitution, as, of course, that clause necessarily has some limitation; and moreover, the use of the mails has been held not to constitute a right but a mere privilege subject to reasonable regulation by Congress.[55]

Over a century earlier, American colonists living under British rule had frequently employed encryption in their letters in order to prevent royal authorities, who routinely tampered with or even destroyed their mail, from learning about their plans and views.[56] Now, the assistant attorney general of the United States was arguing that the federal government should adopt the very mail surveillance and speech censorship practices used by the British that had helped fuel the American Revolution.

While Roosevelt and his key aides would use the press to respond to the political attacks launched by Debs and other socialist leaders, the administration decided not to attempt a head-on assault on *Appeal to Reason*'s mail privileges on grounds of promoting "seditious or revolutionary" calls to action. Instead, government lawyers in the Department of Justice (DoJ) and at the Postal Service would continue to monitor *Appeal to Reason* and look for other potentially prosecutable offenses under different statutes.

Two years later, Roosevelt asked the Justice Department about the prospects of prosecuting the Patterson, New Jersey–based *La Questione Sociale*, an anarchist newspaper highly critical of the administration.[57] The assistant attorney general of the Post Office Department subsequently reported on April 14, 1908, that no mail fraud or other order could be issued against the paper.[58]

Roosevelt's penchant for trying to use the Department of Justice to punish critics wasn't limited to socialists or anarchists.

In July 1906, a citizen in Kenmore, New York, wrote a letter to the chief executive to alert him to an extremely unflattering (and obviously fake) picture of Roosevelt sitting on a toilet published by a man named De la Franier.[59] Writing from the president's summer home, Sagamore Hill, at Oyster Bay, New York, on July 14, 1906, Roosevelt's private secretary, William Loeb, asked the attorney general if "there is any way this man De la Franier can be prosecuted. An action might lie under the New York State statute making it a misdemeanor for anyone to publish another's photograph without his consent."[60] Two days later, the attorney general directed the US attorney in Buffalo, Charles Brown, to

> investigate this matter carefully, and, if necessary, to call upon the Department for the assignment of a Secret Service operative, and to take such action, by search and seizure, if this can legally be done on the facts presented after investigation, and by way of prosecution under the New York State law, referring the matter to the State authorities for that purpose, as you may conclude the situation warrants.[61]

Brown subsequently filed his investigative report with the Department of Justice in August 1906, a copy of which was transmitted to Loeb. No charges were filed against De la Franier at either the state or federal level.[62] Lacking an applicable federal statute to prosecute De la Franier—who clearly was exercising his constitutionally protected First Amendment rights—federal authorities attempted to use state and local law enforcement mechanisms to punish a man for simply printing a photograph that angered the president of the United States.

SURVEILLANCE AND INFILTRATION: SECRET SERVICE TARGETS ANARCHISTS

As the summer of 1906 wore on, William Loeb's attention remained focused on potential threats to Roosevelt, whether they came from the press or from political elements deemed radical and allegedly violence prone. From Oyster Bay, Loeb wrote to Secret Service Chief John Wilkie on September 15, 1906, about his latest concern—convicted British anarchist William "Billy" MacQueen and his newest benefactor—Trenton, New Jersey–based Baptist pastor Reverend Alfred Wishart.[63]

MacQueen, a long-time anarchist and labor organizer in his native Leeds, England, had come to the United States in 1902 to make common cause with American anarchists working in Paterson, New Jersey, and nearby New York. By June 1902, MacQueen and other anarchists (some foreigners, some locals) had successfully convinced the silk dye workers in Paterson to strike.

On June 18, 1902, a confrontation with police led to violence and the arrest of MacQueen and other anarchists.[64] MacQueen fled the country but subsequently returned in 1904, claiming family needs had required his return to England.[65] He was subsequently convicted of inciting to riot and was sentenced to five years in jail. At least as early as 1905, Reverend Wishart began lobbying New Jersey officials to pardon MacQueen and release him, arguing that the case against MacQueen was bogus and that he had committed no acts of violence.[66] By July 1906, Wishart had enlisted the help of Philadelphia soap magnate Joseph Fels in MacQueen's cause.[67]

It was that mounting political pressure that clearly had Loeb concerned.

"Will you please give me for my confidential information any facts you may have about MacQueen?" he asked Wilkie. The Secret Service chief was happy to oblige. In doing so, he revealed exactly how extensive and persistent Secret Service surveillance of anarchists was in the Paterson area.

Wilkie began his September 17 response to Loeb by deriding Reverend Wishart, stating, "In my opinion, the Reverend gentlemen's efforts are the result of absolute ignorance of the real character of the man whose defense he has undertaken."[68] Wilkie went on to say that information on MacQueen obtained from British authorities the week after the Paterson silk dye worker strikes and riots confirmed the Secret Service's own estimate of MacQueen, that "during the whole period of MacQueen's residence in New York and Paterson he was the constant companion, night and day, of the worst element of rabid anarchists. He was a whiskey drinking, loud mouthed incendiary, and in my opinion a dangerous man."[69] Wilkie further alleged that MacQueen and his fellow defendants had tried to get their stories straight before the trial, but that because Wilkie "had advance information of this fact" prosecutors were able to successfully undermine the effort at trial.

The Secret Service chief then went on to describe the details of a meeting held by MacQueen and several other anarchists in Paterson in early October 1902, at which MacQueen allegedly engaged in some inflammatory poetry, saying "Ding, dong, dell, McKinley is now in hell/And Roosevelt soon will go as well."[70] Wilkie then revealed exactly how he had such detailed information on MacQueen and his associates:

> One of our agents in Paterson was in daily contact and on intimate terms with MacQueen during the entire period of his residency there, and the daily reports from this agent . . . demonstrate beyond any question that MacQueen is an enemy to Government. . . . Of course, it would not do to disclose the fact that we maintain this sort of surveillance over MacQueen and his associates, but I think you can safely accept my assurance that the man is absolutely unworthy of consideration.[71]

Wilkie's apparent success in gaining access to the deliberations of MacQueen's defense team is a revelation that strengthens Wishart's case that MacQueen did not receive a fair trial. Moreover, nothing in Wilkie's letter suggests that MacQueen himself was actually responsible for an act of violence during his time in America.

Despite these facts, Loeb made sure that New Jersey's chief executive would turn a deaf ear to Wishart's pleas on MacQueen's behalf. On the basis of Wilkie's information, Loeb wrote him on September 19, "Governor Stokes has been told that our investigations have conclusively shown that MacQueen ought to stay in prison."[72]

MacQueen supporters carried on the campaign to get him freed, finally succeeding in May 1907.[73] But it was a pyrrhic victory. In prison, MacQueen had contracted tuberculosis. As a condition of his release, he was required to leave America and never return. The tuberculosis claimed his life in England in 1908 at age 33. The Secret Service continued its surveillance of anarchists

"WITH CARE, SECRECY, AND DISPATCH"   21

and their associates in the New Jersey–New York area for years after Mac-Queen's departure.[74]

Those closest to Roosevelt remained concerned that anarchists were determined to kill him.

In late July 1907 Loeb again flagged an alleged threat for Wilkie's attention. On July 16, 1907 Professor J.W. Jenks of Cornell University, a Roosevelt appointee to the congressionally created Immigration Commission, wrote to Treasury Secretary George Cortelyou about information Jenks had received from his own "confidential agent" about a burgeoning anarchist plot against the president:

> It is now reported that on the tenth of June, at a special meeting of the highest authorities of the anarchists, it was formally "decided to kill the President and Secretary Taft" and that ". . . some of their agents have positions in the Secret Service of the Treasury."[75]

It was all too much for Wilkie to believe.

Responding to Loeb on July 23, Wilkie assured him that "The information in the possession of this office does not suggest any danger to either the President or Secretary [of War] Taft from any of the anarchist societies."[76] After denigrating the quality of Jenks's information, Wilkie asserted,

> The anarchist societies, as far as I have been able to ascertain, content themselves with talking about the removal of foreign rulers. There has been absolutely nothing in the last two years to cause the slightest suggestion of a "plot" against the President or any cabinet officer, and I am advised by an investigator who has been in close personal touch with the leading spirits, including the so-called terrorists, that any talk of a general meeting of a number of persons to formally decide upon the removal of the President or any other high official of this Government, is the veriest nonsense . . . [77]

Wilkie's message was clear: the SSD had every anarchist organization in the country under surveillance, penetrated by either SSD agents directly or informants. There was no need for concern on that front, no violent threat from any known domestic anarchists. In offering this assessment, Wilkie was also admitting that there was in fact no legitimate case for the ongoing mass surveillance his organization was conducting against anarchists and other political dissidents across the country.

The surveillance and political repression of socialists, labor activists, and anarchists never represented a political threat for Roosevelt. The public, an

22 CHAPTER 1

overwhelming majority of House and Senate members, the courts, and the press broadly shared his antipathy for the relatively new social and political movements that challenged the prevailing political and economic order. But what would happen if the administration used the SSD for domestic surveillance against established, ostensibly respected members of society?

FEDERAL SURVEILLANCE:
TARGETING THE POLITICAL CLASS

In February 1907 during a meeting with members of the California congressional delegation, Roosevelt offered some allegedly off-the-record comments about America's relationship with Japan and the status of Japanese students in American schools, then a hot topic in San Francisco and other California cities. But the comments did not stay off the record for long, as the *Pacific Commercial Advertiser* noted that month, with anonymous administration sources charging "broken faith" on the part of those who attended the meeting with the president.[78]

But the administration's response didn't end with harsh words for the leakers, as the paper noted:

> There has been Secret Service work to find out the names of the men. It is now claimed that one of them certainly was a Senator and that possibly two of the members of the House offended. On top of it all Senator Perkins roiled the President and the Congress by an address he delivered before the National Geographic Society, asserting that war with Japan might be afar off but that it would come in time.[79]

A major American newspaper had revealed that the president had used the Secret Service to investigate House and Senate members for the "crime" of talking to reporters.

Perhaps Roosevelt did indeed start the meeting by stating that his comments were off the record. But in the world of politics, such indiscretions are commonplace. Covering political gossip and back-room meetings is grist for political reporters. Letting it be known that they were in a meeting with the president—and that he thus considered them important enough to be in said meeting—is the kind of access House and Senate members love to peddle to reporters eager for supposedly nonpublic information and insights. But leaking presidential political tidbits was not a crime under any statute much less the Constitution.

What was more revealing was the reaction of House and Senate members generally to the president's use of the Secret Service for such a task—which was exactly nothing. There were no hearings, no howls of protest, no resolutions of censure offered against Roosevelt for using members of his taxpayer-financed bodyguard to investigate members of Congress. As events would show, the administration considered congressional silence on the matter as assent.

Two months before Professor Jenks reported his concerns about potential anarchist threats to Roosevelt, John Wilkie had been in Los Angeles attending to other SSD business that, at the moment, was somewhat less sensational. During his trip, local reporters asked him about the Idaho court case that was making national headlines: the trial of WFM officials charged in the murder of former Idaho Governor Frank Steunenberg. The journalists wanted to know if Roosevelt had directed that the Secret Service investigate whether Haywood and his fellow defendants were getting a fair trial. Wilkie denied any Secret Service involvement in the trial.[80]

It was a half-truthful answer. In reality, for months several SSD operatives had been detailed to the US Attorney's office in Boise on a directly related case: an investigation into a timber fraud scheme allegedly engineered by none other than the late Governor Steunenberg, the supposed victim of Haywood and his WFM associates. Targeting political figures, including members of Congress, in corruption probes—particularly land fraud investigations—had become a major focus of the Departments of Justice and Interior during Roosevelt's first full term in office.

In early 1905, Oregon Senator John Mitchell and Representatives Binger Hermann and John Williamson (all Republicans) were indicted by a federal grand jury in a federal land fraud scheme.[81] Mitchell would be convicted in July 1905 but died later that year while his case was on appeal.[82] The cases of Hermann and Williamson would undergo several twists and turns, with Williamson's conviction being overturned and Hermann's trial ending in a hung jury. In the case of Republican House member Spencer Blackburn of North Carolina, a botched federal prosecution against him led Blackburn to ask the Senate Judiciary Committee to block the reappointment of the federal prosecutor who had originally filed multiple indictments against him.[83] In these cases and others, SSD operatives were the primary means of gathering evidence and conducting physical surveillance, with no external oversight.

As early as March 1907, Roosevelt, ever the anticorruption crusader, had taken a keen interest in the Idaho federal land fraud case. On March 20, Loeb wrote to Attorney General Charles Bonaparte informing him that "the President directs me to ask that you wire to the District Attorney for any information that may be in his possession concerning the matter."[84]

24   CHAPTER 1

Bonaparte replied the same day, telling Roosevelt, "I can find nothing in the Department of Justice to show that ex-Governor Steunenberg's name has been connected with any timber or land frauds" but suggested that the Interior Department or the SSD agents on detail to it might have something.[85] Bonaparte also decided to wire the US attorney in Boise, Norman Ruick, the next day to see what the prosecutor might know.[86]

Ruick responded the next day, and Bonaparte passed along the attorney's findings to Loeb:

> Pending investigation before Grand Jury here involving forty thousand acres timber land, shows Steunenberg as chief promoter and beneficiary of land frauds in this district. Impossible to conduct investigation without showing his connection. Investigation secret and no purpose or intention to allow information obtained to be used in Steunenberg murder case but only in trial of such indictments as shall be returned by the Grand Jury for timber frauds.[87]

The investigation didn't remain secret for long, and it was an SSD operative who not only helped make it public but who would implicate the late Steunenberg's business partner, attorney, and Idaho Republican political powerhouse: recently elected US Senator William E. Borah.

Borah was one of the lead counsels in the Haywood case. If it turned out that he was involved in Steunenberg's land fraud scheme and that fact became public, it would have almost certainly resulted in a mistrial, with Haywood and his codefendants not only being freed but having priceless political ammunition handed to them with which to attack both state and federal authorities.

Bonaparte had sensed that all was not well in Boise well before Ruick's update arrived for Roosevelt. Seeking an independent assessment of the situation, the attorney general had dispatched his own investigator, B.F. Cash, to determine how local reporters had learned that Borah was under scrutiny and possibly facing indictment.

On March 25 Cash submitted his 16-page preliminary report to Bonaparte, which confirmed that a local reporter was a childhood friend of SSD operative Gorman, one of the lead investigators in the case. The reporter had correctly concluded that Borah was a potential target, and Ruick had blamed Gorman for the leak.[88] What neither Cash, Ruick, or Bonaparte addressed was the propriety of having SSD agents conduct close physical surveillance of a US senator who also was an attorney representing the company charged with committing fraud against the US government.

"WITH CARE, SECRECY, AND DISPATCH" 25

The investigation and surveillance of Borah and his associates was so man-power intensive that on April 10, Ruick sent an encrypted telegram to Bonaparte requesting the assignment of six additional SSD operatives.[89] Five days later, Bonaparte informed Ruick that the Treasury Department had no more men to spare and that "it will be necessary for you to get along as best you can with the force you have at present."[90] As it turned out, the case against Borah was circumstantial and weak, and the senator was acquitted in September 1907.

Roosevelt had now repeatedly targeted House and Senate members of his own party in corruption stings, most of which had failed. Other members had been targeted for simply talking to the press. The Secret Service and federal prosecutors had been his preferred weapons of choice every time, and he had taken a personal interest, if not directly involved himself, in each incident. He had angered or embarrassed multiple House and Senate members through these investigations, though most were unwilling to attack him publicly for fear of being accused of trying to block corruption investigations, no matter how questionable.

Shortly before Christmas 1907, a new revelation about Secret Service domestic surveillance would finally give Roosevelt's congressional critics the opening they needed to take action against Wilkie's organization. The ensuing confrontation with Roosevelt would last for the balance of his presidency, and its consequences would be felt up to the present day.

SECRET SERVICE SPYING: EXTRAMARITAL AFFAIR EDITION

On December 13, 1907, the *Washington Times* carried a small front-page story with a headline that read "Elopement Costs Ensign His Job; Divorce Sought."[91] But this was no ordinary story about an extramarital affair.

The naval officer in question, Earl W. Pritchard, had known his love interest, Hazel von Haake Cathcart, since well before her marriage to R. Harry Cathcart in June. Harry Cathcart had suspected his wife's adultery since at least September, and the bride's mother had appealed to the Roosevelt administration to punish Pritchard. The paper noted that Pritchard had

> convinced Assistant Secretary [of the Navy] Newberry of his innocence in connection with the affair and also conferred with Secretary [of the Navy] Metcalfe. The Department was then disposed to drop the matter, but Mrs. von Haake was so insistent that it was decided to put a Secret Service agent on the case.[92]

26   CHAPTER 1

In an effort to keep the story quiet, the Navy pressured Pritchard into resigning, but the *Times* got wind of the incident and made it public. Members of Congress duly took note, and over the next several months the incident was investigated by the House Appropriations Committee, which (along with its Senate counterpart) controlled Secret Service funding.

By the third week of April 1908, both committees had agreed on language that prohibited SSD personnel from being employed on any duties other than defeating counterfeiting and presidential protection. The committee viewed the off-the-books "loaning" of SSD men to other departments (paid for out of the requesting department's funds) to be a flagrant violation of a previously enacted Secret Service–related statute.

The press coverage that week of the committee's findings and proposed legislative prohibition on Secret Service domestic spying was national in scope and damning in tone. "Secret Service Scored as Private Spy" was the April 21 front-page headline of the *Washington Times*.[93] "Espionage Exists: Representatives Contradict Chief Wilkie's Statement," declared the *Washington Evening Star* a day later.[94] And so it went in papers around the country.

By early May, the bill was out of committee and on the House floor for debate. A clear majority of House Republicans found common cause with the argument made by Democrat Joseph Shirley of Kentucky. Referencing the Pritchard incident, Sherley told his House colleagues

> the location of the man was not a question with the Department [of the Navy], to know where that man was while on leave, but the location of the man by the Secret Service was really for the purpose of making charges against him in connection with some scandalous conduct of his. Now, I deny that it is the business of the Secretary of the Navy, or the Secretary of War, or any other Secretary, to employ Secret Service men to dig up the private scandals of men. I do not mean to uphold the scandals, but I do not believe this country has reached the point where it needs that sort of supervision over men's conduct by Government, and by Secret Service methods.[95]

The civil service bill with the new restrictions on the Secret Service passed the House easily on May 1, despite a letter of protest from Roosevelt to House Speaker Joe Cannon.[96] The Senate subsequently approved the bill. The new restrictions on the Secret Service, confining its activities to protecting the president and catching counterfeiters, took effect on July 1, 1908.

Roosevelt's public criticism of the new law was hypocritical. He had personally pushed for Justice Department corruption investigations that had led to the mass employment of SSD personnel in matters they were not, by law, approved to investigate. Using the Secret Service to surveil or even disrupt the constitutionally protected free speech and association actions of anarchists, socialists, and other political dissidents, as well as his own personally directed legal campaigns against offending newspapers and efforts

Figure 1.1. President Theodore Roosevelt. His misuse of the Secret Service for domestic surveillance of political opponents and other Americans led Congress to restrict Secret Service operations to anticounterfeiting investigations and the protection of the president. *Library of Congress*

to keep them out of the mail, revealed Roosevelt's authoritarian core. The victims were people like Nathan Boyd and Earl Pritchard.

As events would show, the publicity surrounding the Pritchard case and the debate over the new law actually did nothing to stop the kind of domestic spying on innocent individuals that had sparked congressional action in the first place. The SSD's campaign against anarchists, socialists, and other political nonconformists continued unabated even as the House Appropriations Committee went about its work.

In January 1908, the New York Police Department asked Wilkie for help in determining whether the Socialist Labor Party was organizing New York tenants upset about their living conditions and rent rates. Wilkie responded by dispatching the SSD's political dissident expert, Maurits Hymans, to investigate.

Hymans reported to Wilkie on January 7 that "the anarchists and socialists are now actively engaged in fomenting trouble among the East Side rent strikers, as well as those in Harlem."[97] Eleven days later, Hymans surreptitiously attended a meeting in support of "Big Bill" Haywood of the WFM. His four-page report to Wilkie included the names of every speaker and key quotes from each.[98] And as the bill restricting the Secret Service to presidential protection and anticounterfeiting operations made its way through the House Appropriations Committee to the House floor, Hymans was busy spying on anarchists and other political dissidents in the Patterson, New Jersey area.[99] The House and the Senate remained oblivious to these activities.

Moreover, Roosevelt's railing about government investigations being hamstrung by the new law was also nonsense. For over a year before the passage of the bill that (in theory) reined in the Secret Service, Roosevelt's attorney general and political confidant, Charles Bonaparte, had been hard at work on a "Plan B" to ensure Roosevelt still had the ability to task government investigators. The new law spurred them to implement it.

FROM ONE SURVEILLANCE AGENCY TO TWO: THE BIRTH OF THE BUREAU OF INVESTIGATION

"In the vast majority of cases," economist Anthony Downs noted, "a bureau starts as the result of aggressive agitation and action by a small group of zealots who have a specific idea they want to put into practice on a large scale."[100]

The description was apt with respect to Roosevelt and Bonaparte. They were not going to let congressional action to restrict Secret Service investigative activities impair the Administration's ability to pursue those deemed to be criminals or political enemies. But the emphasis would be on the detection and prosecution of alleged or actual crimes, not a focus on upholding the Bill of Rights.

In the annual report he submitted to Congress less than two weeks before the Pritchard case became public, Bonaparte made a direct appeal to Congress to authorize the creation of a detective force within the Justice Department.

Bonaparte argued that the expansion of the Department's enforcement responsibilities under a series of laws passed by Congress over the preceding quarter-century had not been matched by the manpower to investigate crimes committed under those laws: "it seems obvious that the Department on which not only the President, but the courts of the United States must call first to secure the enforcement of the laws, ought to have the means of such enforcement subject to its own call; a Department of Justice with no force of permanent police in any form under its control is assuredly not fully equipped for its work."[101]

Bonaparte testified before the House Appropriations Committee in January 1908 and reiterated his request, but Congress ignored it when it passed the civil service bill limiting the Secret Service's activities.[102] With Congress now having denied him the use of SSD agents while providing no alternative, Bonaparte unilaterally created the Bureau of Investigation (BoI) within the Department of Justice on July 26, 1908.[103]

In the absence of a specific legislative authorization and accompanying line-item appropriation, Bonaparte funded the initial force of more than 30 often part-time agents out of the DoJ's general revenue fund. Each request for a "special agent" had to be approved not only by the chief examiner of the BoI, but by either the attorney general or the acting attorney general. Many of the agents hired were Secret Service veterans, including Special Agent Kirk DeBelle, whom Wilkie had notified of his transfer to Justice a month earlier.[104]

The Bureau would begin its existence with no congressional oversight, no limit on the number of agents that could be hired, and no dedicated funding stream. It was a prescription for a repeat of the very same kind of abuses that the Secret Service had perpetrated.

To lead this new unit within the DoJ, Bonaparte chose long-time bank examiner overseer Stanley W. Finch, a Justice employee for 15 years who was well-versed in the nation's banking laws. He coupled managerial experience with an exactitude for detail and adherence to both DoJ policies and his own instructions. He had Bonaparte's ear, had long been an internal advocate for the creation of a Justice-owned detective force, and was more than willing to keep certain investigations "off books" if instructed to do so.

Figure 1.2. Attorney General Charles Bonaparte created the Bureau of Investigation (forerunner of the FBI) in July 1908 on the orders of President Theodore Roosevelt and without congressional authorization. *Library of Congress*

An early example occurred in August 1908, when Finch directed Examiner Charles DeWoody in Detroit to undertake a confidential investigation at the direction of the attorney general. The matter was deemed so sensitive that Finch made no direct mention in the letter to DeWoody of the subject(s) or target(s) of the investigation.

"WITH CARE, SECRECY, AND DISPATCH" 31

After telling DeWoody to conduct the investigation "under cover of your regular examination in eastern Michigan" and to keep him informed daily of his progress, Finch instructed DeWoody to keep their communications out of potentially interceptable channels in order to avoid "the possibility of any leak in our correspondence."[105] Once DeWoody forwarded his report to Finch on August 31, the latter sent the report on to the attorney general and closed his cover letter by noting, "In view of the confidential nature of this report, it has not been jacketed, or recorded in the file room of the Department."[106]

The author could find no follow up to this correspondence, no evidence that any charges were filed in the matter, or that any employee of the Department had been reprimanded or terminated as a result of the investigation.

The fact that Finch made no reference to any violation of a specific federal statute in his correspondence to DeWoody and Gauss, and that he made sure the investigative record was kept out of official DoJ files, suggests that DeWoody was used to investigate a matter of intense personal or political concern to Bonaparte, not an actual federal crime. One or more innocent Americans were likely subjected to illegal government surveillance at the whim of the attorney general of the United States. It was an inauspicious precedent for the new Bureau of Investigation, and it was followed just a few months later by the first Bureau effort to intimidate a journalist.

During the first two decades of the twentieth century, a series of revolutions swept across Latin America, from Mexico to Colombia. Several of those revolutions received either overt or covert support from individuals inside the United States—either foreign nationals here to raise money or smuggle arms to their fellow revolutionists, or Americans who were supporting the aspirations of those seeking to overthrow an existing (and usually tyrannical) government. While the Bureau was interested in both kinds of supporters, in the fall of 1908 it was an alleged American "filibustering expedition" (i.e., a mercenary intervention-for-profit scheme) to Colombia, being organized in the Boston area, that resulted in the first Bureau investigation of its kind.

On October 20, 1908, the State Department forwarded a letter to the Justice Department from the Colombian foreign minister, alleging that several Americans were organizing a paramilitary expedition to the country.[107] The Colombian foreign minister's source was the *Boston Post*. The same day, the Bureau tasked Special Agent Kirk DeBelle—already on assignment in Boston on other matters—to look into the allegations.

The local US attorney, citing the publicity around the incident and the subsequent dissolution of the alleged plot, kept DeBelle on other work until just after Thanksgiving. The agent subsequently interviewed the reporter,

J. Lewis Milmore, and got him to give up his source, a Michael J. Kane, who under interrogation admitted the entire affair was a hoax—he simply wanted good material for a magazine article.[108]

The US government had a legitimate foreign policy reason for preventing American soil from being used as a springboard for privateer-sponsored military expeditions to overthrow foreign governments.

Although Latin American political elites no doubt viewed the Monroe Doctrine as providing nothing more than a political and rhetorical fig leaf for American government interventions in Central and South American countries' internal affairs, it was a policy that at least was promulgated and carried out on behalf of a sovereign nation. Those engaged in "filibustering expeditions" were in it for the rush of adventure and, often, the chance to make money. Washington was not going to tolerate American foreign policy being hijacked by privateers.

However, in seeking to break up what turned out to be a hoax expedition, Justice Department employees clearly engaged in tactics that undermined the *Post*'s First Amendment protections. The implicit threat of prosecution of the paper and its reporter under existing American neutrality laws was used to get the reporter to reveal his source—a source who was subsequently interrogated without counsel present to represent him. The fact that the *Post* did not apparently protest the treatment of its reporter only served to reward the Bureau's tactics.

While the Bureau's initial forays into non–white collar crime investigations and domestic surveillance went unnoticed by the press, public, and federal lawmakers, the confrontation between Roosevelt and Congress that led to the Bureau's creation entered its final act as 1908 drew to a close. The spark was Roosevelt's final message to Congress in December.

Referring to the SSD investigative restrictions passed by Congress in April (but omitting the fact that he did not veto the bill), Roosevelt claimed that, "It is not too much to say that this amendment has been of benefit only and could be of benefit only to the criminal classes."[109]

Falsely claiming that the Secret Service had not been used much for non-counterfeiting investigations, Roosevelt continued that "it is true that the work of Secret Service agents was partly responsible for the indictment and conviction of a Senator and a Congressman for land frauds in Oregon."[110] Arguing that members of Congress should not be beyond the reach of executive branch law enforcement agents, Roosevelt finished by stating that if Congress objected to the use of the Secret Service for that purpose that "a special exception could be made in the law prohibiting the use of the Secret Service force in investigating members of Congress."[111]

"WITH CARE, SECRECY, AND DISPATCH" 33

Within 48 hours of Roosevelt's delivery of his message to lawmakers, senior members of his own party in the House were crafting a censure resolution.[112] On December 11, the House unanimously passed a resolution establishing a temporary committee to report on the incident and recommend legislative language to address Roosevelt's attack on Congress.[113]

Roosevelt fired back, with "high Administration officials" telling the *New York Times* that the chief executive was going to publicly accuse specific House and Senate members of impropriety or misconduct, and that SSD chief John Wilkie had been directed to "get together all these facts and such others as his force can assemble."[114] For Roosevelt's critics, it was proof positive that he was using the Secret Service for exactly the kind of political intelligence gathering and intimidation that they had feared.

On December 16, the Senate passed its own resolution instructing the Appropriations Committee to investigate Roosevelt's use of the Secret Service and whether his claims that the 1908 amendment had impaired the ability of the Department of Justice to find and prosecute criminals.[115] The following day, the House passed a resolution demanding that Roosevelt produce his proof of congressional corruption or malfeasance.[116]

That same week, the *New York Sun*, in a scathing editorial titled "The Perverted Secret Service," stated that Wilkie's unit "today exists as a private and personal vehicle of blackmail and oppression."[117] The paper closed by stating that "if the Congress possesses one last shred of manhood and patriotism the whole structure of spy government will be exposed to the just anger of the nation and will be destroyed in the indignation it will arouse."[118]

Congress had no intention of destroying the Secret Service; too many of its members had appealed to Wilkie to hire their constituents over the years, and counterfeiting was a real problem that needed the full focus of the Service. Even so, absent a retreat by the president, a fresh legislative rebuke seemed certain. As Christmas approached, Roosevelt and his advisors knew he was in a corner; they began implementing their exit strategy.

On December 22, the *Times* reported on the administration's plan to move noncounterfeiting investigations from the SSD to the Department of Justice.[119] The *Times* incorrectly stated that the SSD would be merged with the investigative elements of other executive branch agencies into a single Bureau of Criminal Investigation. In reality, Bonaparte had established the Bureau of Investigation almost six months earlier—without congressional authorization.

In the new year, Roosevelt would backpedal from his previous claims about widespread congressional corruption. Wilkie would face a difficult time with House Appropriations Committee chairman Roger Tawney and other House and Senate members over his previous testimony on SSD activities during February and March 1909, but the controversy died away with the exit of Theodore Roosevelt from the White House in March.

What remained was the new structure Roosevelt and Bonaparte had put in place, and under Roosevelt's immediate successors the Bureau would slowly grow in size, remaining unmolested by Congress. In doing so, Roosevelt created new federal law enforcement structures and operational precedents that shredded the Bill of Rights and provided his successors a template for future crackdowns, a pattern that has repeated itself with regularity for over a century.

In the absence of sustained, probing oversight, the BoI's managers and agents would soon engage in the same kind of political domestic surveillance activities that created the original crisis for the Secret Service. The difference would be that many of those domestic surveillance and political subversion activities—which also involved the SSD, Postal Service, State Department, and other executive branch elements—would not be publicly known for decades, and in cases where they were known, were undertaken with the knowledge and support of Congress. The perceived intensification of pan-national and foreign threats would both drive the growth of the Bureau and other domestic surveillance activities and accelerate a political and legal slide away from an adherence to the Bill of Rights.

NEW PRESIDENT, SAME EMERGING SURVEILLANCE STATE

Theodore Roosevelt left office believing that his hand-picked successor, William Howard Taft, would carry on the policies Roosevelt had put in place over the previous decade. On many issues, Taft would disappoint his predecessor—so much so that Roosevelt would ultimately mount a campaign to unseat him. But on the question of using federal resources to continue domestic surveillance and political persecution of individuals and groups deemed a threat to the prevailing political and economic order, there would be almost complete continuity between the two Administration's. This was especially true regarding the targeting of socialists.

In the 1908 presidential election, Eugene V. Debs almost equaled his 1904 showing, pulling in over 400,000 votes, nearly 3 percent of those cast; in the 1900 election, Debs had received fewer than 90,000 votes. The Socialist Party, despite its own internal struggles, was the fastest growing political

"WITH CARE, SECRECY, AND DISPATCH" 35

party in the nation. Its attacks on the likes of J.P. Morgan, Andrew Carnegie, and other powerful capitalists and the conditions under which their employees worked had struck a chord with an increasing number of American workers and their families.

The political alliance between the socialists and the IWW helped fuel strikes in multiple industries, with calls for better wages and an eight-hour workday gaining the most traction. But it was the calls for the nationalization of industries, along with outbreaks of violence involving striking workers, that most worried the American political class, and thus the federal agencies that answered to leaders in the executive branch and politicians on Capitol Hill. As a result, the nascent Bureau of Investigation was taking an increasing interest in the political activities of American socialists— though to outsiders it would deny such surveillance or investigations were underway.

In May 1909, in response to a letter to the attorney general, Bureau chief Stanley Finch wrote to attorney Sidney Schwartz in Titusville, Pennsylvania, who had requested an investigation of the Socialist Party. Finch replied, "in so far as I am advised, no such investigation is contemplated and that I have no information whatever concerning the 'Independent Order of Americans.'"[120] In fact, Finch had agents around the country investigating socialist organizations and cultivating informants within socialist political circles.

On June 5, Finch wrote to the Chicago special agent in charge, former SSD operative Marshall Eberstein, regarding the desirability of getting close to a journalist working for a socialist newspaper

> I note that, in Agent Quigley's daily report for the 31st ultimo, the statement is made that a telegram was received from a Washington correspondent of the Socialists concerning the intentions of United States Attorney Bone and United States Marshall Mackey. If it can be done without suspicion, or in any way prejudicing the future work of the informant, it seems to be advisable to ascertain the name of the Washington correspondent referred to.[121]

Five weeks later, Finch was directing Special Agent J.W. Vann in Wequetonsing, Michigan, to investigate local socialists, using the US Marshal's office as cover.

> Referring to your letter of the 9th inst., in regard to an organization of socialists at Harbor Springs, you are requested to report fully regarding this matter, and to send to this office copies of the paper mentioned by you. You are advised, also, that the United States Marshal

36   CHAPTER 1

for the western district of Michigan has been authorized to appoint
you as a special deputy marshal, without compensation, and that he
will communicate with you in care of this office.[122]

In none of this correspondence is there any mention of an actual or alleged
violation of federal law, only the fact that socialists were in the area, publishing a newspaper and trying to pick up political support for their positions in favor of unions and worker rights. Like Wilkie, his counterpart at
the SSD, Finch remained obsessed with "radicals" or "revolutionaries" even
in the absence of any articulated violent threat from those who came to his
attention.

In September 1909, Finch wrote a confidential memo to Eberstein in
Chicago regarding a Russian Jewish immigrant by the name of Isaac Hourwich, a "man referred to in certain confidential reports."[123] A former political
prisoner who spent time in a Russian Siberian prison, Hourwich "came to
this country on account of certain evidence found by the Russian authorities
which indicated his connection with a revolutionary movement."[124]

Russian persecution of Jews was a well-known phenomenon (a topic upon
which Hourwich had written, as Finch noted in his memo). Why Finch would
give credence to the claims of an authoritarian regime with a secret police, notorious for using torture and murder to intimidate regime opponents, is baffling.

Finch ended his memo to Eberstein by saying that, "I am informed that
he is now connected with the census office in the capacity of an expert, and
that he is interested in caring for Russian political refugees. I will have further investigation made with reference to this man."[125]

Finch offered no evidence that Hourwich had violated a single federal
law.

The Bureau's chief was also aggressive in using investigative techniques
involving the mass collection of information on American travelers when in
pursuit of a single subject of an investigation.

In January 1910, Finch informed San Francisco–based Special Agent Clayton Herrington that regarding an ongoing investigation (not described in the
correspondence) "the matter of securing the passenger lists therein referred
to has been made the subject of a communication to the State Department
and the Collectors of the various ports mentioned in your letter."[126] Within
two weeks of getting the requests, the State Department and the Customs
Service had provided the full lists of passengers who had sailed from Galves-
ton and New Orleans to Mexico between September 24 and December 1,
1909.[127] Passenger lists of those traveling from Seattle to Mexico for the same
period were sent by Finch to Herrington in early February 1910.[128]

"WITH CARE, SECRECY, AND DISPATCH" 37

The assumption underlying these requests—which were made without resort to a court order—seemed to be that the suspect would actually travel under his real name, a questionable notion. In the process, the names and other personal information of hundreds of innocent Americans (and possibly foreign nationals) were collected and retained by the Bureau.

The presidential penchant for clandestinely gathering information on individuals of interest or to punish critics via federal law enforcement action continued under Taft.

In November 1909, Fred Carpenter, President Taft's personal secretary, had written Wilkie at the SSD to say that, "The President would like to hear from you at as early a date as possible as to what you know about Albert Falck. For your personal information only, I think the matter comes up in some way in connection with the taking of the census."[129] Secret Service operatives in New York dutifully ran down all the data on Falck they could find, but none of them had ever heard of the attorney or dealt with him in any way.[130] Taft had just used the SSD in a way that directly violated the law passed by Congress in 1908 barring such private investigations by the Service.

At the Bureau, Finch had no compunction about using the agents under his command to conduct what amounted to reprisal investigations against those who attacked senior Justice Department officials.

On June 27, 1910, Finch wrote the New York City special agent in charge, Edward Brennan, providing him with "an original anonymous letter, together with the envelope in which it was enclosed, which was received by the Department today and which refers to the Attorney General in highly improper terms. Please make such investigation as may be practicable to ascertain who was the writer of this letter."[131] How writing an anonymous letter to Attorney General George Wickersham that referred to him in "highly improper terms" constituted a federal crime requiring a formal investigation Finch did not explain.

All during the second Roosevelt term and well into Taft's first year in office, these kinds of political or personal investigations by the Bureau and SSD continued, even as both agencies went about their assigned, legally grounded missions of catching white-collar criminals, combating the sex slave trade, or breaking up counterfeiting rings. But the Bureau's misguided and unconstitutional mass surveillance of those deemed political radicals blinded it to a genuine domestic terrorist cell that was operating on a national scale. By 1910, this covert terror campaign featured almost weekly acts of violence targeting commercial infrastructure owned by private interests.

38   CHAPTER 1

Up to this point, no deaths had resulted from the previous infrastructure and industrial sabotage attacks this group had mounted. At 1 a.m. on October 1, 1910, the leaders of this terrorist cell—which up to that point had escaped detection by the Bureau or the Secret Service—conducted another such attack. But this time, they miscalculated.

Instead of an empty building being blown up, the multistory structure that housed the *Los Angeles Times* was filled with staff working on an early edition of the paper. The blast was caused by a time-delayed dynamite bomb in a barrel in the alley next to the building, which subsequently ignited the gas mains feeding the *Times* and surrounding businesses. At least 20 were killed and over 100 injured. The terrorist cell that the Bureau and Secret Service had missed, despite their mass surveillance of socialists, anarchists, and unions, was none other than the leadership of the International Association of Bridge and Structural Iron Workers.[132]

Over the next 18 months, California state officials would pursue the case, charging J.B. and J.J. McNamara, the leaders of the union, as well as dozens of other union members, with murder and conspiracy. During most of this time, the federal government stayed on the sidelines, with Taft administration officials viewing the incident as the latest—albeit most deadly—confrontation between the anti-union ownership of the *Times* and the union.

Indeed, on the very day that the McNamaras found out which of them would go on trial first, the *Washington Evening Star* ran a front-page story about allegations of investigative over-reach and persecution by BoI investigators against the US attorney for Alabama's middle district, Warren Reese, and other officials around the country.[133] Finch and his deputy, Bruce Bielaski, were taken to task by Attorney General Wickersham, and an internal investigation was allegedly launched.

Despite the cloud that now hung over the BoI, by this point President Taft had felt enough political heat from California officials and the *Times*'s ownership that he had the Bureau begin its own investigation of the bombing and the union.

By early October 1911, a federal grand jury had been convened on the case.[134] Legendary defense lawyer Clarence Darrow, hired to represent the McNamaras, so despaired of his chances in court that he attempted to bribe two jurors. The case was hopeless for the defense, and before the jury tampering issue could become public, Darrow and his defense team convinced the brothers to plead guilty, with J.B. getting a life sentence and J.J. getting 10 years for bombing the Llewelyn Iron Works (an earlier incident).

The BoI's conduct in the Reese affair ultimately hastened Finch's departure from the Bureau to a federal commission dealing with human trafficking,

"WITH CARE, SECRECY, AND DISPATCH" 39

but the exile (such as it was) would be temporary. Finch would return as special assistant to the attorney general in 1913.[135] And the Bureau's tactics underwent no changes, despite the damage caused to Reese and other officials wrongly targeted by Finch and Bureau agents.

Between 1911 and the outbreak of World War I in Europe, the BoI and the Secret Service continued to clandestinely monitor politically active Americans concerned with events at home and abroad.

"Big Bill" Haywood's IWW remained a focus of BoI investigation, despite the lack of a true criminal predicate.[136] The political harassment of *Appeal to Reason* and its staff continued throughout Taft's presidency and into that of his successor, Woodrow Wilson. A BoI investigation of an alleged leak of DoJ internal decision-making in a case in Atlanta in 1912 led to BoI harassment of the *Atlanta Constitution* reporter who broke the story.[137]

From November 1913 through at least April 1914, the BoI's San Francisco field office, working at the request of the Canadian Secret Service, investigated Hindu nationalists in the Bay area, including Hindu students and their American academic advisor, at the University of California at Berkeley.[138] Local American socialists were also monitored as part of this particular investigation—in which no allegation of a federal crime had been made by either the BoI or the Canadian government.

As the war in Europe raged, socialists and anarchists found common cause with a new group of Americans committed to keeping the country out of the war and opposed to any return to the draft. At the same time, the BoI, the SSD, and other federal agencies concerned with these and other movements with foreign connections steadily expanded their surveillance operations, with some federal agencies and departments not previously involved in domestic surveillance now getting into the game. For the constitutional rights of thousands of innocent Americans, the results would be catastrophic.

CONCLUSION

Prior to President McKinley's assassination, Secret Service agents had been employed in a very limited, and relatively focused, way on a single domestic political movement with international connections: anarchism—and even that surveillance was largely focused on the Patterson, New Jersey, area. After Leon Czolgosz ended the life of America's twenty-fifth president, the full investigative and legal power of the federal government was hurled at anarchists across the nation. Congress took the extraordinary step of passing a ban on the immigration of anyone known or suspected of being an

40 CHAPTER 1

anarchist, an act federal courts upheld. Nothing like it had happened since the passage of the infamous Alien and Sedition Acts over a century earlier.

Under McKinley's successor, Theodore Roosevelt, the Secret Service was tasked with an increasing number of politically motivated surveillance operations, often untethered to any violation of federal laws, and Roosevelt would even try to get newspapers he found offensive excluded from the mails. Furious at the restrictions placed on his use of the Secret Service after the Pritchard extramarital spying incident, Roosevelt did an end-run around Congress by instructing Attorney General Charles Bonaparte to create a new federal investigative unit inside the Justice Department: the Bureau of Investigation. Congress not only failed to reverse Roosevelt's creation of the BoI, but it also eventually funded it despite the absence of any act of Congress authorizing its creation.

Roosevelt's successor, William Howard Taft, would not be *as* prolific or as brazen as Roosevelt in his use of the Secret Service or BoI, but in the main he didn't need to. Both agencies were developing their own organizational cultures that were focused on threats to the prevailing politico-economic paradigm. Both intensified their surveillance and informant penetration of anarchist and socialist entities throughout American society. Organized labor, particularly the IWW, was also a focus of both federal law enforcement organizations. And as the war in Europe approached, both would develop liaison relationships with friendly foreign law enforcement and intelligence services for the purpose of sharing information on political dissidents with overseas connections. In less than a generation, the structural, legal, and political foundations of the American surveillance state had been laid.

NOTES

1. Letter from Acting Secretary of State Alvin Adey to Treasury Secretary Philander Knox, August 8, 1901. NARA RG 59, Domestic Letters of the DOS, 1784–1906, M40, reel 152.
2. Scott Miller, *The President and the Assassin: McKinley, Terror, and Empire at the Dawn of the American Century* (New York: Random House, 2011).
3. Peter Marshall, *Demanding the Impossible: A History of Anarchism* (Oakland: PM Press, 2010), 45 (iBookstore version).
4. Marshall, *Demanding the Impossible*, 45.
5. James Green, *Death in the Haymarket* (New York: Anchor Books, 2007).
6. Green, *Death in the Haymarket*, 289–294.
7. Letter from Treasury Secretary Lyman Gage to Attorney General John Griggs, August 11, 1900. NARA RG 60, DOJ Straight and Numerical Files, Box 1226, file 11717.

"WITH CARE, SECRECY, AND DISPATCH" 41

8. The available correspondence on this episode can be found in NARA RG 60, DOJ Straight and Numerical Files, Box 1226, file 11717.

9. Letter from Secret Service Division Chief John Wilkie to Treasury Secretary Lyman Gage, November 2, 1900. NARA RG 60, DOJ Straight and Numerical Files, Box 1226, file 11717.

10. NARA RG 87, DOT, SSD, Entry A1/39, Lists of Suspected Anarchists: 1901–1902.

11. Vivian Gornick, *Emma Goldman: Revolution as a Way of Life* (New Haven and London: Yale University Press, 2011), 8–11.

12. Gornick, *Emma Goldman*, 45–52.

13. "Emma Goldman Is Arrested in Chicago," *New York Times*, September 11, 1901.

14. "The Chicago Anarchists," *New York Times*, September 14, 1901.

15. "No Evidence against Emma Goldman," *New York Times*, September 13, 1901.

16. "To Drive Anarchists Out of New York: Detectives Taking a Secret Census of the Brotherhood," *New York Times*, September 11, 1901.

17. "To Drive Anarchists Out of New York."

18. Letter from S. Taliaferro to Attorney General Philander Knox, September 7, 1901. NARA RG 60, MAR, A1 Entry 72B, File number 13658.

19. Letter from S. Taliaferro to Attorney General Philander Knox, September 7, 1901.

20. Letter from S. Taliaferro to Attorney General Philander Knox, September 7, 1901.

21. September 1901 draft of letter to various US attorneys approved by Attorney General Knox. NARA RG 60, MAR, A1 Entry 72B, File number 13658.

22. Memorandum for the Record, October 4, 1901. LOC, TRP, Series 14, 1897–1903, Reel 453.

23. The statutory references for the Commission can be found in *Checklist of United States Public Documents, 1789–1909, Third Edition, Vol. 1, Lists of Congressional and Departmental Publications* (Washington, DC: United States Government Printing Office, March 1911), 1517–1518.

24. Letter from Commissioner Alexander Botkin to COL Cecil Clay, chief clerk of the Department of Justice, November 23, 1901. NARA RG 60, MAR, A1 Entry 72B, File number 13658.

25. "Solicitor General Richards on Anarchy," *New York Times*, November 24, 1901.

26. "The President's First Message," *Washington Evening Star,* December 3, 1901, 1–2.

27. "The President's First Message."

28. Letter from Rep. George Ray to Attorney General Philander Knox, December 18, 1901. NARA RG 60, MAR, A1 Entry 72B, File number 13658.

29. Julia Rose Kraut, "Global Anti-Anarchism: The Origins of Ideological Deportation and the Suppression of Expression," *Indiana Journal of Global Legal Studies* 19, no. 1, (Winter 2012): 177.

30. Public Law 57–162. Ch. 1012, Sec. 39, March 3, 1903.

31. Geoffrey R. Stone, *Perilous Times: Free Speech in Wartime, From the Sedition Act of 1798 to the War on Terrorism* (New York: W.W. Norton & Company, 2004), 133.

32. Kraut, "Global Anti-Anarchism," 182–183.

33. Kraut, "Global Anti-Anarchism,"182–183.

34. Kraut, "Global Anti-Anarchism,"184–186.

35. *Turner v. Williams*, 194 U.S. 279, 294.

36. The Secret Service's correspondence on Boyd is located in NARA RG 87, Records of the SSD, General Correspondence, 1894–1918, Box 2, A1 Entry 18, File number 66830.

42   CHAPTER 1

37. Letter from Nathan Boyd to Theodore Roosevelt, March 17, 1904, 46. NARA RG 87, Records of the SSD, General Correspondence, 1894–1918, Box 2, A1 Entry 18, File number 66830.
38. Letter from Nathan Boyd to Theodore Roosevelt, March 17, 1904, 41–43.
39. Letter from Nathan Boyd to Theodore Roosevelt, March 17, 1904, 107.
40. Report of Secret Service Assistant Operative Clarence Park to Secret Service Chief John Wilkie, November 10, 1904. NARA RG 87, Records of the SSD, General Correspondence, 1894–1918, Box 2, A1 Entry 18, File number 66830.
41. Report of Secret Service Assistant Operative Clarence Park to Secret Service Chief John Wilkie, November 10, 1904.
42. Report of Secret Service Assistant Operative Clarence Park to Secret Service Chief John Wilkie, November 10, 1904.
43. Letter from W.H.H. Llewellyn to J.R. Lucero, January 14, 1905. NARA RG 87, Records of the SSD, General Correspondence, 1894–1918, Box 2, A1 Entry 18, File number 66830.
44. Letter from John Wilkie to Alvey Adee, January 27, 1905. NARA RG 87, Records of the SSD, General Correspondence, 1894–1918, Box 2, A1 Entry 18, File number 66830.
45. Letter from US Postmaster Allen Papen to John Wilkie, March 13, 1905. NARA RG 87, Records of the SSD, General Correspondence, 1894–1918, Box 2, A1 Entry 18, File number 66830.
46. Letter from John Wilkie to Allen Papen, March 17, 1905. NARA RG 87, Records of the SSD, General Correspondence, 1894–1918, Box 2, A1 Entry 18, File number 66830.
47. "Last Act in Elephant Butte Suit," *Albuquerque Morning Journal*, December 11, 1905, pp. 1–2.
48. Letter to C.H. Keep, Assistant Secretary of the Treasury, from Assistant Treasurer Hamilton Fish II, October 11, 1906. NARA RG 87, Records of the SSD, General Correspondence, 1894–1918, Box 15, A1 Entry 18, File number 71299.
49. Letter from NYC Operative in Charge William Flynn to Secret Service Chief John Wilkie, October 16, 1906. NARA RG 87, Records of the SSD, General Correspondence, 1894–1918, Box 15, A1 Entry 18, File number 71299.
50. Report from NYC Operative in Charge William Flynn to Secret Service Chief John Wilkie, October 30, 1906. NARA RG 87, Records of the SSD, General Correspondence, 1894–1918, Box 15, A1 Entry 18, File number 71299.
51. Eugene V. Debs, "If They Hang Moyer and Haywood, They've Got to Hang Me," *Appeal to Reason*, March 10, 1906, 1.
52. Note from President Theodore Roosevelt to Attorney General William Henry Moody, March 19, 1906. NARA RG 60, DOJ Central Files (Straight Numerical Files), File number 77175.
53. Letter from Assistant Attorney General Charles Robb to Attorney General William Moody, March 22, 1906. NARA RG 60, DOJ Central Files (Straight Numerical Files), File number 77175.
54. Letter from Assistant Attorney General Charles Robb to Attorney General William Moody, March 22, 1906.
55. Letter from Assistant Attorney General Charles Robb to Attorney General William Moody, March 22, 1906.

"WITH CARE, SECRECY, AND DISPATCH" 43

56. John A. Fraser III, "The Use of Encrypted, Coded and Secret Communications Is an 'Ancient Liberty' Protected by the United States Constitution," *Virginia Journal of Law and Technology*, 2 (Fall 1997). Accessed at http://www.vjolt.net/vol2/issue/vol2_art2.html#IIIB.

57. White House request to the Attorney General, March 20, 1906. NARA RG 60, DOJ Central Files (Straight Numerical Files), File number 134296. Only the DOJ buckslip on the case was found by the author, not Roosevelt's actual correspondence.

58. Memorandum for the Files in reference to a Recommendation that fraud order be issued against *La Questione Sociale*, Box 1639, Paterson, New Jersey, April 14, 1908. NARA RG 28, Records of the Post Office Department, General Records, 1905–1921, File number 20854.

59. Letter from H.S. Martin to President Theodore Roosevelt, July 9, 1906. NARA RG 60, DOJ Central Files (Straight Numerical Files), File number 85499.

60. Letter from William Loeb to the Acting Attorney General, July 14, 1906. NARA RG 60, DOJ Central Files (Straight Numerical Files), File number 85499.

61. Letter from the Acting Attorney General to US Attorney for Buffalo, NY Charles Brown, July 16, 1906. NARA RG 60, DOJ Central Files (Straight Numerical Files), File number 85499.

62. Letter from the Acting Attorney General to William Loeb, August 13, 1906. NARA RG 60, DOJ Central Files (Straight Numerical Files), File number 85499. The file itself does not contain Brown's report, but a thorough public records and press archive search by the author turned up no mention of de la Franier or charges filed against him in the matter.

63. Confidential letter from William Loeb to John Wilkie, September 15, 1906. NARA RG 87, Records of the SSD, General Correspondence, 1894–1918, File number 71167.

64. "Furious Riots in Paterson Strike," *The World,* June 18, 1902.

65. "Back to Go to Prison," *New York Tribune*, April 11, 1904.

66. "Pastor in Aid of MacQueen," *New York Times*, March 12, 1905.

67. "MacQueen the Anarchist: Wealthy Philadelphian Working to Secure His Pardon," *Washington Evening Star,* July 9, 1906.

68. Letter from John Wikie to William Loeb, September 17, 1906. NARA RG 87, Records of the SSD, General Correspondence, 1894–1918, File number 71167.

69. Letter from John Wikie to William Loeb, September 17, 1906.

70. Letter from John Wikie to William Loeb, September 17, 1906.

71. Letter from John Wikie to William Loeb, September 17, 1906.

72. Letter from William Loeb to John Wilkie, September 19, 1906. NARA RG 87, Records of the SSD, General Correspondence, 1894–1918, File number 71167.

73. "William MacQueen Released," *New York Sun,* May 2, 1907, 1.

74. Correspondence on this between SSD Operative Maurits Hymans and SSD Chief John Wilkie NARA RG 87, Records of the SSD, General Correspondence, 1894–1918, File number 72758.

75. Letter with attachments from William Loeb to John Wilkie, July 22, 1907. NARA RG 87, Records of the SSD, General Correspondence, 1894–1918, File number 72509.

76. Letter from John Wilkie to William Loeb, July 23, 1907. NARA RG 87, Records of the SSD, General Correspondence, 1894–1918, File number 72509.

77. Letter from John Wilkie to William Loeb, July 23, 1907.

44   CHAPTER 1

78. "Westerners Roil President," *Pacific Commercial Advertiser,* February 20, 1907, 1. Accessed via LOCCA.
79. "Westerners Roil President," 1.
80. "Wilkie Makes Denial: Secret Service Chief Not Investigating Boise Case for President," *San Francisco Call,* May 14, 1907. Accessed via LOCCA.
81. "Alleged Senator Mitchell Accepted $2000 from Putter," *East Oregonian,* January 2, 1905, 1. Accessed via LOCCA.
82. "Mitchell Is Dead," *Condon Globe,* December 14, 1905, 2. Accessed via LOCCA.
83. The available body of correspondence on the Blackburn case can be found at NARA RG 60, DoJ Central Files (Straight Numerical Files), File number 69073.
84. Letter from William Loeb to Attorney General Charles Bonaparte, March 20, 1907. NARA RG 60, DOJ Central Files (Straight Numerical Files), File number 59512.
85. Letter from Attorney General Charles Bonaparte to President Roosevelt, March 20, 1907. NARA RG 60, DOJ Central Files (Straight Numerical Files), File number 67015.
86. Telegram from Attorney General Charles Bonaparte to USA Norman Ruick, March 21, 1907. NARA RG 60, DOJ Central Files (Straight Numerical Files), File number 67015.
87. Confidential letter from Attorney General Charles Bonaparte to presidential secretary William Loeb, March 22, 1907. NARA RG 60, DOJ Central Files (Straight Numerical Files), File number 67015.
88. Report of B.F. Cash to Attorney General Charles Bonaparte, March 25, 1907, 1–7. NARA RG60, DOJ Central Files (Straight Numerical Files), File number 67015.
89. Telegram from USA Norman Ruick to Attorney General Charles Bonaparte, April 10, 1907 (Treasury Department copy). NARA RG 60, DOJ Central Files (Straight Numerical Files), File number 67015.
90. Letter from Attorney General Charles Bonaparte to USA Norman Ruick, April 15, 1907. NaRA RG 60, DOJ Central Files (Straight Numerical Files), File number 67015.
91. "Elopement Costs Ensign His Job; Divorce Sought," *Washington Times,* December 13, 1907, 1. Accessed via LOCCA.
92. "Elopement Costs Ensign His Job."
93. "Secret Service Scored as Private Spy: Men Used in Domestic Entanglements, Says House Committee," *Washington Times,* April 21, 1908, 1. Accessed via LOCCA.
94. "Espionage Exists: Representatives Contradict Chief Wilkie's Statement," *Washington Evening Star,* April 22, 1908, 1. Accessed via LOCCA.
95. 42 Congressional Record—House, May 1, 1908, p. 5558.
96. "A Federal Police System," *Washington Herald,* May 7, 1908, 6. Accessed via LOCCA.
97. Letter from Maurits Hymans to John Wilkie, January 7, 1908. NARA RG 87, Records of the SSD, General Correspondence, 1894–1918, File number 73219. The NYPD letter to Wilkie is also located in this file.
98. Letter from Maurits Hymans to John Wilkie, January 18, 1908. NARA RG 87, Records of the SSD, General Correspondence, 1894–1918, File number 73298.
99. Multiple reports from Maurits Hymans to John Wilkie, March 1 through April 25, 1908. NARA RG 87, Records of the SSD, General Correspondence, 1894–1918, File number 73576.
100. Anthony Downs, *Inside Bureaucracy* (Boston: Little, Brown and Company, 1967), 5.
101. *Annual Report of the Attorney General of the United States for the Year 1907* (Washington: Government Printing Office, 1907), 1: 9–10. Accessed via the Hathi Trust at https://babel.hathitrust.org/cgi/pt?id=ucl.b5145514.

"WITH CARE, SECRECY, AND DISPATCH" 45

102. *Hearings before the Subcommittee of the House Committee on Appropriations for Deficiency Appropriations for 1908 and Prior Years on Urgent Deficiency Bill*, 202–203. Extract of testimony from FBI website at https://www2.fbi.gov/libref/historic/history/historic _doc/doc1908jan.htm.

103. Order of Attorney General Charles Bonaparte, July 26, 1908. Accessed via the FBI website at https://www.fbi.gov/history/brief-history.

104. Letter from Secret Service Director John Wilkie to Special Operative Kirk DeBelle, June 27, 1908. LOC, CBP, Box 131.

105. Confidential memorandum from Chief Examiner Stanley Finch to Examiner Charles DeWoody, August 13, 1908. NARA RG 65, Records of the FBI, Letters Sent by the Chief Examiner, October 1907–June 1911, Box 1.

106. Letter from Chief Examiner Stanley Finch to H.C. Gauss, Private Secretary and Assistant to the Attorney General, August 31, 1908. NARA RG 65, Records of the FBI, Letters Sent by the Chief Examiner, October 1907–June 1911, Box 1.

107. Memo titled "In the Matter of the Filibustering Expedition against Colombia," likely date February 27, 1909. NARA RG 65, Records of the FBI, Series M1085, Miscellaneous Records, reel 112.

108. "In the Matter of the Filibustering Expedition against Colombia."

109. "Last Word for My Policies: President's Message Kind to Railroads," *New York Sun*, December 9, 1908, 3. Accessed via LOCCA.

110. "Last Word for My Policies."

111. "Last Word for My Policies."

112. "Congress Prepares Roosevelt Rebuke," December 11, 1908, *New York Times*, 4.

113. "United House Votes Roosevelt Rebuke," *New York Times*, December 12, 1908, 1.

114. "Roosevelt to Tell Congress's Secrets," *New York Times*, December 13, 1908, 1.

115. "Senators Resent Roosevelt Attack," *New York Times*, December 17, 1908, 2.

116. "House Asks Proof from Roosevelt," *New York Times*, December 18, 1908, 1.

117. "The Perverted Secret Service," *New York Sun*, December 19, 1908, 6. Accessed via LOCCA.

118. "The Perverted Secret Service."

119. "To Shift Control of Secret Service," *New York Times*, December 22, 1908, 3.

120. Letter from Stanley Finch to Sidney Schwartz, May 21, 1909. NARA RG 65, Records of the FBI, Letters Sent by the Chief Examiner, October 1907–June 1911, Box 2.

121. Letter from Stanley Finch to Marshall Eberstein, June 5, 1909. NARA RG 65, Records of the FBI, Letters Sent by the Chief Examiner, October 1907–June 1911, Box 3.

122. Letter from Stanley Finch to J.W. Vann, July 14, 1909. NARA RG 65, Records of the FBI, Letters Sent by the Chief Examiner, October 1907–June 1911, Box 3.

123. Letter from Stanley Finch to Marshall Eberstein, September 11, 1909. NARA RG 65, Records of the FBI, Letters Sent by the Chief Examiner, October 1907–June 1911, Box 3.

124. Letter from Stanley Finch to Marshall Eberstein, September 11, 1909.

125. Letter from Stanley Finch to Marshall Eberstein, September 11, 1909.

126. Letter from Stanley Finch to Clayton Herrington, January 12, 1910. NARA RG 65, Records of the FBI, Letters Sent by the Chief Examiner, October 1907–June 1911, Box 4.

46   CHAPTER 1

127. Letter from Stanley Finch to Clayton Herrington, January 25, 1910. NARA RG 65, Records of the FBI, Letters Sent by the Chief Examiner, October 1907–June 1911, Box 4.

128. Letter from Stanley Finch to Clayton Herrington, February 4, 1910. NARA RG 65, Records of the FBI, Letters Sent by the Chief Examiner, October 1907–June 1911, Box 4.

129. Letter from Fred Carpenter to John Wilkie, November 17, 1909. NARA RG 87, Records of the SSD, General Correspondence, 1894–1918, File number 76773.

130. NARA RG 87, Records of the SSD, General Correspondence, 1894–1918, File number 76773.

131. Letter from Stanley Finch to Edward J. Brennan, June 27, 1910. NARA RG 65, Records of the FBI, Letters Sent by the Chief Examiner, October 1907–June 1911, Box 5.

132. The most contemporary account of the union's multiyear bombing campaign is Lew Irwin's *Deadly Times: The 1910 Bombing of the Los Angeles Times and America's Forgotten Decade of Terror* (Guilford: Lyons Press, 2013).

133. "Bureau under Fire," *Washington Evening Star*, October 11, 1911, 1. The McNamara trial story was on the same front page. Accessed via LOCCA.

134. *Deadly Times*, Chapter 38 (Kindle edition). For the available body of FBI records on this case, see NARA RH 65, FBI: Investigative Case Files of the Bureau, 1908–1922, Series M1085, reels 137 and 138.

135. "FBI Directors, Then and Now: Stanley W. Finch, July 26, 1908–April 30, 1912" from the FBI website at https://www.fbi.gov/history/directors/stanley-w-finch.

136. Letter from Stanley Finch to Special Agent William Byron, April 4, 1911. NARA RG 65, Records of the FBI, Letters Sent by the Chief Examiner, October 1907–June 1911, Box 8.

137. See affidavit of E. C. Bruffey, reporter, *Atlanta Constitution*, May 6, 1912, and subsequent report of BoI Agent Lewis J. Baley, May 11, 1912. NARA RG 65, FBI: Investigative Case Files of the Bureau, 1908–1922, Series M1085, reel 144.

138. The available BoI correspondence on this episode can be found at the NARA RG 65, FBI: Investigative Case Files of the Bureau, 1908–1922, Series M1085, reel 175.

CHAPTER 2

"Disloyal Utterances"
1914–1932

At the start of World War I, the United States was only one of many neutral nations watching the carnage engulf Europe. German government espionage in America and German submarine attacks on ships carrying American passengers would, over a two-and-a-half-year period, move the Wilson administration toward entering the war. The military buildup that preceded apace from 1915 onward sparked the creation of antiwar and civil liberties groups and related protests around the country, leading to Secret Service and BoI surveillance of the groups and their leaders. Once war was declared, draconian laws like the Espionage Act were used to prosecute and silence news outlets and political activists opposed to the war, with even the country's first socialist in the House of Representatives prosecuted under the act and denied his seat in Congress.

The initial phase of the interwar period did see the repeal of the Sedition Act and Food and Fuel Control Act, but the Espionage Act remained the law of the land. And while the size of Army and Navy intelligence elements shrank along with the rest of the armed forces, their role in domestic surveillance did not. Even so, the BoI effectively eclipsed them and the Secret Service as the federal government's premier internal security and intelligence gathering arm under the leadership of J. Edgar Hoover. Hoover's role in helping foment the first anticommunist "Red Scare" was an outsized one, and his obsession with Soviet efforts—real or imagined—to undermine American democracy put the Bureau on the path of hunting, persecuting, prosecuting, and where possible, deporting alleged or actual Soviet sympathizers

47

48   CHAPTER 2

throughout the interwar period. And it was in the "Great War" that these tactics and techniques that the Bureau, Military Intelligence Division (MID), and Office of Naval Intelligence (ONI) would use against domestic political leftists were first developed.

FROM GERMAN ESPIONAGE
TO GERMANOPHOBIA

By the end of 1914, the conflict in Europe had settled into a bloody stalemate. American firms were busy supplying war material to the belligerents, almost entirely to Britain and France. The de facto tilt in American policy was clear, but in his annual address to Congress in December 1914, Wilson continued to proclaim American neutrality and good will toward all nations.

"We are at peace with all the world," Wilson said. "No one who speaks counsel based on fact or drawn from a just and candid interpretation of realities can say that there is reason to fear that from any quarter our independence or the integrity of our territory is threatened."[1]

But Wilson was mistaken that no nation was at war with America. Germany was waging a covert war against the United States on American soil.

On the night of February 2, 1915, Werner von Horn, a German army reserve officer, crossed the border from Maine into Canada and attempted—unsuccessfully—to blow up the Canadian Pacific Railway bridge over the St. Croix River.[2] Horn was part of an espionage and sabotage ring operating out of the German embassy in Washington, a fact that would only become clear as the year progressed.

Two days after Horn's failed bombing attempt, the German government declared the waters around Great Britain and Ireland to be a war zone in which any ships—including those of ostensibly neutral nations like the United States—could be attacked.[3] Just over three months later, the British passenger liner *Lusitania* was torpedoed by a German U-boat off the Irish coast, resulting in the loss of nearly 1,200 lives, including over 100 Americans.[4]

The sinking of the passenger liner had a catalyzing effect within the Wilson administration.

A week after *Lusitania*'s loss, Secretary of State William Jennings Bryan wrote to his Treasury Department counterpart, William McAdoo, to request the loan of SSD agents for counterespionage work against known or suspected German government agents and their sympathizers in America.[5] McAdoo agreed, and Wilson approved the plan.[6] But State's foray into domestic surveillance didn't stop there.

"DISLOYAL UTTERANCES" 49

State's number two official, Robert Lansing, was determined that State have its own intelligence gathering capability, which he established in his office, the Office of the Counselor. To run the operation, he selected State veteran Frank Polk. Utilizing a combination of SSD agents and a small cadre of others hired directly, Polk built a small but capable operation that simultaneously monitored German officials and nationals as well as collected intelligence from American diplomatic missions overseas.[7] Wiretapping of German government communications was handled by the SSD. But the larger and more dangerous development was the SSD's renewed domestic surveillance role.

For the first time in nearly a decade, SSD agents would potentially be spying on Americans—effectively violating the 1908 law prohibiting the use of the Secret Service for anything other than catching counterfeiters and protecting the president. The present author found no evidence that Congress was informed of Wilson's authorization of the action.

As the summer progressed, the antiwar Bryan was forced out at State, replaced by the decidedly more hawkish Lansing. By mid-August, Lansing would benefit greatly from Bryan's decision to ask McAdoo for SSD agents to run counterespionage operations.

On July 24, 1915, two New York City–based SSD agents conducted close physical surveillance of German American newspaper editor George Viereck and another man who they didn't initially recognize—the Imperial German commercial attaché, Dr. Heinrich Albert. When the two Germans went their separate ways, one SSD agent, Frank Burke, stayed with Albert.

The day was warm, and Albert dozed on the train until it came to an abrupt halt. Recognizing the stop as his, Albert hastily exited the train—forgetting a large briefcase he'd been carrying. Burke saw his opportunity, took the case, and after successfully evading a belatedly pursuing Albert, brought the case to the SSD office. Inside was a veritable motherlode of documents detailing the German government's clandestine spying and sabotage operations on American soil.[8] It was an amazing find, but it also signaled a massive counterintelligence failure by the American government.

Even after an exhaustive briefing on the contents of Albert's briefcase, Wilson remained reluctant to force the issue with the German government. His long-time friend and chief political confidant, "Colonel" Edward House, had no such hesitation. He secured a pledge of source anonymity from the *New York World*'s Frank Cobb, then gave the newspaper editor the documents.[9] On August 15, the *World* ran the story, which caused outrage across the nation.

That same week, British authorities captured an undercover German naval officer who had also been a key player in the Kaiser's domestic sabotage operations in America—Captain Franz von Rintelen.[10] By the end of the year, German military attachés Karl Boy-Ed and Franz von Papen had been expelled from the United States. Franz von Rintelen would be held by British authorities until America's entry into the war, after which he would be extradited, tried, and convicted of his crimes.[11]

The unmasking of the German government's spy ring triggered a series of policy changes and political shifts that put the United States on a collision course with Germany.

Between August and November 1915, the BoI worked out arrangements with the major telecommunications providers to get copies of incoming and outgoing telegrams of individuals or organizations of interest to investigators. During the Spanish–American War, the Secret Service had secured Spanish government telegrams from the major communications providers, but the BoI's initiative was far more sweeping in its scope.

The year before, the Supreme Court had ruled in *Weeks vs. United States* (232 U.S. 383 (1914)) that federal agents could not simply go into people's homes, seize documents, and use them in prosecutions. But the decision did not address the question of whether copies of cables or telegrams sent to or from the United States and held by the telecommunications companies enjoyed the same protections. The BoI took the position they did not, the telecommunications companies went along, and thus no warrants for those communications were sought.[12] The other major changes included a ramped-up "preparedness" program and increasingly hostile, anti-immigrant (specifically anti–German American) rhetoric coming from the Wilson administration, including the president himself.

In his December message to Congress, Wilson condemned, without naming them directly, German Americans.

"I am sorry to say that the gravest threats against our national peace and safety have been uttered within our own borders," Wilson said.

> There are citizens of the United States, I blush to admit, born under other flags but welcomed under our generous naturalization laws to the full freedom and opportunity of America, who have poured the poison of disloyalty into the very arteries of our national life; who have sought to bring the authority and good name of our Government into contempt, to destroy our industries wherever they thought it effective for their vindictive purposes to strike at them, and to debase our politics to the uses of foreign intrigue.[13]

In reality, the sabotage operation orchestrated by the German government was carried out almost entirely by German nationals, most on the

"DISLOYAL UTTERANCES" 51

Imperial government's payroll. But the national backlash against all things German now included German Americans, and Wilson asked Congress for new legislative powers to go after them.

"Such creatures of passion, disloyalty, and anarchy must be crushed out," Wilson told lawmakers.

> They are not many, but they are infinitely malignant, and the hand of our power should close over them at once. They have formed plots to destroy property, they have entered into conspiracies against the neutrality of the Government, they have sought to pry into every confidential transaction of the Government in order to serve interests alien to our own. It is possible to deal with these things very effectually. I need not suggest the terms in which they may be dealt with.[14]

Wilson and his team did not wait to get new legislative authority to deal with the threat they perceived to be in their midst.

By June 1916, the SSD was conducting surveillance, either directly or via proxies, of both individual German Americans and German American businesses, clubs, and newspapers in Detroit and Baltimore, including the names and alleged political attitudes of key German American community leaders.[15]

The Detroit report described Circuit Court Commissioner Sam May as "a German Jew" and City Clerk Richard Lindsey as "a German Hyphen."[16] The local head of the German American Alliance alleged that "there could be mustered in the Northern [United] States more than half a million [German or German American] men who can be ready for war in a week."[17]

Such unverified reports helped fuel the growing war fears in the administration, and during the balance of 1916, both the press and the administration would increase the anti-immigrant rhetoric, culminating with Wilson's renomination acceptance speech in Sea Girt, New Jersey, in September 1916.

Lamenting how the war in Europe had come home, Wilson noted, "The seas were not broad enough to keep the infection of the conflict out of our own politics." He bemoaned the fact that "The passions and intrigues of certain active groups and combinations of men amongst us who were born under foreign flags injected the poison of disloyalty into our own most critical affairs." While conceding he was "the candidate of a party," he made clear that, "I am above all things else an American citizen. I neither seek the favor nor fear the displeasure of that small alien element amongst us which puts loyalty to any foreign power before loyalty to the United States."[18]

52   CHAPTER 2

ANTIWAR MOVEMENT BEGETS
DOMESTIC SURVEILLANCE

Wilson's change in tone and seeming lurch toward war by advocating an expansion of America's armed forces met with vocal opposition in Congress and across the nation.

Indeed, in 1915 Henry Street Settlement founder Lillian Wald joined other prominent antiwar and civil liberties activists in forming what was known as the Anti-Militarism Committee, who the *Pensacola Journal* promptly labeled "opponents of preparedness" populated by "several ministers and a few more fanatics, who can see nothing but unnecessary expenditure in the [A]dministration plan."[19] By late April 1916, the group had changed its name, rebranding as the American Union Against Militarism (AUAM), a name it would keep for the balance of the decade. In addition to Wald, the group included theologians Rabbi Stephen Wise and Rev. A.A. Berle, who along with other AUAM executive committee members went on a nationwide speaking tour in the spring and summer of 1916, challenging Wilson to meet with them.[20] Surprisingly, he agreed.

On May 8, Wilson spent an hour with key AUAM leaders. The meeting was civil and respectful, but no minds were changed on either side.[21] The divide between Wilson and groups like AUAM only widened as the year passed.

At the opposite end of Pennsylvania Avenue, Wilson's chief congressional opponent on "preparedness" was his one-time Republican admirer and ally, Senator Robert La Follette, Sr. of Wisconsin.

When the war broke out in Europe, Wilson and La Follette were both committed to American neutrality. But following the *Lusitania* incident and the revelations of German government sabotage and espionage operations on American soil, the two men began to diverge in their approach to the European war. By the time La Follette decided to make another run for the Republican nomination to challenge Wilson in 1916, the senator had come out against conscription, attacked most major press outlets as tools of arms manufacturers, and remained adamantly opposed to American entry into the European conflict.[22] La Follette lost the nomination fight to Charles Evans Hughes, but not his willingness to continue opposing what he viewed as the freshly reelected Wilson's seemingly inexorable march toward war.

The resumption of unrestricted submarine warfare by Germany on February 2, 1917, further altered the political dynamic against opponents of intervention like the AUAM and La Follette.

Just days after Germany's announcement, the first version of what would become known as the Espionage Act was introduced in the Senate by Lee

"DISLOYAL UTTERANCES" 53

Overman (D-NC).[23] The bill's scope was radical, as were the punishments to be handed out for violating it. The penalty was life in prison if a person were to "spread or make false reports or statements, or reports or statements likely or intended to cause disaffection in or to interfere with the success of, the military or naval forces of the United States."[24] As written, the bill would literally criminalize opposition to war with Germany.

The 64th Congress failed to act on the bill before adjourning in mid-March 1917, but that did not stop the administration from moving ahead with war preparations on other fronts. By the third week in February 1917, SSD agents were conducting investigations on alleged disloyalty or espionage activity among the German and German American population.

In late February 1917, an Atlanta-based SSD agent investigated a vague tip about a man who was "suspicious acting and talking German" in Titusville, Florida.[25] By March 8, the chief of the SSD had issued formal instructions to all agents to report "matters relating to neutrality and German espionage" via special reports, separately from investigations into counterfeiting or other matters under the purview of the SSD.[26] Even so, SSD Chief Flynn was aware that the Service was no longer the only federal law enforcement agency likely to be tasked with war-related investigations. Accordingly, he cabled all agents on March 25 to "Run out all neutrality matters" but to "not duplicate work of Department of Justice."[27]

Once the Congress granted Wilson's request for a declaration of war against Germany on April 6, the new chief of the SSD, William Moran, attempted to have the SSD reprise its role as the chief wartime investigative body for the federal government. Less than a week after America entered the war, he got all the help he could ask for from the Western Union Telegraph Company.

On the evening of April 10, Moran cabled all SSD field agents that:

> Agents of Western Union Telegraph company everywhere have been instructed to cooperate fully with Agent[s] this service[,] whose addresses have been furnished them. Upon presentation of proper credentials. Don't hesitate therefore to call on the telegraph people for any information you require. Take notice.[28]

Western Union was prepared to hand over to the SSD, without any judicial warrant, any information it wanted on individuals or entities utilizing its services.

And it wasn't just the SSD that was trying to assert primacy in the hunt for domestic enemies.

54   CHAPTER 2

In the weeks leading up to the declaration of war, Justice and Treasury, along with the State Department, had been engaged in a behind-the-scenes struggle over who would handle most war-related investigations, particularly espionage and so-called "disloyalty" investigations.

In his April 6 proclamation announcing the state of war with Germany, Wilson stated, "I do specially direct all officers, civil or military, of the United States that they exercise vigilance and zeal in the discharge of the duties incident to such a state of war."[29] Over two weeks before, Bruce Bielaski, head of the Bureau of Investigation at the Justice Department, got a head start on Wilson.

Bielaski convinced Attorney General Thomas Gregory that because of the Bureau's relatively small size compared to its likely war-time workload, more manpower was needed. Chicago businessman Albert Briggs offered Bielaski a solution: let Briggs raise a force of volunteer investigators to work under and in coordination with the Bureau. Briggs had done something similar during the Spanish–American war on behalf of the government. Gregory signed off on the proposal.[30] And it was that volunteer organization, the American Protective League (APL), that Treasury Secretary McAdoo was now up in arms about.

In a four-page, May 15 letter to Wilson, McAdoo complained that the president had failed to respond to his suggestion that a national "Bureau of Intelligence" be created to coordinate the work of the SSD, BoI, and other civilian federal investigative entities. Further, APL volunteers were effectively masquerading as SSD agents, displaying badges with the words "Secret Service" inscribed on them, in one case ordering a Des Moines, Iowa, resident to raise the American flag over his home.[31]

The extent to which McAdoo had been excluded from key Wilson decisions on domestic surveillance became clear when the Treasury Secretary told Wilson, "I did not know until advised by the Attorney General on April 21 that you had charged him specifically with the duty of executing your proclamation," referring to Wilson's April 6 proclamation on the state of war. McAdoo warned Wilson that if the APL "is allowed to continue to exist, suspicion will be engendered among our people, smoldering race antagonisms will burst into flame, and the melting pot of America will be melting pot no longer, but a crucible out of which will flash the molten lead of suspicion and dissension."[32]

McAdoo's warning proved prophetic, and not simply because of the inept and crude antics of APL members, but because of the actions of the entire federal domestic surveillance and political repression apparatus that Wilson allowed to grow.

THE NASCENT AMERICAN SURVEILLANCE
STATE TAKES SHAPE

As the war progressed, a level of coordination developed between the various civilian and military components of the federal government regarding domestic surveillance and investigations, as well as an entire prowar propaganda office, the Committee on Public Information (CPI), headed by former newspaperman George Creel. But it would be the special assistant to the attorney general of the War Emergency Division, Buffalo lawyer John Lord O'Brian, who would run the show.

Every Wednesday throughout the war, O'Brian hosted a conference that included representatives of ONI, MID, the BoI, State, and Labor where the various departments and agencies divided up the investigative and enforcement workload per Wilson's April 6 proclamation.[33] Treasury and Post Office officials joined when issues clearly within their domain were at stake.

The military intelligence organizations were relative newcomers to the domestic surveillance game. Indeed, the de facto head of MID, Major Ralph van Deman, was almost single-handedly responsible for reviving Army intelligence capabilities after they atrophied in the wake of the Spanish–American War.[34] While all the federal entities involved in the surveillance effort were concerned with so-called "radicals" (generally defined as anarchists or socialists), for the Army and Navy one of the big concerns was American labor—specifically the most militant of the unions, the IWW.

To monitor the workforce in businesses producing war material, working on military installations or in shipyards, both services established "Plant Protection" components, complete with informants working inside the facilities, including the relevant labor unions. In the case of the Navy, in each of the 15 naval districts, an "aide for information" (junior intelligence officers, often enlisted personnel) was responsible for gathering information on the plants, unions, and potentially "disloyal" individuals within their areas of responsibility.[35] The MID Plant Protection Section had branch offices in several major US cities and agents/informants in plants of interest to the Army across the country.[36]

As the civilian and military surveillance bureaucracies expanded across the country, the legal framework that would govern their efforts also grew.

The Espionage Act finally passed the Congress in May 1917, with Wilson signing it into law on June 15. Only four Senate colleagues joined La Follette in voting against it.

Some of the penalties for violating the act had been softened: instead of life in prison for making allegedly false statements, now the maximum was 20 years and a $10,000 fine. But the bill still carried the death penalty for other alleged disloyal acts, and essentially anything that questioned the validity or conduct of the war was banned from the mails.[37]

Postmaster General Albert Burleson wasted no time in applying the new law to America's mail system. On June 16, Burleson sent a memo to all postmasters to keep:

> a close watch on unsealed matter, newspapers, etc., containing matter which is calculated to interfere with the success of any Federal loan which may be offered to the public, or to cause insubordination, disloyalty, mutiny, or refusal of duty in the military or naval service, or to obstruct the recruiting, draft or enlistment services of the United States, or otherwise to embarrass or hamper the Government in conducting the war.[38]

Every Post Office Department employee effectively became a spy—those handling mail at sorting facilities, and those bringing the mail to the homes and businesses of Americans. All were to be on the lookout for material questioning the draft and any other wartime measures.

Burleson's admonition to postal employees to be on the lookout for material that might "embarrass or hamper the government" had no basis in law— no such language was in the Espionage Act itself. Given the sweeping nature of the statute and Burleson's own broad instructions to Post Office employees, it was inevitable that publications with any political content that ran counter to administration policy would be denied mailing privileges or even banned outright, with the publishers facing potential indictment and jail time.

FIRST AMENDMENT ADVOCATES FIGHT BACK

On July 12, Wilson received a letter from three of the leading public intellectuals of the day, denouncing Burleson's actions and asking Wilson to put himself on record on the issue. The authors were former New York County deputy assistant attorney and ex–Bull Moose party member Amos Pinchot; editor and publisher of the socialist magazine *The Masses* Max Eastman (brother of AUAM executive committee member Crystal Eastman); and fellow journalist John Reed. The trio listed over a dozen papers that Post Office Solicitor William Lamar had deemed unmailable under the Espionage Age, including *The Masses*, which Lamar declared unmailable due to the "general tenor" of the publication.[39]

"DISLOYAL UTTERANCES" 57

Eastman, Pinchot, and Reed asked Wilson the only questions that mattered in a constitutional context.

"Is it not of the utmost importance in a democracy that the opposition to the government have a free voice? Can it be necessary, even in war time, for the majority of a republic to throttle the voice of a sincere minority?"[40]

The same day, New York lawyer Gilbert Roe, the primary counsel for the Free Speech League and a slew of other progressive activists and organizations, filed suit in the Southern District of New York seeking an injunction against the Postal Service for prohibiting distribution of *The Masses*.[41] The next day, Wilson wrote to Burleson, asking, "May I not have your advice as to the inclosed? These are very sincere men and I should like to please them."[42]

Burleson would have none of it.

In his July 16 reply to Wilson, Burleson denied any publication had been suppressed but admitted that some issues had been denied mailing privileges because, among other things, they contained material that, "would cause insubordination, disloyalty, mutiny, or refusal of duty" in the military. He failed to provide a single example in his reply to Wilson.[43] And Burleson went further:

> The terms of this law are perfectly plain, and publishers should have no difficulty in avoiding a violation of either the letter or the spirit of the law, but certain of them have not been content with criticism of the policy of the Government, as has been indicated to you, but in their opposition to the war in general and the conscription law in particular have gone far beyond what might properly be termed criticism and have shown a disposition not only in the particular issues on which the Department's action was based, but in previous issues, to obstruct the Government in its conduct of the war in many different ways.[44]

Burleson went on to deny the Department was suppressing "free criticism, right or wrong, of the Government, nor has it been the policy of this Department in any [way] to interfere with legitimate expression of views which do not coincide with those of the Government, in the matter of the war with Germany or any other matter."[45]

It was, of course, a lie. Burleson's use of the phrases "what might be properly termed criticism" and "the legitimate expression of views which do not coincide with the Government" clearly conveyed the reality: any criticism of any wartime policy of the government was, by Burleson's definition, and that of his solicitor Lamar, a violation of the Espionage Act.

Roe successfully convinced Judge Learned Hand to grant the newspaper's injunction against the government, but Hand's order was stayed by the

Second Circuit Court of Appeals, which immediately took the case at the Justice Department's request.[46] Despite making forceful and generally well-reasoned arguments on First Amendment grounds, Roe would ultimately lose *The Masses* case at the Second Circuit Court of Appeals.[47]

Federal officials were not content to simply keep *The Masses* out of circulation, however. They wanted to make examples of the publisher and the staff.

In late November 1917, a federal grand jury handed down indictments against seven staff and some of its columnists for Espionage Act violations. In the course of two trials over 11 months, the federal government lost the case, but *The Masses* was financially destroyed in the process.[48]

Burleson would go on to ban from the mails publications of the IWW and other labor organizations, African American papers that questioned the war or raised issues of racial discrimination, and a veritable host of domestically produced foreign language newspapers that catered to recent American immigrants or the newly naturalized citizen. In one case, he got suggestions on which papers to allow or ban from a sitting federal judge.

On October 25, 1917, the US District Court Judge in Pittsburgh, Joseph Buffington, wrote to Lamar to provide him with "a list of loyal papers and a list of those which are in my judgment not loyal, or at least of such a character that they ought to be looked into very carefully before they are licensed."[49]

The license Buffington referred to was a requirement included in the just passed Trading with the Enemy Act (TWEA) that made it:

> unlawful for any person, firm, corporation, or association, to print, publish or circulate, or cause to be printed, published, or circulated in any foreign language, any news item, editorial or other printed matter, respecting the Government of the United States, or any nation engaged in the present war, its policies, international relations, the state or conduct of the war, or any matter relating thereto.

The TWEA further required all foreign language newspapers to submit certifications to the Postmaster General that nothing contained in their pages was a violation of the law, as well as English-language translations of the paper for verification purposes.[50]

The 23 Slovak-language papers on the judge's list included 18 "loyal" and 5 "disloyal" publications, none of which had thus far been charged under any federal statute. Each of the 23 would receive their own file in the solicitor's office, with Lamar sending the next day a letter thanking Buffington, assuring him that the list he had provided "will be of great benefit to the Department."[51]

"DISLOYAL UTTERANCES" 59

The radically broad reach of the Espionage Act and the TWEA, combined with the pro-war propaganda being churned out daily by Creel at CPI and amplified by most of the American press, created a toxic political and legal climate for anybody opposed to the war, the draft, or related policies. Even former House and Senate members were not safe from prosecution under the new laws.

POLITICAL PROSECUTIONS: THE CONGRESSIONAL TARGETS

Wisconsin native Victor Berger came to the United States from Austria in 1880, and by December 1886, he had become a naturalized citizen.[52] The politically active socialist became a fixture in the state's politics, and in 1910 he ran for and won the 5th District seat in the US House of Representatives, becoming the first socialist ever elected to Congress.[53] He lost in the 1912 cycle but remained active in Socialist Party of America activities (a party he helped found) and gave the lion's share of his attention to his newspaper, the *Milwaukee Leader.*

Berger's antiwar, anticapitalist views were well known before America's entry into the war. Prior to June 1917, neither he nor his paper had ever been targeted for federal prosecution under any statute, and his paper had never been denied typical second-class mailing privileges, much less been excluded from the mails. The passage of the Espionage Act changed all of that.

On October 3, 1917, Burleson affirmed a lower-level Post Office Department appointee's decision to deny second-class mailing privileges to Berger's paper.[54] Berger challenged Burleson's action in court and lost but continued publishing the *Leader* despite the threat of prosecution. On March 6, 1918, Berger and several other Socialist Party leaders were arrested and charged under the Espionage Act.[55]

The indictment sparked a legal battle that would last beyond the war and witness Berger win reelection to the House in 1918, be denied his seat by his House colleagues via Section 3 of the Fourteen Amendment, be convicted, have the conviction overturned by the Supreme Court, and ultimately return to Congress via the 1922 election.[56]

Although they never overlapped in Congress, former Republican South Dakota Senator Richard Franklin Pettigrew came to share at least some of Berger's antiwar and anticapitalist views, which he expressed to the Sioux Falls *Argus-Leader* on October 6, 1917. That interview led to his indictment

60   CHAPTER 2

under the Espionage Act. Among Pettigrew's crimes was suggesting that, "People desire to know if they are living in the United States or in Russia," referring to the Espionage Act and related censorship policies.[57]

Pettigrew managed to get three Chicago area doctors (he was in the city at the time of his indictment) to provide affidavits to the court that he was too ill to stand trial—a practice he would continue throughout the war. The tactic worked. The prosecutor dropped the charges almost one year to the day after the end of World War I.[58]

Even a sitting senator, ostensibly protected by the Constitution's Speech and Debate clause, was not immune from threats of expulsion and prosecution under the Espionage Act.

On September 20, 1917, Robert La Follette attended the convention of the national Nonpartisan League, a grassroots alliance of farmers and laborers that had grown into a real political force in the Plains states and the upper Midwest. Referencing American lives lost on British and other commercial vessels sunk by German U-boats, La Follette told the crowd,

> We had a right, a technical right to ship the munitions. And the American citizens have a technical right to ride on those vessels. . . . I say . . . the comparatively small privilege of the right of an American citizen to ride on a munitions loaded ship flying a foreign flag is too small to involve this government in the loss of millions and millions of lives![59]

The speech not only triggered a wave of national negative press for La Follette, but a backlash among some in his home state for his "unwise and disloyal utterances giving aid and comfort to the enemy," in the words of a petition signed by 423 University of Wisconsin faculty members.[60]

But with the exception of the Civil War, few House or Senate members had been expelled in the nation's history to that point. And the Constitution's Speech and Debate clause (Article I, Section 6) presented a formidable hurdle for going after La Follette. The portion of that applied reads as follows:

> They shall in all Cases, except Treason, Felony and Breach of the Peace, be privileged from Arrest during their Attendance at the Session of their respective Houses, and in going to and returning from the same; and for any Speech or Debate in either House, they shall not be questioned in any other Place.[61]

La Follette could make the case that he was returning from Congress when he gave the speech in question, and he had of course made similar speeches in

"DISLOYAL UTTERANCES" 61

the past, both on and off the Senate floor. And it was another such speech on the Senate floor on October 6, 1917, that La Follette used to defend not only his liberty to speak his mind in wartime, but that of every other citizen as well.

Early on, La Follette made it clear he would not be silenced.

"Neither the clamor of the mob nor the voice of power will ever turn me by the breadth of a hair from the course I mark out for myself," he proclaimed, "guided by such knowledge as I can obtain and controlled and directed by a solemn conviction of right and duty."[62]

After denouncing the attacks on himself by the press and his own colleagues, La Follette talked about the impact of federal surveillance and political repression on ordinary citizens:

> Today and for weeks past honest and law abiding citizens of this country are being terrorized and outraged in their rights by those sworn to uphold the laws and protect the rights of the people. . . . Private residences are bring invaded, loyal citizens of undoubted integrity and probity arrested, cross-examined, and the most sacred constitutional rights guaranteed to every American citizen are being violated. . . . I think all men recognize that in time of war the citizen must surrender some rights for the common good which he is entitled to enjoy in time of peace. But, sir, the right to control their own Government according to constitutional forms is not one of the rights that the citizens of this country are called upon to surrender in time of war.[63]

The speech, generally considered by historians to be one of the greatest in Senate and American history, left La Follette's Senate critics unmoved. On November 26, the Senate Committee on Privileges and Elections voted to launch an investigation into whether the Wisconsin legislator should be expelled from the Senate. The threat would hang over La Follette until a month after the Armistice, when the committee voted to terminate the investigation.[64]

SURVEILLANCE TRIFECTA: FOOD, FUEL, AND PEOPLE

In between the passage of the Espionage Act and the TWEA, Congress passed another bill that not only expanded surveillance over more sectors of the economy but brought federal agents directly into the businesses and even homes of individual Americans, exactly as LaFollette had claimed.

62   CHAPTER 2

The Food and Fuel Control Act (FCA) sought to regulate the agricultural and energy sectors of the economy, particularly coal in the latter case. Two new wartime bureaucracies to oversee the act's implementation—the Food Administration and the Fuel Administration—were also created.[65]

The law's passage also meant federal authorities would need the manpower to conduct compliance inspections and, when deemed necessary, prosecutions for violations. Over a month before the law's passage, Herbert Hoover, who had been named by Wilson in May to coordinate food and fuel matters on Wilson's personal authority, reached out to SSD Chief William Flynn to ask for the Service's help "should the unfortunate occasion arise where we might require such services as you could render."[66]

Through the annual Sundry Civil Service spending bill Wilson signed into law on June 12, Congress had provided increased flexibility to Wilson regarding the use of the Secret Service. Now, it was legal for Wilson to use Treasury Department funds to pay for SSD agents detailed to State for counterespionage and other missions. The bill also authorized Wilson "to direct, without reference to existing limitations, the use of the persons employed hereunder if, in his judgment, an emergency exists which requires such action."[67]

Wilson could now lawfully employ SSD agents for TWEA and FCA investigations, but the receiving agencies would have to pay the salaries and expenses of agents detailed to them. Even so, it represented a radical departure from the 1908 bill that had barred SSD agents from doing anything other than chasing counterfeiters and physically protecting presidents.

By the fall of 1917, SSD agents were conducting a large number of investigations for both the Food Administration and the War Trade Board (WTB), a workload that only grew in 1918. In many cases, the "tips" sent to SSD agents working on these investigations were driven by personal vendettas or attempts to snuff out competition.

An April 28, 1918, report from an SSD agent working FCA cases noted that the manager of the Hankow Tea Company claimed that local German nationals of the Haegar Coffee Co. were "buying and selling coffee bags throughout the county and poisoning same." In fact, the entire Haegar family were naturalized American citizens who had, in the words of the SSD agent:

> been bothered by these hysterical patriotic people and by officials of the American Patriotic [Protective] League. They have gone so far as to ask the chief of police to immediately arrest Haegar and could not understand when the chief told them he had no charge to place before him and could not understand why a man like Haegar should be left at liberty.[68]

In St. Louis, a neighbor of one Josephine Guhman alleged that the widow with four children was hoarding food and had allegedly claimed Guhman spoke admiringly of the Kaiser and said she "knew he would win the war." The SSD agent who investigated Guhman reported she denied ever making the remarks and allowed the agent to search her home. The agent noted that Mrs. Guhman "showed me all her groceries on hand and made no attempt at concealment of anything."[69]

War Trade Board investigations conducted by the SSD had a similar character and tone. Before the war was over, SSD agents would conduct over 3,200 such investigations for the WTB. Some would uncover real efforts to violate the law, but as the final report of the WTB noted, "As a result of these investigations it was found that most of the evasions and violations were committed either through carelessness or ignorance."[70]

The overwhelming number of German American–owned businesses scrutinized by SSD agents were loyal establishments, many with family members serving in the US Armed Forces. And it wasn't just German American businesses that could be targeted by the WTB.

The War Trade Intelligence (WTI) unit of the WTB maintained a confidential "blacklist" of companies barred from doing business with the government on the basis of Espionage Act or TWEA violation allegations. Among those who could be blacklisted were, "Any individual, partnership or corporation in this country which is engaged in propaganda favorable to Germany or her Allies."[71]

Just as German American business owners were under often invasive investigation by SSD agents at the WTB's request, German American workers in factories received intense scrutiny from the respective "plant protection" components of the Army and Navy intelligence branches.

SURVEILLANCE AND ETHNIC BIAS

Between July and September 1917, ONI, in coordination with the Sperry Gyroscope Company's owner and the New York Police Department, investigated every single one of the employees at the plant with any German heritage, whether naturalized American citizens or German or Austrian nationals. By late September 1917, the 96 German and 90 Austrian nationals working at the plant had been arrested and interned as enemy aliens.[72] The cooperation of the owner and the late-night nature of the raids kept the story out of the press at the time. But ONI and the Navy leadership were not satisfied with simply expelling German and Austrian nationals from Sperry.

64   CHAPTER 2

Via a December 4 letter to Elmer Sperry (the company's founder), Secretary of the Navy Josephus Daniels had asked that Sperry plant superintendent Otto Meitzenfeld be dismissed (he had already been demoted from plant superintendent and his job given to a native-born, non–German American). Even though the German American Meitzenfeld had been accused of disloyalty and radically favoring German American or German nationals among the Sperry workforce, the allegations against him were disproven, a point Sperry made in a December 10, 1917, letter to Daniels.[73] Sperry noted Meitzenfeld's "very unusual technical knowledge and ability" and the fact that throughout his employment at Sperry he had "proved most remarkably efficient." Nevertheless, Sperry acquiesced to Daniels's demand that Meitzenfeld be fired.[74]

By the spring of 1918, anti-German hysteria was at an all-time high across the country, and weekly MID "Suspect List" reports told the tale in terse but graphic terms.

The March 11, 1918, MID Suspect List noted not only the indictment of Victor Berger and several of his associates but stated that University of Maine Law School Dean William Walz was "dismissed after discussion of 'Kultur.'" Harry Wormst of New York, described as a "noisy Austrian" was "forced to kiss [the] U.S. flag." John Lindberg of St. Paul lost his job as a result of "disloyalty charges." Dr. F.K. Krueger of Atchison, Kansas, was a "college professor under arrest as pro-German."[75]

The March 11 MID Suspect List also included the German American mayor of Michigan City, Indiana, Fred C. Miller, who was characterized as "Alien enemy mayor" who was "told not to interfere."[76] Miller had come to the attention of Wilson himself when Indiana's two US Senators, Harry New and James Watson, wrote to him on January 4, 1918, complaining that Miller was "a native of Germany who has not completed his naturalization papers and is therefore an alien enemy."[77] Judge Albert B. Anderson of the federal circuit had already told New and Watson there was nothing he could do, so the senators asked White House Secretary Joe Tumulty if he would "place the matter before the President" in the hopes he could block Miller from taking office again.[78]

Four days later, Wilson wrote to Attorney General Gregory about the matter.

"I dare say you have seen various things in the papers about the question of the election of an alien enemy as Mayor of Michigan City, Indiana," Wilson said. "Is there no way, do you think, in which we could prevent his occupying this office?"[79]

Gregory took nearly three weeks to reply to Wilson, perhaps concerned that his response would not be what the president wanted to hear.

"DISLOYAL UTTERANCES" 65

In the second paragraph of his letter to Wilson, Gregory cautioned the president that, "I do not believe that any action should be taken on the part of the government."

Miller's citizenship status was in question, as his claims to have filed the necessary paperwork could not be proven or disproven. Even so, Gregory noted, "Miller, to be on the safe side, applied to the US Marshal of the district for an enemy alien permit, which was granted to him by the Marshal."

While Gregory opined that, "In my opinion however, you have the power, under the alien enemy statute, to make a regulation which would preclude an alien enemy from performing the functions of a municipal office," he noted that this was the third time Miller had been elected mayor of Michigan City, and that the voters had done so "with full knowledge of the facts." He reiterated his advice to Wilson to avoid "any interference in this case."[80] Wilson let the matter drop.

The Constitution sets standards for who is eligible to run for and hold federal office, not at the state or local level. Those had always been viewed as under the purview of the states, per the Tenth Amendment. Gregory's failure to recognize, and remind Wilson, that the Tenth Amendment barred federal interference in state or local elections—even in wartime—was bad enough. But his suggestion that Wilson could, via executive fiat, ignore the Tenth Amendment and overturn the results of a local or state election was legal malpractice on Gregory's part. Fortunately, Wilson never tested the proposition.

The daily MID Suspect Lists during March 1918 catalogued rights violations not only against German Americans, but others as well.

On March 9 in Globe, Arizona, an E.D. Sexton of the International Bible Students Association was "forbidden to make [an] address."[81] On March 14 in Brooklyn, Mary McDowell was the "Quakeress teacher suspended, charged with opposing war and Red Cross work."[82] On March 19, Henry Krenning of St. Louis was "[a]rrested on charge of calling President Wilson a traitor during a theatrical performance."[83] On March 23 in the author's home town of Springfield, Missouri, nationally renowned socialist and feminist activist Rose Pastor Stokes was "arrested for addressing meeting of socialists after having been forbidden; forfeits bail."[84] On March 27, Joe String of Tulsa, Oklahoma, was "killed by [a] member of [the] County Council of Defense for pro-German utterances."[85]

And so it went in Woodrow Wilson's America throughout 1918.

The intensity of the attacks and rancor were only heightened by the passage of the Sedition Act in May 1918, an amendment to the Espionage Act.

66   CHAPTER 2

Among other things, the law made it a felony, punishable by a fine up to $10,000 and up to 20 years in prison, to

> willfully utter, print, write, or publish any disloyal, profane, scurrilous, or abusive language about the form of government of the United States, or the Constitution of the United States, or the military or naval forces of the United States, or the flag of the United States, or the uniform of the Army or Navy of the United States, or any language intended to bring the form of government of the United States, or the Constitution of the United States, or the military or naval forces of the United States, or the flag of the United States, or the uniform of the Army or Navy of the United States into contempt, scorn, contumely, or disrepute.[86]

The same month, the director of the Selective Service, General Enoch Crowder, issued a "work-or-fight" regulation targeting unemployed men for military call-up under the draft. Organized labor was outraged but given the nation-wide crackdown against unions over the past year, especially the IWW, the willingness of union members to strike was somewhat blunted after Secretary of War Newton Baker said strikers would not be counted as members of the unemployed for enforcement purposes.[87]

By fall of 1918, all but two members of the AUAM's staff and executive committee were under surveillance by the BoI, and one—Executive Director Roger Baldwin—would be convicted of violating the Selective Service Act for failing to register and get a physical examination. Federal agents also raided the offices of the AUAM-affiliated National Civil Liberties Bureau (NCLB), looking for evidence upon which to convict not only AUAM and NCLB staff but the clients and supporters of the two organizations.[88] Despite the attacks, the AUAM and NCLB not only endured throughout the war but went on to become the most well-known constitutional rights advocacy organization in American history—the American Civil Liberties Union.[89]

The worldview conveyed by historian Roy Talbert, Jr.'s account of MID during the war applied to federal, state, and local officials as well:

> The enemies were varied: Socialists, pacifists, supporters of pacifists, Germans, German Americans, Americans suspected of being pro-German, Americans suspected of being neutral, the IWW, black activists, and labor agitators active in too many sensitive industries.[90]

Figure 2.1. As America's chief executive during World War I, Woodrow Wilson pushed through draconian laws such as the Espionage Act, Sedition Act, and Food and Fuel Control Act. The expansion of the modern American federal domestic surveillance apparatus began with his administration. *Library of Congress*

68   CHAPTER 2

To that list would be added suffragettes, some of whom continued to push for passage of a constitutional amendment during the war to give women the vote. Also targeted were Irish Americans, who were viewed as potential pawns of German agents because of the British occupation of Ireland. But the highest profile political and legal cases continued to involve American socialists.

SOCIALISTS IN THE DOCKET

Among American socialists, only Eugene Debs had a higher political profile than Wisconsin's Victor Berger, and like Berger, Debs would be charged under the Espionage Act—in Debs's case for a speech he gave in Canton, Ohio, in June 1918 condemning the war. For Debs, Berger, and others charged under the Espionage Act, the end of the war on November 11, 1918, did not halt their legal troubles or the political repression targeting those as perceived by federal authorities as challenging the prevailing political and economic order. Indeed, several key wartime free speech cases would not be decided by the Supreme Court until the late winter of 1919. Among them would be the case of Socialist Party Secretary Charles Schenck and his Party associate Elizabeth Baer.

In August 1917, Schenck and Baer had prepared and mailed some 15,000 leaflets to draft-age men in the Philadelphia area, urging them to oppose the newly passed conscription law.[91] In September 1917, the pair were indicted by a federal grand jury on charges of "urging insubordination, disloyalty, mutiny and obstruction of the selective draft act."[92] The pamphlet that had been circulated did not, in fact, call for outright obstruction of the draft, but for political action to get the law repealed.[93] Beyond a straightforward First Amendment argument, Schenck and Baer contended that the conscription law represented a form of involuntary servitude and thus was unconstitutional per the Thirteenth Amendment.[94]

The case made its way to the Supreme Court in January 1919, and in one of the most infamous and consequential decisions in the history of the nation's highest court, the nine justices handed down a unanimous verdict in March, upholding Schenck and Baer's convictions.

Delivering the opinion for the Court, Associate Justice Oliver Wendell Holmes conceded that the pamphlet in question "in form, at least, confined itself to peaceful measures such as a petition for the repeal of the act." But he and his colleagues inferred, despite the plain language of the pamphlet, that its authors had much more in mind.

"DISLOYAL UTTERANCES" 69

"Of course," Holmes wrote, "the document would not have been sent unless it was intended to have some effect, and we do not see what effect it could be expected to have upon persons subject to the draft except to influence them to obstruct the carrying of it out. The defendants do not deny that the jury might find against them on this point."[95]

Holmes went on to acknowledge that "in many places and in ordinary times" sending the pamphlet "would have been within their constitutional rights." But he then pivoted, arguing that the First Amendment should not be construed as an absolute, unchanging standard. For Holmes and his fellow justices, the context mattered: "The most stringent protection of free speech would not protect a man in falsely shouting fire in a theatre and causing a panic. . . . The question in every case is whether the words used are used in such circumstances and are of such a nature as to create a clear and present danger that they will bring about the substantive evils that Congress has a right to prevent."

He went on to advance a line of argument that has remained an executive branch mantra ever since.

"When a nation is at war," Holmes contended, "many things that might be said in time of peace are such a hindrance to its effort that their utterance will not be endured so long as men fight, and that no Court could regard them as protected by any constitutional right."[96]

COMMUNISTS (ALLEGEDLY) EVERYWHERE: THE FIRST "RED SCARE"

Even as most Americans were celebrating the end of the "war to end all wars," American officials were gearing up to fight a new one.

The Russian revolution in 1917 had devolved into a civil war between a political patchwork of socialists, monarchists, and others on the one hand versus Vladimir Lenin and his Bolsheviks on the other. While Marxist and socialist theories and political activism had been around for over half a century, nowhere had they been implemented on a national, much less international, scale. Lenin and his compatriots sought to do exactly that, cultivating adherents in virtually every country in the West, including the United States.

But whereas most American socialists generally sought to use existing institutions to advance their political and economic agenda, Lenin and his adherents sought to dismantle those institutions altogether. The Bolsheviks' wholesale confiscation of private property in Russia, their murder of the ousted Romanov dynastic family and other Russian aristocrats, as well as their relentless

70   CHAPTER 2

anticapitalist propaganda and recruiting efforts in the United States sparked a fear that fueled what became known in America as the first Red Scare.

But while in previous eras the assignment of dealing with domestic radicals or related threats would have fallen to the Secret Service, the war had changed the bureaucratic pecking order in Washington.

The BoI, as well as MID and ONI, had borne the brunt of the domestic investigative workload against German agents, German Americans, and naturalized American citizens who had emigrated previously from other Central Power nations, and of course the IWW and socialists. The SSD, on the other hand, had largely had its domestic wartime work confined to WTB or Food Administration investigations. With that work now over, the SSD reverted largely to focusing on its primary missions: protecting the president and pursuing counterfeiters.

During the war, federal civilian and military intelligence and law enforcement organizations had been augmented by the APL, as well as a vast host of volunteer patriotic organizations that were little more than organized vigilante squads. Once the war was over, those private organizations were disbanded, and both federal military and civilian intelligence organizations underwent a postwar downsizing. But their domestic surveillance and political repression operations continued, with the Bolshevik threat now the prime, but not exclusive, focus.

Within the Navy leadership, the circulation of an investigative report on alleged IWW and Bolshevik penetration of the Marine Transport Workers union led one Navy official to send a memo to the Chief of Naval Operations on February 6, 1919, suggesting "A declaration of war on the present Bolsheviki Government of Russia" as well as "Trial for treason of all spreaders of Bolsheviki doctrine and literature" and the "immediate deportation of all foreign agitators or suspects."[97]

In fact, the Allied governments, including the United States, had already dispatched military forces to Russia to try to help the anti-Bolshevik forces militarily eradicate Lenin and his followers.[98] That effort failed, but the domestic war against the IWW and known or alleged communists would be waged with a vengeance in 1919 by Wilson's new attorney general and the former wartime alien property custodian, A. Mitchell Palmer. Aiding Palmer at Justice was a young attorney he made head of the new "Radical Division" at the BoI: J. Edgar Hoover.[99]

Hoover was a vehement anticommunist, but his antipathy to any ideas that challenged the prevailing political and economic order was hardly unique. As historian Beverly Gage has noted, "in the turmoil of 1919, with millions of workers on strike and enthusiasm for socialist revolution

Figure 2.2. John Edgar Hoover at the Justice Department in 1924. Hoover would, through his fifty-year tenure as FBI director, become the most feared government bureaucrat of the twentieth century. *Library of Congress*

sweeping through Europe, plenty of Americans shared a basic desire to suppress revolutionary thought and social disorder."[100] Hoover would go on to make a career out of going after those who challenged the prevailing political and economic order.

The Justice Department also got help from the Army, which was employed in multiple communities affected by strikes.

During 1919, there were major steel industry strikes and related violence in a dozen states. In early October 1919, elements of the Army's 4th Division were dispatched to Gary, Indiana, under a proclamation of martial law issued by Major General Leonard Wood, commander of the Army's Central Department. On the night of October 12, 1919, two separate groups of soldiers conducted a warrantless search of a home based on an allegation that dozens of "Reds" met in the basement every night.[101]

The only people home were the owners, Mr. and Mrs. John Werner, who admitted the first group of soldiers voluntarily. A search of the basement revealed nothing, the on-scene Army officer apologized for the obvious error, and the troops left.

72   CHAPTER 2

The second group of soldiers showed up hours later and tried to force their way into the house, causing the wife to scream wildly. A second search was conducted and likewise found no evidence of Reds at the premises.[102] It took pressure from the homeowner's House member, Rep. William R. Wood (R-IN), to get a written apology sent to the Werners 18 months after the unconstitutional raid on their home. Wood subsequently learned that the individual who originally claimed the Werners' home was a Red meeting place "was either overzealous or mentally unbalanced at the time."[103]

As strikes and violence gripped the country in the spring and summer of 1919—including a failed assassination attempt via a bomb placed at his own home—Palmer, with the aid of MID, ONI, and state and local law enforcement organizations, began a series of warrantless raids and arrests targeting those deemed "radicals" allegedly seeking to overthrow the government. Initially cheered on by federal lawmakers, the public, and the press, by the end of 1919 Palmer's antiradical campaign had ensnared enough innocent Americans and flouted American immigration law to the point where he was clashing publicly with Secretary of Labor William Wilson.

Palmer, and his young Justice Department assistant and head of the newly formed Radical Division, J. Edgar Hoover, did have their victories along the way.

Using the Anarchist Exclusion Act of 1903 and the 1917 update of the act passed by Congress, Palmer and Hoover succeeded in securing the deportation of Emma Goldman and her ideological fellow traveler, Sascha Berkman, on December 21, 1919, along with almost 50 other alleged or known anarchists and 184 members of the Union of Russian Workers.[104] Palmer and Hoover would score another victory in late January 1920, when Labor Secretary Wilson agreed with Justice's assertion that noncitizen members of the recently formed Communist Party of America and Communist Labor Party could be deported because the organizations represented "a revolutionary party seeking to conquer and control the State in open combat."[105]

But after Palmer and Hoover sought and got sign off from the Labor Department to detain for deportation thousands of individuals, Assistant Labor Secretary Louis Post had second thoughts and began denying deportation warrant requests. Post believed the evidence submitted in too many cases was questionable or even nonexistent. Enraged, Palmer and Hoover conspired to have Post impeached. It was an epic miscalculation, as it gave Post the very public platform he needed to bring real scrutiny to Palmer and Hoover's activities at Justice.[106]

After Palmer's prediction of massive May Day 1920 violent leftist uprisings failed to materialize, his star began to wane. He failed to secure the

Democratic nomination for president in 1920, and his political career effectively imploded.

Palmer tried to salvage his reputation with an act of mercy: a recommendation in January 1921 to Wilson that Debs, then aged 65 and in failing health, be pardoned. After all, during Thanksgiving week 1920, Wilson had pardoned German saboteur Franz von Rintelen—a man who had orchestrated real acts of violence and sabotage on American soil.[107] In what can only be characterized as a hypocritical and vindictive act, Wilson refused to pardon his one-time presidential opponent, a man who had never committed a violent act in his life.[108] It would fall to incoming Republican president Warren Harding to set Debs free.

For Hoover, the scandal over the Palmer Raids and other excesses in 1920 earned his unit budget cuts and scorching press coverage. He tried to change the narrative by changing the name of the Radical Division to the General Intelligence Division, but after Senate testimony, in which Palmer fingered Hoover as being responsible for the unconstitutional warrantless immigration raids, he was lucky to keep his job.[109]

THE ILLUSION OF THE RETURN TO NORMALCY

The day before his inauguration, the 66th Congress gave Warren G. Harding legislation that would help him fulfill his campaign pledge of "a return to normalcy" in America. House Joint Resolution 382 officially ended the war with Germany and repealed most of the Food Control Act and the Sedition Act of 1918.[110] That Christmas of 1921, Harding would free his 1920 presidential rival Eugene Debs—he had conducted his campaign from his prison cell in Atlanta—and welcome him to the White House. Harding would go on to commute the sentences of those remaining in prison from convictions under the Espionage, Sedition, or Selective Service Acts.[111]

But the limited legislative rollback of war-time government powers and presidential clemency actions belied the real change.

The American national security state, created in peace and vastly expanded during war, would now become a permanent feature of national life, complete with enduring, draconian national security laws in the form of the Espionage Act and TWEA, with others to follow. And while that national security apparatus had been downsized in the immediate postwar era, it remained operational and active in its pursuit of those deemed a threat to the prevailing political or economic order.

74   CHAPTER 2

A nearly 240-page, May 1920 BOI review of the "radical" situation in the country in the post–Palmer Raids era revealed the mindset that would continue to dominate not just the Bureau but MID and ONI as well for the next seven decades. The report's introduction claimed that

> Bolshevism as a revolutionary doctrine is now embraced by practically the entire radical element in the United States and even advocated and condoned by many in other circles. These revolutionary forces have also succeeded in assimilating and directing most of the radical press in the United States.[112]

The report's assessment that the Communist Party of America and the Communist Labor Party were effectively Soviet controlled had a credible factual basis, but the notion that the political left as a whole was controlled and directed by Moscow ignored the diversity of opinion and activism on the left.

One method the Bureau, MID, and ONI developed to battle those they deemed a threat was a classic divide-and-conquer strategy.

Within the African American community, this involved intimidating potentially pliable editors and publishers like Robert Abbott of the *Chicago Defender*. Established in 1905, Abbott's *Defender* focused on racial inequality and violence against African Americans, especially lynchings and race riots.[113] The *Defender*'s tone during the war angered federal authorities, who leaned on Abbott to back off of publishing articles that government officials claimed stoked racial tensions. The tactic worked to the point that Abbott effectively became an FBI collaborator, helping the Bureau investigate rival publisher and African nationalist leader Marcus Garvey in the early 1920s.[114]

Indeed, the federal government's legal and political assault on Garvey, along with Garvey's own inability to get along with fellow African American political activists, created the kinds of inter-community wedges the Bureau, State Department, and other federal entities needed to ultimately bring Garvey down, jail him in 1925, and deport him in 1927. As historian Theodore Kornweibel, Jr. noted:

> Early in the Garvey case the Bureau of Investigation mistakenly believed Garvey to be a communist. Disproof of this allegation did not diminish one whit its zeal to eliminate him from America. His real "crime," in the eyes of J. Edgar Hoover and the Justice Department, was in being a racial agitator. Garveyism was hardly less threatening than Bolshevism in 1919 and 1920, for his challenge came from within, from the place where white Americans sensed their vulnerability.[115]

"DISLOYAL UTTERANCES" 75

Claims of communist connections, infiltration, or cooptation were also employed against women political activists even after the passage of the Nineteenth Amendment to the Constitution.

Hull House founder Jane Addams's three decades of public advocacy for international peace and women's equality had made her many enemies in the federal government, particularly in the BoI and the War Department. Her Women's International League for Peace and Freedom (WILPF) continued to campaign for general disarmament and international mediation of disputes after the peace treaty with Germany went into force. In April 1922, Secretary of War John Weeks was so enraged by a WILPF pamphlet attacking the 1920 Army Reorganization Act that he asked Attorney General Harry Daugherty to advise him whether "there is anything in this propaganda which would justify legal action by your Department."[116]

Daugherty's reply, if any, is missing from the MID records, but what is clear is that the BoI was tasked to investigate WILPF and its key members starting at least as early as 1922, that BoI agents attended every WILPF meeting they could get into, and that they catalogued the names, addresses, and relationships of WILPF members at least into the 1940s.[117]

For its part, the War Department was not above using politically conservative organizations like the Daughters of the American Revolution (DAR) to help monitor or even politically counter WILPF and affiliated organizations.

On July 22, 1931, Fredrick J. Libby, executive director of the National Council for Prevention of War, wrote to Secretary of War Patrick Hurley, criticizing Hurley's apparent referral of incoming letters to MID on WILPF to DAR for response.

"I have reason to think that such reference is not so helpful as I am sure you would wish all of the services of the War Department to be," Libby wrote. "I am sure that no peace organization would endorse a policy which you say is the regular routine policy of the War Department."[118]

Libby then got to the core issue.

"Speaking quite seriously, it seems to me grossly improper for the Military Intelligence Division of our Government in time of peace to make the Daughters of the American Revolution in effect one of its official bureaus."[119]

It was a tactic MID had used extensively during the war that it had carried over into its peacetime operations. There were many "grossly improper" surveillance and political repression activities that took place during the 1920s. One of them involved what may well have been the Bureau's first foray into presidential election interference.

76   CHAPTER 2

SURVEILLANCE AND POLITICAL SHENANIGANS: THE FBI AND THE 1924 ELECTION

Warren G. Harding's administration is primarily remembered for two things: the untimely death of the president himself, and the multiple corruption scandals involving key members of his cabinet. The most infamous was the so-called Teapot Dome federal oil reserve scandal and corruption allegations leveled at Daugherty.

By March 1924 Montana Democratic Senator Burton K. Wheeler had been named to lead the investigation into Daugherty's alleged misconduct—a move that prompted Daugherty and the BOI Director William Burns to initiate their own investigation of Wheeler, allegedly for oil lease irregularities. Wheeler's indictment triggered a Senate inquiry into his activities.[120] By early May, Burns was forced to admit in Senate testimony that then–Attorney General Daugherty had specifically instructed Burns to "get evidence on Senator Wheeler."[121] Later that month, more witnesses came forward to confirm the scheme to frame Wheeler and derail the Daugherty investigation.[122]

Even so, the Coolidge administration refused to drop the case. Wheeler, who would go on that fall to become the vice-presidential running mate of Senator Robert M. La Follette, Sr. on the Progressive Party ticket, spent the rest of the election under a legal and political cloud created by what was clearly a bogus and politically motivated investigation by the Justice Department and the FBI. The incident did trigger Burns's resignation as BoI director. His replacement turned out to be none other than J. Edgar Hoover of Palmer Raids infamy. And Hoover had apparently learned little from Burns's ill-considered foray into investigating members of Congress.

On September 17, 1924, Hoover sent a startling message to Arthur Bliss Lane, special assistant to Undersecretary of State Joseph Grew. The Soviets, Hoover warned Lane, had directed that:

> all Soviet institutions should indirectly aid Senator La Follette in his election campaign, as it is believed that if Senator La Follette is victorious in his campaign, then the recognition of the Soviet Government will follow immediately, and on the basis of this supposition all the Trade Institutions of the Soviet Government are instructed to utilize all their force and influence to aid the La Follette campaign. However, at the same time it is directed that no official statement should be made and no personal opinions expressed in connection

"DISLOYAL UTTERANCES" 77

with the elections in general, in order that the enemies of the Soviet Government may have no opportunity to say that the latter is interfering in the internal affairs of a foreign nation, and conducting propaganda therein.[123]

Evan Young, chief of Eastern European affairs at State, disputed Hoover's report. He told Lane that the *Daily Worker*, the Soviet propaganda paper published in the United States, had actually spent more time attacking La Follette than either Coolidge or other potential presidential contenders, a fact that Lane communicated to Grew in a note the next day.[124]

Anticommunist opponents of La Follette already had ample public ammunition to use against the venerable Wisconsin senator.

La Follette had vehemently opposed Wilson's decision to join the Allied intervention in the Russian civil war, and he supported recognition of the Soviet Union.[125] Hoover's explosive missive of September 17 suggested that Soviet authorities might indeed be seeking to capitalize on La Follette's previous statements. But Hoover failed to mention the fact that earlier in 1924, La Follette had repudiated communism and had urged his political supporters not to join organizations with known or alleged Soviet connections.[126]

Coolidge's political allies somehow got wind of the alleged Soviet scheme and sought to take advantage of it in the run-up to the November elections.

In a "Strictly Confidential" memo to Grew on September 23, Lane relayed that:

> Mr. Evan Young told me this morning that the National Defense Committee had communicated with the White House to the effect that they had $500,000 available to spend in running a campaign to defeat Mr. La Follette; that they were anxious to unearth any material which would show that La Follette was supported by the Soviet Government or by its agents and that they would be grateful if the [A]dministration would facilitate their obtaining any facts along these lines.[127]

As Young had already seen Hoover's original September 17 memo (and presumably shared its contents with unidentified National Defense Committee members), Lane checked with Justice officials to see if they had "further information of this character."[128]

Justice officials had nothing new at that point, except to clarify that internal divisions among American communists over who to support in the election had somewhat muddied the waters. Lane noted to Grew that, "Mr. Young is handling this matter direct with the Secretary."[129]

78   CHAPTER 2

Career State Department employees, acting at the behest of the Secretary of State, were helping funnel derogatory (but conflicting and possibly false) information to an outside group targeting a rival presidential candidate. And a month before the general election, Hoover gave Lane an update on Soviet efforts to "help" La Follette.

In his October 6 letter to Lane, Hoover conceded that there was "a difference of opinion" among Workers (i.e., Communist) Party members about whether to support their own ticket or La Follette. Party members had been instructed "to take advantage of all La Follette meetings for the purpose of disseminating propaganda and distributing circulars relative to the candidacy of Foster and Gitlow."[130]

But Evan Young at the State Department obtained perhaps the most detailed and damning evidence of direct Soviet efforts to back La Follette's candidacy.

On the morning of October 20, Senator George Pepper (R-PA) called on Young at the State Department, accompanied by a constituent who was a close friend of a State employee at the American Embassy in Paris. The State employee had obtained and passed along to Pepper's constituent an alleged abstract of meeting minutes of the Executive Committee of the Communist International in March 1924 that told a remarkable story, if true.

At the alleged meeting, the abstract read, the "Committee also approved a proposal 'to the central office of the Federation to become affiliated with the greatest circumspection with the La Follette radical party'" and that "subsequent contributions by Moscow to the 'La Follette radical party' to date have exceeded $2,000,000 from gold credits previously established in the United States via London."[131] Young set down the explosive allegations in a memo to Secretary Hughes and attached the alleged Communist International meeting minutes summary to it.

Two days later, at a Senate hearing focused on campaign finance irregularity allegations, Chairman William Borah (R-ID) pressed T.V. O'Conner, chairman of the Shipping Board, to clarify allegations O'Connor had made that Soviet money was flowing to La Follette's campaign via Mexico or other sources, which he characterized as a "common rumor."

> "Where did these 'common rumors come from?" Borah asked O'Connor.
> "Some of them came from the crews of boats running into Russia," O'Connor replied.
> "Do you have any information that money has been sent here by Soviet Russia for political purposes?" Borah pressed.

"DISLOYAL UTTERANCES" 79

"I could not say positively," O'Connor said. Borah then asked O'Connor to speculate.

"Do you believe such is the case?"

"I believe in my own heart, yes."[132]

On Election Day, La Follette would finish a distant third behind Democrat John Davis and the incumbent, Calvin Coolidge. He would blame his loss in part on unidentified "slush funds" and voter intimidation, among other things.[133] How much allegations of Soviet support for his campaign cost him with voters is unknown.

Hoover got in one final, post-election dig at La Follette.

On November 13, he sent Lane at State another letter containing information from "an exceedingly delicate and confidential source" who claimed, among other things, that "La Follette, while in Russia, promised recognition to the members of the Russian government, if he became President of the United States."[134]

There is no evidence in available public records that Hoover ever sought to warn La Follette about Soviet attempts to influence or manipulate his campaign.

CHASING REDS: BIRTH OF THE CONGRESSIONAL WITCH HUNT COMMITTEE

As the Roaring 20s gave way to the Great Depression, Herbert Hoover's administration faced increasing domestic unrest as the ranks of the unemployed soared. Not surprisingly, communist political organizers tried to make the most of the situation, which led conservative anticommunist organizations like the National Civic Federation to lobby Congress to investigate. On May 22, 1930, the House obliged, passing House Resolution 220, authorizing the creation of what would formally be known as the Special Committee to Investigate Communist Activities in the United States, but which would ultimately be referred to as the Fish Committee for its chairman, Rep. Hamilton Fish (R-NY).[135]

During the balance of 1930, the committee held field hearings at multiple locations around the country where actual or alleged communist activities were reported. Not surprisingly, the ACLU became a major target of the committee.

Roger Baldwin had remained the public face of the ACLU during the years after World War I, and both Baldwin and the ACLU had already been

80 CHAPTER 2

through one legislative inquiry-turned-witch hunt at the hands of the New York state's Lusk Committee in the immediate aftermath of the war.[136] Now, a decade later, Baldwin and his organization were once again in the cross-hairs of a legislative committee, this time at the federal level.

Baldwin was a reluctant witness; the Fish Committee had used a sub-poena to compel his testimony. His opening statement made clear why:

> I declined to accept the invitation of your chairman to appear vol-untarily as a witness, because the American Civil Liberties Union is opposed to your committee and its work. . . . Far more important in our view of the country's best interest is the maintenance of the right of agitation by communists and all others who have a griev-ance. The country is not menaced by communist propaganda. It is menaced far more by the economic conditions causing unemploy-ment, poverty, and unrest. It is those conditions which bring about protests and demands for change in our economic and political life. A congressional committee could do far better, in our judgment, to determine those evils of which communist propaganda is a mere reflection.[137]

Briefly, some committee members advocated cutting Baldwin off and refus-ing to allow him to finish his statement, but Fish insisted Baldwin finish what he started.

Baldwin went on to give a spirited defense of the organization he had devoted his life to. He categorically denied that the ACLU was a communist led or infiltrated organization:

> Concerning the work of the Civil Liberties Union itself, we state to you that we have no connection whatever with communist organi-zations, except to defend their rights of freedom of speech, press, and assemblage on precisely the same basis as we defend the rights of others. That we have had more occasion to defend communists than others is due solely to the fact that they are the chief victims of attack. Several communists have served upon our national or executive committees just as do many Republicans, Democrats, and Socialists. We accept in our membership anybody who believes in the right of free speech, regardless of his political views. We have on occasion defended the rights of reactionaries to free speech, notably cases affecting the Ku-Klux Klan and the American Fascisti in the South, just as we have defended the rights of radicals.[138]

"DISLOYAL UTTERANCES" 81

After Baldwin completed his prepared statement, Fish started with his big question.

> "Mr. Baldwin, does your organization uphold the right of an American citizen to advocate force and violence for the overthrow of the Government?"
>
> "Certainly," Baldwin replied, "in so far as mere advocacy is concerned."
>
> "Does it uphold the right of an alien in this country to urge the overthrow and advocate the overthrow of the Government by force and violence?"
>
> "Precisely on the same basis as any citizen," Baldwin responded.
>
> "That is not your personal opinion?"
>
> "That is the organization's position."
>
> "That is the position of the organization?" Fish asked.
>
> "Also the position of two Justices of the Supreme Court," Baldwin noted.[139]

In response to Fish's inquiry as to whether the ACLU would defend someone who committed an overt act of violence aimed at the federal government, Baldwin was clear: "We draw the line for either the overt act, or attempted act."[140]

In the end, the distinctions Baldwin and the ACLU drew between speech and acts were seen as meaningless by the Fish Committee's majority.

In the section of their final report dealing with the ACLU, the majority stated that:

> The American Civil Liberties Union is closely affiliated with the communist movement in the United States, and fully 90 per cent of its efforts are on behalf of communists who have come into conflict with the law ... it is quite apparent that the main focus of the A.C.L.U. is to attempt to protect the communists in their advocacy of force and violence to overthrow the Government, replacing the American flag by a red flag and erecting a Soviet Government in place of the republican form of government guaranteed to each State by the Federal Constitution.[141]

Fish Committee member and Maine Republican Rep. John Edward Nelson would have none of it. The lone dissenter among the five House members on the panel, Nelson refused to sign the majority report and instead insisted the committee include his lengthy rebuttal in the final report. Nelson noted that the committee's investigation had found almost no communists where legions of American Reds allegedly existed. Regarding the American armed forces, Nelson noted:

> Since the birth of communism in the United States but two communists have been discovered in the enlisted personnel of the Army. . . . As regards the Navy, an investigation covering a period of six months revealed the presence of but from 12 to 15 communists in the enlisted personnel of the Navy, comprising some 85,000 men.[142]

Nelson noted that the same miniscule communist presence prevailed in American schools and the labor force.

The committee's dissenter also had a warning for his House colleagues, and the public at large, even as he conceded the Soviets and their American communist sympathizers represented a threat:

> Communist aims and methods arouse our righteous indignation, yet we should proceed to put needed reforms into effect sanely and sensibly, without hate or haste or hysteria. Freedom should be the rule in America rather than restrictive legislation, and we should approach with reserve the consideration of any criminal statutes that seek to fetter the operations of the human mind or to encroach in the slightest degree on those rights guaranteed in our Constitution to the lowliest individual in the United States.[143]

Nelson's articulate defense of the Bill of Rights fell largely on deaf ears. While the committee itself came to an end, the political demonization of individuals and groups it had targeted endured. The Fish Committee's baseless smear of the ACLU would dog the organization for decades.

SURVEILLING AND REPRESSING THOSE WHO SERVED: THE BONUS MARCH

One group with long-standing grievances against the federal government consisted of the veterans of America's last war. And in the wake of the Fish Committee report, they too would be labeled as tools of Soviet agitation and subversion.

In the years immediately following World War I, veterans service organizations like the American Legion and Veterans of Foreign Wars (VFW)

"DISLOYAL UTTERANCES"   83

mounted a political campaign to secure additional payments to veterans for their wartime service. Over President Coolidge's veto, Congress passed in May 1924 the World War Adjusted Compensation Act.[144] As originally enacted, the bill structured the payments to be paid 20 years after the legislation's enactment, but the onset of the Great Depression caused thousands of veterans and their families to demand that Congress make the payments immediately.

President Hoover opposed the push for expedited payments, and as a result, veterans organized themselves into the Bonus Expeditionary Force (BEF), a takeoff on the name given the US Army in Europe during the war—the American Expeditionary Force. By May 1932, veterans, their families, and supporters were beginning to head toward Washington.

On May 25, 1932, the Army Chief of Staff, through MID and the relevant G-2 (Intelligence) components, issued a memo claiming that the Communist Party of the United States was behind what would soon be called the June 8 Bonus March and that the

> mass demonstration is to be held under the camouflage of the Worker's Ex-Servicemen League, supposedly making demand for the immediate payment of the Adjusted Compensation Certificate, but in reality as a forerunner and foundation of a series of national demonstrations planned to agitate the recognition of Russia by the United States.[145]

The memo directed that addressed commands "send any information you may have on this matter or that you may obtain, direct to G-2, War Department, in the form of an informal daily air mail report until we inform you that the reports are no longer needed."[146]

The current generation of soldiers was ordered to spy on their predecessors. Before long, they would be used to crush their largely peaceful protests.

From late May through late July, Army elements dutifully tracked the movement of Bonus Marchers, sending in detailed reports that MID drew from to publish its own daily summaries. The daily summary for May 31, 1932, noted among other things that, "So far, the veterans here have expelled all radicals found among them, and two men distributing Red literature are reported to have been given ten welts over the back with a strap and expelled from the group."[147]

The BEF's size—and militancy—grew to the point that by late July, District of Columbia officials appealed to Hoover to send in the troops and disperse the marchers.[148] Hoover obliged, the Army destroyed the marchers'

84   CHAPTER 2

encampments, and the press dutifully reported "arrests of radicals who have been active with the Bonus Expeditionary Force . . ."[149] While perhaps 1,000 marchers remained in and around DC after the Army crackdown, the BEF was effectively obliterated. American veterans would not take to the streets again in significant numbers to protest federal policies for decades.

CONCLUSION

Prior to World War I, America's only dedicated federal domestic intelligence-gathering entities were the civilian Secret Service Division of the Treasury Department and the Bureau of Investigation in the Department of Justice. By the war's end, the SSD and BoI would have full-fledged domestic spying counterparts in the Army's Military Intelligence Division and the Navy's Office of Naval Intelligence. Precedents for effectively deputizing select, politically conservative civil society organizations, such as the American Protective League, as federal surveillance partners were also set during the war. Cable, telegram, and phone companies also became regular government partners in domestic surveillance operations, either willingly or via court orders.

In contrast to the Theodore Roosevelt era, Congress became a willing and enthusiastic partner in expanding executive branch power during the war not only to conduct domestic surveillance but also to punish allegedly disloyal speech or other forms of antiwar activism via the draconian Espionage Act, Sedition Act, and Food and Fuel Control Act. Federal courts invariably upheld those laws when challenged by those targeted with them. These were the pivotal events that effectively laid waste to the Madisonian construct of checks and balances between the three branches of government as a means of preserving individual liberty during times of national crisis.

The repeals of the Sedition Act and the Food and Fuel Control Act during the Harding administration were welcome developments, but the other World War I Bill of Rights–shredding statutory holdovers, the Espionage Act and Trading with the Enemy Act, endured, as did the fear-driven political and psychological mindset that produced the emergent American surveillance state. The newly created USSR gave the BoI, SSD, MID, and ONI a new, potent adversary on which to focus during much of the interwar period, and thus reason to continue and expand domestic surveillance targeting those known or believed to harbor pro-Soviet sympathies—even if they were not active Soviet intelligence agents. And by the early 1930s, yet another series of overseas political developments would give the civilian and

"DISLOYAL UTTERANCES" 85

military intelligence components of the federal government reason engage in renewed forms of ethnically focused domestic spying.

On January 30, 1933, a former Austrian corporal and virulent antisemitic political agitator was sworn in as the new chancellor of Germany. His future political nemesis, Franklin Delano Roosevelt, would become America's thirty-second president less than six weeks later. In the Far East, the military junta in Tokyo, already committed to an expansionist policy through its invasion of Manchuria some two years earlier, was busily expanding Japan's power projection capabilities and eyeing American, British, French, and Dutch colonial possessions from Malaya to Hawaii. America's civilian and military intelligence organizations were watching all these developments, laying the groundwork for an intensified wartime domestic surveillance campaign that would be every bit as consequential as the last one.

NOTES

1. *Washington Evening Star*, December 8, 1914, 4.
2. "German Rocks C.P.R. Bridge with Dynamite," *New York Tribune*, February 3, 1915, 1. Accessed via LOCCA.
3. "Waters about Great Britain Are Declared a War Zone," *Washington Evening Star*, February 5, 1915, 1. Accessed via LOCCA.
4. "Lusitania Torpedoed by German Submarine," *The New York Evening Sun*, May 8, 1915, 1. Accessed via LOCCA.
5. Letter from William Jennings Bryan to William McAdoo, May 14, 1915. NARA RG 59, Microfilm Series T-914, reel 4.
6. Treasury Department Comptroller "Memorandum to the Secretary," November 20, 1917. NARA RG 87, Treasury/Secret Service Division General Correspondence, 1894–1918, File number 97131, Box 91.
7. A fairly large body of this material can be found in the NARA RG 59, Records of the Department of State, Office of the Counselor.
8. Howard Blum, *Dark Invasion 1915: Germany's Secret War and the Hunt for the First Terrorist Cell in America* (New York: HarperCollins, 2014), 340–349.
9. Blum, *Dark Invasion 1915*, 346.
10. Synopsis of the Franz von Rintelen Mission, 1915–1918. NARA RG 87, Records of the U.S. Secret Service, Box 1.
11. Synopsis of the Franz von Rintelen Mission, 1915–1918.
12. See NARA RG 65, Records of the FBI, Series M 1085, reel 182.
13. Woodrow Wilson, Third Annual Message, December 7, 1915. Accessed via *The American Presidency Project* at http://www.presidency.ucsb.edu/ws/index.php?pid=29556.
14. Woodrow Wilson, Third Annual Message, December 7, 1915.
15. NARA RG 87, Field Agents' Reports & Correspondence, 1887–1936, Boxes 6–7, reports titled "German Activities: Description of Detroit, MI" and "German Activities: Agents in U.S. Army."

86 CHAPTER 2

16. NARA RG 87, Field Agents' Reports & Correspondence, 1887–1936, Box 6, "German Activities: Description of Detroit, MI."

17. NARA RG 87, Field Agents' Reports & Correspondence, 1887–1936.

18. Woodrow Wilson, Address at Sea Girt, New Jersey Accepting the Democratic Nomination for President, September 2, 1916. Accessed via The American Presidency Project at http://www.presidency.ucsb.edu/ws/index.php?pid=65393.

19. "Organizes to Oppose Preparedness," *Pensacola Journal*, December 27, 1915, 4. Accessed via LOCCA.

20. "Pacifists Ask Hearing, Desire to Present Anti-Militarist Views at White House," *Washington Evening Star*, April 29, 1916, 3. Accessed via LOCCA.

21. "President Hears about Perils of Militarism," *Washington Evening Star*, May 8, 1916, 10. Accessed via LOCCA.

22. See Nancy Unger, *Fighting Bob La Follette: The Righteous Reformer* (Chapel Hill: University of North Carolina Press, 2000), 235–238.

23. A Bill to Define and Punish Espionage, S. 8148, 64th Congress (2nd Session), 1917.

24. A Bill to Define and Punish Espionage, 5.

25. NARA RG 87, Daily Reports of Agents, 1876–1936, Series T915, reel 325. Daily Reports of Agents for April 11, 1917, Atlanta District.

26. Daily Reports of Agents for March 11, 1917, Atlanta District. NARA RG 87, Daily Reports of Agents, 1876–1936, Series T915, reel 325.

27. National Archives RG 87, Daily Reports of Agents, 1876–1936 reel 364. Daily Report of Agent for March 25, 1917.

28. National Archives RG 87, Daily Reports of Agents, 1876–1936 reel 364. Daily Report of Agent for April 11, 1917.

29. Proclamation 1364—Declaring That a State of War Exists between the United States and Germany, April 6, 1917. Accessed via the American Presidency Project website at http://www.presidency.ucsb.edu/ws/index.php?pid=598.

30. For a dated but still relevant look at the interdepartmental battle over domestic spying and the creation of the American Protective League, see Joan Jensen, *The Price of Vigilance* (New York: Rand McNally & Company, 1968).

31. LOC, Papers of William McAdoo, May 15, 1917, letter to Wilson, Box 522.

32. LOC, Papers of William McAdoo, May 15, 1917, letter to Wilson, Box 522, 4.

33. Document titled "An Article on the Office of Naval Intelligence," by RADM Roger Welles, U.S.N., 1919, 16. LOC, JDP, ONI Files, Reel 96.

34. Van Deman's role in Army intelligence is told well by Alfred W. McCoy in *Policing America's Empire: The United States, the Philippines, and the Rise of the Surveillance State* (Madison: University of Wisconsin Press, 2009).

35. LOC, JDP, ONI Files, Reel 96 in a document titled "An Article on the Office of Naval Intelligence," by RADM Roger Welles, U.S.N., 1919, 12–16.

36. Memo for Colonel Van Deman, December 10, 1917, Subject: Plant Protection Section, Military Intelligence, History. NARA RG 165 (NM 84, Entry 109), MID Plant Protection Officer's Correspondence 1917–18, Box 2.

37. Public Law 65–24, June 15, 1917. Accessed via Legisworks at http://www.legisworks.org/congress/65/publaw-24.pdf.

38. Postmaster General Confidential memo to Postmasters of the First, Second, and Third Classes, June 16, 1917. NARA RG 28, Post Office Department, Records of the Solicitor, File 47594, Box 36.

"DISLOYAL UTTERANCES" 87

39. Letter of Amos Pinchot, John Reed, and Max Eastman to Wilson, July 12, 1917. NARA RG 28, Post Office Department, Records of the Solicitor, File 47594, Box 36.

40. Letter of Amos Pinchot, John Reed, and Max Eastman to Wilson, July 12, 1917, 1.

41. Eric B. Easton, *Defending the Masses: A Progressive Lawyer's Battles for Free Speech* (Madison: University of Wisconsin Press, 2018), 132.

42. Wilson letter to Burleson, July 13, 1917. NARA RG 28, Post Office Department, Records of the Solicitor, File 47594, Box 36.

43. Burleson letter to Wilson, July 16, 1917. NARA RG 28, Post Office Department, Records of the Solicitor, File 47594, Box 36.

44. Burleson letter to Wilson, July 16, 1917, 2.

45. Burleson letter to Wilson, July 16, 1917, 3.

46. Easton, *Defending the Masses,* 137–138.

47. Easton, *Defending the Masses,* 138–146.

48. Easton, *Defending the Masses,* 146–148.

49. Letter of Judge Jospeh Boffington, United States Court in Pittsburgh, to Lamar, October 25, 1917. NARA RG 28, Post Office Department, Records of the Solicitor, File 49547, Box 142.

50. Public Law 65–91, Sec. 19. Accessed via Legisworks at http://www.legisworks.org/congress/65/publaw-91.pdf.

51. Letter from Lamar to Buffington, October 26, 1917. NARA RG 28, Post Office Department, Records of the Solicitor, File 49547, Box 142.

52. Bureau of Investigation Report "In Re: Victor L. Berger et al, Alleged violations of the Espionage Act," July 24, 1918. NARA RG 165, MID Correspondence and Reports, File 10110–120, Box 2721.

53. Drawn from the United States House of Representatives "History, Art, & Archives" website, accessed via http://history.house.gov/Historical-Highlights/1851-1900/Representative-Victor-Berger-of-Wisconsin,-the-first-Socialist-Member-of-Congress/.

54. Burleson Telegram to Berger, October 3, 1917. NARA RG 28, Post Office Department, Records of the Solicitor, File 49841, Box 144.

55. March 5, 1920, Memo from Brigadier General Marlborough Churchill, Director of Military Intelligence to Captain Frothingham, Assistant Chief of Staff of Intelligence for the Northeaster Department, "Subject: Victor L. Berger." NARA RG 165, MID Correspondence and Reports, File 10110–120, Box 2721.

56. A brief but informative summary of Berger's life and career can be found on the University of Wisconsin Digital Collections website at http://digicoll.library.wisc.edu/cgi/f/findaid/findaid-idx?c=wiarchives;view=reslist;subview=standard;didno=uw-whs-mss00798;focusrgn=bioghist;cc=wiarchives;byte=243167173.

57. Indictment of Richard Franklin Pettigrew, United States District Court for the District of South Dakota, October 17, 1919, 2. NARA RG 21, Records of the District Courts of the United States, Records of the Southern District, District of South Dakota, Case 1704.

58. NARA RG 21, Records of the District Courts of the United States, Records of the Southern District, District of South Dakota, Case 1704.

59. Unger, *Fighting Bob La Follette,* 254.

60. Unger, *Fighting Bob La Follette,* 257.

61. Constitution of the United States, Article I, Section 6.

88   CHAPTER 2

62. Senator Robert M. La Follette, Sr., "Free Speech and the Right of Congress to Declare the Objects of the War," *Congressional Record—Senate*, October 6, 1917, 7878.

63. La Follette, "Free Speech and the Right of Congress to Declare the Objects of the War."

64. Unger, *Fighting Bob La Follette*, 257–261.

65. The text of the Food and Fuel Control Act, Public Law 65–41, can be found on Legisworks.org at http://www.legisworks.org/congress/65/publaw-41.pdf.

66. Letter from Herbert Hoover to SSD Chief William Flynn, July 3, 1917. NARA RG 87, Treasury/SSD General Correspondence, 1894–1918, Box 89, File 96386.

67. Public Law 65–21, Sundry Civil Service bill, June 12, 1917, 120. Accessed via Legisworks at http://legisworks.org/congress/65/publaw-21.pdf.

68. SSD St. Louis Agent Report to SSD Chief William Moran, April 28, 1918. NARA RG 87, DOT/SSD Field Agent Reports and Correspondence, 1887–1936, Box 8.

69. Letter from the St. Louis SSD Agent in Charge to Missouri Food Administrator W. F. Gephart, May 28, 1918. NARA RG 87, DOT/SSD Reports of Agents on Special Investigations, 1871–1933, Box 1.

70. *Report of the War Trade Board* (Washington: Government Printing Office, 1920), 275.

71. War Trade Intelligence Confidential Instructions: Confidential Consignor List, January 19, 1918. NARA RG 87, DOT/SSD Reports of Agents on Special Investigations, 1871–1933, Box 2.

72. NARA RG 38.4, ONI, "CAP File," Box 18.

73. Letter from Elmer Sperry to Navy Secretary Josephus Daniels, December 10, 1917, 1. LOC, JDP, Reel 38.

74. Letter from Elmer Sperry to Navy Secretary Josephus Daniels, December 10, 1917, 2.

75. Suspect List for March 11, 1918. NARA RG 165, MID Reports and Correspondence, 1917–1941, File 9140-5862-42, Box 2126.

76. Suspect List for March 11, 1918.

77. Letter of Senators James Watson and Harry New to Wilson, January 4, 1918. LOC, WWP, File 1938, Reel 328.

78. Letter of Senators James Watson and Harry New to Wilson, January 4, 1918.

79. Wilson note to Attorney General Thomas Gregory, January 8, 1918. LOC, WWP, File 1938, Reel 328.

80. Letter from Attorney General Thomas Gregory to Wilson, January 28, 1918. LOC, WWP, File 1938, Reel 328.

81. Suspect List for March 9, 1918. NARA RG 165, MID Reports and Correspondence, 1917–1941, File 9140-5862-41, Box 2126.

82. Suspect List for March 14, 1918. NARA RG 165, MID Reports and Correspondence, 1917–1941, File 9140-5862-46, Box 2126.

83. Suspect List for March 19, 1918. NARA RG 165, MID Reports and Correspondence, 1917–1941, File 9140-5862-49, 2, Box 2126.

84. Suspect List for March 23, 1918. NARA RG 165, MID Reports and Correspondence, 1917–1941, File 9140-5862-52, Box 2126.

85. Suspect List for March 27, 1918. NARA RG 165, MID Reports and Correspondence, 1917–1941, File 9140-5862-55, Box 2126.

86. Public Law 65–150, Sec. 3, May 16, 1918. Accessed on August 1, 2018 via Legislworks at http://www.legisworks.org/congress/65/publaw-150.pdf.

87. See David M. Kennedy, *Over Here: The First World War and American Society* (Oxford: Oxford University Press, 2004), 269.

"DISLOYAL UTTERANCES"   89

88. The assessment of the BoI's surveillance of AUAM staff and executive committee members is drawn from the author's examination of AUAM-related files in NARA RG 65, Records of the BOI, 1908–1922, Series M1085. For an account of federal operations against AUAM, NCLB, and Baldwin, see Robert C. Cottrell, *Roger Nash Baldwin and the American Civil Liberties Union* (New York: Columbia University Press, 2000).
89. Cottrell, *Roger Nash Baldwin*, 119–134.
90. Roy Talbert, Jr., *Negative Intelligence: The Army and the American Left, 1917–1941* (Jackson: University Press of Mississippi, 1991), 19.
91. *Schenck v U.S.*, 249 U.S. 47 (1919) at 50.
92. *Albuquerque Morning Journal*, September 9, 1917, 2. Accessed via LOCCA.
93. Stone, *Perilous Times*, 193.
94. *Schenck v U.S.*, 249 U.S. 47 (1919) at 50.
95. *Schenck v U.S.*, at 51.
96. *Schenck v U.S.*, at 52.
97. Memo of H. E. Yarnell to the Chief of Naval Operations, February 6, 1919. LOC, JDP, Reel 38.
98. See Robert M. Willett, *Russian Sideshow: America's Undeclared War, 1918–1920* (London: Brassey's, 2003).
99. Beverly Gage, *G-Man: J. Edgar Hoover and the Making of the American Century* (New York: Viking, 2022), 61.
100. Gage, *G-Man*, 62.
101. Report of Acting Inspector General J. L. Chamberlin to the Adjutant General, March 24, 1921, War Department File A.G.O. 250.23, 1. NARA RG 60, DOJ Records, Records Regarding a Study of the Use of Force in Internal Disturbances by the Federal Gov (Glasser File), Box 5.
102. Report of Acting Inspector General J. L. Chamberlin to the Adjutant General, March 24, 1921.
103. Report of Acting Inspector General J. L. Chamberlin to the Adjutant General, March 24, 1921, 2.
104. See Kenneth D. Ackerman, *Young J. Edgar: Hoover, the Red Scare, and the Assault on Civil Liberties* (New York: Carroll & Graf Publishers, 2007), 155–163.
105. Ackerman, *Young J. Edgar,* 207–212.
106. Ackerman, *Young J. Edgar,* 263–269.
107. "Wilson Pardons Rintelen, Who Set Fire Bombs," *New York Herald*, November 25, 1920, 8. Accessed via LOCCA.
108. Ackerman, *Young J. Edgar,* 351.
109. Gage, *G-Man*, 88.
110. 41 Stat. 1359, March 3, 1921. Accessed via Legislworks at http://legisworks.org/sal/41/stats/STATUTE-41-Pg1359.pdf.
111. Records of those commutation actions can be found in NARA RG 204, Records of the Pardon Attorney.
112. *Memorandum on the Revolutionary Movement in the United States: Its Origin, Development, and Present Status.* Division of Radical Publications of the Bureau of Investigation, Department of Justice, May 24, 1920. NARA RG 28, Post Office Department, Records of the Solicitor, Espionage Act cases, 1917–21, Box 181, File 50616.
113. Theodore Kornweibel, Jr., *Seeing Red: Federal Campaigns against Black Militancy* (Bloomington: Indiana University Press, 1998), 37.

90   CHAPTER 2

114. Kornweibel, *Seeing Red*, 39–41.
115. Kornweibel, *Seeing Red*, 131.
116. Letter from Secretary of War John Weeks to Attorney General Harry Daugherty, April 26, 1922. NARA RG 165, MID Correspondence and Reports, 1917–1941, Box 2826, File 10110-1935-14.
117. NARA RG 165, MID Correspondence and Reports, 1917–1941, Box 2826. File 10110–1935 Has a Wealth of Material on BoI and War Department Surveillance and Correspondence Involving WILPF in the 1920s and 1930s.
118. Letter from Fredrick J. Libby to Secretary of War Patrick Hurley, July 22, 1931. Letter from Secretary of War John Weeks to Attorney General Harry Daugherty, April 26, 1922. NARA RG 165, MID Correspondence and Reports, 1917–1941, Box 2826, File 10110-1935-82.
119. Letter from Fredrick J. Libby to Secretary of War Patrick Hurley, July 22, 1931.
120. "Senate to Probe Jury Accusation Against Wheeler," *Washington Evening Star*, April 9, 1924, 1. Accessed via LOCCA.
121. "U.S. Agent Ordered to 'Get' Wheeler, Burns Declares," *Washington Evening Star*, May 7, 1924, 4. Accessed via LOCCA.
122. "Effort to 'Frame' Wheeler and Foil Probe Described," *Washington Evening Star*, May 21, 1924, 1. Accessed via LOCCA.
123. Letter from J. Edgar Hoover to Arthur Bliss Lane, September 17, 1924. NARA RG 59, Records of the Secretary of State, Classified Records of the Office of the Counselor, 1916–27, Box 10.
124. Handwritten note from Lane to Undersecretary Robert Grew, September 18, 1924. NARA RG 59, Records of the Secretary of State, Classified Records of the Office of the Counselor, 1916–27, Box 10.
125. Unger, *Fighting Bob La Follette,*, 268–269.
126. Unger, *Fighting Bob La Follette,*, 299. See also David Lawrence, "La Follette Attack on Reds Held Shrewd Political Move," *Washington Evening Star*, May 29, 1924, 1. Accessed via LOCCA.
127. "Strictly Confidential" Memo from Lane to Grew, September 23, 1924. NARA RG 59, Records of the Secretary of State, Classified Records of the Office of the Counselor, 1916–27, Box 10, 1.
128. "Strictly Confidential" Memo from Lane to Grew, September 23, 1924.
129. "Strictly Confidential" Memo from Lane to Grew, September 23, 1924, 2.
130. Hoover letter to Lane, October 6, 1924. NARA RG 59, Records of the Secretary of State, Classified Records of the Office of the Counselor, 1916–27, Box 10.
131. Evan Young Memo to Secretary of State Charles Evan Hughes, October 20, 1924. NARA RG 59, Records of the Secretary of State, Classified Records of the Office of the Counselor, 1916–27, Box 10.
132. "Labor Delegation Expenses to D.C. Paid by O'Connor," *Washington Evening Star*, October 22, 1924, 1. Accessed via LOCCA.
133. Unger, *Fighting Bob La Follette,* 300.
134. Hoover letter to Lane, November 13, 1924. NARA RG 59, Records of the Secretary of State, Classified Records of the Office of the Counselor, 1916–27, Box 10.
135. H. Res. 220, Providing for an Investigation of Communist Propaganda in the United States, as found in *Hearings before a Special Committee to Investigate Communist Activities*

"DISLOYAL UTTERANCES" 91

in the United States, House of Representatives, 71st Congress (Second Session), Part 1, Vol. 1 (Washington, DC: GPO, 1930) 1.

136. For the Lusk Committee's rather selective and skewed view of the ACLU, see *Report of the Joint Legislative Committee Investigating Seditious Activities,* Part 1, Vol. 1, 1077–1104. Accessed via the Hathi Trust at https://catalog.hathitrust.org/Record/001134234.

137. *Investigation of Communist Propaganda: Hearings Before a Special Committee to Investigate Communist Activities in the United States,* House of Representatives, 71st Congress (Second Session), Part 1, Vol. 4 (Washington, DC: GPO, 1930), 406–407.

138. *Investigation of Communist Propaganda,* 409.

139. *Investigation of Communist Propaganda,* 409.

140. *Investigation of Communist Propaganda,* 409.

141. *Investigation of Communist Propaganda,* House Report No. 2290, 71st Congress (Third Session) (Washington, DC: GPO, 1931), 56.

142. *Investigation of Communist Propaganda,* 95–96.

143. *Investigation of Communist Propaganda,* 96–97.

144. The World War Adjusted Compensation Act, H.R. 7959, May 19, 1924. Accessed via LOC at https://www.loc.gov/law/help/statutes-at-large/68th-congress/session-1/c68s1ch157.pdf.

145. Memorandum for the Assistant Chief of Staff, G-2, First Corps Area from the Army Assistant Chief of Staff, G-2, May 25, 1932. NARA RG 165, MID Correspondence and Reports, 1917–1941, Box 2832, File 10110-2452-280.

146. Memorandum for the Assistant Chief of Staff, G-2, First Corps Area from the Army Assistant Chief of Staff, G-2, May 25, 1932.

147. Memorandum for the Chief of Staff: Subject: Daily Report on "Bonus March," May 31, 1932. NARA RG 165, MID Correspondence and Reports, 1917–1941, Box 2832, File 10110-2452-292.

148. Letter from the Commissioners of the District of Columbia to President Hoover, July 28, 1932. NARA RG 165, MID Correspondence and Reports, 1917–1941, Box 2832, File 10110-2452-444.

149. "Hoover Demands D.C. Preserve Order," *Washington Evening Star,* July 29, 1932. Accessed via LOCCA.

CHAPTER 3

"The Spirit of the Concentration Camp" 1933–1941

Franklin Delano Roosevelt's four terms in office as the nation's thirty-second president resulted in a dramatic, permanent increase in the size, power, and reach of the federal domestic surveillance apparatus. The process began, and ran in parallel with, developments abroad that raised concerns about Soviet, Nazi, and Imperial Japanese efforts to both steal American government and defense sector secrets as well as attempts to create or amplify divisions in American society to the benefit of those same hostile foreign powers. His own wartime experience with intelligence operations is one thing that set FDR apart from his predecessors. One incident illustrates the point.

On October 6, 1917, FDR, then assistant secretary of the Navy, gave a specific intelligence tasking to Commander Edward McCauley, Jr., in the Office of Naval Intelligence. "I received the following information today and believe it should be investigated," he wrote McCauley.[1]

The incident in question was the September 28, 1917, grounding of the battleship *USS Texas* a few hundred yards off of Block Island, New York.[2] Roosevelt wanted the lookout on duty on the ship at the time investigated as a potential pro-German saboteur, even though the same informant reported "a heavy mist" at the time the *Texas* ran aground.

No final report on the incident exists in FDR's files, but the available records do show his interest in and regular receipt of intelligence reports during his time in the Wilson administration, an interest that only increased once he became the nation's chief executive. And in the period between the world wars, the American intelligence apparatus that FDR inherited as president had continued its surveillance of enemies—real, suspected, or imaginary. By the end of FDR's second term in office, plans were in place to round up not only German, Italian, and Japanese foreign nationals but American citizens with the same ethnic identities.

Roosevelt's insatiable need for information extended well beyond potential wartime opponents, however. Always on the lookout for attacks from his domestic political enemies, FDR made liberal use of J. Edgar Hoover and his agents for the collection of political intelligence on individuals and groups opposed to Roosevelt's rearmament program and his efforts to help Great Britain survive Hitler's onslaughts in the air and on the seas. Roosevelt focused at least as much of his political intelligence gathering on members of his own party who opposed him as he did on anti-interventionist Republicans. And well before he was elected to the nation's highest office, the intelligence bureaucracy he subsequently inherited was already at work gathering information on individuals or entire groups of Americans deemed potential threats to internal security or wartime operations.

ETHNIC AND RACIAL SURVEILLANCE

Just four months before the 1932 election, MID elements in the New York region conducted a "Survey of the Negro Population in New York City," utilizing Census data and other direct sources to assess the alleged threat of communist penetration of the Black population throughout the city or its likelihood to otherwise protest ongoing racial discrimination. The accompanying maps had the numbers of Black people labeled on a block-by-block level.[3]

The memo's author, Major Joseph Quittner, revealed much about his mindset when describing the situation in Harlem:

> A class distinction exists between the American negro and the West Indian and Spanish speaking negro. The latter are conceded to be more intelligent and progressive and by reason of their controlling numbers, are assuming a dominating position in the control of the political life in Harlem and also by reason of their greater intelligence and capacity, are embarking on substantial business enterprises while the American negro in contrast is essentially stagnant.[4]

Exactly how Quittner and his white MID colleagues concluded that one group of Black people were somehow "more intelligent and progressive" than any other was absent from the memo.

94   CHAPTER 3

After conceding that "due to many causes, included among which is lack of training and opportunity, the negro is unable to compete with the white man" in securing jobs paying a living wage, Quittner went on to say that while the Black "deplores the discrimination which exists between him and the whites, it does not reach the point where it amounts to a resentment."[5]

The report made no mention of the relatively recent suppression of the Garvey movement, much less the continued growth of the National Association for the Advancement of Colored People (NAACP) and the Urban League, among other Black political organizations. The reality is that racial tensions in Harlem were acute, reaching a boiling point less than three years later in the first major race riot in the city since the Civil War draft riots.[6]

MID interest in Black political activities remained strong throughout the 1930s, and its tracking of the constitutionally protected political activities of Black people, even if only through press accounts, had no legitimate national security-related basis.

By the fall of 1933, MID, FBI, ONI and other federal agencies were working on a new surveillance angle: alleged Japanese government attempts to foster racial unrest among Black people.

The US Navy recruiting office in Kansas City, Missouri, provided ONI with the first tip off about the alleged Japanese government scheme on September 12, 1933, with the reporting officer claiming that "a Japanese visited Kansas City with the object of organizing among the negroes an Anti-White Race Movement."[7] The report contained no evidence that the agitator was actually a paid agent of the Japanese government.

By late October 1933, the VII Corps Area G-2 had reached a more refined conclusion: the Japanese agitator was nothing more than a con man.

In an October 25, 1933, "Special Report on 'Pacific Movement' (Jap-Negro)," Major F. M. Moore wrote that the Japanese agitator (who in reality was a Philippine communist) was charging Black people who attended his meetings money to join the "Pacific Movement" and help fund "a proposed colored aviation school. . . . While still watching this matter, I think now it is simply a racket."[8]

In deriding the alleged threat, Moore noted that "The 'Pacific Movement' has almost as many investigators as it has members: Immigration Service, Secret Service, Dept. of Justice, and Kansas City Detective Squad, while the Navy is in full cry. . . . There has been so much uncoordinated and largely ill-advised activity in this present matter that, if it were serious, the valuable chance of quiet investigation would have been lost."[9]

Even as multiple federal agencies were bumbling their way through the Pacific Movement episode, a northeastern Democratic House member was preparing to launch another congressional witch hunt "investigation" focused on a familiar ethnic group.

THE MCCORMACK–DICKSTEIN COMMITTEE

By the fall of 1933, New York Democrat Samuel Dickstein had a reputation among his House colleagues as a hothead. In February 1933, he had accused the US attorney for the Southern District of New York with allowing two employees in his office to conspire with a federal judge in a racketeering scheme—without presenting a bit of concrete evidence to back up the charges.[10] Dickstein's behavior should have precluded him from being taken seriously, much less being awarded the chairmanship of the House Immigration and Naturalization Committee. It didn't.

Whatever misgivings the House Democratic leadership might have had about Dickstein as a committee chairman, he got the job—and with it the platform he needed to go after his next target. In October 1933, he shifted his focus to German dictator Adolph Hitler and alleged German government efforts to undermine American democracy.

As a Jewish immigrant, Dickstein's fear of Hitler's rabid antisemitism was understandable and rational. It was a fear shared by the national Anti-Defamation League (ADL).

On October 12, ADL Director Richard Gutstadt wrote to Dickstein about

> Nazi representatives in this country. We have for some time been watching carefully the various movements. Our people have attended several meetings and reported to us, particularly where reactionary or anti-Semitic sentiment was openly expressed. We submit herewith the attached list of names of those reported to us as very active in the Nazi movement, and we trust that this may be of some help to your committee.[11]

More than 50 people, including in most cases their addresses, were on the ADL list supplied to Dickstein. No information was contained indicating whether they were German nationals or Americans, and no context was provided about what, if anything, a given individual had said or done to represent an actual security threat to the United States. Despite the hearsay nature of the ADL's accusations, it clearly reinforced Dickstein's view that Germans, regardless of citizenship, were a menace.

96   CHAPTER 3

In an October 17, 1933, radio address on NBC, Dickstein told his listeners:

> I do not want our people to be deceived as to the scope of the Hitler movement. Do not be deluded by utterances coming from official German sources which seek to make it appear as though this movement were confined to Germany. On the contrary, just as there is a Communist "Internationale," so there is a Hitler "Internationale," which operates in many countries of the world, and which seeks to convert all people of German blood or descent to the philosophy of Hitler.[12]

While promising that his committee would conduct a "fair and impartial" investigation of alleged Nazi connections to domestic individuals and groups, Dickstein's view of the threat revealed both his anti-German bias and ignorance. Dickstein's approach also ignored the lessons of World War I. Wild claims about German Americans being in league with the Kaiser proved false, at great cost to the safety, liberty, and livelihoods of Americans of German ancestry.

In mid-December 1933, Dickstein went back on NBC Radio to update the public on the status of his inquiry, wasting no time in making sweeping charges while presenting no concrete evidence to back them up, claiming "Poor Germans in this country are literally being blackmailed into lending their moral and financial support to the issues of their chancellor."[13]

At no point in this radio address did Dickstein identify any specific Nazi government employee who had blackmailed or paid off a specific German American organization, nor did he indicate that he had contacted the FBI about alleged Nazi subversion.

By March 1934, Dickstein not only had the headlines he wanted, he had also convinced his House colleagues to create a special select committee to investigate further his allegations of Nazi infiltration of American society.[14] During the debate on the House floor on March 20, New Jersey Republican Fredrick Lehlbach spoke in support of the resolution, stating,

> an organization, growing by leaps and bounds ... has as its basic principle the subversion of constitutional government in the United States. ... We also had evidence that agents of this organization, carrying credentials from Nazi agents in the United States, went to Berlin in order to refinance this movement. This is a proposition that is not general, but quite concrete, and deserves investigation.[15]

"THE SPIRIT OF THE CONCENTRATION CAMP" 97

The organization in question was the Silver Shirts, the brainchild of rabid antisemite William Dudley Pelley—a descendant of English immigrants to Massachusetts. Pelley had never been to Germany.[16]

Pelley was an outspoken admirer of Hitler and did advocate the effective dismantlement of constitutional government in America. But he was also a bizarre, erratic public figure, obsessed as much with the occult as Nazism. Pelley was never a serious threat to the federal government.

Dickstein's failure to find any real evidence of Nazi-controlled German American organizations on US soil should have been a warning sign that his ethnically driven approach to finding Nazis was dangerously flawed. Instead, he got the special select committee he wanted—but not the chance to lead it.

In passing over Dickstein, the House Democratic leadership chose the more junior but far better liked John W. McCormack of Massachusetts as the new chairman. But while McCormack wielded the gavel, Dickstein remained the driving force behind the committee as its vice chairman.

Throughout 1934, the committee conducted multiple field hearings and executive sessions, interviewed hundreds of witnesses, and produced over 4,000 pages of testimony. But in a radical departure from decades of House practice and precedent, McCormack and Dickstein also used tactics and techniques generally employed by Hoover and his FBI agents.

By the summer of 1934, committee investigator Florence Shrieve was on the payroll of the Friends of the New Germany, filing regular reports on her activities, including "Typing more copies of letters to churches and clubs for Mr. Ferenz for his publicity work in connection with Nazi activities."[17] F. K. Ferenz was the head of the Friends of New Germany.

Shrieve's illicit undercover exploits were tame compared to those of other committee investigators.

William Lucitt impersonated a police officer—complete with Lieutenant of Detectives badge—to the German vice consul in Los Angeles to acquire information.[18] Another investigator was Irwin Rothberg, who operated under the alias of Richard Rollins and was also an undercover investigator for the American Jewish Congress. Rothberg wrote in an undated (but likely early 1934) letter to Dickstein regarding the Nazis and American fascists that noted, "I am levelheaded and sincere and not fanatical on the subject, but events have occurred that brand me as an alarmist, and I will be one in all my written reports till I have enough on them to expose their activities."[19]

Rothberg's incoherence and bias were red flags and should have disqualified him for a position on the committee staff. By August 1934 he had been fired by the committee and was found to have altered his official committee credential to include the phrase "United States Secret Service."[20]

98   CHAPTER 3

The committee also used third parties to conduct investigations on individuals.

On May 4, 1934, Ralph Alexander of the Boston Better Business Bureau's (BBB) Financial Division wrote McCormack that the BBB's inquiries regarding an Irvin L. Potter produced

> no information or record in our files on the above name. Upon making inquiries we have ascertained that one Irvin L. Potter has resided at various addresses in Boston starting in about 1927. His occupation is given as that of teacher. At the present time he resides at 337 Huntington Avenue, Boston, Mass. . . . We understand from inquiries made that 337 Hunting Avenue is an apartment house building and that Potter carries on some kind of teaching or instruction from that address. We have been unable to learn the nature or the subject of Potter's teaching or instruction. We are continuing our inquiries and if information is secured, it will be forwarded to you.[21]

Whatever the nature of the allegation against Potter or any of his clients, the willingness of the committee to solicit the BBB—and the BBB's eagerness to help—spoke volumes about the low regard by both entities for Mr. Potter's free association rights under the Constitution. The committee files also show that the Boston BBB was a regular source for such intelligence.

The committee also had no scruples about using its subpoena power to try to get the private communications of at least one its targets.

It began with the April 1934 trip of committee member Charles Kramer (D-CA) to the home base of William Dudley Pelley's Silver Shirt organization: Asheville, North Carolina. While there, Kramer, with McCormack's approval, issued a subpoena for the records of the Silver Shirts. He also held a closed hearing in which he took testimony from several former and some current Silver Shirt members or business associates.[22] Western Union was also pressed for Pelley's telegram traffic.[23]

Nearly 50 years earlier, the Supreme Court had ruled in *Kilbourn v. Thompson* (103 U.S. 168) that congressional subpoena power did not extend to citizens' private matters.[24] While the committee's inquiry into Nazi propaganda had a legal legislative basis, the same cannot be said for its coercion of Pelley and Western Union to produce private business records or communications. Pelley predictably "blamed the Jews" for being behind the committee inquiry, but he did not file suit in federal court to challenge the committee's actions under the *Kilbourn* precedent.[25] The committee's tactics went legally unchallenged, setting a radical new and dangerous precedent in congressional overreach.

"THE SPIRIT OF THE CONCENTRATION CAMP" 99

The McCormack–Dickstein Committee's final report, issued in February 1935, was a mere 24 pages. While the German government-funded "Friends of the New Germany" was certainly very active in pushing the Nazi Party line in the United States and trying to recruit from among the German American population, the committee conceded that "the twenty-odd-million Americans of German birth or descent . . . have refused to participate in the Nazi movement and propaganda in this country, which the evidence plainly shows have been founded, in the main, on racial and religious prejudices."[26]

The only committee finding that gained traction with House members was the recommendation to require agents of foreign governments to register with federal authorities. Even that idea would languish until 1938.

FDR AND CIVIL LIBERTIES: PREVARICATION AND DECEPTION

The investigative excesses of the McCormack–Dickstein Committee and the political climate it fostered did not go unchallenged.

On May 15, 1935, James Myers, Industrial Secretary of the Federal Council of the Churches of Christ, forwarded to White House Secretary Marvin McIntyre a letter signed by 250 religious leaders to Senate Judiciary Chairman Henry Ashurst (D-AZ) urging him to "make an investigation of conditions throughout the country that limit the liberties guaranteed to citizens of the United States under the Constitution."[27]

Protestant, Catholic, and Jewish clergy expressed in vivid terms the dangers of the kinds of legislative witch hunts—at the federal and state levels—that had spread across the country during the McCormack–Dickstein Committee's tenure:

> Some of the organizations sponsoring this repressive legislation are no doubt sincere in their patriotic purpose of defending Americanism, but they appear to be strangely ignorant of this country's historic principles of freedom and are now advocating measures which would in the end tend to destroy the very foundations of the Republic. . . . We are opposed to the use of force and violence. It is for that very reason that we feel impelled to point out that to enact measures which would exclude any political party—no matter what its aims—from the ballot, would have the effect of encouraging violent action on the part of those groups against whom the door to orderly political action had been closed.[28]

100   CHAPTER 3

One prominent member of FDR's cabinet shared the clergymen's concerns, particularly after Rep. Dickstein introduced legislation that summer to revive his moribund committee.

On July 11, 1935, Dickstein had introduced H. Res. 293, which would authorize the Speaker to appoint a seven-member committee to investigate "the extent, character, objects, and sources of any un-American propaganda and un-American activities in the United States."[29] Although the committee would only be authorized for the balance of the 74th Congress, its subpoena powers and mandate would have dwarfed the original McCormack–Dickstein Committee.

A week later, Interior Secretary Harold Ickes wrote FDR about the danger of Dickstein's proposal and the forces pushing it:

> As you know, this resolution was inspired by Victor Watson, Managing Editor of Hearst's *Herald Examiner* of Chicago ... At this time when liberals generally throughout the country are solidly behind the Administration, it would seem to me the height of folly to proceed with an investigation that would put to their defense men and women whose only fault is that they dare to be liberal in their views at a time when Hearst, and those like him, would drive us all into the dark caverns of reaction.[30]

Whether FDR actually contacted House Speaker Joseph Byrns (D-TN) about Dickstein's bill is unknown, but the measure went nowhere during the balance of the 74th Congress.

The malevolent spirit that had animated it and similar bills remained, however. And FDR himself seemed subject to some of those same dark impulses.

On March 17, 1936, Roger Baldwin, Arthur Garfield Hays, and Harry Ward of the ACLU wrote FDR about an April 1935 ONI memo titled "Communist-affiliated and Communist-aiding organizations" that had

> Cited under such a head not only the Federal Council of Churches, but the American Civil Liberties Union, the National Council for the Prevention of War, the Women's International League for Peace and Freedom, together with a number of well-known leaders in religious and peace movements ... You were quoted as assuring your callers that no further efforts by the Army and Navy to criticize civilian organizations would be permitted without your express authority ... We urge that the Administration go further by a positive order that no agency of the Military and Naval forces should engage in any propaganda whatever, intended to create prejudice on political issues.[31]

"THE SPIRIT OF THE CONCENTRATION CAMP" 101

FDR's March 23, 1936, response was disingenuous and alarming. The president began by claiming that the kind of "hard and fast rule" of not investigating domestic groups was "not exactly practical." He then invoked a familiar refrain, one used repeatedly by his predecessor and former boss, Woodrow Wilson:

> As the head of the government, I cannot for the safety of the nation agree never to look into the affairs of any organization. . . . The difficulty is that all pacifist, progressive and other organizations do not live up to their professional ideals. A few of them go to one extreme, a few to the other and, unfortunately, they sometimes disseminate false information and false teachings which are contrary to our democratic ideals and the objectives of a republican form of government.[32]

FDR's use of the phrase "disseminate false information and false teachings" was a clear echo of the language of the Espionage and Sedition Acts from World War I.

Two weeks later, the ACLU's Ward called out FDR for his misrepresentations and tone:

> we did not request you to "agree never to look into the affairs of any organization. What we requested was that the Naval Intelligence Department be stopped from circulating or issuing statements which reflect injuriously upon persons and organizations, and which tend to incite political prejudices and passions and to prevent freedom of discussion. . . . It seems to us altogether contrary to our traditions and sound public policy that a Naval or Military Intelligence Department should deal with such matters.[33]

FDR ignored the ACLU's request. MID, ONI, and FBI continued to surveil various "subversive" individuals and organizations. Indeed, years before FDR's presidency began, they had been targeting another American ethnic minority: Japanese Americans.

DOMESTIC SURVEILLANCE AND COUNTERINTELLIGENCE: THE JAPANESE ANGLE

American military concerns about Japanese Americans as a potential "fifth column" that could be directed from Tokyo emerged shortly after World

War I. On March 20, 1920, MID director Brigadier General Marlborough Churchill issued a memo to all department-level military intelligence elements simply titled "Japanese Situation." His opening sentence conveyed the scope of the project:

> It is desired to establish in each Department headquarters a card index showing the names, occupations, and residences of all male Japanese within the several Departments, both in the United States and in the foreign possessions.[34]

Churchill made no distinction between Japanese foreign nationals, naturalized Japanese Americans, or Japanese Americans born in the United States. He ended his memo with the admonition that "Extreme caution should be taken to secure this information in a manner as to excite the least amount of suspicion."[35]

By April 1920, MID had secured the cooperation of the Census Bureau, which would "furnish us with a list of all Japanese in the United States showing their age, sex, and occupation."[36] Throughout the spring and summer of 1920, index cards containing data on Japanese males of any nationality flowed into MID headquarters in Washington. Within a year, the BoI was having its agents collect similar data on Japanese employees of the Union Pacific Railroad and the Northern Pacific Terminal Company.[37]

Whether MID's Japanese male tracking project extended beyond the first year is unclear from existing records. What FBI, MID and ONI files do show is that for the balance of the 1920s and into FDR's administration, American civilian and military intelligence organizations continued to surveil a range of Japanese individuals and organizations, including the largest and most prominent, the Japanese American Citizens League (JACL).

A March 1933 MID memo asserted—in the absence of any evidence—that, "The policy of *The Pacific Citizen* [JACL's publication] indicates a tendency to use the organization in support of Japan's policies, regardless of their effect on the interests of the United States and the responsibilities of United States citizens."[38] As the Commission on Wartime Relocation and Internment of Civilians (CWRIC) would note decades later, "The League was too young and poorly organized to achieve much success in improving the social and economic status of the Nisei [second-generation Japanese Americans] before the war . . ."[39]

Although the majority of Japanese Americans lived either in Hawaii or on the US Pacific coast, American intelligence monitoring of the minority community was national in scope.

"THE SPIRIT OF THE CONCENTRATION CAMP" 103

On September 28, 1935, the Commandant of the 9th Naval District (head-quartered at Great Lakes, Illinois) sent a memo to ONI about his investigation of Japanese American businesswoman Faye Watanabe.[40] None of Watanabe's activities violated any federal law, and ONI had no information linking her to known or suspected Japanese government intelligence agents. Despite the lack of evidence, ONI had the Postal Department maintain a "mail trace" (i.e., intercepting and copying the to/from information on letters, packages, etc.) on her incoming and outgoing correspondence for years.[41]

The alleged espionage threat from the overwhelming majority of Japanese Americans was a figment of the imagination of federal officials, driven by racial bias and cultural ignorance. In contrast, Japanese government spying on the US military was real, and its effects made the plight of Japanese Americans worse.

Some of FDR's cabinet members were concerned that the administration wasn't doing enough to ferret out potential spies and saboteurs.

As early as January 1936 then–Secretary of War George Dern had written Attorney General Homer Cummings on what Dern viewed as a growing espionage and sabotage threat. While falsely claiming that, "The policy of the War Department has been to conduct no investigations among the civilian population," Dern expressed concern that

> It appears that at the present time there is no agency conducting a counter-espionage service among civilians to prevent foreign espionage in the United States and to collect information so that in case of emergency any persons intending to cripple our war effort by means of espionage or sabotage may be taken into custody.... I would appreciate it very much if you would communicate to me your views in regard to the reestablishment of this agency.[42]

Dern was advocating the revival of the Bureau's Radicals Division that had scandalized the Justice Department during and after the infamous Palmer Raids carried out under Cummings's predecessor almost 20 years earlier.

In pushing the proposal, Dern had a ready-made ally inside Justice: FBI Director J. Edgar Hoover.

On January 27 Hoover sent his own missive to Cummings attached to which was a clip from the January 26 edition of the *Washington Herald* with the headline, "Spies Are Active in America." Hoover closed by saying, "I thought you might wish to have this article called to your attention in order to consider the same in reaching a final decision relative to the request of the Secretary of War."[43]

Dern took nearly a month to reply to Hoover, sending him a note on February 19 that he had talked with Dern and that "there was no particular urgency about the matter, and I also rather thought he was not particularly interested. . . . Under these circumstances, there is nothing further to be done about the matter, at least until we hear from it again."[44]

Hoover's setback proved temporary. Events in the Pacific gave new impetus to Hoover and Dern's push for a ramped up domestic counterintelligence (CI) capability.

Between February and April 1936 several Imperial Japanese Navy (IJN) oil tankers made port calls at Oahu, Hawaii. On three occasions during that period, members of the crews of the tankers took photographs of key US Navy installations from various vantage points around Pearl Harbor. Another IJN tanker crew took detailed measurements of the docks at Hilo. These were the acts of spies, not tourists.[45]

Their brazenness angered Navy officials, and by August 1936, Navy Secretary Claude Swanson asked his judge advocate general (JAG) whether future incidents could be prosecuted under US law. The JAG assured Swanson that those who engaged in similar activities in the future, "whether a citizen of the United States or an alien," were prosecutable under the Espionage Act.[46]

FDR was informed and by August 10 had instructed the War and Navy departments to come up with a plan to create "concentration camps in the Hawaiian Islands for dangerous or undesirable aliens or citizens in the event of a national emergency."[47] Even before Roosevelt's election, the Army had already planned for such a contingency.

A 1932 joint exercise held in Hawaii postulated a "BLACK" opposing force (Japanese) in control of the islands, with "BLUE" force (US) Army and Navy forces assigned the task of liberating the islands. The Army's official operations order included the following for the exercise:

> Counter-Espionage.—It will be brought to the attention of all ranks that many OAHU civilians are BLACK [i.e., Japanese] nationalists and that firm measures are necessary to combat the enemy's espionage activities. All BLACK nationalists and suspected BLACK nationalists will be interned and held under guard for examination and disposition.[48]

No distinction was made between Japanese nationals and Japanese Americans. Now, in the event of war with Imperial Japan, FDR was making such roundups and internments national policy. Absent armed conflict both departments were to stop, or at least discourage and mitigate, Japanese government espionage efforts in the Hawaiian Islands.[49]

"THE SPIRIT OF THE CONCENTRATION CAMP" 105

On October 22, 1936, Navy Secretary Swanson and his War Department counterpart, Harry Woodring, sent FDR their preliminary recommendations. The two secretaries advised FDR against taking extreme measures, such as "an increase in the local garrison" or "the closing of the important Hawaiian commercial ports to the commerce of the world." Instead they confirmed that "lists of [espionage] suspects are maintained by those responsible for military intelligence and such suspects will normally be the first interned in the event of trouble." They also told FDR that:

> it is expected that vacancies occurring hereafter in military or naval civil service positions in Hawaii will be filled by selected citizens of unquestionable loyalty rather than by citizens generally of alien extraction whose loyalty may be questionable.[50]

Thus a core response to foreign espionage activity was to recommend penalizing Japanese Americans by denying them civilian jobs with the Army or Navy. And in the event of war with Japan, Japanese Americans deemed "dangerous or undesirable" would be rounded up and put into concentration camps.

FDR must have been underwhelmed by the two secretaries' recommendations, as he issued no implementing instructions between the fall of 1936 and the spring of 1937. It was not until May 1937 when he designated Woodring to chair an expanded working group to come up with better ideas to deal with Japanese government espionage in the Hawaiian Islands. On November 17, 1937, Woodring submitted revised recommendations agreed upon by the Departments of War, Navy, Treasury, Labor, State, Interior, and Justice.

In addition to their recommendations of October 1936, the working group urged limiting Japanese public vessels to visiting only the Honolulu port. They also recommended additional surveillance measures:

> Various governmental agencies, particularly the Immigration and National Defense authorities, acting separately, but under the coordination of the Navy Department, unobtrusively to check all individuals leaving and boarding Japanese public vessels visiting Honolulu. Customs authorities to observe carefully Japanese public vessels visiting Hawaii, in order to discover any undue advantages being taken of the courtesies accorded under international practice.[51]

On November 26 FDR approved the recommendations and directed that "the measures recommended be put into effect as quickly as possible."[52]

106   CHAPTER 3

In doing so, FDR was authorizing federal agencies to warrantlessly surveil any American boarding or leaving any Japanese vessel, including passenger liners or other purely commercial vessels—all without probable cause and a court order, as required by the Fourth Amendment. And if war with Japan broke out, Roosevelt had no qualms about imprisoning—without charge—an entire class of citizens simply on the basis of a shared racial ancestry with another country.

REDS AND FASCISTS: THE HUNT INTENSIFIES

During the summer of 1936, as FDR and his military chiefs debated how to inhibit Imperial Japanese government espionage operations in Hawaii and on the West Coast, the president returned to an issue members of his cabinet had raised over two years earlier: the extent to which alleged domestic subversives were in league with Soviet Russia or Nazi Germany.[53]

As he had been for nearly two decades, J. Edgar Hoover remained obsessed with communists. During his August 24–25, 1936, meetings with FDR and Secretary of State Cordell Hull, Hoover painted a picture of Soviet subversion aimed at taking control of major labor unions and the Newspaper Guild.[54] FDR directed Hoover to inform Attorney General Homer Cummings about FDR's new instruction to collect intelligence on "subversives" and to coordinate such intelligence operations with his Army and Navy counterparts.[55] That FDR initially kept Attorney General Cummings out of the discussions and dealt directly with Hoover spoke to the latter's effectiveness in cultivating a strong relationship with the president over the preceding three years.

Shortly after Labor Day 1936, Hoover issued an order to all FBI field offices to begin collecting data on communist, fascist, as well as "other organizations or groups advocating the overthrow or replacement of the Government of the United States."[56]

The broad nature of Hoover's directive meant that suggesting even peaceful changes to the existing political or economic order in America guaranteed that those advocating such changes would be surveilled and have their name, address, place of work, business and personal connections, and other information entered into FBI files. Hoover's directive and approach also suffered from built-in confirmation bias. The FBI director and his agents saw foreign connections to domestic groups where none existed.

While his cabinet officers carried out his domestic spying requests, FDR kept up the public pretense that he and his administration were adhering to the Constitution and the Bill of Rights. Writing to Louisiana Governor

Richard Leche on April 5 regarding freedom of the press, FDR noted, "The institutions of our democratic form of Government are secure in just such proportion as the government guarantees those bulwarks of freedom—a free press, free speech and freedom of assembly. Without these there can be no national life, no assurance of liberty or attainment of happiness."[57]

The administration's attacks on civil liberties, conducted in secret, continued. Congressional assaults on the Bill of Rights matched, and occasionally exceeded, those carried out by executive branch authorities.

HOOVER AND THE FBI: LOOKING FOR SPIES IN ALL THE WRONG PLACES

By the end of 1935 the glare of the McCormack–Dickstein investigation had proven too much for Hitler. He ordered any German nationals who were members of the Friends of the New Germany to leave the organization at once.[58] The Fuehrer's order seemingly killed the Friends of New Germany, but it did not lessen the concerns of FDR or many in Congress about potential Nazi or Soviet espionage or subversion efforts in the United States. Several key events in 1936 fueled those worries. The first was Hitler's March 1936 reoccupation of the Rhineland region, in violation of the Treaties of Versailles and Locarno.[59]

Hitler's willingness to threaten the use of force to achieve his political objectives, and his rejection of post–World War I treaties designed to contain Germany, raised the specter of another European war.

Although in no way coordinated, Hitler's move coincided with the rebirth of the Friends of the New Germany under a new leader, German American immigrant and virulent antisemite Fritz Kuhn. The organization also changed its name to Der Amerikadeutscher Volksbund—the German American Bund.[60]

Under Kuhn's bombastic leadership, the Bund would over the next several years draw the attention of federal and state officials, as well as federal law enforcement and intelligence organizations. But the FBI's focus on Bund members caused it to miss a genuine Nazi government spy ring operating on American soil, one that did involve a number of naturalized German Americans.

When Admiral Wilhelm Canaris took over German military intelligence (the Abwehr) in 1935, he found a service with no effective espionage network in the United States.[61] By early 1937, he had at least partially remedied the situation by recruiting additional officers and agents, one of whom was a South African named Fredrick Joubert Duquesne.[62] Duquesne exploited his relationship with a German American employee of the Carl Norden

108   CHAPTER 3

optical company, Herman Lang, to get blueprints for the Norden bomb sight—intended for American heavy bombers like the B-17—smuggled out of the United States in 1938. It was a German intelligence coup that would go undetected until Duquesne's Abwehr-supported spy ring was exposed in 1941. Of the 33 members of the Duquesne ring who either pled guilty or were convicted at trial, 22 were naturalized German Americans.[63] The German American Bund itself had no connection to the Abwehr operation.

A TEXAN'S SEARCH FOR THE DISLOYAL: BIRTH OF THE HOUSE UN-AMERICAN ACTIVITIES COMMITTEE

House Democrat Martin Dies of Texas was both an opponent of FDR's New Deal and a fervent anticommunist. Ever since the formal end of the McCormack–Dickstein Committee in 1935, Dies had used his position on the Immigration and Naturalization Committee to champion anti-alien legislation based on alleged or actual political beliefs—in this case fascism or communism. Dies, Dickstein, McCormack, and like-minded House members sought to revive a committee on "un-American" activities, pass legislation outlawing communist or fascist political parties, or both.[64]

Dies's fellow Texan and House member Tom Blanton had managed, in 1935, to secure passage of an appropriations rider barring federal money for public schools from being used to teach or advocate communism.[65] This so-called Red rider had been ruled by the comptroller general to require public school employees, every time they were paid, to affirm via oath that they had not taught or advocated communism.[66]

Attempts to pass legislation undermining the Bill of Rights dated back to the Alien and Sedition Acts of the early nineteenth century but had been rare prior to the twentieth century. Dies, McCormack, Dickstein, Blanton, and others clearly saw no contradiction between their oath to uphold the Bill of Rights and supporting legislation that gutted it. In the late spring of 1938, Dies scored his most important victory when the House agreed to create a successor to the McCormack–Dickstein Committee.

House Resolution 282 empowered the speaker to appoint a seven-member special committee to investigate:

(1) the extent, character, and objects of un-American propaganda activities in the United States, (2) the diffusion within the United States of subversive and un-American propaganda that is instigated

from foreign countries or of a domestic origin and attacks the principle of the form of government guaranteed by the Constitution, and (3) all other questions in relation thereto that would aid Congress in any necessary remedial legislation.[67]

On May 27, 1938, the House passed H Res 282 by a vote of 191–41. Dies now had the platform he wanted to go after anyone or any organization he deemed "subversive" or "un-American"—terms that were never defined in the authorizing legislation.[68]

A month later, Dies demanded that FDR supply him with FBI investigators and other staff support. Responding for the president, acting Attorney General Thurman Arnold declined, reminding Dies that, "As you are of course aware, the principal duties of the Bureau are the investigation of violations of laws of the United States."[69] Arnold likewise declined Dies's request for a Justice Department attorney to be assigned to his committee.[70] But FDR agreed to an even more troubling request by Dies: access to the tax returns of Americans targeted by the committee.

On June 17, Dies wrote to FDR requesting that his committee be given access to taxpayer and organizational tax returns. Within two weeks, Treasury Secretary Henry Morgenthau had drafted and proposed an executive order and related Treasury department implementing regulations for FDR's approval.[71] On July 9, Attorney General Cummings transmitted to the White House the draft executive order authorizing the Dies Committee access to the tax returns of American citizens and organizations.[72] Roosevelt signed Executive Order (EO) 7933-A on July 14, 1938.[73]

No previous president had ever granted a congressional committee such sweeping, largely unfettered access to the sensitive personal financial information of American taxpayers. Moreover, what American Nazi sympathizer would report to the IRS any funds received from the German government? The notion was ludicrous.

What getting the tax returns did allow Dies and his staff to do was employ another method of harassment against those being targeted by the committee or retaliate against those who attacked Dies. Although the access granted via EO 7933-A had to be renewed annually, it became a pro forma matter for the balance of FDR's presidency.

The committee's first hearing on August 12 was aimed squarely at German Americans and the Bund specifically. Committee chief investigator John Metcalfe made two demonstrably false statements that, amazingly, went unchallenged. The first involved the history of German government espionage in America during World War I:

110   CHAPTER 3

In this connection, it must be borne in mind that in 1916, prior to the entrance of the United States into the World War, Germany had practically no espionage organization or sabotage machine in this country.[74]

In the two years prior to America's declaration of war against Germany in April 1917, the Imperial German government ran multiple, often improperly coordinated, espionage and sabotage operations on American soil via its embassy in Washington and via Franz von Rintelen's covert operations. The names of Boy-Ed, von Papen, and von Rintelen were well known to millions of Americans, but apparently not to Dies's chief investigator.

Metcalfe went on to claim that the Bund's activities were "to avoid a duplication of this mistake" (i.e., not having an active espionage and sabotage operation in America) and that "We will show, as we go along, the activities here which will support this statement."[75]

In fact, neither the remainder of Metcalfe's testimony nor that of any other witness would show any connection between the Abwehr and the Bund.

The August 12 hearing would be the committee's only hearing on alleged or actual Nazi propaganda activity in the United States until after Hitler's invasion of Poland over a year later. And while the committee was certainly able to show that fascist or Nazi-inspired groups like the Bund or William Dudley Pelley's Silver Shirts were prolific in spewing hate-filled, anti-Semitic propaganda, Dies could never demonstrate a link between either group and German military intelligence. For the balance of 1938 and through most of 1939, Dies turned his attention to a range of domestic groups with alleged Soviet ties, especially labor unions.[76]

Dies also had no compunction about targeting FDR's political allies.

In hearings in August and October 1938, Dies invited testimony from former Michigan state officials who criticized Governor Frank Murphy's handling of "sit down" strikes in 1937. Former Flint city manager John Barringer went so far as to characterize Murphy's allegedly inadequate response to the strikes as "treasonable action."[77] No witness produced any evidence that Murphy was influenced by, much less a member of, the Communist Party.

At an October 25, 1938, press conference, FDR was asked whether he was concerned about the charges.

"Yes, I certainly am concerned with that kind of testimony. I would like to say something about it, but I think it probably would be better if I wrote something out instead of trying to talk extemporaneously."

The resulting two-page press release issued later that day was a head-on attack at Dies and his committee:

"THE SPIRIT OF THE CONCENTRATION CAMP" 111

I was very much disturbed. I was disturbed not because of the absurdly false charges made by a coterie of disgruntled Republican officeholders against a profoundly religious, able and law-abiding Governor; but because a Congressional Committee charged with the responsibility of investigating un-American activities should have permitted itself to be used in a flagrantly unfair and un-American attempt to influence an election.[78]

FDR went on to describe, in considerable (and flattering) detail, how Murphy had handled the 1937 strikes.

FDR's final broadside at the Dies Committee was clearly aimed at discrediting the chairman and the process that gave him a platform to attack individual Americans or groups with innuendo and hearsay:

Most fair-minded Americans hope that the committee will abandon the practice of merely providing a forum to those who for political purposes, or otherwise, seek headlines which they could not otherwise obtain. Mere opinion has been barred in court since the American system of legislative and judicial procedure was started.[79]

Dies issued an angry rebuttal to FDR's charges:

While I deeply regret the President's bitter attack on a Congressional committee of an independent department of the Government, and while I regret that the President did not read the testimony before issuing this statement, I wish to make it plain that I shall continue to do my duty undeterred and unafraid.[80]

Dies's complaints were baseless.

State political and law enforcement matters were, per the Tenth Amendment, not the province of the federal government. Murphy and his administration's action in resolving a Michigan labor dispute were none of the committee's business. The committee's investigation of Murphy's actions had no legitimate federal nexus.

Moreover, Dies's requests for FBI agents, Department of Justice attorneys, or other executive branch staff were also inappropriate on practical and constitutional grounds.

Having executive branch agents working as investigators for a congressional committee would have represented a potential violation of separation of powers under the Constitution. Moreover, had Dies truly thought the

112   CHAPTER 3

matter through, he would have realized that having executive branch offi-cials of FDR's administration in his midst would have been a security and political nightmare.

Every committee confidential federal informant critical of FDR would have been at risk of exposure and retaliation via information fed back from FBI or DoJ committee detailees to their parent department, or even the White House itself. Every notional committee investigation of the FBI or another executive branch component could have been reported back by executive branch detailees on the committee—allowing the targets of an investigation to prepare for, and possibly preempt, committee actions. A review of Dies Committee files by the author revealed no awareness of those risks by the chairman.

Finally, if Dies wanted more staff, he and his fellow House committee members and supporters could have asked for the necessary additional funds to hire truly qualified investigators—former FBI or Secret Service agents, former federal prosecutors, and so on. If he lacked for qualified staff, the fault lay with Dies himself, not FDR.

Ironically, while Dies and his staff were targeting all manner of innocent Americans, they missed an actual Soviet spy right in their midst: Representative Samuel Dickstein.

Even though it was Dickstein who had been the most relentless advocate for reviving the committee he led with John McCormack, the House leadership instead turned to Dies. Dickstein was denied even a back-bencher slot on the new Un-American Activities Committee. Despite being frozen out of the official inquiry, Dickstein continued his antifascist campaign via legislative proposals and speeches. What he also ran was an illegal immigration-related racketeering scheme, which is how in July 1937 he came to the attention of the Soviet civilian intelligence service, the NKVD.[81]

For the two-and-a-half years that Dickstein was on the NKVD payroll, he constantly demanded more and more money for the information he provided or the speeches and actions he took on behalf of the Soviets. His handlers gave him an appropriate code name—"Crook."[82]

Dickstein was never able to get access to FBI, ONI, or MID materials that would have been of value to the Soviet government, but he was able to get them information on a range of alleged Nazi or fascist sympathizers and agents in the United States. In the end, his ceaseless demands for more cash and highly argumentative posture with his handlers finally caused the Soviets to cut off Dickstein in early 1940.[83] How long Dickstein simultaneously worked for Polish and British intelligence agencies while receiving money from the NKVD is unknown.[84]

A review of MID and ONI files by the author revealed no material suggesting any awareness by either intelligence service of Dickstein's espionage or racketeering activities. The Department of Justice was another matter.

In 2017, through a Freedom of Information Act request filed by researcher John Greenewald, it was revealed that the Justice Department got a credible tip in February 1939 about Dickstein's racketeering operation but didn't direct the FBI to pursue the lead.[85]

An investigation of Dickstein's "pay-to-play" scheme targeting desperate Jewish immigrants fleeing Nazi persecution might not have surfaced his work for the NKVD. But the failure of Attorney General Frank Murphy to direct Hoover to investigate Dickstein forfeited the best chance of exposing him. For his part, Dickstein played the role of public booster of Hoover and the FBI throughout his time in Congress,[86] developing a warm personal rapport with the FBI director that may well have played a role in the decision not to pursue the racketeering allegations.

SURVEILLING JAPANESE (AND OTHERS) BY LAND, SEA, AND AIR

The year 1938 not only marked the launch of Dies's witch hunt committee, it also saw a significant escalation of domestic surveillance activities by the War and Navy departments. Roosevelt's November 1937 directive to his cabinet heads to increase surveillance of persons of Japanese ancestry engaged in travel to or from Hawaii opened the door to other, more sweeping intelligence collection operations.

A March 30, 1938, report from the 13th Naval District (13th ND) headquarters in Seattle listed 61 individuals labeled as "pro-Japanese propagandists" who represented "only those who have up to 20 March 1938 come to the attention of this district. Many, but not all, of those listed are undoubtedly financed by the Japanese government."[87]

Of the 61 persons listed, nine were current or former Japanese government officials (including members of the Diet). With the exception of a Canadian school teacher, the remaining 51 persons were all American citizens, including five schoolteachers, two university professors, two ministers, three attorneys, and six persons engaged in publishing or otherwise connected with journalism.[88]

Simply going on a cultural exchange trip sponsored by the Japanese government (as many on the list had done) or writing an opinion piece or giving

114   CHAPTER 3

a speech viewed by Navy officials as favorable to the Japanese government (true or not) was enough to get one on the list. Each person's activities were tracked via numbered cards maintained by the naval district responsible for monitoring the individual, indicating the practice was likely Navy-wide.

By May 1938, the 13th ND DIO had compiled a multi-hundred-page "Japanese Monograph" that catalogued every Japanese-owned or -operated entity, as well as "Japanese employed by White Concerns," in the states of Washington, Oregon, and Idaho.[89] The Japanese American Citizens League was characterized as

> decidedly pro-Japanese and takes an active part in protesting and lobbying against any anti-Alien or anti-Japanese legislation and it is known that the Japanese Consuls and their staff as well as first generation Japanese exert considerable influence "behind the screens" and actually go a long way to formulate the policies and activities of the association.[90]

No data was provided to back up the allegations of JACL collusion with Japanese government political or espionage activities.

Indeed, Secretary of War Woodring on multiple occasions ordered surveillance against individuals or even groups of people by race.

On July 20, Woodring instructed MID to send a confidential radiogram to Major General John H. Hughes, commanding general of the Army's Philippine Department. In it, Woodring directed Hughes to

> Radio complete passenger and crew list of east bound Pan American Clipper which left Manila July 7 with description, mission or other identification of any passengers of oriental race.[91]

Woodring's request to MID had come verbally through the chain of command, and MID files reviewed by the author shed no light on why Woodring was interested in the identities of any Asians on that particular flight, much less the Pan Am Clipper crew itself—all of whom were Americans.

The next day, Hughes's staff sent back the complete list of crew and passengers, by nationality. Besides the American crew, there were American, British, and Chinese passengers on the flight, but no Japanese.[92] If Woodring ordered further surveillance of any of the passengers or crew, or requested such surveillance by the FBI, no record of it exists in the MID files reviewed by the author.

In at least one case, Woodring directed the surveillance of the manager of the *New York Journal of Commerce*.

"THE SPIRIT OF THE CONCENTRATION CAMP" 115

On August 26, Woodring directed MID to cable the American military attaché in Tokyo that "Alexander R. Sharton sailed from San Francisco August 5 on the CHICHIBU MARU for Yokohama. Will be in Japan about five weeks. Observe and report by pouch his activities, speech and writing."[93]

Three days later, Major Harry Creswell filed his report on Sharton from Tokyo, covering everything he learned about Sharton's activities since arriving at Yokohama on August 20.

Creswell's sources opined that Sharton's activities were exclusively focused on "making money for his paper" through "arrangements for advertising space with some of the firms having large interests in Manchuria." Creswell concluded, "As far as can be determined, he has made no speeches, nor has he done any writing for publication since his arrival in Tokyo."[94]

Sharton was an innocent American businessman, not a spy. The Secretary of War had directed the surveillance of an American publisher conducting legitimate international travel and business on behalf of his company.

The fact that Woodring was able to determine Sharton's sailing date, the name and destination of the Japanese merchant vessel on which he traveled, the duration and key itinerary items on the publisher's agenda, as well as the identities of any Japanese government officials with whom Sharton had met, showed the detailed level of surveillance that was employed against Americans traveling to or from Japan. It also demonstrated that FDR's November 1937 order to surveil anyone traveling to or from Japan, particularly on Japanese aircraft or merchant vessels, had been interpreted to apply beyond the Hawaiian Islands to the US mainland.

COUNTERINTELLIGENCE CONCERNS MOUNT

By the fall of 1938, FDR was concerned that the level of continuity and coordination was lacking among the federal law enforcement and intelligence services in counterintelligence (CI) matters. At an October 14 cabinet meeting, Roosevelt expressed concern about personnel turnover at ONI and MID was creating problems in ensuring foreign spies were being monitored, caught, and where possible prosecuted. At the meeting, the president directed Cummings to head an interdepartmental group that would include among its principals the secretaries of War, Navy, State, and Treasury to examine how to improve intelligence sharing and cooperation across involved departments and agencies.[95]

Cummings's memo noted that the FBI's General Intelligence Section was already monitoring major American industrial sectors (steel, automobile,

116   CHAPTER 3

coal, and mining, among others), maritime activities, the armed forces, educational institutions, actual or alleged fascist or Nazi entities, organized labor, the Black community, young Americans, and the press. The Army and Navy were primarily concerned with CI threats to their own institutions, but the Navy's CI program was also aimed at curbing "divulgence of information . . . to persons when such divulgence is contrary to the interests of our national defense."[96] In addition to using its own agents, the Army also relied on "contact with other governmental agencies and patriotic citizens in matters relating to the security of information."[97]

According to Cummings's contemporaneous account of the meeting, Secretary of War Woodring expressed concern that "we might be open to criticism as setting up O.G.P.U."[98] The OGPU was the Soviet secret police, predecessor to the NKVD.

Cummings noted that in response, FDR "said it should be confined to investigation of espionage on the part of foreigners" and that "there should be supplied a fund to be distributed under the direction of the Attorney General, with the approval of the President." Treasury Secretary Morgenthau felt that regarding such funding, "it should also be provided that no report need be given as to the disposition of the fund so that there would be no publicity in the matter."[99] Roosevelt and his key advisors had conspired to set up a secret slush fund for domestic surveillance and conceal it from public scrutiny.[100]

The departure of Cummings in early 1939, along with other pressing domestic priorities, slowed down the effort to decide which agency or department would lead federal counterintelligence and antisubversive activities. In the interim, the continued activities of the Dies Committee and related threats to the rights of Americans prompted one New York University professor to write a brief but prophetic letter to FDR shortly after the new year began.

On January 6, two days after FDR's State of the Union message to Congress, political science professor Winchester H. Heicher wrote to the president to say, "I agree with you that there is nothing more vital than the preservation of civil liberty. Like you, I want no concentration camps in America."[101] But while Heicher welcomed FDR's soothing tone on protecting the constitutional rights of Americans, he was skeptical of Roosevelt's commitment should America go to war again:

> If you become a war-time President, will you help preserve freedom of speech and opinion? To be more concrete, I can imagine no situation within the limits of practical possibility in which I could support the United States in war. If we go to war, will you do all in your power to preserve my freedom to present my point of view? Will you support

my refusal to go to war if every dictate of my conscience argues against my participation? Or will you defend, as other Presidents have done, the suppression of civil liberty at the time it has most value—and thus support the spirit of the concentration camp?[102]

A White House staff colleague of presidential private secretary Marvin McIntyre wrote in a cover note to him, "I don't know what in the world to do with a letter like this."[103]

Because of government secrecy, Professor Heicher would not learn until after Pearl Harbor that his fears were well founded. FDR had already embraced the spirit of the concentration camp.

DOMESTIC SURVEILLANCE TURF WARS: FDR'S MANAGEMENT DILEMMA

When Roosevelt finally decided who would have the domestic surveillance and CI lead, it simply formalized the prior informal arrangements between the FBI, ONI, and MID.

On June 26, 1939, FDR issued a memorandum to the secretaries of War, Navy, State, Treasury, and Commerce, the postmaster general, and the attorney general directing that:

> the investigation of all espionage, counter-espionage, and sabotage matters be controlled and handled by the Federal Bureau of Investigation of the Department of Justice, and the Military Intelligence Division of the War Department, and the Office of Naval Intelligence of the Navy Department. The directors of these three agencies are to function as a committee to coordinate their activities. . . . I shall be glad if you will instruct the heads of all other investigative agencies than the three named, to refer immediately to the nearest office of the Federal Bureau of Investigation any data, information, or material that may come to their notice bearing directly or indirectly on espionage, counter-espionage, or sabotage.[104]

Nominally, the FBI had the lead, but in practice all three federal intelligence agencies would be hunting for "subversives" and spies.

The FBI, ONI, and MID got an assist in their efforts to target allegedly disloyal federal employees via legislation offered by Senator Carl Hatch (D-NM) that made it unlawful for any federal employee "to have membership

118   CHAPTER 3

in any political party or organization which advocates the overthrow of our constitutional form of government in the United States."[105]

The Hatch Act was ostensibly designed to prevent the return of any kind of "spoils system" and election interference or partisan political malfeasance by government workers. But the lack of the qualifier "violently" before the word "overthrow" meant that almost any effort to change an established federal policy, regulation, law, or constitutional provision could result in the federal employee or the civil society group advocating the change being designated a threat. It was the first piece of authorizing legislation that would ultimately lead to the creation of what would become known as the Attorney General's List of Subversive Organizations (AGLOSO).

In August 1939, Hoover arranged for American air carriers to let the Bureau know about "the air travel of all Japanese in this country."[106] The air travel surveillance was ostensibly focused on Japanese nationals, but any Japanese Americans flying with family or friends visiting from Japan would naturally have been swept up in such surveillance, and thus potentially become targets of surveillance themselves.

Hoover's Japanese air travel surveillance program was just one example of how the executive branch's three lead intelligence agencies ramped up their domestic surveillance activities after the outbreak of war in Europe. Even so, the actions of the Dies Committee in the fall of 1939 overshadowed all three.

HUAC TARGETS: CIVIL SOCIETY GROUPS AND FEDERAL EMPLOYEES

The Constitution does not give Congress police powers, particularly the authority to conduct seizures and searches of private property. Beginning in October 1939, the Dies Committee ignored that prohibition and began raiding the offices of organizations in its crosshairs.

On October 10, committee investigators raided the Washington and Chicago offices of the League for Peace and Democracy, a group labeled a communist front by Dies. In a letter to FDR, League executive secretary Thomas Harris condemned the raids as a "complete disregard of [the] legal rights and civil liberties of American citizens and organizations," according to the White House memo on the letter.[107] Eight days later, the League issued a press release announcing that it had instructed all of its offices to resist, "with legal force if necessary," any further Dies Committee raids.[108]

On October 23, the League's chairman, Methodist minister and ACLU founding chairman Harry F. Ward, Jr., was grilled by Dies and his colleagues

"THE SPIRIT OF THE CONCENTRATION CAMP" 119

about the League's alleged Soviet ties, its activities, and membership, among other things. The day after his testimony, Ward demanded Congress disband the Dies Committee, noting the danger of Dies's proposal that the Communist Party and others be outlawed:

> If we permit the restriction of political parties in this country, whether they be Nazis, Communists, Republicans or Democrats, then we are no longer capable of governing ourselves and the essence of American democracy has been killed.[109]

Ward's high-minded rhetoric was at least somewhat undermined when he admitted under oath that the League received $2,000 to $3,000 annually from the Communist Party of the United States, which Dies asserted "represents approximately 15 per cent of the total annual budget" of the League.[110]

The subsequent publication in the *Congressional Record* of the names of almost 600 federal employees whose names appeared on League membership lists prompted Dies Committee member Jerry Voorhis (D-CA) to condemn his committee colleagues, noting the action "will lead to casting doubt upon the findings of the committee even when they are of the most substantial and important sort."[111]

Rep. John Coffee (D-WA) was blunter, stating that Dies and his investigators "were guilty of the very practices we are prone to inveigh against Germany and Russia. They secured these documents by illegal means when they could have gone down there and merely asked them to produce them."[112]

FDR condemned the publication of the names of federal employees on the League's membership and mailing lists as a "sordid procedure."[113] Presidential verbal attacks notwithstanding, the administration did nothing to stop the raids carried out by Dies Committee staff. For the balance of FDR's presidency, the Texas congressman and his supporters on and off the Hill would be a thorn in Roosevelt's side and a menace to innocent Americans.

WAR PLANS: FACTORY "SURVEYS," INTERNMENT TARGETS, AND STILL MORE DOMESTIC SURVEILLANCE

Hitler's invasion of Poland, followed by declarations of war by England and France, not only plunged Europe into a new war, it resulted in increased FBI scrutiny of anyone of German ancestry in federal government jobs.

120   CHAPTER 3

During World War I, the Army and Navy had the responsibility for monitoring the potential counterintelligence threats in American factories producing war material. Now, the FBI assumed the job as part of Hoover's quest to put even more of American domestic life under the gaze of his agents in the hunt for subversives or saboteurs.

In late January 1940, Hoover received a tip that two German nationals working at the Frankford Arsenal in Pennsylvania were potential Nazi saboteurs. Hoover wrote to Colonel E. R. Warner McCabe of MID that:

> It is also alleged that two experts were brought to the United States from Germany for employ in the Mechanical Time Fuse Department of the Frankford Arsenal, and that one of the above experts has returned to Germany, the other being presently in charge of the Mechanical Time Fuse Department at the arsenal. It is alleged that during the past summer considerable difficulty was encountered with the time fuses manufactured in the Mechanical Time Fuse Department, inasmuch as thousands of such fuses proved defective shortly after the commencement of hostilities in Europe.[114]

Had Hoover bothered to check with the Army Ordnance Department before writing to McCabe, he would have learned that the fuse manufacturing problems "were thoroughly investigated at the time of their occurrence and there was no evidence whatsoever of any attempt at willful destruction of Government property or interference with manufacturing operations."[115]

Hoover's blundering in the Frankford Arsenal case did not alter the fact that concerns about potential sabotage by foreign agents were legitimate. Imperial German army and navy attachés had done exactly that in World War I. But Hoover and his Army and Navy counterparts wanted to go much farther than simply investigating allegedly suspicious or dangerous foreign nationals. In the event of war, they wanted to round them up for the duration of any conflict.

At a January 4, 1940, conference FBI Deputy Director Edward Tamm asked his Army and Navy counterparts where and under what circumstances they intended to intern aliens in the event of war.[116] The next day, MID generated and distributed a memo noting that "a maximum of 1500 enemy aliens were interned by the Army" during World War I, and that the Army was "very anxious to keep the number to be interned by the military authorities low."[117] Army officials were concerned about the sheer number of personnel that might be required for any large-scale internment program.

By mid-June, Hoover reported to the conference attendees that the FBI was proposing to detain a minimum of 7,500 Germans, at least 6,000

Italians, and roughly 5,000 communists. He also offered a list of 21 potential concentration camp sites spread across the country from Massachusetts to California. The glaring omission was the proposed internment of Japanese, and Hoover admitted that as of that moment the Bureau had not made plans for a Pacific war and related internment options.[118] Realizing the magnitude of the error, Hoover acted quickly, telling his counterparts at the June 25 meeting of his plans "for tripling of the investigative staff in the Hawaiian Islands" and the work they would be doing.[119]

Beyond the internment of alleged or actual enemy nationals, and possibly Americans of German, Italian, or Japanese ancestry, throughout the balance of 1940 the conferees also planned for an extensive censorship and radio communications monitoring regime, as well as nationwide FBI defense plant "surveys" designed not just to assess potential vulnerabilities to sabotage but to facilitate surveillance of the workforce. Yet even as these steps took place behind a veil of secrecy, other federal government war

Figure 3.1. From left to right: Special Assistant Attorney General for Immigration and Naturalization Lemuel Schofield; Solicitor General Francis Biddle; Attorney General Robert Jackson, June 14, 1940. Within a year, Biddle would succeed Jackson as attorney general and become a key player in the plans for wartime internment of Axis power citizens and Japanese, German, and Italian Americans. *Library of Congress*

preparation efforts unfolded publicly. And just as it had been the case with the Wilson administration in the run up to World War I, the actions of FDR and his key advisors helped fuel a growing antiwar movement. Like Wilson, FDR would use federal intelligence and law enforcement organizations to target those opposed to his policies.

Hoover's aggressive foray into industrial plant "surveys" for counterintelligence purposes caused an uproar when the practice became public. During testimony before the House Appropriations Committee on January 5, 1940, Hoover acknowledged that employees working for companies with Army or Navy contracts were being fingerprinted by their employers and the fingerprints and related information were being given to the FBI to determine "whether any of these individuals have been engaged either in criminal or subversive activities."[120]

While it was certainly understandable that a company like Boeing would want to screen out prospective employees with prior criminal histories, Hoover considered virtually any individual or group that challenged the prevailing political or economic paradigm to be subversive by default. Many of the workers in defense-related industries were union members. Hoover's indexing system was a form of unconstitutional political surveillance, enabled and encouraged by the owners of companies with contracts with the War and Navy departments.

RAIDS, MAIL INTERCEPTS, WIRETAPS, AND WORSE

Another major event that shaped American foreign and domestic policy during the late 1930s—and thus domestic surveillance priorities—was the Spanish Civil War. The proxy war fought between the Soviet and Nazi governments within the Spanish Civil War from 1937 to 1939 motivated nearly 3,000 left-leaning, antifascist Americans to volunteer their services. Those Americans often found their way into various leftist combat formations that unsuccessfully battled General Francisco Franco's Nazi-backed military machine.

The survivors—who referred to themselves as Veterans of the Abraham Lincoln Brigade—returned to the United States in 1939 and resumed their lives, usually in the service of organized labor or other left-leaning causes. And it was their combat background and experience, along with their left-leaning political activities, that made them targets of Hoover and his men.

In a series of highly publicized raids on February 6, 1940, Hoover's agents arrested over a dozen former Lincoln Brigade members for violating

"THE SPIRIT OF THE CONCENTRATION CAMP"   123

a World War I–era law barring US citizens from enlisting in foreign armies.[121] The raids drew immediate and sustained criticism from members of Congress, editorial boards, and a range of civil society organizations. Once he took over at Justice, Attorney General Robert Jackson dismissed the charges to avoid rekindling "the animosities of the Spanish conflict" so many years after the fact.[122]

The raids prompted a major rhetorical attack on Hoover and the FBI from anti-interventionist Senator George Norris (R-NE). In late February 1940, Norris labeled the Bureau's tactics "rather abhorrent to one who believes in constitutional liberty" and inserted into the *Congressional Record* a *New Republic* editorial that likened the FBI to the infamous Soviet OGPU.[123]

Norris would likely have been even more outraged had he known that senior Bureau officials were giving MID license to conduct mail surveillance of Americans.

At the March 19, 1940, MID-ONI-FBI conference, Army Captain W. E. Crist asked FBI Deputy Director Edwin Tamm if it was legal for Army officers to ask the Post Office Department to conduct "mail tracings" on the Army's behalf. Tamm reportedly replied the answer was yes because the request was made by a department or agency "of the executive department of the Government."[124] Only the Attorney General could issue such an opinion upon the written request of the department or agency in question, and no such written opinion had been sought. Tamm had engaged in extraconstitutional legal freelancing.

Moreover, senior Bureau officials were neither impressed nor intimidated by verbal blasts from House or Senate members or their staffs over the raids against the former Abraham Lincoln Brigade members.

On March 12, Senator Norris had announced his intention to launch a Senate investigation into allegations that law enforcement officials, including the FBI, had used wiretaps against targets in violation of the Communications Act of 1934.[125] At the March 26, MID-ONI-FBI conference, the FBI's Tamm referred to Senate Interstate Commerce Committee investigator and attorney Max Lowenthal as "a very slick Jew" who "probably obtains his money from Russia."[126] He went on to claim without evidence that Lowenthal cowrote the *Washington Evening Star* piece that covered Norris's announcement and allegations, and he asked his MID and ONI colleagues to check "what connection, if any, Lowenthal . . . has with the Communists."[127] For Hoover, Tamm and other senior FBI leaders, any attacks on the Bureau had to be the work of Reds or communists or those inspired by them.

124   CHAPTER 3

In April 1940, the Conference on Civil Rights of the Washington Committee for Democratic Action passed a resolution—transmitted to FDR—condemning the FBI's labor union "subversives" card index system as "clearly an unjustifiable assumption of power not authorized by law" and "tantamount to a plot against the peace and security of the American people."[128] The investigation of Hoover and the FBI also requested by the conference never took place.

Hoover's counterattacks against his critics involved both his own public defense of the FBI as well as private appeals to Hill allies like Dies to speak out. It also involved another well-honed Hoover tactic: painting his enemies as FDR's as well.

On April 13, 1940, Hoover sent a memo to Roosevelt's chief private secretary, Brigadier General Edwin A. "Pa" Watson, in which he alerted FDR and Watson to "a proposed meeting to be held in Washington on April 14, 1940, to protest to the President against the alleged unlawful activities of the Federal Bureau of Investigation."[129] Hoover went on to list dozens of leftist or communist-affiliated organizations with whom one of the organizers, 80-year old Professor Franz Boas—the father of the American academic discipline of anthropology—was allegedly affiliated.[130]

A month later, the FBI director sent an even more overt piece of political intelligence to the White House, one that intimated Nazi intrigue with FDR's GOP opponents.

On May 14, 1940, Hoover wrote to Watson about a "confidential source heretofore found to be reliable" that August Gausebeck, the head of a major investment banking firm that handled "much of the German business" in America, wanted to "donate $500,000 to the Republican Presidential Campaign."[131] Gausebeck's reasoning was, according to Hoover's source, that "if a Republican were elected, there would then be established favorable trade treaties between the United States and Germany, whereas if President Roosevelt were reelected this would be impossible."[132] Hoover told Watson that "In view of the international aspect of this situation I thought the President should be informed of it."[133]

Yet even though Hoover went on to describe Gausebeck's proposed scheme to launder the $500,000 through a large number of small donors to try to conceal the size and source of the illegal contribution, he did not say that he had informed the attorney general or even initiated a formal counterintelligence investigation of Gausebeck. Hoover simply ended his note to Watson by saying, "If I receive any further information about this situation I will advise you."[134] For Hoover, Gausebeck's alleged illicit political activities were a political weapon to be used to curry FDR's favor, not a credible foreign plot to influence a US presidential election.

"THE SPIRIT OF THE CONCENTRATION CAMP" 125

Despite Hoover's nearly always questionable instincts on who or what actually constituted a real threat, FDR trusted him enough to authorize FBI wiretaps—in direct violation of Supreme Court rulings barring the practice.

The 1928 Supreme Court decision in *Olmstead v United States*[135] held that the use of secret government wiretaps against criminal targets did not, in fact, violate the Fourth Amendment's prohibition on warrant-less seizures and searches. Congress disagreed, and in 1934 it passed the Communications Act, which its authors believed created a blanket pro-hibition on government wiretapping. Hoover, as well as his MID and ONI colleagues, had complained about the law's constraints ever since, even though Justice allowed wiretaps to continue so long as their use was not disclosed.[136] Their complaints reached a crescendo after the Supreme Court ruled in *Nardone v. United States* in December 1939 that the Com-munications Act was indeed a complete bar to the use of wiretaps or their evidence at trial.[137]

During the first five months of 1940, Nazi victories on the European con-tinent only intensified Hoover's concerns that the law was denying the FBI potential intelligence on Axis spies and saboteurs. With the aid of his friend Treasury Secretary Henry Morgenthau, Hoover waged a campaign inside the administration to resume wiretapping, over the objections of Attorney General Robert Jackson.[138] Morgenthau's appeal to FDR worked, and on May 21, 1940, FDR issued a one-page confidential memo to Jackson autho-rizing and directing him to "secure information by listening devices" target-ing "persons suspected of subversive activities against the Government of the United States, including suspected spies."[139]

Roosevelt rationalized his decision by claiming "I am convinced that the Supreme Court never intended any dictum in the particular case which it decided to apply to grave matters involving the defense of the nation."[140] Not surprisingly, he never sought the opinion of Chief Justice Charles Evans Hughes on the matter. Also of note was his decision to only allow the Justice Department, through the FBI, to conduct such wire taps; MID and ONI were excluded from the order. Why remains a mystery.

While some House members sought to create a carve-out to authorize national security–related wiretaps, the legislation went nowhere. A year later, Jackson would be elevated to the Supreme Court, never revealing while alive his failed opposition to or knowledge of the unconstitutional wiretap-ping program.[141]

At least some in the Justice Department were contemplating more extreme measures than wiretapping.

Figure 3.2. President Franklin Delano Roosevelt's May 1940 memo authorizing warrantless wiretapping in cases involving subversive activities as well as espionage violated a 1939 Supreme Court decision banning the practice. Every man who followed FDR in the presidency would use that same authority throughout the Cold War. *FDR Presidential Library*

A May 1940 memo to FDR prepared for Jackson's signature but never sent advocated that an "'Internal Defense Unit', headed perhaps by J. Edgar Hoover" be created and function under the War Department in order to combat "fifth column" elements, which represented "a form of undeclared war." This was necessary, the memo's author argued, because a fifth column

Figure 3.3. As attorney general under FDR, Robert Jackson acquiesced to Roosevelt's insistence that national security wiretapping was within a chief executive's constitutional powers, despite the Supreme Court's *Nardone* decision in 1939 upholding the 1934 Communication Act's ban on the practice. *Library of Congress*

must be met "by a use of war powers and defensive and preventative tactics—not punishment after the fact."[142]

The memo's author advocated this approach because "the bulk of the work is counter-espionage and circumvention" and that "Broad search and seizure, wiretapping, economic pressures, and other police methods that will not be tolerated in general enforcement will be conceded to national defense.... Many who would be glad to cooperate in national defense are cool to the Department of Justice because it prosecutes under many business, and other, statues."[143]

Because the memo was never sent, the program it advocated was not implemented during FDR's tenure. But the concepts it advanced to go after alleged fifth column elements or those otherwise deemed subversive—wide-ranging, warrantless search and seizures, intensive wiretapping, and "circumvention" (perhaps better understood as "preemption")—would be techniques that the FBI would eventually adopt during the Cold War.

128   CHAPTER 3

DEFINING "CIVIL LIBERTIES,"
IGNORING THE CONSTITUTION

The White House apparently made no direct response to the Conference on Civil Rights' letter and resolutions condemning the FBI's backdoor surveillance activities against labor, but in May 1940 the Justice Department issued new guidelines to all US attorneys regarding the handling of civil liberties cases.[144] The 41-page memo described the term "civil liberties" as "a phrase of popular currency applied somewhat indiscriminately to a miscellaneous group of rights, interests, and situations."[145] According to the memo—authored by Assistant Attorney General O. John Rogge—"There is no law of civil liberties as such."[146]

Groups such as the Conference on Civil Rights clearly viewed the Bill of Rights as exactly such a law, and the memo's attempt to circumscribe what constituted a violation of civil liberties was clear throughout. Absent from the memo was any mention of the *Weeks* case from 1914, which explicitly made the warrantless seizure of telegrams and cables from a person's home unconstitutional.[147] No mention was made of the Communications Act of 1934, which made it a federal crime for any individual to wiretap the communications of another.[148] Also missing from the memo was any reference to the very recent (and legally dubious) FBI raids on the homes of former Abraham Lincoln Brigade members and the attorney general's subsequent dismissal of the charges.

If any Justice Department lawyers or FBI agents deployed around the country had any qualms about the Department's "light touch" approach to upholding the Bill of Rights, the president and Hoover had none—especially when critics called into question FDR's dramatic call for vastly greater spending on military preparedness. As was usually the case, Roosevelt used events in the European war to advance his argument.

In April 1940, the German navy (augmented by German paratroopers) successfully executed a daring—and costly—assault on Norway.[149] A month later, German armored and mechanized formations accomplished what French generals thought impossible: an offensive through the Ardennes Forest that bypassed the fortified but static Maginot Line.

Between May 10 and May 25, German forces penetrated deep into France while simultaneously encircling the British Expeditionary Force (BEF), the French First Army, and Belgian troops in Belgium.[150] The BEF, along with remnants of the French and Belgian troops, were squeezed into an ever-shrinking pocket around the besieged French port of Dunkirk. The

"THE SPIRIT OF THE CONCENTRATION CAMP" 129

fall of France was now inevitable. If the BEF surrendered, Britain would be wide open to a German invasion across the English Channel. By the time FDR began a "fireside chat" on May 26, British Prime Minister Winston Churchill had already ordered the evacuation of the BEF and as many other Allied troops as possible from Dunkirk.

It was against this ominous backdrop that Roosevelt appealed to Americans to not only donate to the Red Cross, but to get behind his defense buildup. And he made it clear that those who opposed his request for another $1 billion for the Army and Navy were unpatriotic and nothing more than tools of Nazi propaganda.

Roosevelt denounced those engaged in "a dissemination of discord . . . a group that may be sectional or racial or political is encouraged to exploit its prejudices through false slogans and emotional appeals. . . . Sound national policies come to be viewed with a new and unreasoning skepticism, not through the wholesome debates of honest and free men, but through the clever schemes of foreign agents."[151] Five days later, FDR sent his formal request to Congress for the vast military funding increase.[152]

The White House received an avalanche of letters and telegrams in response to Roosevelt's speech and message to Congress, many of them highly critical of the president's language and actions. That Roosevelt was angered by the tone and volume of the negative mail became apparent when he directed one of his key aides, Stephen Early, to transmit the offending letters and telegrams to the FBI to determine if the Bureau had derogatory information on any of the senders. On June 8, Hoover sent Watson information from the Bureau's files on 63 groups or individuals who sent letters or telegrams to the White House in response to FDR's military funding increase push.

Hoover disingenuously caveated the Bureau's work, telling Early, "Although the names appearing on the telegrams and letters are similar to the names appearing in the files of this Bureau, there is no indication that the individuals are identical with the senders of the communications directed to the President."[153]

If Hoover could not confirm a relationship between the Bureau's holdings and those who wrote to FDR, why send the president uncorroborated information? More importantly, why agree to a file search at all on people who exercised their First Amendment rights to petition the president?

The author's review of the incoming letters and telegrams in this episode revealed that none in any way threatened the president. Had any done so

130   CHAPTER 3

the referral would have gone to the Secret Service for follow up, not the FBI. FDR's purpose in having Hoover crosscheck the Bureau's files was purely political: he wanted as much information as possible on those he clearly deemed domestic political opponents.

A coalition calling itself the American Peace Crusade was among those who sent a telegram to FDR. Organized by the Los Angeles Industrial Union Council, the California Youth Legislature and the Hollywood Peace Council, the group conducted a peace rally on the steps of the Los Angeles city hall and demanded "No guns, no credits, no men to foreign wars."[154] The tone of cable clearly annoyed the president. On June 11, 1940, he sent a note to Watson along with the telegram, "Will you ask Edgar Hoover to investigate the attached?"[155]

By June 25, Hoover had delivered a five-page report on the coalition, highlighting the role of alleged or known communist political activists in organizing and leading the demonstration.[156] The organizers had claimed 30,000 in attendance, but the Bureau memo described it as a "straggling crowd."[157] No directs threats of violence against the president or the federal government were reported, and the event itself garnered no follow-up media coverage. The president had directed the FBI to investigate a peaceful political gathering that threatened no one.

HOOVER VERSUS DIES AND HUAC

If international events in the first half of 1940 had presaged the triumph of Hitler's forces on the battlefields of Europe, the second half of the year demonstrated that he and his fellow fascist allies in Italy and Japan harbored ambitions of global domination.

By June 4, the last of the BEF and what French and other Allied troops could be saved had been evacuated from Dunkirk. Sensing that France was doomed, Italian dictator Benito Mussolini ordered Italian forces into southeastern France on June 10. On June 22, 1940, the Third French Republic surrendered to Adolph Hitler's Third Reich. Less than a week later, Congress passed and FDR signed the Alien Registration Act (Public Law 76–670), which required any nongovernmental foreigner seeking entry to the United States to register and be fingerprinted.[158] The law also made it a crime for anyone, whether a citizen or not, to "advise, counsel, urge, or in any manner cause insubordination, disloyalty, mutiny, or refusal of duty by any member of the military or naval forces of the United States."[159] The law only intensified paranoia over German, Italian, or Japanese nationals, or any associations with them.

"THE SPIRIT OF THE CONCENTRATION CAMP" 131

Over the next three months Hitler would try but fail to bomb England into submission in what would become known as the Battle of Britain. Expanding their war of conquest from China, by late September 1940 Japanese forces had occupied the French colonial possession of Vietnam—bringing their forces ever closer to American bases in the Philippine Islands and the British naval base at Singapore on the Malay peninsula.

That same month FDR and Churchill signed a deal transferring 50 obsolete American naval destroyers to Britain in exchange for nearly century-long basing rights in Bermuda and Newfoundland, bases that would soon host US Navy ships on secret convoy escort missions in the Atlantic war zone.[160] One day after FDR made the destroyer-for-bases deal public, his anti-interventionist opponents made an announcement of their own—the creation of the America First Committee (AFC).[161]

Founded by Yale University graduate R. Douglas Stuart, Jr. and led by retired Army General Robert E. Wood, AFC attracted support from prominent citizens ranging from Alice Roosevelt Longworth to Charles Lindbergh to Lillian Gish.[162] Once the group began radio broadcasts in the fall of 1940, an FBI informant in Birmingham suggested to the agent in charge that the group was spreading Nazi propaganda.[163] The AFC was a major FBI target until after the Pearl Harbor attack.

By the late summer and throughout the fall of 1940, Hoover was again facing a Capitol Hill problem: Martin Dies. The Texas Democrat and chairman of the Select Un-American Activities Committee had once again ordered his staff to raid the offices of another organization, in this case the German Railroad Information Bureau in New York City in August 1940.

In his August 26, 1940, memo to Jackson on the episode, Hoover noted that "Books, films, radio, and cablegram files were seized for examination, according to information received through a confidential source. This appears to be another instance where action of this Committee was taken to the detriment of the long-range plan for intelligence work which this Bureau has been pursuing."[164]

Hoover's agents had been gathering data on the same organization prior to Dies sending his staffers to raid it and seize its records. Dies's actions sabotaged the Bureau's surveillance activities targeting the organization, and Hoover now knew—from the same informant—that Dies was about raid the German Library of Information in New York City, an organization also under FBI surveillance "for a considerable period of time," Hoover wrote Jackson. Hoover complained that additional Dies's raids on such organizations "will further handicap activities of Special Agents . . . in the field of general intelligence."[165]

132   CHAPTER 3

"There can obviously be but one principal motive for such action as that taken by representatives of the Committee in question," Hoover told Jackson, "and that is publicity."[166]

Interestingly, Hoover's complaint was not that the Dies Committee's actions were unconstitutional—they clearly were—but that they had blown or could blow FBI intelligence operations. Why Hoover failed to suggest that Jackson tell Dies further raids might lead to criminal indictments against him and his staff for unconstitutional search and seizures under the Fourth Amendment is a mystery.

Hoover's August 26 memo to Jackson about Dies and his raids was the first in nearly a dozen such missives the FBI director sent to the attorney general between September 11 and November 22. On October 11, Hoover suggested to Jackson that "a grand jury in the District of Columbia invite Congressman Dies to immediately turn over . . . all and any evidence which he may have indicating any violation of the Federal Statutes. . . . To call him before a Grand Jury divorces the action from any so-called Executive Department and at the same time precludes the issuance of statements during the consideration of the matter by the Grand Jury."[167]

Legally and politically, Hoover's suggestion seemed a masterstroke. It would, as he put it to Jackson, force Dies to "lay his cards on the table" before a "properly constituted legal body" while simultaneously silencing Dies publicly over anything pending before a federal grand jury.[168] Unfortunately for Hoover, Dies was just smart enough not to take the bait, instead continuing his highly publicized raids on organizations while simultaneously claiming the FBI—and by inference, Hoover—were falling down on the job of protecting the public from spies and subversives.

Just before Thanksgiving, Jackson had had enough.

On November 24, he issued a five-page press release, praising Hoover and his agents, cataloguing a number of instances where the Bureau had long since looked at organizations targeted by Dies, and in one instance alleging that the committee had been duped by a known fabricator trying to pass himself off as a former Gestapo agent.[169]

Jackson said it was "highly regrettable" that Dies "should seek to undermine the confidence of the American public in the Federal Bureau of Investigation," which Jackson characterized as "the finest investigative organization in the world." The Bureau, Jackson said, would continue to go about its many tasks "in a workmanlike manner without alarmist tactics and without sensationalism." In a parting shot at Dies, Jackson said "Efforts to arouse public sentiment or emotion, if that be desirable, will have to come from other sources."[170]

A RACIST PRISM: SURVEILLANCE AND INTERNMENT PREPARATIONS

While the war of words raged between Hoover and Dies in the fall of 1940, the prelude to a real shooting war in the Pacific began with Imperial Japanese forces occupying the French colony of Vietnam on September 22, a potential jumping-off point for future military action against British and Dutch colonies in the region. Four days later, FDR ordered a steel and scrap metal embargo against Japan. Twenty-four hours after Roosevelt's move, the official alliance between Nazi Germany, Imperial Japan, and Fascist Italy was announced as the "Rome-Berlin-Tokyo Axis."[171] The president and his senior advisors knew the nation was now clearly a step closer to being caught in a two-front war. On October 9, Navy Secretary Frank Knox sent a secret memo to FDR in which it was clear Knox was concerned about another front in any future war: the home front.

After informing FDR that he had ordered a call-up of Navy and Marine Corps reservists and other limited defensive measures, Knox offered a series of 15 other recommended actions. Number 12 was, "Prepare plans for concentration camps (Army-Justice)."[172]

At the FBI, Hoover would soon direct his agents to operationalize the first phase of Knox's proposal by conducting massive, generalized intelligence collection operations that were unequivocally racial or ethnic in character.

On October 21, 1940, Hoover sent a memo to all FBI field offices directing them to conduct "general intelligence surveys" on persons of German, Italian, or Japanese ancestry, as well as organizations representing the ethnicities of the three Axis powers.[173] The effort was an officially sanctioned parallel to the American Legion Contact Program formally established in the late fall of 1940.[174] Under the latter, and with the approval of Attorney General Robert Jackson, Legion members of German, Italian, French and Russian ancestry were asked to monitor any potential "subversive" activities of their respective ethnic groups in their communities.[175] Leads were fed to the local Bureau office, which would then investigate the allegations.

Both programs proceeded from the baseless assumption that generalized, mass surveillance and monitoring of specific ethnic communities would lead to the discovery of potential spies or saboteurs. That mentality was shared by British intelligence, which issued its own report in December 1940 on the Japanese espionage system that claimed

134 CHAPTER 3

Every Japanese has a quite childish delight in spying. If he is not doing under orders or because he is merely expected to do it by the local Japanese club or association, he is spying for the fun of spying; they are all enthusiastic amateurs. Spying is in fact a part of the Japanese character. A Japanese who is not addicted to spying is not a typical Japanese. And so the conclusion that every Japanese is a potential, if not an actual spy, is, therefore not surprising.[176]

The Bureau's own General Intelligence Surveys of such communities resulted in the acquisition of the names, addresses, and in many cases related organizational affiliations and activities of thousands of Americans and foreign nationals alike. Most of the information generated from such mass surveillance and intelligence gathering operations was of no actual intelligence value.

In the case of the Honolulu Field Office's massive December 1940 report, it took Special Agent N.J. Alaga over three weeks of work to canvas the island of Oahu. By the time he was done, Alaga had catalogued every significant business, educational, religious, and social organization frequented by the tens of thousands of persons of Japanese ancestry—foreign nationals and American citizens. And while some were deemed suspicious, the report itself failed to identify a single confirmed Japanese government spy or any Japanese Americans working in an espionage capacity for the Imperial government.

Without question, the 250 or so Japanese consular agents located at various points throughout the Hawaii chain acted as the eyes and ears for the Honolulu consulate to the extent they could. But Alaga and his Honolulu Field Office colleagues had the names and other personally identifying information on all those agents.[177] They were too easily monitored to be effective intelligence collectors, and because those consular agents spent the overwhelming majority of their time among the local Japanese, they were not privy to the kind of secrets or information the FBI, MID, or ONI needed to protect the Pacific Fleet or the Army's airfields and barracks. Yet Bureau agents expended considerable time and energy keep track of them and any other individuals the handful of "confidential informants" working for the FBI fingered as spy suspects.

In the Duquesne spy ring case, the Bureau's error had been focusing on ethnic German organizations instead of looking for clear links between confirmed Nazi government officials and those in the United States with access to sensitive defense technology, regardless of nationality. In its sweeping, racialized mass surveillance operation in the Hawaiian Islands and on the

"THE SPIRIT OF THE CONCENTRATION CAMP" 135

American mainland, the Bureau was repeating the same error, this time with regard to Japanese. Hoover got reinforcement for his mentality from his new friends in British intelligence, as the excerpt from the UK report referenced earlier makes clear. The race-based, mass surveillance approach of US and British intelligence guaranteed actual threats would go unexamined until it was too late.

CONCLUSION

Between the start of FDR's first and third terms in office, the world had transitioned from a global economic depression to another world war, with Britain barely hanging on against the Nazi onslaught. By the beginning of 1941, the United States had moved, in ways obvious (like Lend-Lease and the reinstitution of the draft) and secret (intelligence sharing with Britain, preparations to intern enemy aliens and Americans of alleged suspect loyalty), closer to joining the conflict. A number of techniques and approaches adopted during World War I were prepared for employment in the new one: censorship, mail intercepts, and the employment of select civil society organizations (in this case, the American Legion) to help with mass surveillance of suspect ethnic populations. But FDR and his key cabinet and subcabinet officials were prepared to go much further.

Roosevelt's complete circumvention of the Supreme Court on the issue of wiretapping—even in limited circumstances—represented a radical, unilateral, and illegal expansion of presidential surveillance-related power. And the decision to plan for the internment of American citizens of German, Italian, and Japanese ancestry absent a valid criminal predicate was a step well beyond the surveillance, harassment, and ostracization meted out to German Americans during World War I. But as German and Italian Americans were so large in number and so heavily represented in multiple sectors of American society, large-scale internment of them was both logistically and politically impossible. Instead, it was the relatively tiny Japanese American minority that was at greatest risk of a wholesale round up and confinement, a fact reflected in Army surveillance and planning dating from 1920 and that would become even clearer as 1941 unfolded.

Finally, the emergence of the congressional witch hunt committee in the House of Representatives—first with the Fish Committee, then the McCormack–Dickstein Committee, and finally the House Select Committee on Un-American Activities—guaranteed that civil society organizations had far more to worry about than the FBI. The willingness of Texas

136   CHAPTER 3

Democrat Rep. Martin Dies, the Un-American Activities Committee chairman, to employ his staff in raids on civil society groups' offices represented unconstitutional searches and seizures, none of which were prosecuted by FDR's Justice Department. The administration's failure to prevent further Dies Committee raids on private organization set a dangerous precedent that would lead to even worse abuses in 1941.

NOTES

1. Confidential Memorandum of Assistant Navy Secretary Franklin Roosevelt to CMDR Edward McCauley, Jr., October 6, 1917. FDRL, Papers as Assistant Secretary of the Navy, 1913–1920, Official Files, Box 2.
2. "U.S. Battleship Aground on the Atlantic Coast," *New York World*, September 28, 1917, 1. Accessed on August 21, 2018, via LOCCA.
3. "Survey of the Negro Population in New York City," Memorandum from Major Joseph Quittner, M.I. Reserve to Colonel Kenyon A. Joyce, G-2, 2nd Corps Area, August 18, 1932. NARA RG 165, MID Reports and Correspondence, 1917–41, File 10110-2662-15, Box 2842.
4. "Survey of the Negro Population in New York City," 2.
5. "Survey of the Negro Population in New York City," 3.
6. "One Dies, 30 Hurt in Harlem Rioting," *Washington Evening Star*, March 20, 1935, A-4. Accessed on August 21, 2018, via LOCCA.
7. US Naval Recruiting Station Kansas City, MO, memo to Director of Naval Intelligence, Subject: Japanese Organizer—Visit of to Kansas City, Missouri, September 12, 1933. NARA RG 165, Correspondence of the Military Intelligence Division Relating to "Negro Subversion," 1917–1941, microform series M1440, reel 4, File number 10218-261-81.
8. Special Report on "Pacific Movement," Major F. M. Moore, Acting Chief of Staff, G-2, October 25, 1933. NARA RG 165, Correspondence of the Military Intelligence Division Relating to "Negro Subversion," 1917–1941, microform series M1440, reel 4, File number 10218-261-85.
9. Special Report on "Pacific Movement."
10. "Graft Quiz Asked in U.S. Dry Cases," *Washington Evening Star*, February 16, 1933, A6. Accessed on November 24, 2018, via LOCCA.
11. Letter of Richard Gutstadt, ADL to Dickstein, October 12, 1933. NARA RG 233, Records of the U.S. House of Representatives, HR73A-F30.1, Special Committee on Un-American Activities on Nazi Propaganda, Box 369.
12. Transcript of radio address by Rep. Samuel Dickstein, 2–3, October 17, 1933. NARA RG 233, Records of the U.S. House of Representatives, HR73A-F30.1, Special Committee on Un-American Activities on Nazi Propaganda, Box 358.
13. Transcript of radio address by Rep. Samuel Dickstein, 4–5, December 15, 1933. NARA RG 233, Records of the U.S. House of Representatives, HR73A-F30.1, Special Committee on Un-American Activities on Nazi Propaganda, Box 358.
14. H. Res. 198, 73rd Congress (Second Session).

"THE SPIRIT OF THE CONCENTRATION CAMP" 137

15. *Congressional Record*, March 20, 1934, H4941.

16. For more on Pelley, see Scott Beekman, *William Dudley Pelley: A Life in Right-Wing Extremism and the Occult* (Syracuse: Syracuse University Press, 2005).

17. Memo of Florence Shrieve to the Committee on Un-American Activities, July 12, 1934, 1. NARA RG 233, Records of the U.S. House of Representatives, HR73A-F30.1, Special Committee on Un-American Activities on Nazi Propaganda, Box 366.

18. Memo of William P. Lucitt to Rep. John McCormack, July 5, 1934. NARA RG 233, Records of the U.S. House of Representatives, HR73A-F30.1, Special Committee on Un-American Activities on Nazi Propaganda, Box 366.

19. Undated letter of Irwin Rothberg to Rep. Samuel Dickstein. NARA RG 233, Records of the U.S. House of Representatives, HR73A-F30.1, Special Committee on Un-American Activities on Nazi Propaganda, Box 359.

20. Correspondence on this episode can be found in NARA RG 233, Records of the U.S. House of Representatives, HR73A-F30.1, Special Committee on Un-American Activities on Nazi Propaganda, Box 359, folder titled "Reinhardt-Rothberg."

21. Letter of Ralph Alexander of the Boston Better Business Bureau to Rep. John McCormack, May 4, 1934. NARA RG 233, Records of the U.S. House of Representatives, HR73A-F30.1, Special Committee on Un-American Activities on Nazi Propaganda, Box 358.

22. Beekman, *William Dudley Pelley*, 106.

23. Letter from Committee Secretary Frank P. Randolph to F.J. Prince, May 25, 1934. NARA RG 233, Records of the U.S. House of Representatives, HR73A-F30.1, Special Committee on Un-American Activities on Nazi Propaganda, Box 358.

24. *Kilbourn v Thompson*, 103 U.S. 168.

25. Beekman, *William Dudley Pelley*, 106.

26. *Investigation of Nazi and Other Propaganda, Report No. 153*, February 15, 1935, United States House of Representatives, 74th Congress (First Session), 3.

27. Letter from James Myers to Marvin McIntyre, May 15, 1935. FDRL, OF 1581, Civil Liberties 1933–1945.

28. May 11, 1935, letter from 250 clergymen to Senator Henry Ashurst, 1. FDRL, OF 1581, Civil Liberties 1933–45.

29. H. Res. 293, 74th Congress (First Session), 1. FDRL, OF 4453—Propaganda.

30. Letter of interior Secretary Harold Ickes to FDR, July 18, 1935. FDRL, OF 4453—Propaganda.

31. Letter from ACLU to FDR, March 17, 1936. FDR Presidential Library, OF 2111—ACLU, 1933–45.

32. FDR letter to Harry Ward, ACLU, March 23, 1936. FDRL, OF 2111—ACLU, 1933–45.

33. Letter of Harry Ward, ACLU to FDR, April 4, 1936. FDRL, OF 2111—ACLU, 1933–45.

34. Memo "Japanese Situation" from BG Marlborough Churchill to the Assistant Chief of Staff for Military Intelligence, Eastern Department, Governor's Island, New York, March 20, 1920. NARA RG 165, MID Reports and Correspondence, 1917–41, File 1766-Z-45, Box 556. Identical memos to several other Army departments can be found in this box.

35. Ibid.

36. Memo from Acting Director of Military Intelligence to the Assistant Chief of Staff for Military Intelligence, Southeastern Department, Charleston, S.C., April 15, 1920. NARA RG 165, MID Reports and Correspondence, 1917–41, File 1766-Z-45 (11), Box 556.

138   CHAPTER 3

37. Reports of BoI agent T.M. Word, September 6 and 7, 1921. NARA RG 165, MID Reports and Correspondence, 1917–41, File 1766-Z-45 (138–139), Box 556.

38. MID memo, "Japanese American Citizens League," March 1933, National Archives Record Group 165, MID Reports and Correspondence, 1917–41, File 1766-Z-522 (1), Box 564.

39. *Personal Justice Denied: Report of the Commission on Wartime Relocation and Internment of Civilians* (Seattle: University of Washington Press, 2000), 41.

40. Memo from Commandant/9th Naval District to ONI, "Subject: Miss Faye Watanabe— Activities of," September 28, 1935, 1. NARA RG 38, Records of the Chief of Naval Operations, ONI Formerly Classified Administrative Correspondence, 1921–1946, Box 218.

41. NARA RG 38, Records of the Chief of Naval Operations, ONI Formerly Classified Administrative Correspondence, 1921–1946, Box 218.

42. Letter from Secretary of War George Dern to Attorney General Homer Cummings, January 6, 1936. Papers of Homer Stille Cummings, Albert and Shirley Small Special Collections Library, University of Virginia, Box 174.

43. Letter from J. Edgar Hoover to Attorney General Home Cummings, January 27, 1936. Papers of Homer Stille Cummings, Albert and Shirley Small Special Collections Library, University of Virginia, Box 191.

44. Memo of Attorney General Home Cummings to J. Edgar Hoover, February 19, 1936. Letter from J. Edgar Hoover to Attorney General Home Cummings, January 27, 1936. Papers of Homer Stille Cummings, Albert and Shirley Small Special Collections Library, University of Virginia, Box 191.

45. Navy Judge Advocate memo to Secretary Claude Swanson, "Subject: Activities of Japanese naval and civil personnel in Hawaii," September 18, 1936, 1–2. NARA RG 38, Office of Naval Intelligence, CI Branch—Sabotage, Espionage, and Counterespionage Section, Box 1.

46. Navy Judge Advocate memo to Secretary Claude Swanson, "Subject: Activities of Japanese naval and civil personnel in Hawaii," September 18, 1936, 2.

47. August 24, 1936, memo from the Chief of Naval Operations to the Army Chief of Staff, "Subject: Espionage in Hawaiian Islands." NARA RG 38, Office of the Chief of Naval Operations, War Plans Division, Records Relating to Naval Activity during World War II, 1916–1948, Box 89.

48. *Report of Army Participation in Grand Joint Exercise No. 4, Hawaii, February 1932*, by Major General Malin Craig, USA, Commanding General, BLUE Army Expeditionary Force, March 15, 1932. NARA RG 494, Records of U.S. Army Forces in the Middle Pacific, 1942–1946, Box 5.

49. Joint memo to FDR from Secretary of War Harry Woodring and Secretary of the Navy Claude Swanson, October 22, 1936, p. 1. NARA RG 59, Records of the Department of State, Decimal Files, 1930–39, File number 894.20211A/34, Box 7316.

50. Joint memo to FDR from Secretary of War Harry Woodring and Secretary of the Navy Claude Swanson, October 22, 1936, 1–2.

51. Memo from Secretary of War Harry Woodring to FDR, November 17, 1937, 2. FDRL, PSF, State Department, 1933–37, Box 8.

52. FDR memo to Secretary of War Woodring, November 26, 1937. FDRL PSF, State Department, 1933–37, Box 8.

53. See Athan Theoharis, *The FBI and American Democracy: A Brief Critical History* (Lawrence: University of Kansas Press, 2004), 44.

"THE SPIRIT OF THE CONCENTRATION CAMP" 139

54. Theoharis, *The FBI and American Democracy*, 45.
55. Theoharis, *The FBI and American Democracy*, 45–46.
56. Theoharis, *The FBI and American Democracy*, 46.
57. FDR letter to Governor Richard Leche, April 5, 1937. FDRL, PPF 4765, Box PPF 4763–4801.
58. See Arnie Bernstein, *Swastika Nation: Fritz Kuhn and the Rise and Fall of the German-American Bund* (New York: St. Martin's Press, 2013), 40–41.
59. R.A.C. Parker, "The First Capitulation: France and the Rhineland Crisis of 1936," *World Politics* 8, no. 3 (April 1956): 355–373.
60. Bernstein, *Swastika Nation*, 45–49.
61. See André Brissaud, *Canaris: The Biography of Admiral Canaris, Chief of German Military Intelligence in the Second World War* (New York City: Grosset & Dunlap, 1974), 44.
62. Brissaud, *Canaris*, 46–47.
63. For the FBI's account of the Duquesne episode, see "Fredrick Duquesne: Interesting Case Write Up," March 12, 1985. Available on the FBI "Vault" website.
64. August Raymond Ogden, *The Dies Committee: A Study of the Special House Committee for the Investigation of Un-American Activies, 1938–1944* (Washington, DC: Catholic University Press, 1945), pp. 38–44.
65. Ogden, 39.
66. Ogden, 39.
67. H. Res 282, introduced June 21, 1937, via Ogden, 43.
68. Ogden, 45.
69. Letter from Acting Attorney General Thurman Arnold to Rep. Martin Dies, June 27, 1938. FDRL, OF 320—Americanization, Box 4, folder "Dies Committee, 1938."
70. Letter from Acting Attorney General Thurman Arnold to Rep. Martin Dies, June 27, 1938.
71. White House memo, June 20, 1938, on Secretary Morgenthau's Proposed Response to Representative Dies. FDRL, PPF 3458.
72. White House memo, July 9, 1938, on Attorney General Cummings' Proposed Executive Order "Inspection of Income, Excess-Profits, and Capital Stock Tax Returns by the Special Committee on Un-American Activities, House of Representatives," FDRL, PPF 3458.
73. EO number and Federal Register page number reference available via the National Archives Executive Orders Disposition Tables at https://www.archives.gov/federal -register/executive-orders/1938.html.
74. *Investigation of Un-American Propaganda Activities in the United States: Hearings before a Special Committee on Un-American Activities*, House of Representatives, 75th Congress (Third Session) (Washington, DC: GPO, 1938), 1: 25.
75. *Investigation of Un-American Propaganda Activities in the United States*, 25.
76. *Investigation of Un-American Propaganda Activities in the United States*, 106.
77. *Investigation of Un-American Propaganda Activities in the United States: Hearings before a Special Committee on Un-American Activities*, House of Representatives, 75th Congress (Third Session) (Washington, DC: GPO, 1938), 2: 1689.
78. White House Press Release, October 25, 1938. FDRL, PPF 3458 (Dies, Martin), 1.
79. White House Press Release, October 25, 1938, 2.
80. Text of Dies' statement as carried by the *Washington Evening Star,* October 26, 1938, A5, via LOCCA.

140   CHAPTER 3

81. See Allen Weinstein and Alexander Vassiliev, *The Haunted Wood: Soviet Espionage in America—The Stalin Era* (New York City: Random House, 1999), 141.
82. Weinstein and Vassiliev, *The Haunted Wood,* 142.
83. Weinstein and Vassiliev, *The Haunted Wood,* 144–149.
84. Weinstein and Vassiliev, *The Haunted Wood,* 149.
85. Justice Department and FBI correspondence on Dickstein released to John Greenewald, founder of TheBlackVault.com, dated June 23, 2017, at http://documents .theblackvault.com/documents/fbifiles/politicians/samueldickstein-fbi1.pdf.
86. Justice Department and FBI correspondence on Dickstein released to John Greenewald.
87. Report from Commandant, 13th Naval District to the Chief of Naval Operations (Director of Naval Intelligence), March 30, 1938, cover page. NARA RG 38, ONI Formerly Classified Administrative Correspondence, Box 218.
88. Report from Commandant, 13th Naval District to the Chief of Naval Operations (Director of Naval Intelligence), March 30, 1938, 1–8.
89. 13th Naval District "Japanese Monograph," May 1938, I–IV. NARA RG 38, ONI Sabotage, Espionage, and Counterespionage Section—Oriental Desk (OP16-B-7-0), 1936–46, Japanese Organization and Intelligence in the U.S., Box 1.
90. 13th Naval District "Japanese Monograph," May 1938, 24–1.
91. Memorandum from Colonel E. R. W. McCabe to the Adjutant General, "Subject: Passenger List of East bound Pan American Clipper," July 20, 1938. NARA RG 165, MID Reports and Correspondence, 1917–41, file 2801–2840 (1), Box 1842.
92. Radiogram from Philippine Department to the Adjutant General, July 21, 1938. NARA RG 165, MID Reports and Correspondence, 1917–1941, File 2801–2840 (3), Box 1842.
93. Memorandum from Colonel E. R. W. McCabe to the Adjutant General, "Subject: Radiogram to Military Attaché, Tokyo, concerning A. R. Sharton," August 26, 1938. NARA RG 165, MID Reports and Correspondence, 1917–41, file 2801–49 (3), Box 1842.
94. Cable from Major Harry Creswell, military attaché, US Embassy Tokyo to Assistant Chief of Staff/G-2, "Subject: Report on Alexander R. Sharton," August 29, 1938. NARA RG 165, MID Reports and Correspondence, 1917–1941, File 2801–2849 (4), Box 1842.
95. Memorandum of record by Attorney General Homer Cummings, October 14, 1938, 1. Papers of Homer Stille Cummings, Albert and Shirley Small Special Collections Library, University of Virginia, Box 100.
96. Memorandum of record by Attorney General Homer Cummings, October 14, 1938, 1–2.
97. Memorandum of record by Attorney General Homer Cummings, October 14, 1938, 3.
98. Memorandum of record by Attorney General Homer Cummings, October 14, 1938, 3.
99. Memorandum of record by Attorney General Homer Cummings, October 14, 1938, 3.
100. Memorandum of record by Attorney General Homer Cummings, October 14, 1938, 3.
101. Letter of Winchester H. Heicher to FDR, January 6, 1939. FDRL, OF 1581—Civil Liberties.
102. Memorandum of record by Attorney General Homer Cummings, October 14, 1938, 3.
103. Cover note from "R.B." to Marvin McIntyre, January 11, 1939, to Heicher letter. FDRL, OF 1581—Civil Liberties.

"THE SPIRIT OF THE CONCENTRATION CAMP" 141

104. Memo from FDR to the Secretaries of War, Navy, State, Treasury, Commerce, the Postmaster General, and the Attorney General on Espionage, Counter-Espionage, and Sabotage Responsibilities, June 26, 1939. NARA RG 38, Records of the Office of the Chief of Naval Operations, Office of Naval Intelligence, Office of the Director, Director's Subject File, Box 4.

105. Section 9(A)(1) of Public Law 76–252, more commonly known as the Hatch Act.

106. Hoover to Watson Memo, November 13, 1941, 2. FDRL, OF 10B, Box 15, File 980.

107. White House memo of Stephen Early, Secretary to the President, October 12, 1939. FDRL OF 320—Americanization, Box 4, folder "Dies Committee, 1939."

108. "League for Democracy to Resist Dies Agents," *Washington Evening Star*, October 18, 1939, A2. Accessed via LOCCA.

109. "League for Peace Asks Abolition of Dies Committee," *Washington Evening Star*, October 24, 1939, A7. Accessed via LOCCA.

110. "Roosevelt Hits League List Use as 'Sordid' Step," *Washington Evening Star*, October 27, 1939, A17. Accessed via LOCCA.

111. "Dies Probers Condemned for Peace League List," *Washington Evening Star*, October 26, 1939, A3. Accessed via LOCCA.

112. "Dies Probers Condemned for Peace League List," A3.

113. "F.D.R. Displeased with Dies Action," *The Key West Citizen*, October 27, 1939, 1. Accessed via LOCCA.

114. Letter of J. Edgar Hoover to Colonel E. R. Warner McCabe, G-2, War Department, January 22, 1940. NARA RG 165, MID Reports and Correspondence, 1917–1941, File 2801–2826 (12), Box 1840.

115. Letter from War Department Ordnance Office to the Assistant Chief of Staff, Counter Intelligence Branch, G-2, February 7, 1940. NARA RG 165, MID Reports and Correspondence, 1917–41, File 2801–2826 (12), Box 1840.

116. Notes on conference at FBI headquarters, January 4, 1940. NARA RG 165, MID Reports and Correspondence, 1917–41, File 9794–186A-1, Box 2200.

117. Memo for Colonel J. M. Churchill, January 5, 1940. NARA RG 165, MID Reports and Correspondence, 1917–1941, File 9794–186A-1, Box 2200.

118. June 22, 1940, FBI memo "Conference between Representatives of State Department, Military Intelligence Division of War Department, Naval Intelligence and the Federal Bureau of Investigation on June 18, 1940," 5–7. NARA RG 165, MID Reports and Correspondence, 1917–41, File 9794–186A-5, Box 2200.

119. July 1, 1940, FBI memo "Conference between Representatives of State Department, Military Intelligence Division of War Department, Naval Intelligence and the Federal Bureau of Investigation on June 18, 1940," 2. NARA RG 165, MID Reports and Correspondence, 1917–41, File 9794–186A-6, Box 2200.

120. *Hearings before the Subcommittee of the Committee on Appropriations*, House of Representatives, 76th Congress (Third Session) on the Department of Justice Appropriation Bill for 1941, H.R. 8319, 119.

121. See Curt Gentry, *J. Edgar Hoover: The Man and the Secrets* (New York: W. W. Norton & Company, 1991), 214–216. The law at the time was §10174 of the United States Combined Statutes. Today, it is codified at 18 U.S.C. § 958–960.

122. Gentry, *J. Edgar Hoover*, 216.

123. "Norris Fears F.B.I. Is 'American OGPU'; Suggests Inquiry," *Washington Evening Star*, February 27, 1940, A2. Accessed via LOCCA.

142 CHAPTER 3

124. MID-ONI-FBI interagency meeting minutes, March 19, 1940, 1. NARA RG 165, MID Reports and Correspondence, 1917–41, File 9794–186, Box 2200.
125. "Senators Charge Wire-Tapping for Political Ends," *Washington Evening Star*, March 12, 1940, A1, A6. Accessed via LOCCA.
126. MID-ONI-FBI interagency meeting minutes, March 26, 1940, 1. NARA RG 165, MID Reports and Correspondence, 1917–41, File 9794–186, Box 2200.
127. MID-ONI-FBI interagency meeting minutes, March 26, 1940, 1.
128. Letter and resolutions from the Conference on Civil Rights to FDR, April 26, 1940, 6. FDRL, File OF 1581—Civil Liberties, 1933–45.
129. Letter from J. Edgar Hoover to Brigadier General Edwin Watson, April 13, 1940. FDRL, OF 10b—Department of Justice, Box 11, File number 55.
130. Letter from J. Edgar Hoover to Brigadier General Edwin Watson, April 13, 1940.
131. Letter from J. Edgar Hoover to Brigadier General Edwin Watson, May 14, 1940. FDRL OF 10b—Department of Justice, Box 11, File number 69, 1.
132. Letter from J. Edgar Hoover to Brigadier General Edwin Watson, May 14, 1940.
133. Letter from J. Edgar Hoover to Brigadier General Edwin Watson, May 14, 1940.
134. Letter from J. Edgar Hoover to Brigadier General Edwin Watson, May 14, 1940.
135. *Olmstead v. United States*, 277 U.S. 438 (1928).
136. For an excellent discussion of the background on the wiretapping debate, see Neal Katyal and Richard Caplan, "The Stronger Case for the Legality of the NSA Surveillance Program: The FDR Precedent," *Stanford Law Review* 60, no. 4 (2008): 1023–1076.
137. *Nardone v United States*, 308 U.S. 338 (1939).
138. Katyal and Caplan, "The Stronger Case," 1047–1052.
139. FDR confidential memo to the Attorney General, May 21, 1940. NARA RG 263, Records of the Central Intelligence Agency, Troy Papers, Box 8, Folder 15—"FBI Docs."
140. FDR confidential memo to the Attorney General, May 21, 1940.
141. Katyal and Caplan, "The Stronger Case," 1051–1052.
142. Undated, unsigned Jackson to FDR memo, May 1940, 1. LOC, Robert H. Jackson Papers, Box 87.
143. Undated, unsigned Jackson to FDR memo, May 1940, 1, 1–2.
144. Based on the author's examination of the relevant files at the FDR Presidential Library.
145. Department of Justice Circular No. 3356, Supplement No. 1, May 21, 1940, 1. FDRL, OF 1581—Civil Liberties, 1933–1945.
146. Department of Justice Circular No. 3356, Supplement No. 1, May 21, 1940, 1.
147. *Weeks v. United States*, 232 U.S. 383 (1914).
148. Public No. 416, 73rd Congress, S. 3285, Sec. 605, enacted June 19, 1934. Currently codified at 47 U.S.C. § 605.
149. See Edward P. Von Der Porten, *The German Navy in World War Two* (New York: Ballantine Books, 1974), 72–92.
150. See General Sir David Fraser, *And We Shall Shock Them: The British Army in the Second World War* (London: Sceptre, 1988), 54–80.
151. Address of President Franklin D. Roosevelt to the nation, May 26, 1940. FDRL, Master Speech File, 1898–1945, Box 52, File 1283-A, Fireside Chat #15—National Defense, 13.
152. President Franklin D. Roosevelt Message to Congress, May 31, 1940. FDRL Master Speech File, 1898–1945, Box 52, File 1284.

"THE SPIRIT OF THE CONCENTRATION CAMP" 143

153. Letter and attachments from J. Edgar Hoover to Stephen Early, June 8, 1940. FDRL, OF 10b—Department of Justice, Box 12, folder "FBI Reports, 1940," File number 121.

154. Telegram of American Peace Crusade to FDR, June 10, 1940. FDRL, OF 10b—Department of Justice, Box 12, folder "FBI Reports, 1940," File number 164.

155. FDR note to Brigadier General Edwin M. Watson, June 11, 1940. FDR Presidential Library, File OF 10b—Department of Justice, Box 12, folder "FBI Reports, 1940," File number 135.

156. Letter from J. Edgar Hoover to Brigadier General Edwin M. Watson, June 25, 1940. FDRL, OF 10b—Department of Justice, Box 12, folder "FBI Reports, 1940," File number 164.

157. Letter from J. Edgar Hoover to Brigadier General Edwin M. Watson, June 25, 1940, 2.

158. Viewable online at https://www.loc.gov/law/help/statutes-at-large/76th-congress /session-3/c76s3ch439.pdf.

159. https://www.loc.gov/law/help/statutes-at-large/76th-congress/session-3 /c76s3ch439.pdf.

160. See Brian F. Hussey, Jr., "The U.S. Navy, the Neutrality Patrol, and Atlantic Fleet Escort Operations, 1939–1941," Trident Scholar Project Report, United States Naval Academy, May 1991.

161. See Wayne S. Cole, *Roosevelt and the Isolationists, 1932–1945* (Lincoln: University of Nebraska Press, 1983), 379.

162. Cole, *Roosevelt and the Isolationists*, 380.

163. See Douglas M. Charles, *J. Edgar Hoover and the Anti-Interventionists: FBI Political Surveillance and the Rise of the Domestic Security State, 1939–1945* (Columbus: Ohio State University Press, 2007), 63.

164. Memo from J. Edgar Hoover to Attorney General Robert Jackson, August 26, 1940. LOC, Papers of Robert H. Jackson, Box 89.

165. Memo from J. Edgar Hoover to Attorney General Robert Jackson, August 26, 1940.

166. Memo from J. Edgar Hoover to Attorney General Robert Jackson, August 26, 1940.

167. Memo from J. Edgar Hoover to Attorney General Robert Jackson, October 21, 1940, 1. LOC, Papers of Robert H. Jackson, Box 89.

168. Memo from J. Edgar Hoover to Attorney General Robert Jackson, October 21, 1940, 1.

169. Justice Department press release, November 24, 1940, 1–3. LOC, Papers of Robert H. Jackson, Box 89.

170. Justice Department press release, November 24, 1940, 5.

171. See R. Ernest Dupuy and Trevor N. Dupuy, *The Encyclopedia of Military History* (New York: Harper & Row, 1977), 1126–1127.

172. Memo from Navy Secretary Frank Knox to FDR, October 9, 1940, 2. FDRL, PSF (Safe File), Box 4, Navy Department, 1934–February 1942.

173. The memo itself has not, so far as the author is aware, been declassified and made public but it is referenced in multiple FBI field division reports from the period, including the 103-page December 9, 1940, "General Japanese Intelligence Survey in the Honolulu Field Division," written by Special Agent N. J. Alaga. NARA RG 165, MID Reports and Correspondence, 1917–41, File 2327-H-60, Box 1246.

174. See Athan G. Theoharis and John Stuart Cox, *The Boss: J. Edgar Hoover and the Great American Inquisition* (New York: Bantam Books, 1990), 224–229.

144   CHAPTER 3

175. Theoharis and Cox, *The Boss*, 224–229.
176. NARA RG 65, FBI HQ Investigative Records Classified Subject Files Released Under the Nazi & Japanese War Crimes Disclosure Acts, PL 105–246, Box 235, Folder 65-40048-Section 1 (2 of 2)
177. December 9, 1940, "General Japanese Intelligence Survey in the Honolulu Field Division," written by Special Agent N. J. Alaga. NARA RG 165, MID Reports and Correspondence, 1917–41, File 2327-H-60, Box 1246.

CHAPTER 4

"We Are Developing a Gestapo in This Country and It Frightens Me"
1941–1945

For FDR and his key advisors in early 1941, the anxieties over the prospect of a two-front overseas war were matched by concerns about real or imagined vulnerabilities on the home front, seen as directly connected to the threats posed by the Nazi and Imperial Japanese governments. The president viewed opponents of his Lend-Lease proposal, such as Senator Burton Wheeler (D-MT) and the rapidly growing America First Committee, as enemies to be targeted with surveillance and public discreditation. J. Edgar Hoover continued to look for Soviet spies or agents of influence within the growing civil rights movement, taking particular interest in Black civil rights leaders and organizations like A. Philip Randolph and the National Negro Congress, as well as Walter White and the NAACP.

The FBI, along with Army and Navy intelligence elements, intensified their surveillance of German, Italian, and Japanese aliens and American citizens with such ancestries as the year progressed, adding still more names to the growing lists of those to be rounded up in the event of war with the Axis powers. A national gun registration and confiscation scheme, to be carried out in the name of internal security, was also on the table, albeit briefly. But it was the growing perception of the military threats from Germany and Japan, and the potential for sabotage or fifth-column activity, that was on the minds of Roosevelt's advisors and even many ordinary citizens at the start of 1941.

146   CHAPTER 4

THE INTERNAL JAPANESE THREAT: PERCEPTION VERSUS REALITY

It wasn't just Roosevelt who got mail from the public about the deteriorating security situation in the Pacific. Some of his key cabinet secretaries were hearing from citizens too.

"There is a strong public sentiment here in favor of building cantonments back on the desert for the concentration of most of the 250,000 Japanese on the Pacific Coast, real soon," H.M. Gallagher of Los Angeles wrote Secretary of War Henry Stimson on January 22, 1941. After suggesting that the interned Japanese be used as hostages in any peace negotiations with Japan, Gallagher expressed a view that mirrored the one contained in the British intelligence report from late 1940.

"Many of these Japs are born here, BUT Japanese are ALWAYS loyal to the 'Rising Sun,' to the Mikado, regardless of the place of birth."[1]

There is no record in the file indicating Stimson replied, but Gallagher needn't have worried. As previously noted, almost a decade before Stimson's arrival at the War Department, the Army already had plans for interning Japanese in the event of a war in the Pacific.

While one could argue that military exercises against hypothetical opponents were not necessarily dispositive of an intent to commit mass violations of constitutional rights in wartime, military forces generally train the way they intend to fight. Moreover, many US government officials—including FDR—had direct experience during World War I in overseeing surveillance and detention operations targeting both foreign nationals and American citizens. The reality was that the mass surveillance and intelligence collection targeting Germans, Japanese, and Italians persons and entities—including Americans—that Hoover had ordered his agents to begin in the fall of 1940 would be the cornerstone of the future detention program.

For some in Congress who believed Japan was preparing for war, potential recruitment of dual citizen Japanese Americans as soldiers or even spies was a special concern.

On January 3, Senator Guy Gillette (D-IA) wrote to Secretary of State Hull about "complaints by certain representatives of the Sino-Korean Peoples League relative to an alleged conscription list of American citizens of Japanese ancestry which is taking place at the present time in Hawaii and on the mainland."[2] Gillette pressed Hull for a quick answer in light of the "very difficult situation in the relationship of the racial groups in our territory where our Pacific fleet is based and where the territory's security is synonymous with our racial security."[3]

"DEVELOPING A GESTAPO IN THIS COUNTRY" 147

The Sino-Korean Peoples League was, in the words of historian Richard Kim, largely "a one-man outfit with few Korean or Chinese members in the United States" headed by one Kilsoo Haan, an ardent Korean independence activist.[4] Haan wanted the Japanese occupation of Korea, ongoing since 1910, ended. Anything he could do to cause trouble between Japan and the United States served his ends. Gillette was being played, but the question remained: was the Japanese government really trying to conscript Japanese Americans?

Hull responded to Gillette on January 8, telling the Iowa senator that State was "without evidence" that such Japanese government conscription efforts were underway.[5] To be certain, Hull sounded out ONI, MID, and the FBI. The Bureau had no evidence of such conscription, but Hoover wrote Assistant Secretary of State Adolph Berle, Jr. on January 14 that he had "instructed that additional investigation be conducted in this matter."[6] Knox wrote Hull on January 24 that the Navy was "without evidence ... that the Japanese authorities are engaged in actual military conscription of the Japanese in the United States for duty in Japan. However, it is known that Japanese male nationals who reside in the United States must make application each year for postponement of military service in Japan."[7] A week earlier, Stimson had written Hull that the War Department "has never at any time found any evidence that the Japanese Government itself was actively engaged in conscripting American citizens of Japanese parentage."[8]

Indeed, MID knew that the Japanese diplomatic and intelligence services had been instructed generally to avoid the use of Japanese nationals or Japanese Americans for intelligence gathering, propaganda, or related purposes.

On February 12 Colonel C.H. Mason, the head of MID's Intelligence Branch, sent a memo to his counterpart in the Counterintelligence Branch noting that "a highly reliable source" indicated a reorganization and enlargement of the Imperial Japanese Intelligence Service in the United States was underway. Close coordination between Japanese, German, and Italian intelligence services was directed, and of particular note was the directive that "Investigation to be made of all anti-Semitism, communism, Negro movements, and labor movements" for the purpose of utilizing "citizens of foreign extraction (other than Japanese), aliens (other than Japanese), communists, Negroes, labor union members, and anti-Semites, in carrying out investigations, to get best results. These agents should have access to governmental establishments, laboratories, governmental organizations of various sorts, factories, etc."[9]

However, military and Foreign Ministry leaders in Tokyo warned Japanese government officials in the United States that "Utilization of second generation Japanese to be made with utmost caution as a slip in this phase would subject Japanese in America to considerable persecution."[10] The government in Tokyo was telling its operatives in America to go out of their way to avoid using Americans of Japanese heritage due to a fear that should a Japanese American be enlisted for espionage and subsequently caught, every person of Japanese ancestry on American soil would risk retaliation.

That warning from Tokyo to its personnel in America did nothing to dissuade Hoover from directing FBI field offices, especially the Honolulu office, from making surveillance and investigation of Japanese persons and organizations a high priority.

Since the establishment of the FBI Honolulu field office in August 1939, the staff had steadily grown under the supervision of the special agent in charge, Robert Shivers. So had the workload. As of the end of January 1941 Shivers and his team of seven agents and six clerical staff were managing nearly 1,000 security-related cases, including over 240 targeting the consular agents operating out of the Japanese consulate in Honolulu.[11] Missing from Shivers's rather expansive target list—which included literally every Japanese civic society, business, school, and religious organization in the islands—were the Japanese Americans working at the Japanese consulate in Honolulu. The reality was that Shivers made no effort to try to recruit or otherwise exploit the seven Japanese Americans working at the Honolulu consulate. It was a failure that would have lethal consequences.

FDR VERSUS THE ANTI-INTERVENTIONISTS

The potential Imperial Japanese threat to American territory and interests in the Pacific was still, at least in the first half of 1941, of lesser daily concern to FDR and his advisors than the menace of Nazi Germany. Roosevelt's push to save England from Hitler began in earnest on January 6 with his State of Union message to Congress, calling for "authority and for funds" to provide nations fighting the Axis powers the equipment and supplies they needed— what would become known as the Lend-Lease program. Enabling legislation was introduced in the House and Senate on January 10.[12] That night FDR's principal isolationist nemesis in the Congress, Senator Burton K. Wheeler (D-MT), began organizing other House and Senate anti-interventionists to try to defeat the proposal, and just two days after the Lend-Lease bill debuted in Congress he told a radio audience that if enacted it would "plough under every fourth American boy" in another European war.[13]

"DEVELOPING A GESTAPO IN THIS COUNTRY" 149

FDR was enraged but undeterred by Wheeler's remarks. The Lend-Lease battle would be a major test of wills and political power between FDR and his anti-interventionist opponents, particularly Wheeler and the AFC. FDR benefited from political intelligence on both, courtesy of Hoover and his FBI agents.

Wheeler of course had been the subject of unconstitutional FBI surveillance and investigation in the 1920s—including a sexual entrapment scheme—as a result of his role in exposing the Teapot Dome scandal and in retaliation for blasting the Justice Department's failure to investigate the bribe-for-leases scheme involving then-Interior Secretary Albert Fall.[14] FDR availed himself of FBI and Post Office department surveillance of Wheeler's franked congressional mail to monitor Wheeler's antiwar and anti-interventionist communications with constituents and others. The Bureau's surveillance operations included other anti-interventionist House and Senate members on a bipartisan basis, including Senators Rush Holt (D-WV) and Gerald Nye (R-ND) among others.[15]

The Bureau began monitoring the activities of the AFC in the fall of 1940. By December 16, 1940, the Bureau was receiving information from AFC meeting attendees about the key officers of the organization, as well as insights into the group's public relations strategy.[16] On December 19, Hoover received information about at least two major donors to AFC, including car maker Henry Ford.[17] By the end of January 1941, FBI official J.B. O'Leary had completed a five-page memo on AFC that listed 26 well-known Americans as key AFC officers or supporters. On the list were Ford, former World War I flying ace Eddie Rickenbacker, Jay Hormel of Hormel Foods, Alice Roosevelt Longworth (daughter of the late President Teddy Roosevelt and wife of the late House Speaker Nicholas Longworth), and of course Wheeler.

The initial intelligence work done by the Bureau on AFC served Hoover well when, on February 21, FDR tasked his secretary, Stephen Early, to "find out from someone—perhaps FBI—who is paying for this?" referring to an AFC bulletin headlined "Are you willing to give up democracy?"[18]

Hoover's initial response on February 26 was a report on an event sponsored by the Los Angeles chapter of AFC, at which one

> Paul Von Gontard, who is also under investigation by this Bureau, displayed a cashier's check for $2000 issued by the St. Louis Trust Company of St. Louis, Missouri, which he turned over to Mr. John Wheeler as a contribution to the America First Committee. In this connection the informant stated that Wheeler had been able to raise only $200 in Los Angeles in connection with this work.[19]

150   CHAPTER 4

Hoover subsequently sent a memo to Early on March 1 for FDR's attention on the AFC national funding question, then followed up on March 3 with an eight-page memo on AFC that went into some detail about the organization, key officers and board members, recent activities, and plans.[20]

The FBI director also ensured that FDR and his key senior advisors had political intelligence regarding coordination between Senate anti-interventionists and AFC on legislative and publicity matters.

On February 21 Hoover advised Watson that "I have received information from a strictly confidential source to the effect that the debate in the Senate on the Lend-Lease Bill will last for about two weeks or longer. It is reported that there are eleven Senators who have pledged themselves to filibuster in opposition to this bill."[21]

Via "Information of a strictly confidential character," Hoover informed Watson on March 19 that "plans are presently underway to have Senators, Congressmen, and various peace and patriotic organizations travel throughout the United States to reach all areas for the purpose of opposing any plans that the President might have in bringing this country into war."[22] The effort was "in cooperation with the America First Committee" and that "General Robert Wood and Senator Burton K. Wheeler" were leading the effort.[23]

FDR received similar kinds of information from the White House legislative affairs and public relations staff based on public announcements by AFC and conversations with House and Senate members and staff on an informal basis. But the Bureau's covert surveillance of congressional anti-interventionists like Wheeler, Nye, Holt, and others, as well as the spying on AFC, gave FDR information he might otherwise not have obtained. The Bureau's warrantless surveillance of the anti-interventionists was also flagrantly unconstitutional. Indeed, even as Roosevelt benefited politically from the illegal surveillance, there was a movement afoot in Congress to radically expand legal federal wiretapping powers.

On January 16 Rep. Samuel Hobbs (D-AL) introduced H.R. 2266, a bill that would have eliminated the Communications Act's ban on wiretapping by the federal government and permitted the head of any federal agency or department to do so if, in the judgment of the senior official, a felony "may have been committed, is being committed, or may be about to be committed" by a suspect.[24] The proposal was as sweeping as it was terrifying to both other House and Senate members and civil society organizations.

To ensure his existing secret unilateral warrantless wiretapping program continued uninterrupted, FDR took measures to get the issue off the table legislatively and out of the papers.

"DEVELOPING A GESTAPO IN THIS COUNTRY"   151

On February 21 James Rowe, FDR's administrative assistant, informed Attorney General Jackson that Rep. Hatton Sumners (D-TX) was telling fellow members that Hobbs's bill was in fact "an Administration bill." To help kill the bill's momentum, Rowe had enlisted the help of a known opponent of H.R. 2266, Rep. Tom Eliot (D-MA), who wrote FDR for his views on the bill.[25] The president then engaged in the prearranged legerdemain.

"I have read the bill and I have no hesitation in saying that it goes entirely too far and that its provisions are unnecessarily broad," Roosevelt wrote Eliot on February 21. After opining on the judicial history of previous wiretapping decisions and debates, FDR told Eliot, "I have no compunction in saying that wiretapping should be used against those persons . . . who today are engaged in espionage or sabotage against the United States" but that any legislation on the topic should be confined "to the Department of Justice and to no other department" and that the AG should in each case of wiretapping "sign a certificate indicating such necessity."[26] The letter was subsequently released to the press by the White House.

The gambit worked. While Congress continued to debate wiretapping for the balance of the year, neither the Hobbs bill nor any other on the topic moved to the floor of either chamber.

Yet even as the debate on whether or not to limit executive branch wiretapping unfolded, *a House committee* was engaged in wiretapping and other forms of surveillance: the Dies Committee.

WIRETAPPING RUN AMOK: THE DIES COMMITTEE AND THE NAVY

On February 27, Hoover informed Jackson that the Dies Committee was opening an office in Philadelphia to "conduct a 15-month surveillance of the workers in National Defense industries in the Pennsylvania-New Jersey-Delaware area." He noted that "Employees of such industrial concerns will . . . have their names checked against thousands of names of Communists and Bund members in the Committee files."[27] These files were notorious for containing innuendo, gossip, and outright falsehoods.

The Dies Committee had no constitutional basis for conducting surveillance of American workers at either private companies or government facilities, yet Jackson took no action in the matter after Hoover flagged it for his attention.

On May 12 the FBI director sent the attorney general a memo in which Hoover revealed that "I have today learned from a reliable source that representatives of the Dies Committee have in Philadelphia placed a telephone tap upon the telephone lines of the Communist Party headquarters there." The tap was allegedly located "in the office of a lawyer who maintains an office in the North American building in Philadelphia."[28]

If true, Dies and his committee were in direct violation of Section 605 of the 1934 Communications Act. It was, if verified by investigation, a clearly prosecutable act.

And it was also a political hand grenade, in that the debate over executive branch wiretapping authority was well underway in Congress at that very moment, with Hoover noting that a revelation of such activity would "result in some serious embarrassment to the Federal Government."[29]

Indeed, earlier that very day, Hoover had brought Jackson other alarming news: the Navy was engaged in illegal wiretapping as well.

Hoover's five-page May 12 memo on the matter revealed that ONI personnel had tried but failed to persuade a Chicago area phone service provider to tap the line of the German and Japanese consulates in that city. The phone company had tipped off the FBI Chicago field office but asked that the company's cooperation be kept confidential. The second incident was even more serious, with ONI having tapped the phone of a female American citizen in Los Angeles and also obtaining some of her telegram traffic. Hoover had managed to get some of the transcripts and included them in his memo to Jackson.[30]

The FBI director also included a draft letter for Jackson's signature to Navy Secretary Frank Knox, which reminded Knox that "Because of the specific prohibition of such conduct by statute as well as by judicial decision, I am obligated to bring this matter to your attention in the sincere belief that you will readily appreciate the embarrassment which might arise if acts of this kind were consummated or continued."[31]

A May 17 Hoover to Jackson "Strictly Personal and Confidential" memo contained still more information on the Dies Committee wiretapping operation, including confirmation of the tap by a Pennsylvania State Police officer who assisted with its placement.[32] Hoover then presented Jackson with two options on how to proceed:

> If you deem it desirable, I could approach the head of the Pennsylvania Motor Police and advise him that the Bureau has received information indicating the existence of this telephone tap, point out that the Bureau must investigate matters of this kind since they constitute possible violations of Federal Statutes, and ask for full details concerning this situation in view of the reported participation therein of a representative of the Pennsylvania Motor Police. I will not,

however, make this approach without your specific authorization in view of the fact that immediate publicity might follow the contacting of the head of this organization.[33]

Jackson orally directed Hoover to drop the matter, according to a handwritten note on Hoover's memo.[34]

The attorney general of the United States knowingly turned a blind eye to clear violations of the Communications Act's prohibition on domestic wiretapping, probably because he feared that if these incidents were surfaced, FDR's confidential wiretapping order—issued in violation of the Supreme Court decision in the *Nardone* case—might also become public.

Whether Jackson ever privately confronted Knox over the ONI incidents is not recorded in either man's public papers. What is known is that ONI's use of microphones and telephone surveillance on US soil, in direct violation of the Communications Act of 1934, continued in various locations right up to the attack on Pearl Harbor.[35]

And the Navy was not the only military service giving Jackson headaches over actual or potentially unconstitutional acts. Senior War Department officials wanted to effectively suspend the Bill of Rights even before the outbreak of hostilities.

On April 26 Hoover alerted Jackson to a meeting he had just had with Assistant Secretary of War John J. McCloy, in which McCloy—acting on orders from Undersecretary of War (and former federal appeals court judge) Robert Patterson—was seeking "evidence that the obvious slowdown in certain plants was inspired by foreign sources." After informing McCloy that the kind of evidence he sought, under current law and Supreme Court rulings, "could not be obtained by legal, ethical investigations," McCloy made clear he and Patterson would seek a meeting with Jackson to secure his approval to have the FBI "disregard technicalities" and get the needed information.[36]

Patterson and McCloy got their meeting with Jackson on April 28, and after it the attorney general was so shaken by the encounter that he fired off a memo to FDR the next day.

"I call the matter to your attention," Jackson began, "because they stated you had given a 'green light' to a proposition which seems to me extremely dangerous."[37]

The War Department duo had "complained that the Federal Bureau of Investigation has confined its investigations within the limits of the law, whereas they believe that normal methods should be abandoned and that investigators should be unrestrained in wiretapping, in stealing of evidence, breaking in to obtain evidence, in conducting unlimited search and seizures, use of dictaphones, etc., etc."[38]

Jackson was vehemently opposed to the plan, noting that "Lawless methods temporarily productive will rapidly demoralize the Department of Justice," reminding FDR of the "descent of the Department in public estimation and in trustworthiness" following the Palmer Raids and related actions, which were "a permanent blot on the Wilson administration" and that "nearly wrecked the Department."[39] Jackson was adamant that "definite standards" mattered and that "a Department which is constantly in court cannot lay down standards which do not meet the test of legality."[40]

Patterson and McCloy's most radical suggestion prompted a not-so-veiled resignation threat from Jackson.

"They suggested the establishment of what one of them termed a 'suicide squad' to conduct investigations by methods outside the law," Jackson wrote. "I told them that this could not be in the Department of Justice because it would contaminate the ordinary administration of the law, and I certainly would not be the type of man to run that sort of unit."[41]

Jackson drove home his argument to FDR by noting that "I know that Navy Intelligence is already tapping wires and has listened in on the conversations of O.P.M. officials dealing with labor matters. The intensive drive now is to use methods which I think lawless in labor situations." While acknowledging Patterson and McCloy's frustrations with strikes and slowdowns at some defense production plants, Jackson advised FDR that the administration could not afford "to become characterized as lawless. These methods, if resorted to, will be known soon and will be the subject of bitter controversy."[42] Jackson ended by exhorting FDR to "adhere to the legal and ethical standards" of the day.

Jackson ultimately prevailed in preventing a wholesale abrogation of the Bill of Rights by the War Department before being elevated to the nation's highest court two months later.

IN SEARCH OF "NEGRO SUBVERSION"

Roosevelt's stated concern over "those persons . . . engaged in espionage and sabotage" ostensibly meant Nazi or Imperial Japanese agents. In reality, his key subordinates—particularly Hoover at FBI and his counterparts and MID and ONI—took a far more expansive view of the alleged threat. Always high on the list was "Negro subversion."

On March 6, 1941, Hoover sent—via special courier—a letter to Assistant Secretary of State Adolph Berle, Jr. alerting him to "a planned

"DEVELOPING A GESTAPO IN THIS COUNTRY"   155

demonstration to take place today at Brooklyn, New York."[43] According to Hoover,

> the American Peace Mobilization and the National Negro Congress, through Communist agitation, are organizing a mass demonstration to take place at two o'clock this afternoon. The basis for this demonstration is the alleged refusal of the Sperry Gyroscope Company at Brooklyn, New York, to employ Negroes. The demonstration is reportedly going to center around the Brooklyn plant of the Sperry Gyroscope Company and then spread throughout Brooklyn.[44]

Formed in early 1936 as an umbrella organization, the National Negro Congress (NNC) "combined several strands of protest movements from African American history, the labor movement, and radical political parties into a black-led, interracial, mass movement" with a public, militant antiracist agenda.[45] And since the NNC did in fact have communist members and publicly partnered with communist organizations, its activities fit neatly with Hoover's long-standing narrative that communists were behind all manner of labor disputes and strikes in the United States.

However, Hoover chose to interpret NNC's communist ties as evidence of communist control of the organization, which was never the case. And by 1941, the NNC had lost its leading light and former president, A. Philip Randolph, to what became known as the March on Washington Movement.[46]

The African American drive for full civil and constitutional rights encompassed a range of organizations, not a Moscow-controlled monolith. Hoover chose to either ignore or deliberately misrepresent the reality of the impact of systemic racism in fueling the rise of organizations like NNC. In the federal national security establishment, he was hardly alone in that regard.

The author of an April 3 Army Ordnance Corps memo writing about NNC calls for African American workers to not cross picket lines at the Ford Motor plant speculated "that this negative position results from the activities of subversive aliens" designed to create "obstruction through the medium of inciting unsatisfactory labor relations and policies affecting Negroes."[47]

At the Army's Lowry Field, an NNC flyer targeting African Americans in the Works Progress Administration doing construction work at the airfield was obtained by the base commander and forwarded to the Eighth Corps Area G-2, MID Counterintelligence Branch in Washington, and the FBI Denver field office. The flyer was a call for, among other things, "the right of the Negro people to be free from jim-crowism, segregation, discrimination, lynching and mob violence, and to work for the enactment of federal anti-lynching legislation." There were no calls for the violent overthrow of the federal government, only actions that clearly involved constitutionally protected free speech and association.[48]

The National Association for the Advancement of Colored People (NAACP) got similar treatment and characterization in the spring of 1941.

The March 11, 1941, FBI Washington field office report on the NAACP, report number 100–893, carried the designation of "Internal Security (C)"—the letter "C" short for "Communist."[49] The opening summary paragraph of the report claimed "Indication of increased communist tendencies among some local branches and officers. The various local connections with the communist party and other communist controlled organizations determine extent of subversive activities NAACP may be engaged in."[50]

The report also noted that "the NAACP has allied itself with the National Negro Congress, the American Civil Liberties Union, and the American People's Mobilization and other communist front organizations on specific issues in several respects" though the report offered that "any subversive or un-American activities which the NAACP may be engaged in are determined for the most part by the local relationship of its various branches with the local communist element."[51]

DETENTION PROGRAM PLANNING ACCELERATES

Throughout this period the hunt for alleged sympathizers of hostile foreign powers among the American population expanded on virtually a weekly basis. If there was one area where the level of cooperation was excellent, particularly between the FBI and MID, it was in deciding who would be detained and interned in the event of war.

On March 20 Hoover wrote to his opposite number at the War Department, Army G-2 Brigadier General Sherman Miles, to follow up on their conversation of the day prior about implementing a "custodial detention" program should the country go to war with Germany, Italy, Japan, or all three.

"In line with our discussion in conference yesterday, I would appreciate it if you would furnish me at the earliest possible time with a list of those individuals regarded by you as proper subjects for consideration for custodial detention in the event of a national emergency," Hoover wrote. To speed up the process Hoover asked Miles to furnish the Bureau "with a summary of the information in your files with respect to each of these persons, together with your recommendation as to the action to be taken with regard to him,

"DEVELOPING A GESTAPO IN THIS COUNTRY" 157

so that this information may be coordinated with any information available in our own files and then forwarded to the appropriate office in the Department of Justice for consideration."[52]

In addition to asking Miles for lists of people—foreigners and American citizens—that the Army would like rounded up, Hoover sent over his own lists of names, seeking anything the Army had on them.

Between March 20 and March 31 Hoover sent Miles the names of nearly 300 persons for derogatory information checks. The names on the lists were of German, Irish, and other European origin and included Silver Shirt founder and antisemitic extremist William Dudley Pelley, as well as the Rev. J. Vint Laughland, a two-time British Labor party candidate and leftist political organizer living in Buffalo, New York.[53] Neither man was wanted for a federal crime at the time, and neither were any other people on Hoover's lists. Before 1941 was over similar measures coordinated between FBI, MID, and ONI would result in thousands of people being preemptively selected for internment in the event of war.

The administration also considered another measure to defeat any fifth-column sabotage or violence: the legal framework for a national gun confiscation program.

On April 9 FDR sent AG Jackson a memo asking, "What do you think?" regarding a suggestion from the Bureau of the Budget for legislation "requiring the registration and fingerprinting of the owners of all firearms in the U.S. to be administered by the F.B.I."[54] Bureau of the Budget Director Harold Smith reported back to FDR that Attorney General Jackson "has expressed the opinion that the information obtained, should the bill be enacted, would place a weapon against 'fifth column' activities in the hands of law enforcement" but that he questioned "the value to national defense or crime prevention measures of such a volume of information relating to shotguns and low-grade rifles."[55]

The Department of Justice estimated that over 30,000,000 such weapons were in private hands, and "considering the resentment which might be aroused among our law-abiding citizens," Smith advised FDR and Jackson to drop the idea, which they did. Left unsaid was an even more pertinent problem with the idea: hardcore Nazi or Japanese sympathizers, or actual enemy agents bent on sabotage, would secretly stockpile weapons and never declare them.

FDR VERSUS DIES COMMITTEE

While FDR and his advisors worried about real fifth-column activity from German or Japanese government operatives, some were accusing the president and those around him of being the fifth column itself. Roosevelt didn't take the insult well.

On February 7 FDR directed his chief private secretary, Edwin Watson, to ask the FBI to investigate the origins and individuals associated with a pamphlet titled "The Fifth Column and the Dies Committee," published by the Constitutional Education League (CEL).[56] In it, the League alleged that the Justice Department was blocking FBI investigations into "spies, saboteurs, and Fifth Columnists."[57] A previous CEL publication had labeled Attorney General Jackson, Interior Secretary Harold Ickes, and Labor Secretary Frances Perkins as being on "List number 1 of America's Fifth Column."[58] According to the FBI report, another CEL publication accused First Lady Eleanor Roosevelt "of heading the Communist movement by her financial assistance to the Highlander Folk School at Monteagle, Tennessee."[59]

The CEL's founder, Joseph Kamp, was characterized as believing Justice Department officials, and thus the administration, were deliberately impeding the work of the Dies Committee. Because FDR and Watson had raised the issue, in his response of April 15 Attorney General Jackson felt obliged to lay out the legal realities facing the administration should FDR want to go after Kamp in court:

> A study made in this Department of the legal aspects of the matter, leads to the conclusion that publication and distribution of the pamphlet does not constitute any violation of any Federal criminal statute. There is always, of course, the possibility of libel proceedings. I should hardly recommend criminal prosecution for libel, however, without further consideration of the questions of policy involved. A civil action for libel on the part of one of the many individuals defamed by the pamphlet would be another matter.[60]

Jackson was willing to let FDR's secret, warrantless wiretapping slide, but an open assault on the First Amendment rights of a publisher was, at that point at least, a step too far for the attorney general.

As for the Dies Committee, its chairman continued to have no compunction about making wild, unsubstantiated, and even racist claims about communists running amok around the country.

In the months since FDR's reelection Dies had not let up on his attacks on the administration's alleged (and wholly imaginary) communist leanings, or that of civil society organizations Dies deemed subversive. His committee staff, led by chief of staff and lead investigator Robert Stripling, had, by late April 1941, concluded that the "Washington Branch of the American Peace Mobilization . . . is highly organized in the Government. At the recent American People's Meeting in New York City, which was sponsored by the American Peace Mobilization, 150 of the delegates who attended from Washington were Government employees."[61]

Not surprisingly, the FBI also was monitoring the group.[62] But the FBI was monitoring literally hundreds of groups and thousands of individuals on the basis of leads, innuendo, and accusations just as spurious as those fueling Dies's congressional witch hunt committee.

In his telegram to his boss, Stripling provided no explanation as to how he knew 150 people at the meeting were both (1) US government employees and (2) communists. He did offer more salacious gossip with blatantly racist overtones:

> Young white girls in the American Peace Mobilization are instructed to play up to Negroes, by sleeping with them if necessary, in order to bring them into the movement. . . . Both at the general sessions of the American People's Meeting and at individual delegation meetings, white girls were observed "necking" and "petting" with Negro men.[63]

The reports on the interracial encounters at the meetings were supplied by "undercover agents who attended this Convention."[64] The year before, Dies had sent his investigators to break into the offices of civil society organizations targeted by the committee. Now, Dies was running his own private spy operation against groups like APM.

THE MARCH ON WASHINGTON MOVEMENT

A. Philip Randolph, former head of NNC and the head of the Brotherhood of Sleeping Car Porters, planned a July 1 March on Washington to protest discrimination against African Americans in the defense industry. The NAACP, under Walter White's leadership, was also participating, as was the Urban League. On May 24 Hoover sent a memo to ONI head Captain Alan Kirk, copying Brigadier General (BG) Miles at G-2/MID, stating that "because of alleged discrimination against negroes in the defense program the Communist Party is undertaking an intense campaign of agitational work, which, it is reported, will cause a great deal of trouble in the United States."[65] Hoover went on to claim that Nazi and Soviet agents were providing varying levels of money and operational support for the proposed march, but ended his memo by admitting, "These data have been obtained confidentially and are without verification by investigation."[66]

The head of the FBI was passing along unverified gossip suggesting that organic African American political activities were somehow influenced, if not controlled, by two hostile foreign governments rather than considering that the protest, like the movement itself, was authentic and purely American in origin and character.

Hoover's brief follow-up to Kirk of May 31 mistakenly stated June 1 as the target demonstration date and that "the Negroes assembling in Washington, D.C., will demonstrate against alleged 'Jim Crow' practices."[67] By the end of the first week in June, FDR was sufficiently alarmed at the prospect of 100,000 African Americans marching in Washington that he instructed his private secretary, Marvin McIntyre, to tell Dr. F.O. Williston—a local pharmacist and prominent African American political activist—that

the President is much upset to hear (yesterday) that several negro organizations are planning to March on Washington on July first, their goal being 100,000 neg[r]oes and I can imagine nothing that will stir up race hatred and slow up progress more than a march of that kind. The best contribution Williston can make is to stop that march.[68]

The march leaders refused to back down.

Two weeks before the scheduled march date, FDR invited A. Philip Randolph and Walter White to the executive mansion to try to talk them out of it. The African American leaders insisted on an executive order banning workplace discrimination on the basis of race, at least in defense plants. FDR resisted, but when it became clear to New York Mayor Fiorello La Guardia, who along with Knox and Stimson attended the meeting at FDR's request, that things were going nowhere, he suggested to FDR that "we all begin to seek a formula" for ending the standoff. On June 25 Randolph, White, and Williston got the presidential action they were looking for in the form of EO 8802, which barred defense industry job discrimination on the basis of race. The order also applied to federal hiring.[69] Randolph and White cancelled the march.

What did not end was federal surveillance targeting NNC, NAACP, and other African American organizations and their leadership.

Just one day after the White House meeting between FDR, Randolph, and White, Hoover sent Watson a confidential memo on Randolph and the

"DEVELOPING A GESTAPO IN THIS COUNTRY" 161

proposed march, which Hoover claimed the Communist Party (CP) was try-ing to convert "into a Communist demonstration."[70] Other than CP public statements of support for the cause of African American civil rights, Hoover offered no evidence of CP financial or logistical support for the march or any role in its origination or direction.

The day before FDR signed EO 8802, Army officers at Fort Myer, Vir-ginia, and the War Department were preparing to implement War Plan WHITE—domestic unrest contingency plans for the use of troops in the event the march took place. According to a June 24 MID memo, "The troops will be the 3rd Cavalry Regiment of Fort Meyer, plus one battery of 75mm guns, Military Police Battalion at Arlington Cantonment, a battalion from Fort Meade which has been added to Brigade from the 29th Division, which will come over by trucks."[71] One of the senior officers involved in the plan-ning process reportedly didn't "feel justified in taking any chances on the repetition of the race riots of 1921."[72]

Secretary of War Stimson had been in the meeting with FDR, Randolph, and White on June 18. He therefore knew a peaceful resolution to the crisis was in the works. Why Stimson allowed the Army to continue preparing to use at least 5,000 armed troops, plus 12 field artillery guns, against unarmed demonstrators is unknown.

THE FBI, ARMY, AND NAVY AS DOMESTIC POLITICAL INTELLIGENCE COLLECTORS

Even as FDR and his key advisors were trying to contain labor and race-related protests and demands for political and economic changes, the effort to help Britain survive Hitler's onslaught and prepare the United States for what Roosevelt and his team viewed as the inevitable confrontation with the Nazis remained front and center—even in the face of negative public opin-ion and organized, vocal political opposition. As was often the case, Hoover and the Bureau were a key source of domestic intelligence for FDR on the issue.

On May 12, Hoover sent Watson the results of a *Look* magazine poll over a week before the official publication date, supplied by a source at the mag-azine, that spelled trouble for key administration defense and foreign policy initiatives. The poll found that 80 percent of Americans opposed American convoys of aid to Britain.[73] Americans also refused to believe Roosevelt would actually take America to war against either Germany (58 percent "no") or Japan (73 percent "no").[74] Those who answered the *Look* poll might have felt differently about the prospects for war if they had known that at the recommendation of Stimson, Knox, and the Joint Army-Navy Board,[75] FDR had ordered the Federal Works Agency and the Bureau of the Budget to identify and ready funding for a 32,000 square foot space for an office of National Censorship of International Communications.[76]

As the administration continued to push its rearmament and prepared-ness programs in the media and on Capitol Hill, the FBI, MID, and ONI also collected a steady stream of domestic intelligence on civil society orga-nizations and individuals whose potential links to agents of hostile foreign powers were at best tenuous and at worst nonexistent.

On June 4, the III Corps Area G-2 passed to MID in Washington a report by an undercover Army intelligence source that the president of the Virginia Fencibles fencing club at Gadsby's Tavern in Alexandria, Virginia, a Colonel Edwin Emerson, was "known to the Dies Committee to have Nazi tendencies" and that the FBI Richmond field office "has the case of Colonel Emerson under active investigation."[77] There was no evidence in the MID report, or the attached FBI report from May 1940, that Emerson or anyone associated with the fencing clubs under investigation in Virginia, D.C. or Pennsylvania were sources of known Abwehr or other Nazi intel-ligence agents.[78] Equally fanciful was an MID report of May 23, 1941 that claimed that AFC was receiving financial support from "German singing societies."[79]

Sometimes false accusations of Bund membership or other alleged pro-Nazi sentiments by a disgruntled neighbor were enough to cause profes-sional and reputational damage that could not be undone.

Heinz Schultze, a naturalized American citizen from Germany, was working on a government-funded contract for the construction of an air-base in Trinidad in mid-May 1941 when he was told to return to Washington immediately.[80] When Schultze discovered that he had been accused of being a Bund member and pro-Nazi, he sought the help of the man who repre-sented him in Congress, Rep. Leonard W. Hall (R-NY).

Hall requested that Schultze be given a hearing by MID as a means of clearing his name, even though, according to the investigating MID officer, "the allegations mentioned in the original report were not substantiated" prior to Schultze's dismissal from his employer in Trinidad.[81] Schultze's accuser was a woman who had previously worked with Schultze's wife at a Bund camp near Yaphank, New York.[82]

As 1st Lieutenant William Slayden of MID began the interview with Schultze—who appeared without legal counsel present—the German American laborer and AFL member's true concerns became clear:

SLAYDEN:	You know your constitutional rights? That is, whatever information you give us might be used against you; you understand that is possible? You don't have to give the information—
SCHULTZE:	Now, I have folks on the other side. No harm from any of this information I give you will come to my mother or folks at home in Germany?
SLAYDEN:	No information you give here will get outside the War Department.
SCHULTZE:	After all, you know the conditions over there and I don't want any harm to befall my mother.[83]

Having been falsely accused of being a Nazi sympathizer or even an agent, Schultze's top concern was protecting his mother and other relatives from retaliation by Hitler's government should his interrogation by MID ever become public.

Despite Slayden's report clearing Schultze of any Nazi connections or sympathies, the War Department ordered a further investigation into Schultze on June 12.[84] The results of that investigation, along with Schultze's fate, are unknown. The same cannot be said of coppersmith and former Philadelphia Navy Yard employee Max Hirth, who was ordered fired by Navy Secretary Knox because Hirth was "reliably reported to have views antagonistic to the policies of this country and the principles upon which it was founded" and because Hirth was "believed to be active in the membership of organizations which have a primary interest in promoting [Nazi] policies."[85] Hirth was completely innocent of any crime under federal law.

JOHN FRANKLIN CARTER: FDR'S PRIVATE SPYMASTER

Even as the FBI, MID, ONI and the State Department churned out reports on potential threats at home and abroad, FDR was not entirely satisfied with what he was getting. Each of the major federal elements producing intelligence products had a bureaucratic incentive to push the agenda and priorities of the officials running them. This was especially true of Hoover and the FBI, with the incessant emphasis—nearly always wrong—that malign foreign actors or communists were responsible for racial or labor unrest. FDR wanted his own intelligence capability, one not under the control of Hoover, Stimson, Knox, or Hull. So he created it for himself.

164   CHAPTER 4

It began with FDR calling upon an old friend and former administration official turned columnist, John Franklin Carter (pen name Jay Franklin), to organize a private, covert intelligence operation that would report directly to FDR.[86] The initial $10,000 in operating cash came from a de facto general fund in the 1940 military appropriations bill (for fiscal year 1941) but would ultimately be administered out of the State Department under Assistant Secretary Adolph Berle, Jr.[87]

Carter and the team he assembled gathered information from both public and private sources, relying heavily on a range of contacts Carter had accumulated over several decades, as well as developing new ones. Some of the data obtained by Carter came from Nazi occupied territory. One of his first reports was a March 1, 1941, memo on the raw materials situation in German-occupied Belgium—a report FDR had Carter share with Knox, Stimson, Hull, and the British ambassador to the United States.[88] Carter's reports on a range of issues flowed to FDR on a regular basis during the balance of 1941, including a spying operation targeting the CIO convention.[89] Clearly feeling Carter's operation was of value to him, in late July 1941 FDR directed Berle to ensure Carter got at least $40,000 per year for his work.[90]

The other component of FDR's attempt to get a better coordinated intelligence picture involved recruiting another long-time friend—this one a Republican—to become what would be known as the coordinator of information (COI). The man in question was William J. Donovan, a fellow New Yorker (born in Buffalo), Medal of Honor winner, and former Justice Department assistant attorney general of the Criminal Division during the Coolidge administration.[91]

After FDR secured a third term in the 1940 election, he began 1941 by dispatching his close aide Harry Hopkins to meet with Churchill in London and Donovan to meet with British operatives in the Balkans in an attempt to organize resistance against an expected Nazi invasion of Greece that spring.[92] Over the next several months, Donovan developed a concept that he ultimately put on paper for FDR in June 1941—a proposal for the creation of a "Service of Strategic Information" that would "constitute a means by which the President, as Commander-in-Chief, and his Strategic Board would have available accurate and complete enemy intelligence reports upon which military operational decisions could be based."[93] Donovan's proposal also emphasized the need for psychological warfare and other non-conventional approaches to battling the Nazi and Imperial Japanese threats.

In essence Donovan was proposing a structure similar to that being employed by FDR confidant and Naval Reserve officer Vincent Astor in the New York region, but on an international scale and strictly for foreign intelligence. But FDR's creation of the Carter and Donovan operations ensured

"DEVELOPING A GESTAPO IN THIS COUNTRY"   165

not a streamlining but an overlap—and potential duplication—of effort, not only between the two new organizations, but between existing intelligence collection agencies like MID, ONI, FBI and to a degree the State Department. Conflict over, and opposition to, Donovan's operation from MID, ONI, and FBI was inevitable.

Unrest over the arrangement surfaced less than three weeks after FDR made Donovan COI. On July 30 a Carter source reported that ONI Director Captain Alan Kirk felt that "he should be called on by the White House to give information directly on strategic matters" and he was jealous "of the new Donovan set-up."[94] That FDR let Carter run a de facto political espionage operation against senior American military officers was yet another line the president was willing to cross.

Carter would also become a rival of another senior government official: J. Edgar Hoover. The arena was domestic intelligence collection on FDR's political opponents. Long-time FDR nemesis Senator Burton Wheeler was among Carter's first targets.

Wheeler had aroused FDR's ire by revealing on July 3 administration plans to send US troops to Iceland without congressional authorization.[95] The Montana senator's charges—which were accurate—were explosive because they came as Army Chief of Staff George Marshall was begging Congress to renew the military draft for 18 months. Most existing draftee terms were set to expire soon.[96] Ickes would subsequently rail to his diary that

> Some traitor had tipped it off to Wheeler that this occupation was in prospect and he had made an open allegation to this effect on the Senate floor. Fortunately, he fixed the probable date as two or three weeks later than the actual one. If the Germans had known in advance of this expedition, there might have been casualties and the sinking of one or two ships. This made it doubly important to keep it quiet.[97]

In reality and as Carter would report to FDR on July 11, "Information on Iceland expedition was supplied by a number of Boston mothers who wrote Wheeler protesting that their sons were being loaded on board transports with equipment, etc., which suggested a polar type of expedition."[98]

Wheeler was also "believed to get some information from the Navy—both officers and enlisted men—where there is said to be hostility to Secretary Knox." Carter's source was Eddie Cooper, who Carter referred to as "the Jewish boy Wheeler has hired to prove that he (Wheeler) is not

166   CHAPTER 4

anti-Semitic."[99] The anti-Wheeler political intelligence from Carter continued flowing to FDR, with Carter reporting on July 16 that Wheeler's connections to the Great Northern Railway company indicated that the Senator "may command substantial economic and political support from this and similar interests with a commercial stake in trade with the Axis."[100]

FDR, through Carter, now had an informant in the office of one of his biggest political opponents, paid for with American tax dollars. Carter's network also yielded valuable information on the leading anti-interventionist organization of the day: the America First Committee.

On July 22, Carter forwarded to FDR a nine-page confidential memorandum prepared by a *Fortune* magazine reporter who had been on assignment in Chicago looking into the AFC's activities, organizational structure, and political power. Carter's operative reported that "the backbone of this Committee are the vitriolic Roosevelt-haters associated with 'big business.' It is they who supply most of its funds; they who shape its policy; and they who, with the support of the *Chicago Tribune*, have made it virtually impossible for any prominent Chicagoan to assume the leadership of an interventionist drive."[101] While Carter's source felt that "the East's attitude . . . of loftily patronizing the Middle West as 'isolationist'" was problematic, he offered the view that in the event of war Chicagoans and others in the Midwest would be "as patriotic and just as ready to accept its share of the responsibility."[102]

While there were many anti-interventionist voices in Congress and elsewhere in the public sphere, it was the tag-team of Wheeler and AFC that clearly gave FDR and his key advisors their biggest challenge. However, Wheeler's own missteps often gave FDR openings to blunt the Senator's attacks on the Administration's foreign and defense policy, and even threaten him with prosecution.

In mid-July 1941 Wheeler sent 1,000,000 anti-interventionist postcards to Americans across the country, asking recipients to write to FDR that they were against American entry into the European war.[103] Two of those postcards made their way to Staff Sergeant William L. White at Fort Benning, Georgia, and 1LT Alford T. Hearns at Fort McIntosh in Laredo, Texas. On July 24, Stimson had the War Department's public relations bureau send to Watson at the White House copies of the postcards received by White and Hearns. FDR had requested copies to use at a press conference the next day to denounce Wheeler's alleged use of his congressional franking privilege to urge troops to oppose their commander-in-chief's policies. Stimson and the War Department would go farther, in direct violation of the Constitution.

Not only was MID keeping its own file on Wheeler and his public activities; in coordination with Post Office officials, Miles set up a secret operation

"DEVELOPING A GESTAPO IN THIS COUNTRY" 167

to monitor any franked mail the Montana senator sent to Army bases around the country. Miles classified the order SECRET and sent it encrypted to major commands, including the II Corps Area G-2 at Governors Island, New York:

> Under cover of utmost secrecy request you take immediate action to cover mails arriving at the two largest troop concentration centers in your corps area for purpose of determining names of all military recipients of correspondence of Senator Burton K Wheeler. This action must be given greatest discretion and be handled by two selected individuals in your office. Request report of action and results thereof at earliest practicable date.[104]

Stimson led the public counterattack against Wheeler on July 25, telling reporters that Wheeler's action came "very near the line of subversive activities against the United States, if not treason."[105]

In fact, Wheeler noted that the mailing had been financed by AFC and was based on a mailing list provided by a former Wilkie campaign staffer.[106] Wheeler's use of his Senate franking privilege was lawful under Senate rules at the time.[107] Miles's secret order for mail covers for any Wheeler correspondence to any servicemembers remained in force until July 28.[108]

Wheeler and the AFC were exercising their First Amendment rights under the Constitution, and since the postcards quoted material allegedly previously printed in the *Congressional Record*, Wheeler was also acting lawfully under the Constitution's Speech and Debate clause. None of that mattered to Roosevelt and Stimson, and the mail and telegrams FDR received attacking Wheeler—some called for the Senator's imprisonment or even execution—helped fuel the Administration's determination to pound away on the "Wheeler is a traitor" narrative.[109] It also gave FDR just enough political momentum to get the draft extended for 18 months by a 45–30 vote in the Senate, but by only a one vote margin in the House, 203–202.[110]

ONI: SURVEILLING JAPANESE, RECRUITING JAPANESE AMERICANS

In May, ONI had sent to FBI a report confirming that Hidenari Terasaki, the ostensible secretary of the Japanese embassy in Washington, was in fact the head of all Japanese espionage operations in the United States.[111] Among Terasaki's American government contacts were State Department Foreign

168   CHAPTER 4

Service Officer Eric Wendelin and Senator Theodore Green (D-RI) on the Senate Foreign Relations Committee.[112] Terasaki's relationship with the two men went back many years, and both were in a position to give him information—probably unwittingly—that could be valuable from a political and potentially military perspective. Accordingly, the counterintelligence threat posed by Terasaki and his operation was real.

A follow up ONI report of June 11 was even more revealing regarding the instructions and targets Japanese intelligence operatives were to focus on, and in one key case, avoid:

> all consulates within the United States were instructed to concentrate . . . on obtaining early information of United States naval movements. To this end they were instructed to minimize their propaganda and cultural activities, to concentrate their funds on the employment of agents and saboteurs, and they were specifically enjoined to avoid the use of second-generation Japanese domiciled in the United States in order that there would be no retaliatory measures taken against this group. They were specifically urged to employ Americans of foreign extraction, disloyal native-born Americans and to utilize to the fullest extent possible the Communist party and underprivileged racial groups such as the Negroes.[113]

The Japanese intelligence organization's emphasis on avoiding the use of Japanese Americans while trying to recruit disgruntled Caucasians, Blacks, or communists simultaneously confirmed and refuted some core assumptions by the heads of ONI, MID, and FBI.

The report certainly seemed to validate Hoover's emphasis on monitoring and going after communists, a view generally shared by Kirk at ONI and Miles at MID. But the revelation that Imperial Japanese intelligence operatives were to avoid the recruitment or use of a segment of the Japanese American population for fear of US retaliation was also a signal that Japanese Americans overall were almost certainly not an espionage or sabotage threat.

For its part, the 14th Naval District Intelligence office in Honolulu attacked the Imperial Japanese espionage threat in the Hawaiian Islands in a way no doubt deemed radical by most in ONI: it actively recruited Japanese Americans as spies.[114] As Navy Commander C.H. Coggins noted in his report on what became known as the "Japanese Undercover Organization,"

> In the 14th Naval District, citizens of Japanese ancestry are more closely associated throughout their lives with white Americans than

in any other district. This fact enabled a few of the younger Japanese businessmen to be selected upon the basis of unqualified recommendations made by lifelong white associates. All possible information was obtained; a few who first were qualified assisted in the remaining investigations until finally a nucleus of one dozen intelligent, loyal Nisei was assured.[115]

The race-based nature of the vetting process was simply a different form of discrimination. Instead of excluding Japanese Americans from federal service on the basis of race and potential family or other ties to Imperial Japan, a select group were being invited to become spies because their white friends believed them intrinsically loyal to the United States.

At the direction of the 14th ND District Intelligence Officer (DIO), Captain Irving Mayfield, the unit got off the ground in July 1941 with one junior, white 14th ND intelligence agent Joseph P. McCarthy assigned to form and lead the initial group on a part time basis from an office separate from the 14th ND intelligence office. By October 1941, McCarthy was on the task full time.[116] As events would show, however, the unit was formed too late to develop any leads that would point to an impending attack on Pearl Harbor—but it would play a major counterintelligence role in the months after America entered the war.

OPPOSING CONCLUSIONS ON JAPANESE AMERICAN LOYALTY: THE FBI VERSUS JOHN FRANKLIN CARTER

For his part Hoover continued to believe that Japanese Americans and the organizations that represented them were a potential fifth-column threat. In fact since March 1941, the JACL had become a collaborator with 11th Naval District Intelligence Officer LCDR Kenneth Ringle.[117] It was thus a sign of the lack of coordination between Ringle and the FBI that on July 11, 1941, San Francisco field office agent D. J. Griffin sent his 17-page report on the JACL not only to Hoover but to FBI field offices in Seattle, Portland, Los Angeles, Phoenix, Salt Lake City, Butte, and of course Honolulu. The ONI office in San Francisco and the MID component at the Presidio were also copied.[118]

Griffin had opened his investigation "to ascertain whether or not it had any subversive tendencies, and also to obtain the purpose of the organization."[119] Saburo Kido, the JACL national president, gave Griffin everything

170   CHAPTER 4

he asked for: copies of the organization's bylaws, the list of its chapters and key officers, the organization's purpose, and copies of its monthly newspaper, *Pacific Citizen*. Griffin conceded in his report that the publication's contents "were very pro-American."[120]

Despite the fact that Griffin's extensive investigation of the JACL uncovered no evidence of connections to Imperial Japanese espionage operations, he ended his report with a designation of "Pending"—meaning that the organization would remain under FBI surveillance and investigation despite its cooperation with Ringle and ONI.[121]

The FBI's monitoring of Japanese of any nationality continued into the fall, occasionally revealing clues about Imperial Japanese war preparations and also offering confirmation of the Empire's general anti-Japanese American bias from an espionage and security standpoint.

On October 29, Hoover sent Watson a report on Japanese government evacuation policy regarding persons of Japanese ancestry in the United States, which was being overseen by Imperial Japanese Naval authorities. Executives and employees of Japanese firms, as well as temporary visitors to the United States or those only resident in America for a short period of time would be permitted to leave for Japan. Japanese "who have lived in this country for [a] very long period" or those who "have (or have applied for) a US re-entry permit" were refused passage.[122] A Hoover follow-up report to Watson on November 13 noted that "Instructions have emanated from one of the Japanese Consulates on the West Coast that it should be informed of all Nisei, or Second-Generation Japanese, who may book passage to Japan on any of the NYK vessels since there is some belief that the United States authorities may attempt to employ them for espionage purposes in Japan."[123] Potential Nisei disloyalty was an obsession of both governments.

In the same memo to Watson, Hoover confirmed that the Bureau had "conducted extensive investigations of Japanese residents in the states of California, Oregon and Washington, and in the territories of Alaska and Hawaii, who might be considered for custodial detention pending investigation in the event of a national emergency."[124]

Even as Hoover and his agents were conducting surveillance operations and informant recruitment targeting both Japanese nationals and Japanese Americans, FDR sought a second opinion from John Franklin Carter and his operatives.

Beginning in mid-October, a member of Carter's team, Curtis Munson, began what would become a multi-week journey through the West Coast, the southwestern United States, northern Mexico and ultimately the Hawaiian Islands to essentially confirm or deny existing estimates on Imperial

"DEVELOPING A GESTAPO IN THIS COUNTRY" 171

Japanese espionage operations and the loyalty of Japanese Americans. On October 22 Carter forwarded Munson's initial report, dated October 18, to FDR. In his cover letter to Roosevelt, Carter summed up Munson's findings, which proved eerily prophetic:

> The essence of what he has to report is that, to date, he has found no evidence which would indicate that there is danger of widespread anti-American activities among this population group. He feels that the Japanese are more in danger from the whites than the other way around.[125]

Munson's sources in Honolulu—which as of October 22 he had not yet visited—estimated that 98 percent of the Japanese in Hawaii were "loyal to the U.S. and that those who are not, the Navy and F.B.I. has ticketed."[126] By "ticketed" Munson meant marked for custodial detention in the event of war with Japan.

Carter would submit several additional reports to FDR on the "Japanese Situation" during November and December, the last pre-war report of Munson not reaching FDR until the day after the Pearl Harbor attack. In it, Munson was again prophetic:

> In summarizing, we cannot say how loyal the Japanese in the Hawaiian group would be if there were an American Naval disaster and the Japanese fleet appeared off the Hawaiian Islands. Doubtless great numbers of them would then forget their American loyalties and shout "Banzai" from the shore. Under those circumstances if this reporter were there, he is not sure that he might not do it also to save his own skin, if not his face. Due to the fact that there are more than enough soldiers in the Islands to take care of any Japanese, even if not so inclined, the Japanese will doubtless remain quietly at their tasks. However, in fairness to them it is only right to say that we believe the big majority anyhow would be neutral or even actively loyal.[127]

As news reached Los Angeles of the Japanese Navy's successful and devastating surprise attack at Pearl Harbor, 21-year-old Japanese American gardener Harry Fukuhara's employer emerged from her house to announce, "Japan has attacked Pearl Harbor." He acknowledged her comment but was, probably like most young Americans, clueless as to where Pearl Harbor was or its significance. The woman returned a short time later to state, "Japan has invaded Pearl Harbor. I think maybe you should go home." Fukuhara,

172   CHAPTER 4

apparently sensing his Japanese ancestry was now the issue, responded that he had nothing to do with the attack. It didn't matter. She fired him.[128]

Over the next three months, it would go from bad to nightmarish for Japanese Americans like Fukuhara, in Hawaii and especially on the mainland.

AMERICA AT WAR: CENSORSHIP AND INTERNMENT BEGIN

Attorney General Francis Biddle was in Detroit about to give a speech at 2:30 p.m. local time when he received word of the Pearl Harbor attack. He managed to get back to Washington in time for the 8:30 p.m. cabinet meeting FDR had called at the White House.

"The President is his usual calm self," Biddle recorded, "but most of us were deeply shocked at the terrific loss. . . . The President, at my suggestion, will issue a directive to Hoover that he take charge of all censorship pending some permanent arrangement."[129] Japanese government communications in the United States were immediately cut.[130]

At the same December 7 late evening cabinet meeting, FDR signed Proclamation 2525, "for the immediate detention of all suspected Japanese."[131] By Monday, 736 of the 800 suspect Japanese on the initial target list had been arrested by the FBI and detained by the Immigration and Naturalization Service (INS).[132]

The same day, proclamations targeting German and Italian citizens deemed a threat were also issued as part of what would become officially known as the Enemy Alien Control Program.[133] It was also the day FDR asked for and got a declaration of war against Japan.

In Milwaukee, FBI agent (and future assistant director) William Sullivan noted that, "The declaration of war brought to the surface much suspicion among and about the German population in Milwaukee, the overwhelming majority of whom were entirely loyal to the United States."[134] Sullivan noted that in the days after war was declared, the Milwaukee field office picked up 56 alleged enemy aliens for questioning and possible internment. One of them confided to Sullivan that he was a German Jew who had fled the Nazi regime.

"I told him to go home," Sullivan would later write. "As I walked him to the door, I asked why he had chose me to talk to. 'I thought you looked more sympathetic than the others,' he replied. I never knew his name and never saw the man again."[135] Thousands of other German and Italian persons, including German and Italian American citizens, would not be so lucky.

"DEVELOPING A GESTAPO IN THIS COUNTRY" 173

By December 11, Hoover reported to Watson that in Hawaii alone 345 Japanese aliens had been detained, as had "22 [U.S.] citizens of Japanese extraction."[136] None of the US citizens so detained had actually been charged with committing a crime.

It was all the more ironic then that ACLU National Committee Chairman Edward Ross and ACLU Board Chairman John Haynes Holmes wrote FDR the next day that, "The celebration in these ominous days of war of the 150th anniversary of the adoption of the Bill of Rights highlights the imperative obligation on us all to maintain without compromise in wartime the principles of those guarantees."[137] Ross and Holmes went on

> We have all learned, we trust, the lessons of the First World War in which an excess of zeal produce the savage prosecutions under the Espionage Act of thousands of pacifists, Socialists, I.W.W.'s and others. The prosecution and control of opinions held to be anti-war went far beyond the necessities of national morale. We are confident that no such record, now almost universally condemned, will be repeated, nor that reactionary forces will be permitted to take advantage of the war to weaken the democratic cause.[138]

If anything, it was the ACLU and civil liberties advocates who had failed to learn from history—namely that in war, federal officials viewed the Bill of Rights as optional at best.

Four days before Ross and Holmes sent their letter to FDR, the press had already announced the initial censorship actions.[139] And on December 9, the *Washington Evening Star* reported the FBI's Los Angeles field office had announced "the arrest for investigation of 70 men and women, 60 of them identified as German or of German extraction."[140] Four days after receiving the ACLU's letter, implementation of a full censorship program was well underway, with FDR selecting Associated Press executive news editor Byron Price to become the new director of censorship.[141] Congressional passage of the War Powers Act of 1941 had given FDR explicit authority to censor any communications.[142]

One report that did not get censored involved a confirmed case of a Japanese American aiding one of the Pearl Harbor attackers.

On December 17, the *Washington Evening Star* carried a story about a downed Japanese pilot on the tiny Hawaiian island of Niihau who, with the help of a local Japanese American, terrorized the inhabitants for nearly a week before being killed by a local married couple.[143] The story was a tip off for ONI, MID, and the FBI, and its implications would loom large in the months ahead.

174   CHAPTER 4

Two days after the Niihau incident became public, Curtis Munson reported to John Franklin Carter about the situation on the West Coast for Japanese Americans. As Carter relayed to the White House, Munson's report was dire in tone:

> Curtis Munson reports from Los Angeles that already five L.A. Japanese Americans have committed suicide because their honor could not stand suspicion of their loyalty. He is rushing to Washington a program, which is based largely on the ONI (Commander Ringle) proposals for maintaining the loyalty of Japanese Americans and establishing wholesome race relations. Its essence is to utilize Japanese filial piety as hostage for good behavior.[144]

Munson blasted comments made by Knox on December 15 to the *Los Angeles Times* that, "I think the most effective Fifth Column work of the entire war was done in Hawaii with the possible exception of Norway," a reference to Norwegian Nazi collaborators who helped German forces take over the Scandinavian country in April 1940.

Munson said that he doubted "that outside of sabotage, organized and paid for by the Imperial Japanese Government beforehand (i.e., professional work), that there was any large disloyal element of the Japanese population which went into action as a Fifth Column, running around and intentionally disrupting things on their own hook."[145]

Munson's broad assessment of Japanese American loyalty would be validated, and he made excellent suggestions, including vetting Nisei for work in defense plants. But the Niihau incident—the details of which were widely circulated in American intelligence circles in early 1942—helped fuel the stereotype promoted by British intelligence a year earlier that every Japanese was a potential or actual spy or saboteur. None of Munson's suggestions or warnings were heeded. Among the dominant Caucasian American population—civilian and military—anti-Japanese sentiment boiled over.

JAPANESE AMERICAN INTERNMENT: THE ROAD TO EO 9066

Hawaii began 1942 under martial law and military control, but by January 8 MID at Fort Shafter had decided that in the interest of "promulgating military orders, information and propaganda to the Japanese element of the population which does not speak English" the Japanese language papers *Nippu*

Jiji and *Hawaii Hochi* would be allowed to resume publication—under censorship.[146] It was the most enlightened action US military authorities would take that year toward any organization with ties to Japanese persons or culture.

On January 23 the War Department's adjutant general issued a directive titled "Training and Assignment of Soldiers of Japanese Descent," which directed that upon completion of their basic training, Japanese American soldiers

> will not be assigned to units of the Air Force, the Armored Force, the Signal Corps, or the Chemical Warfare Service. They may be assigned to units and installations of the Zone of the Interior in the continental United States and to units in theaters of operations which may be designated specifically by the War Department in the future. They will not be assigned positions in units or installations where they might gain valuable information or be able to execute damage to important installations; nor will they be grouped in specific units.[147]

Not a single Japanese American soldier had been implicated in espionage or any other activity that threatened the lives or security of American persons, property, or installations. It didn't matter. At the most senior levels of the War Department, the loyalty of Japanese Americans in uniform was now suspect simply because of their race.

Meanwhile, on the mainland, political pressure on FDR to round up and intern Japanese Americans had passed the breaking point. The catalyst was the report on the Pearl Harbor attack issued by a commission headed by Associate Supreme Court Justice Owen Roberts.

The Roberts Commission, as it was known in the press, delivered damning indictments of Admiral Kimmel and General Short, while largely letting the War and Navy Department leadership off the hook for their own failures in making the tragedy possible. But as historian Richard B. Frank has noted, a key passage in the report likely helped give the public the false impression that many local Japanese had somehow acted as spies prior to the attack:

> There were, prior to December 7, 1941, Japanese spies on the island of Oahu. Some were Japanese consular agents and others were persons having no open relations with the Japanese foreign service. These spies collected and, through various channels transmitted, information to the Japanese Empire respecting the military and naval establishments and dispositions on the island.[148]

176   CHAPTER 4

As Frank wrote, "The greatest significance of this passage lay in what it did not say: it failed to affirm the basic loyalty of persons of Japanese descent." Prior to the release of the Roberts Commission report, the public generally had a favorable view of Japanese Americans. After its release, the public turned against persons of Japanese heritage—citizens or Japanese nationals—by almost 7 to 1.[149]

During January and February 1942, right-wing, anti-immigrant groups like the Native Sons and Daughters of the Golden West and the American Legion, along with white-owned agricultural businesses, essentially tag-teamed to first pressure California state legislators and then federal House and Senate members to get behind their call for the internment of Japanese.[150]

Within the Administration, and perhaps surprisingly, it was Attorney General Biddle and FBI Director Hoover who argued against mass internment. Lieutenant General John DeWitt, commander of the Western Defense Command (which encompassed the US West Coast) was strongly in favor of it. Although Biddle reputedly said that Justice would have nothing to do with the evacuations if they were ordered, neither he nor Hoover threatened to resign over the issue.[151]

On February 19 FDR made it official via the promulgation of Executive Order 9066, which gave the Secretary of War or his designee the authority "to prescribe military areas in such places and of such extent as he or the appropriate Military Commander may determine, from which any or all persons may be excluded, and with respect to which, the right of any person to enter, remain in, or leave shall be subject to whatever restrictions the Secretary of War or the appropriate Military Commander may impose in his discretion."[152] While the text itself did not mention any particular racial or ethnic group, Japanese Americans did not need to have it explained to them that they were the target.

As more Japanese were seized and detained by federal authorities in preparation for relocation to concentration camps far from the West Coast, many appealed to FDR to release their loved ones. On March 12, Hoshi Arimoto of Salinas, California, wrote to the president seeking the release of her father, World War I veteran Katsuichi "Tom" Yuki, who was suffering from a long-term illness. Arimoto spoke of her father's loyalty to America and her own.[153]

Arimoto's desperation to prove her family's loyalty—a feeling no doubt shared by the entire Japanese American community—could not overcome the racism-driven government juggernaut of detention and removal. Six days after Arimoto's letter arrived at the White House, FDR issued Executive Order 9102, formally creating the War Relocation Authority (WRA) and giving the Army the mission of rounding up and interning over 100,000 Japanese American citizens.[154]

INTERNMENT: THE GERMAN AND ITALIAN AMERICAN EXPERIENCE

German and Italian Americans would not endure the kind of wholesale relocation and incarceration experience by their Japanese American counterparts, but they would not escape unscathed either. Even as Emmons in Hawaii was trying to get the War Department to back off on relocating and interning Hawaiian Japanese, nearly 5,000 miles away his counterpart, Eastern Defense Command's LTG Hugh Drum, was telling the press that the War Department was going to declare the entire East Coast a military area, complete with exclusion zones and surveillance of persons of German or Italian heritage.

The *Wilmington Morning Star*'s front page headline—"Entire Atlantic Coast to Become Military Area"—on April 27 got the attention of many of FDR's allies in New York and Washington. He was not pleased. On May 5, he sent Stimson a note about

> complaints from the Hill and from New York about General Drum's statement creating a "military area" along the East Coast. From what I hear, the German and Italian people up there are in a state of confusion and believe this means another evacuation like that on the West Coast. American citizens with German and Italian names are also worried. I am inclined to think this may have a bad effect on morale . . . Will you make sure that no action is taken by General Drum under this Executive Order in relation to alien enemies without your talking to me first?[155]

Bureaucratically, Drum was clearly violating the existing agreement that the FBI and INS would handle civilian aliens of German or Italian origin, as had been the case after FDR issued his proclamations regarding German and Italian citizens in the United States.

Politically, FDR was concerned about the fallout among the millions of German and Italian Americans who were politically active and who also had representation in business and elsewhere throughout civil society. A wholesale round-up of German and Italian Americans was off the table, but that did not mean all German and Italian American families were spared.

178   CHAPTER 4

Imperial German Army veteran Bruno Victor Stiller had left his Berlin home in 1921 seeking a better life in the United States. In 1929 he married Alice Muschinske (born in Sheboygin, Wisconsin), and the couple settled in Prairie View, Illinois, establishing the Green Duck restaurant and having four children between 1934 and 1942.[156] The one thing Stiller had not done prior to FDR issuing his proclamation regarding German "enemy aliens" was become a US citizen. He did have a shortwave radio, something that noncitizens were prohibited from having after Pearl Harbor. In late May 1942 the FBI took Stiller into custody, and by early June he was at the Camp McCoy, Wisconsin, internment camp.[157] He would spend the next three years being periodically moved between detention centers in the United States while his wife was left to care for their four children and try to keep the family restaurant afloat.

The Jacobs family of Brooklyn, New York, was effectively destroyed by the internment policy targeting Germans.

Lambert Jacobs and Paulina Knissel arrived in America within less than a year of each other in the late 1920s. The German immigrants met, married and by February 1933 had two sons—Lambert, Jr. and Arthur.[158] And until the Pearl Harbor attack, the Jacobs family lived a relatively normal American family existence. After FDR issued the German enemy alien declaration, the Jacobs family, like tens of thousands of other households of German ancestry, wondered if they would be targeted by the federal government for surveillance, internment, or even deportation. An anonymous and baseless accusation of Nazi sympathies triggered the first FBI raid on the Jacobs home in June 1943.[159]

Over the next two years there would be further raids, multiple interrogations, the loss of their home, internment, and finally deportation of the entire family—including the American-born children—on December 1, 1945, nearly seven months after the defeat of Nazi Germany. The Jacobs boys would not be returned to the United States until November 1947; they would not see their parents again until June 1958.[160]

In the days immediately following the Pearl Harbor attack, hundreds of persons of Italian ancestry were also arrested and interned, including six naturalized American citizens; three were denaturalized.[161] Even the families of famous Italian Americans were not immune to federal restrictions on resident noncitizens. New York Yankee Joe DiMaggio's father, Giuseppe, was "subject to a ban on fishermen that prevented him from fishing out of Fisherman's Wharf in San Francisco."[162]

All told, nearly 11,000 persons of German ancestry and nearly 4,000 persons of Italian ancestry would be interned during the war, clearly including American citizens—in most cases on flimsy evidence or even pure hearsay.[163]

KEEPING TABS ON HIS OPPOSITION: FDR AND WARTIME DOMESTIC POLITICAL SURVEILLANCE

The administration's ethnically focused surveillance, internment, and deportation policy represented only a portion—albeit a large one—of the overall surveillance, censorship, and related actions targeting individuals and organizations. For FDR, getting a steady stream of intelligence on his domestic political opponents remained a high priority.

For well over a year before the Pearl Harbor attack, AFC had waged an unrelenting, but usually unsuccessful, effort to prevent FDR from moving America ever closer to involvement in Churchill's struggle against Hitler. On February 13, 1942, Hoover claimed to Watson that while AFC "ostensibly went out of existence" after the United States entered the war, Hoover claimed "I am informed that the Committee has in reality gone underground, under the leadership of Charles A. Lindbergh."[164]

In fact the organization had officially disbanded on December 11, 1941, and its key figures—General Robert Wood, General Tom Hammond, Robert Stuart, and Lindbergh—had all volunteered for various kinds of government service after the attack.[165] A simple check by Hoover with the War Department would have confirmed those facts in short order. The continued collection of information on AFC after its disbandment was another example of FBI's incompetence and misplaced priorities.

In the case of the *Chicago Tribune*, the Bureau was getting copies of the personal telegrams sent by the paper's owner and publisher, Robert McCormick—a long-time GOP supporter and relentless critic of FDR and the New Deal. In this case, Hoover relayed to Watson a February 18 telegram from McCormick to Arthur Sears Henning, the *Tribune's* DC bureau chief, that "A meeting of the American and British Army staffs had been held, at which time there had been violent disagreement relative to the sending of American troops to various foreign ports and that the President had had to intervene and as a result there was serious disagreement between the British and American staffs."[166]

This was not censorship of a pending story on government policy—a constitutionally dubious proposition in its own right—but the FBI intercepting and monitoring the communications of a publisher with one of his reporters so Hoover could curry presidential favor.

Roosevelt also wanted as much intelligence as he could get on his congressional opponents. Hoover obliged.

On May 5 Hoover forwarded to Watson a report on Senator Rufus Holman (R-OR), another anti-interventionist opponent of the president,

180   CHAPTER 4

and his secretary, Mrs. Anna Marie Kurtz. Holman was characterized by Hoover's source as "extremely radical in his opinions and an isolationist." Kurtz was alleged "to have refused to obey blackout regulations. It is also reported that she made light of the speeches made by the President of the United States and made slurring remarks concerning them."

After reading the memo, FDR instructed Watson to "Tell Edgar Hoover this should be followed up and to keep us in touch." Watson sent a memo to Hoover on May 13 instructing him to get more on Holman, and on May 30 Hoover submitted his five-page follow up.[167] The investigation revealed that the previous allegations of blackout noncompliance were false, and the issue of statements about FDR was not even mentioned by anyone interviewed by the Bureau. The cover note accompanying the report, presumably by Watson to FDR, stated that "previous allegations may not have been founded on facts."[168]

On May 11 FDR sent a memo to Attorney General Biddle referencing the May 2 edition of *The Hour* newsletter, published by Albert E. Kahn (a Communist Party member and Soviet agent not yet revealed as such), which contained an article entitled "U.S. Fifth Column [E]ndorsement of Senator."[169] In the White House file referencing the column, no precise description of the allegations or the specific senator is present, but FDR was clearly exercised by the piece:

> Please read this number of "The Hour" of May second and return for my files. I think very definitely that the FBI can run down things like this. Senators and members of the Congress are, of course, protected in a sense by the Constitution, but this must be strictly construed. There is absolutely no valid reason why any suspected subversive activities on their part should not be investigated by the Dept. of Justice or any other duly constituted agency.[170]

It was up to federal courts, not FDR or any other president, to determine whether a particular act of a House or Senate member fell outside of the protections of the Constitution's Speech and Debate clause or the First Amendment. Roosevelt's attitude here, like his disregard of the Supreme Court's wiretapping prohibition in the Nardone case, was equally outrageous and antidemocratic.

On June 30 Hoover sent to Watson a January 14, 1942, letter from Senator Nye to Horace Haase of the School of Democracy in New York City that had been "confidentially furnished to this Bureau." Hoover claimed that Haase was seeking to consolidate "peace groups and it is further reported that he is collaborating with and receiving support from some of the extremist element of the former America First Committee, as well as other anti-war and anti-Administration organizations in New York City."[171] In his letter to

"DEVELOPING A GESTAPO IN THIS COUNTRY" 181

Haase, Nye agreed on the need for a revived AFC-type of organization but cautioned that, "What we need right now is patience lest we move too soon and before there is sufficient understanding with a loyal opposition organization throughout the country."[172]

The president had clearly viewed the efforts of congressional anti-interventionists like Wheeler and Nye to stop Lend-Lease and related administration initiatives as "subversive," and Wheeler's anti-interventionist congressional mailings, in concert with AFC, had led to War Department monitoring of the Wheeler's franked congressional mail. Now, FDR was getting—albeit belatedly—some of Nye's private correspondence as well.

As American war production kicked into high gear to meet the demands of US and Allied forces, the focus on monitoring the workforce for signs of disloyalty intensified as well.

On March 28 Hoover was able to report to Watson that as of the end of February, "the Federal Bureau of Investigation has established a total of 17,067 confidential informants in 2389 industrial plants throughout the country"—an average of about seven FBI spies in each plant.[173] By July, Hoover's industrial plant informant network had grown to nearly 21,000 in some 4,000 factories nationwide "and in each instance the industrial establishment is engaged in the preparation of war materials," Hoover told Watson.[174] It was the most sweeping network of government informants in the business sector in American history.

For his part, John Franklin Carter and his network continued to supply FDR with political intelligence on key labor leaders, particularly John Lewis of the United Mine Workers (UMW). In his April 10 memo to FDR, Carter operative Jim Gillan previewed the upcoming UMW convention and the power struggle between Phil Murray, the UMW vice president and FDR supporter, and UMW president John Lewis.[175] A follow-up report of May 14 noted that "Lewis has lost influence because his word is no longer regarded as being good."[176] Generally, reports from Carter and his operatives were short enough to be quickly and easily digested by FDR, Watson, and other senior advisors but also detailed enough to allow Roosevelt to decide whether further information tasking was required regarding key unions and their leaders.

RACIAL AND ETHNIC SURVEILLANCE IN WARTIME

Issues of race, surveillance, and loyalty to the federal government remained a dominant theme throughout 1942, even as the tide of the Pacific War turned decisively in America's favor.

182 CHAPTER 4

In May Pearl Harbor's "Station Hypo" Navy codebreakers had provided the intelligence needed to blunt the Japanese advance in the South Pacific in the Battle of the Coral Sea. A month later, the same unit cracked enough of the IJN's code to allow Admiral Raymond Spruance to ambush four of the six Japanese aircraft carriers that had raided Pearl Harbor seven months earlier, sinking all of them at the Battle of Midway.[177] The war would go on for over three more bloody years, with the Japanese making the United States pay dearly in killed and wounded to eject their forces from the across the Pacific, but after Japan's shattering defeat at Midway any invasion threat to Hawaii and the West Coast vanished.

The changed military and geopolitical situation did not lead to a reevaluation of the exclusion of Japanese Americans from military service in the Pacific.

Earlier in the year, the Hawaiian Department commander, LTG Delos Emmons, had suggested that the War Department put together an all-Nisei unit and send it to fight in Africa or Europe. The War Department shot down the idea. When the War Department asked Emmons to supply the number of Army Reservist officers of Japanese descent who had not been called to active duty, his assistant adjutant general, Chief Warrant Officer W.H.P. Purdin, duly compiled a list of 32 such officers and sent it to Washington.

In his memo, Purdin noted that the failure to order those men to report for duty created "the ever-present possibility of alienated loyalty upon the part of young men capable of assuming military leadership of civilian Japanese or otherwise aiding the enemy."[178] Purdin did offer that the Hawaiian Department had "no objections" to the 32 officers on the list being called up and deployed to the mainland or another theater of operations.[179] The Army G-1 (Personnel Division) subsequently declared that "None of these officers will be ordered to active duty unless specifically requested for duty with the Military Intelligence Service."[180] Racism didn't simply deny over 30 loyal Army officers the chance to serve their country; it was allowed to override even the Army's critical manpower needs.

The Army leadership's racially motivated loyalty concerns extended to African American soldiers as well.

In May 1942 the Fourth Corps Area G-2 ordered undercover Army Counterintelligence Corps (CIC) agent Thornton Greene to investigate the cause of "several upheavals . . . involving Colored military personnel and White civilians" in and around Hattiesburg, Mississippi, near Camp Shelby. The agent was "instructed to find if subversive groups or elements were behind the trouble . . . and to study Colored civilian and military personnel relationship" in the area.[181] In two weeks on the ground in Hattiesberg,

Greene found "no eminent danger and no subversive groups" and that any "upheavals" were likely due to "individuals with various attitudes."[182]

A May 15 report by the 4th Army G-2 at the Presidio in San Francisco titled "Negro Situation at Ft. Huachuca" (in Arizona) claimed that an MID study on "Japanese Racial Agitation among American Negroes" offered multiple "Ft. Huachuca Parallels" indicating Japanese agents were responsible for the "present difficulties among the Negro troops of the 93rd Division" based at Huachuca.[183]

Noting that Japanese propaganda "is aimed toward the creation of dissatisfaction among American Negroes to foster race riots and organize revolt against the United States Government and authority," the report pointed to "agitation and threatened riots in towns adjacent to Post . . . tense situation developed as a result of alleged discrimination against colored soldiers by civilian population of Arizona."[184]

While the report criticized various African American media outlets, it provided no actual proof that any confirmed Japanese agent was involved in the racial tensions and incidents between African American troops at Huachuca and members of the local white community. Like the FBI, many Army officials were incapable of seeing the root cause of African American political disaffection—the systemic racism in American society and government.

By the fall of 1942, MID, ONI, and FBI were all putting out their own domestic intelligence summaries on various racial, foreign, or religious groups. A reading of the reports reveals unambiguous violations of the Bill of Rights, particularly the Fourth Amendment.

The October 31, 1942, 14th ND "Counterintelligence Summary" covered not only the Japanese population in Hawaii but German, Korean, French, Portuguese, Spanish, and Italian populations as well. The new Jehovah's Witnesses chapter made the list because of its "continued resistance to all government and constituted authority except the will of God," which was considered as "acting contrary to the best interests of the war effort."[185]

The November 30 14th ND CI Summary added "The Gospel of Salvation" and "Technocracy, Inc." to its list of subversive organizations—the former for the same antiwar reasons as the Jehovah's Witnesses, the latter because of its avowed goal of overthrowing the US government so that "engineers and scientists may govern the nation."[186] Hoover's end-of-year, 52-page "General Intelligence Survey" covered much of the same ground as the 14th ND reports but usually in greater detail and with the addition of "Filipino Activities" and the "Nationalist Party of Puerto Rico."[187]

The year also witnessed some Japanese Americans trying to overturn in federal courts their status as second-class citizens of suspect loyalty who needed to be effectively quarantined from the rest of the population.

184   CHAPTER 4

JAPANESE AMERICAN INTERMENT CHALLENGED IN FEDERAL COURT

On March 28, 1942, 25-year-old Army Reserve officer Minoru Yasui entered a Portland, Oregon, police station around 11 p.m. in violation of the Army Western Defense Command (WDC) 6 p.m. curfew for all persons of Japanese ancestry.[188] Yasui later said he acted out of the conviction that the curfew order was clearly discriminatory "because it makes distinctions between citizens on the basis of ancestry. That order infringed on my rights as a citizen."[189]

Yasui's situation was complicated by the fact that for a year prior to the Pearl Harbor attack, he had been on the staff of the Japanese consulate in Chicago. The young lawyer had been unable to secure a job with any American law firm or company after graduating law school, so his father used his Japanese government connections to get Minoru the consulate job. After the attack, he resigned his post and tried to get on active duty with the Army but was refused because of his race.[190]

A few weeks before the curfew order went into effect, Yasui's father had been interned as an "enemy alien" by federal authorities.[191] The JACL's subsequent public denunciation of him as a "propaganda agent for a foreign government" left the Army Reservist and lawyer feeling very much alone as he awaited trial, the first test case in a legal challenge to the detention of Japanese Americans. He soon had company.

Gordon Kiyoshi Hirabayashi was a member of a religious order known as the Friends of the World—effectively a Japanese version of the Quaker faith. Hirabayashi was thus antiwar and antimilitary service in outlook and also had a strong sense of justice, which is what caused him to refuse to comply with the WDC relocation order on May 16, 1942. Hirabayashi declared his refusal in the Seattle FBI field office, no less.[192]

Hirabayashi made it clear to the FBI agent that "he could not reconcile the will of God, a part of which was expressed in the Bill of Rights and the United States Constitution, with the order discriminating against Japanese aliens and American citizens of Japanese ancestry."[193] On May 28 a federal grand jury handed down a two-count indictment against Hirabayashi for violating Public Law 77–503, the legal enforcement mechanism for FDR's EO 9066 evacuation and internment edict.[194]

The third challenger of the restrictions on Japanese Americans was not a voluntary legal test case subject, at least in the beginning.

When Fred Korematsu was apprehended by San Leandro, California, police on May 30, he attempted to pass himself off as another person of Spanish–Hawaiian extraction. When that failed, the former welder and Boiler Makers Union member gave up his real name and revealed that his efforts to physically alter his appearance—via surgery—was to help him to try to escape the evacuation and detention order with his then-girlfriend and fiancé, Ida Boitano.[195] The local police turned Korematsu over to military authorities pending trial.

Yasui, Hirabayashi, and Korematsu had all violated existing law and regulation. A fourth Japanese American who challenged internment, Mitsuye Endo, complied with the evacuation and internment orders but, on the advice of her attorney, James Purcell, decided to file a habeas corpus petition in federal court in San Francisco on the grounds that race-based detention violated her fundamental constitutional rights.[196]

By the end of 1942, the three men in the cases had lost their first rounds in federal court, while a federal judge left Endo in limbo without a ruling on her habeas writ.

HABITUAL DOMESTIC SPYING, EMPLOYEE LOYALTY SCREENING, AND DIES COMMITTEE CONTRETEMPS

By the beginning of 1943 the domestic security situation in the United States had settled into a pattern that would remain largely unchanged for the balance of the war. On virtually a monthly basis, MID, ONI, and FBI produced reports on the various ethnic, political, or religious groups that were deemed potential security threats. The industrial plant informant network created by the FBI provided a steady stream of intelligence on alleged Axis sympathizers or others viewed as undesirables from a security standpoint. Japanese Americans and foreign nationals of Japanese, German, or Italian heritage identified as threats had either been interned or were otherwise under surveillance. One group that would get renewed, intense, and infamous attention was prospective or actual federal workers.

Attorney General Biddle had, in October 1942, proposed to FDR the creation of an executive branch–wide body to advise the president and federal department and agency heads on cases involving workers accused of being members of subversive organizations. The draft executive order made no attempt to define what constituted a subversive organization or activity, but it did contain a limited employee appeal mechanism.[197] The final version issued by FDR on February 5, 1943, Executive Order 9300, omitted the employee appeal mechanism entirely.[198]

186   CHAPTER 4

If anyone in the administration thought the creation of the new board would stop Rep. Martin Dies and his congressional allies from looking for subversives in the federal government, they were quickly disabused of that idea.

On February 1 Dies went to the House floor and gave a more than 90-minute-long invective-filled screed, attacking his critics and claiming that nearly 40 federal employees—who he named—were subversives, communists, or both.[199] By February 9 the House has passed a resolution (H. Res. 105) authorizing the House Appropriations Committee to examine

> any and all allegations or charges that certain persons in the employ of the several executive departments and other executive agencies area unfit to continue in such employment by reason of their present association or membership or past association or membership in or with organizations whose aims or purposes are or have been subversive to the Government of the United States.[200]

Nowhere in the bill was the phrase "subversive to the Government of the United States" defined.

Four of the employees targeted by Dies worked at the Interior Department, and in his letter to Dies—whom he addressed as "Mr. Dies" vice "Chairman Dies"—Interior Secretary Harold Ickes noted the effort to defund the salaries of the employees in question via the Treasury–Post Office Appropriations bill, telling Dies that "it would be un-American to take summary action and brand these employees as undesirable citizens without an opportunity to defend themselves."[201]

Separately, Eleanor Roosevelt was receiving word from multiple sources that former members of the Abraham Lincoln Brigade—the volunteer unit that had fought on the side of the Loyalists in the Spanish Civil War—were being discriminated against in their efforts to serve in either the military or elsewhere in the government war effort.

"I get this from so many sides," she wrote her husband, "and the FBI and Dies hound them in government work. We are developing a Gestapo in this country and it frightens me."[202]

Dies and his supporters were unmoved by administration complaints. Through the special committee created via H. Res. 105—known as the Kerr Committee, as House Appropriations Committee Chairman John Hosea Kerr (D-NC) chaired both the full committee and the special investigative body—they got the inquiry they sought. They also got a fight from the administration over it.

"DEVELOPING A GESTAPO IN THIS COUNTRY" 187

By early April Dies and others were attacking Attorney General Biddle for allegedly slow-rolling the provision of FBI reports on the individuals named by Dies, even as Dies's own committee failed to turn over everything it allegedly had on the so-called subversives at Interior, the FCC, and elsewhere.[203] On May 14 the Kerr Committee issued a mere 14-page report that was long on hypocritical rhetoric and demonstrably misleading in its presentation of alleged evidence of subversive activities by those so charged.[204]

The committee's targeting specific federal employees for termination on the basis of tenuous, one-time associations with organizations deemed subversive or questionable by Justice Department officials—despite none of the named organizations having been "adjudged by the courts or by Congress as subversive"—was more than a travesty. It was blatantly unconstitutional.

Article I, Section 9 of the Constitution states "No Bill of Attainder or ex post facto Law shall be passed."[205] In the Revolutionary era, bills of attainder were legislative acts authorizing the taking—without trial or other form of judicial process—of the personal property or money of an individual. In *Federalist 44*, Madison wrote that the inclusion of the bill of attainder language in the Constitution was added as a "bulwark in favor of personal security and private rights."[206] In the 1810 Supreme Court case *Fletcher v. Peck*, Chief Justice John Marshall wrote that "A bill of attainder may affect the life of an individual, or may confiscate his property, or may do both. In this form the power of the legislature over the lives and fortunes of individuals is expressly restrained."[207] In the 78th Congress, it was not restrained.

On July 12 via a special emergency war funding measure, Dies got the salary defunding action he wanted, specifically targeting three federal employees—Goodwin B. Watson, William E. Dodd, Jr., and Robert Morss Lovett—by mandating that none of the three men could receive any federal salary or other compensation after November 15, 1943, unless FDR appointed them to government jobs subject to Senate confirmation.[208]

In his subsequent statement on the bill—which he signed on September 14—Roosevelt noted that "There is no suggestion that the three named individuals have not loyally and competently performed the duties for which they have been employed. They are sought to be disqualified for Federal employment because of political opinions attributed to them."[209] After lamenting that the Senate had yielded to such a constitutional and human outrage, FDR conceded that he too was yielding to Dies "to avoid delaying our conduct of the war."[210] Going on to declare the provision "not only unwise and discriminatory, but unconstitutional," the president ended

188   CHAPTER 4

by declaring the punitive rider "an unwarranted encroachment upon the authority of both the Executive and judicial branches under out Constitution. It is not, in my judgment, binding upon them."[211]

But FDR would voluntarily be bound by it. While the three men were kept on briefly after the November 15 deadline, they received no salaries or other compensation. By early December, the trio had filed suit in federal court, seeking back pay and to have the law invalidated as unconstitutional.[212] It would not be until June 1946 that the Supreme Court would rule in *U.S. v. Lovett* that Dies and his colleagues had indeed violated the Constitution's prohibition on passing bills of attainder.[213] The three men received back pay but not restoration to federal service.

"THE ENTIRE JAPANESE POPULATION IN THE UNITED STATES SHOULD BE EXTERMINATED"

Many Caucasians in the Army and Navy were not onboard with Roosevelt's directive that "Every loyal American citizen should be given the opportunity to serve this country wherever his skills will make the greatest contribution."[214] A memo memorializing a March 12, 1943, discussion between Army officers from the Provost Marshal General's Office (PMGO) and officers working for the Chief of Naval Operations regarding trip reports and impressions of two Army officers who had visited concentration camps in Arkansas and Colorado revealed the mindset.

The memo's author, Naval Reserve Ensign Don Gorham, recorded that the Army officer who visited the Colorado camp—a Captain Fairchild— had, prior to his trip, been "of the firm conviction that the entire Japanese population in the United States should be exterminated" but that after his visit came to believe, grudgingly, that "there was a possibility that some of the nisei might be loyal."[215] His counterpart who had visited the Arkansas camp, Captian Holbrook, was "firmly convinced that the great majority of the [N]isei were bitter because of being evacuated and that practically none of them could be trusted outside of a Relocation Center."[216] Holbrook "was convinced that the nisei, apparently as one of their racial characteristics, hold a deep grudge against Americans generally and would probably knife an American in the back any time an opportunity was given to do so."[217]

Reflecting on "the rather obviously narrow minded viewpoints" of the PMGO delegation, Gorham wrote that "the present program of relocating Japanese Americans into industry will be an extremely slow process, if

"DEVELOPING A GESTAPO IN THIS COUNTRY" 189

carried out at all . . . as long as the policy of investigating all nisei having 'Japanese' connections is followed, we will never abolish relocation centers."[218] The problem had almost certainly been made worse by an Army colonel who told a group of interned Japanese Americans that "unless the nisei volunteered for duty with the armed forces they would be put in jail or in regular concentration camps and sent to Japan after the war." Gorham finished his memo by stating "The undersigned believes that Colonel Scobey was the Army officer in question who is reported to have made this thinly veiled threat."[219]

There was nothing "thinly veiled" about the threat, which was also clearly unconstitutional and beyond the power of any War Department official to impose.

And those who spoke out against the internment program or proposals to expel all Japanese Americans from the United States could find themselves the target of federal surveillance, especially if their fiancé was a Japanese American. Such was the fate of a young Army private and aspiring singer-songwriter named Pete Seeger.

Seeger's bride-to-be was Toshi Aline Ohta, a Japanese American woman, and the California American Legion's passage of a resolution calling for the deportation of all Japanese—including American citizens— after the war, as well as a ban on citizenship for Japanese descendants, had outraged the young soldier. In his letter to the Legion, which was forwarded to the FBI San Francisco field office and thence to MID, Seeger wrote, "If you deport Japanese, why not Germans, Italians, Rumanians, Hungarians, and Bulgarians? If you bar from citizenship descendants of Japanese, why not descendants of English? After all, we once fought them too."[220]

By November 1942, local MID elements at Keesler Field, Mississippi (where Seeger was posted) had begun an investigation of him and were intercepting his mail through at least June 1943. It was the beginning of an intelligence file on Seeger that would, by the 1970s, run more than 1,700 pages.[221]

Within the administration, many officials were at best uncomfortable with what had been perpetrated against Japanese Americans, and others were clearly hostile to the policy. As was the case with so many issues, Interior Secretary Harold Ickes, Jr. was the most vocal. In an April 13, 1943, letter to FDR, he made his feelings clear.

Ickes noted that "Native-born Japanese who first accepted with philosophical understanding the decision of their government" to round up all of Japanese ancestry on the West Coast and send them inland "have been

190   CHAPTER 4

pretty generally disappointed with the treatment they have been accorded." The result, Ickes wrote, was:

> the gradual turning of thousands of well-meaning and loyal Japanese into angry prisoners. I do not think that we can disregard, as of no official concern, the unnecessary creating of a hostile group right in our own territory consisting of people who are engendering a bitterness and hostility that bodes no good for the future.... I am unwilling to believe that a better job in general could not have been done than has been done. Neither do I believe that we can't do better from here out, especially if we tackle the job in a different spirit and with real determination without further delay.[222]

Roosevelt took nearly two weeks to reply to Ickes, and when he did so evaded responsibility for his decision to intern Japanese Americans in the first place.

"Like you I regret the burdens of evacuation and detention which military necessity has imposed on these people," FDR wrote. He admitted that "some measure of bitterness is the inevitable consequence of a program involving direct loss of property and detention on grounds which the evacuees consider to be racial discrimination." Roosevelt went on to say he was "glad to endorse" the effort to give internees the chance to work in war industries and that the "best hope for the future lies in encouraging the relocation of the Japanese-Americans throughout the country." He ended by noting that Ickes's "own recent action in employing a Japanese family on your farm seems to me to the best way for thoughtful Americans to contribute to the solution of a very difficult and distressing problem."[223]

Two days earlier, Office of War Information Associate Director Milton Eisenhower—the first leader of the War Relocation Authority and General Eisenhower's brother—had reminded FDR that with respect to Japanese American internees,

> States in which they are now located have enacted restrictive legislation forbidding permanent settlement, for example. The American Legion, many local groups, and city councils have approved discriminatory resolutions, going so far in some instances as to advocate confiscation of their property. Bills have been introduced which would deprive them of citizenship.... They also know that some of the military leaders responsible for evacuation were motivated by a conviction that all persons of Japanese blood in this country cannot be trusted. Public statements to this effect have appeared in the press

"DEVELOPING A GESTAPO IN THIS COUNTRY" 191

only recently.... Under such circumstances it would be amazing if extreme bitterness did not develop.[224]

FDR's suggestion to Ickes that most of his fellow Americans could be encouraged to welcome Japanese Americans was a disingenuous form of magical thinking.

The "military necessity" of the round-up and detention of over 100,000 American citizens had never been demonstrated. FDR had personally received estimates and reports from Carter and others before and immediately after Pearl Harbor that stated clearly and with high confidence that Japanese Americans as a group were as loyal as any other citizens. Japanese American soldiers in Hawaii fought back against Pearl Harbor's attackers on December 7 and had continued to serve honorably since, despite the systemic racism clearly extant in the American military. Still more were volunteering for the newly formed Nisei Army regimental combat team.

The "difficult and distressing" reality of Japanese American bitterness and anger over a clearly unconstitutional mass detention program that had destroyed their professional and personal lives was of FDR's making. He passed on the opportunity to quickly end their ordeal and help them try to rebuild their lives.

JAPANESE AMERICAN INTERNMENT: ADMINISTRATION OFFICIALS LIE TO FEDERAL COURTS

Interned Japanese Americans would get no help from the Supreme Court in 1943, either. On June 1 the Court remanded Korematsu's case back to the Court of Appeals to give a judgment on whether the exclusion order was legal.[225] On June 21 the high court ruled first in the Hirabayashi case, and then in the Yasui case, that the charges against the two men were valid under the Constitution.

In Hirabayashi the Court stated "The adoption by Government, in the crisis of war and of threatened invasion, of measures for the public safety, based upon the recognition of facts and circumstances which indicate that a group of one national extraction may menace that safety more than others, is not wholly beyond the limits of the Constitution, and is not to be condemned merely because, in other and in most circumstances, racial distinctions are irrelevant."[226] And the Court went further still:

The fact alone that attack on our shores was threatened by Japan, rather than another enemy power, set these citizens apart from others who have no particular associations with Japan. . . . We cannot close our eyes to the fact, demonstrated by experience, that, in time of war, residents having ethnic affiliations with an invading enemy may be a greater source of danger than those of a different ancestry.[227]

What the Court did not know is that Justice Department lawyers deliberately withheld the pre- and post-Pearl Harbor attack reports on Japanese American loyalty prepared by Kenneth Ringle of ONI—a move one Justice Department official conceded "might approximate the suppression of evidence."[228]

If the records noted previously had been released via a truthful discovery process, they would have obliterated the executive branch's "military necessity" argument regarding the mass evacuation and detentions of Japanese Americans and exposed their hypocritical, disparate treatment compared to others who actively aided prewar Nazi propaganda efforts.

Indeed, in the months following the Supreme Court decisions, administration officials would make further statements internally that had they been made public would likely have resulted in the cases against all four Japanese Americans being tossed.

In October 1943 Assistant Secretary of War John McCloy wrote to Army Deputy Chief of Staff LTG Joseph McNarney regarding the 442nd Regimental Combat Team (Nisei) and the issue of accepting other Japanese American volunteers and the Japanese American population as a whole:

> We have now assembled about as complete a set of records on Japanese Americans as has ever been gathered together for any segment of our population, sufficiently so that loyalty can be determined pretty accurately. . . . As soon as we start treating these people like everyone else, three-quarters of our difficulties disappear . . . the studies which have been made thus far show that birthplace alone has little significance with respect to loyalty.[229]

McCloy's statement further undermined the notion that the relocation and internment of Japanese Americans had any military legitimacy at all.

Three months later, Attorney General Biddle would explicitly state that the Japanese American "problem" was purely political in nature.

In a December 30, 1943, memo to FDR on the Japanese internment situation, Biddle noted that right-wing groups and "the Hearst press" were working overtime "discrediting the Japanese minority so completely that they will be set apart permanently from the rest of the population and encouraged or force to go to Japan after the war and discouraged or prevented from returning to California."[230] Biddle believed that transferring control of the interned Americans from the War Relocation Authority to the Department of the Interior—which Ickes had reluctantly agreed to since most of the camps were already on Interior-controlled land—would help move along the release and resettlement process.

"The present practice of keeping loyal American citizens in concentration camps on the basis of race for longer than is absolutely necessary," Biddle wrote, "is dangerous and repugnant to the principles of our Government."[231] Racism, not military necessity, was why loyal Japanese Americans were experiencing political repression.

And it was not simply the racism exhibited by WDC commander LTG DeWitt, but of the American public at large, that represented the real political obstacle to the release and resettlement of interned Japanese Americans. Biddle noted:

> The amount of interest in the Japanese problem on the West Coast makes it a general political problem. A poll recently conducted by a Los Angeles paper indicated that Californians would vote ten to one against permitting the United States citizens of Japanese ancestry ever to return. Congressmen and others are tempted to make political capital by urging harsh regulation of the Japanese in response to the public clamor which has been fostered. It is necessary to conduct the administration of the program so that the least possible ground for public sensation and such political action is available.[232]

FDR took no immediate action on Biddle's recommendations. The internees ended the year as they had begun it—behind barbed wire.

SURVEILLANCE, SUBVERSION, AND THE DETROIT RACE RIOTS

Roosevelt's 1942 executive order regarding nondiscrimination against African Americans in defense plant jobs had only come about as a result of direct political pressure by the Black community. The leaders of that community had no intention of settling for an executive order that could be rescinded, or tolerating still more acts of brutality against African Americans, whether

194   CHAPTER 4

committed by civilian racists or government officials. The race riots that took place in the late spring and summer of 1943 in several American cities only steeled their determination. The Detroit riots, which occurred between June 20 and 22, were particularly lethal.

Hoover's June 29 report to White House secretary Marvin McIntyre conceded up front that "the trouble was of a spontaneous nature and not planned or organized"—a contrast to Hoover's usual claim of communist or foreign agitation as the catalyst for racial violence.[233] As the fighting in Detroit raged, Walter White of the NAACP telegrammed FDR with a very different view, blaming racist "Axis and other propaganda" for fueling racial violence from Los Angeles to El Paso to Philadelphia that had the effect of denying "minorities, Negroes in particular, the opportunity to participate in the war effort on the same basis as other Americans."[234] White warned FDR "that unless you act, these outbreaks will increase in number and violence."[235]

Michigan Governor Harry Kelly waited until roughly 6 p.m. on June 21 to ask FDR for a declaration of martial law and federal troops, hoping Michigan state police, Detroit police, and Michigan state troops (National Guard equivalent) could handle the situation. They could not.

Over the four-day period of rioting and fights between Black and Caucasian Detroit residents, 34 died (28 Blacks) and over 700 (both races) were injured. Over 2,500 Caucasian federal troops were deployed for riot control duty and to assist local law enforcement. Nearly 300 troops in the 543rd Quartermaster Battalion (an all-Black unit) mutinied at Camp Custer, Michigan, and attempted to head to Detroit in Army trucks loaded with rifles and ammunition but were stopped and disarmed before they left the post.[236]

Hoover relayed to McIntyre that his agents in Detroit had been hearing for at least two years that the city had become a racial tinderbox, "that sooner or later there is going to be a blow-up." Housing discrimination by local officials, an influx of Caucasians from the South in search of defense-related jobs, "the average white man's normal antipathy toward close and intimate association with Negroes," and "the Negro's natural desire to receive complete equality with white people" ensured that the slightest incident could trigger violence.[237]

Not satisfied with just having Hoover's version of events in Detroit, Biddle dispatched his special assistant, C.E. Rhetts, to make an on-the-ground assessment of the situation and provide recommendations. His 12-page report painted a far bleaker picture than Hoover's.

Of the 25 Black people killed during the riots, "The [Detroit] police accounted for 23," with Rhetts noting that "the negro community and many white people have condemned the conduct of the Police Department as

"DEVELOPING A GESTAPO IN THIS COUNTRY" 195

inefficient, partial to the white rioters, and characterized by brutality towards the negroes."[238] Rhetts stated that while he was not prepared "to make any such general characterization" he was "inclined to believe that a thorough investigation would provide some support for each of these charges."[239]

Rhetts also noted that the draft and war industries had taken the best men and that police recruiting standards had thus been lowered, likely contributing to problems plaguing a force than was nearly 300 officers below its budgeted strength. He recommended that state and local police officers be exempted from the draft, and he also recommended that Biddle pressure state and local officials to convene grand juries to investigate the 34 deaths and 340 injuries "with a view to bringing to justice any persons who may be found to have violated local laws."[240]

Biddle passed along to FDR and endorsed Rhetts' call for police to be exempted from the draft, but instead of pushing state and local officials to investigate the murders, the attorney general told Roosevelt that

> careful consideration be given to limiting, and in some instances putting an end to, negro migration into communities which cannot absorb them, either on account of their physical limitations or cultural background. . . . It would seem pretty clear that no more Negroes should move into Detroit. Yet I know of no controls being considered or exercised.[241]

Over 20 years earlier the Supreme Court had ruled that the very thing Biddle was recommending was unconstitutional. In *United States v. Wheeler*, 254 U.S. 281 (1920), the high court ruled 8–1 that neither the federal government nor the states could prohibit the free movement of anyone not wanted for a crime.[242]

In the wake of the riots Black leaders renewed their political push for action from FDR on the issues Hoover, Biddle, and Roosevelt himself had ignored or slow rolled. Once the situation in Detroit and other cities that had experienced racial conflict seemingly stabilized into an uneasy peace, a familiar pattern resumed: continued political agitation for change by Black leaders and organizations and intensified federal surveillance of those same leaders and organizations.

As the National Urban League convened in September in Chicago for its annual meeting, its national president, William Baldwin, telegrammed FDR seeking a welcome message for the delegates. Bureau of the Budget Director Elmer Davis strongly supported such a statement, characterizing the League as "a reputable and constructive organization."[243] There was a two-day delay

196   CHAPTER 4

in getting a message prepared for Roosevelt's signature, by which time the League's convention was over and the chance to publicize FDR's message had passed. During the interregnum Hoover had submitted a report on the organization which claimed that "several sources" charged that "individual leaders in the local branches of the National Urban League have either been members of the Communist Party or have been strong Communist sympathizers who were affiliated with Communist front groups."[244] Among the alleged Reds was League Chairman William Y. Bell.[245]

In the letter FDR sent to the League, he said at one point "We cannot stand before the world as a champion of oppressed peoples unless we practice as well as preach the principles of democracy for all men."[246] In a post-mortem note to William Hassett on the episode, Watson observed, "In view of the attached report from J. Edgar Hoover which mentions Wm. Y. Bell, Chairman of the National Urban League, perhaps it is just as well their request for a message came too late."[247]

The fact that Watson, Hassett, and others in FDR's inner circle were willing to take Hoover's unverified allegations that communists were controlling the Urban League or its key leaders at their word was a way of absolving themselves for their own role in perpetuating the ongoing political repression—and indirectly, the murder—of Black Americans.

POLITICAL AND DOMESTIC SURVEILLANCE, 1943–1944

As FDR geared up to run for an unprecedented fourth term as the nation's chief executive, John Carter and his organization continued to provide Roosevelt a regular stream of domestic political intelligence.

In July 1943 Carter claimed that multiple House and Senate members were likely in violation of the Federal Corrupt Practices Act based on their campaign expenditure filings, including Senators Albert Hawkes (R-NJ), Homer Ferguson (R-MI), and Charles "Curly" Brooks (R-IL).[248] Carter promised to keep investigating the allegations.

He followed up in September with a detailed report about the GOP conference at Mackinac Island, a prequel to the GOP convention in 1944. At the Makinac Island meeting, Carter's operative reported that

> The meeting of the Governors was significant in that the stronger ones made it plain that the day of GOP isolationism is done and if the delegates to the national convention of the party follow the trend

"DEVELOPING A GESTAPO IN THIS COUNTRY" 197

of their thinking, I expect to see a solid platform and witness a tight election fight.[249]

One thing the GOP attendees apparently agreed on, according to Carter's operative, was that "No one but Roosevelt can win again for the Democratic Party."[250]

Carter also provided FDR political intelligence on reactions to decisions by his cabinet-level officers that could increase Roosevelt's political vulnerability.

In October 1943 Treasury Secretary Henry Morgenthau suggested that significantly increased tax rates would be necessary to help fund the war effort. Carter's network got negative feedback on the Morgenthau proposal from multiple Wall Street and business sector sources, some of whom had been FDR backers since his first presidential campaign:

> A banker who has been an administration supporter on most of the progressive steps taken since 1932 said, "Unfortunately the Morgenthau plan seems obviously one to free the low income earner from the Victory Tax because of the inherent voting power—estimated between 8,000,000 and 9,000,000 persons—and at the same time impose additional burdens on the incomes of the middle and upper bracket groups . . . a large part of any additional tax revenue must come from those who have heretofore been virtually exempt from onerous tax burdens and that even those in the lower brackets must bear their share."[251]

The November election results in New York and New Jersey—where GOP state-level candidates won—caused Carter to report that "Republican and anti-New Deal Democrats in the New York area" had concluded that "Tuesday's elections were an indication of the average American's weariness with the home front bungling of the Administration" that left some key FDR supporters in the business and banking sectors worried whether the "trend is a fair sample of the national temper."[252]

Carter's political intelligence work for FDR continued into 1944, but for his broader domestic intelligence needs he continued to rely on the FBI, MID, and ONI.

The 4th Naval District (headquartered in Philadelphia) took an extremely expansive view of domestic intelligence targets and threats. In a February 15, 1944, memo to ONI, District Intelligence Officer W.T. Smith listed more than 400 categories and subcategories of intelligence collection

198   CHAPTER 4

targets. Included under "Communists" were "Russian nationals (not Communist)," "Anarchists," "IWW Members," "Negro," "German," and so on.[253] Also targeted were multiple unions, companies, media outlets, and even local city government entities focused on race issues.[254]

An April 17 intelligence report for the commanding general of Army Service Forces (ASF) titled "Racial Situation in the United States" only examined "Agitation by Negro organizations, the Negro Press, Negro leaders" and Communist Party efforts to exploit racial tensions between African Americans and Caucasians; Japanese Americans and other minorities were not mentioned.[255]

A May 12 report by the Second Service Command/ASF in New York City stated that "Additional indication of the increasing racial consciousness of Negro-Americans is seen in the report that at least one Negro and possibly four will enter the fall elections in the Jamaica-Rockaway area of Queens County, New York."[256] Meanwhile, the FBI had long had an interest in another Black House seat seeker: the Reverend Adam Clayton Powell, Jr.

The 35-year-old Powell had been a Bureau target for several years, as was the Black newspaper he cofounded, *The People's Voice*, which published its first issue on February 14, 1942—the day Fredrick Douglass had chosen as his birthday.[257] Powell had for years used his pastoral leadership position at Harlem's Abyssinian Baptist Church as a platform to attack segregation, Jim Crow laws, and discrimination against Black people generally. The new publishing venture amplified his influence and helped set the stage for his congressional run.

Within a year of the paper's launch, the FBI's New York field office was claiming that Powell's "nationalistic tendencies" were "communistic" and his praise of the Communist Party for having had "the courage to run Negro people in national, state and county elections" ensured further FBI surveillance of him, the paper, and his associates.[258] During and after his election in 1944 and for over a quarter-century after, Bureau spying on Powell and those close to him, personally and professionally, would become routine.

JAPANESE AMERICAN INTERNMENT: RESOLUTION AND CONSEQUENCES

By early February 1944 FDR had accepted Biddle's recommendation that the WRA be taken out of the War Department and placed in another federal department—in this case, Interior, still under the direction of relocation and internment critic Harold Ickes. On February 16 FDR issued EO 9423,

"DEVELOPING A GESTAPO IN THIS COUNTRY" 199

which formally transferred the WRA from the War Department to Interior.[259] Ickes and his staff then began trying to figure out how to end the internment altogether. Shortly before Easter he issued a statement on the status of his review. He used it to both attack WRA's critics and praise Americans who had at least verbalized support for ending Japanese American internment.

"WRA did not persecute these people," Ickes rather disingenuously claimed, "and it made no attempt to punish those of a different race who were not responsible for what has been happening in the far Pacific." The Interior Secretary continued in this vein, noting that WRA "has been criticized for not engaging in this sort of a lynching party. Under my jurisdiction, it will not be stampeded into undemocratic, bestial, inhuman action. It will not be converted into an instrument of revenge or racial warfare."[260]

On these points, Ickes was at best shading the truth.

Nobody at WRA or the War Department had ever resigned in protest over the continued detention of Japanese Americans. And there had been incidents of violence, one of the most serious at the Manzanar, California, concentration camp, when in December 1942 two internees were killed and nine wounded during a demonstration about the deplorable conditions at the camp.[261] What was true was that Ickes was trying to prevent any further deterioration of the situation, and he was furious with those in American society who continued to call for retribution against fellow citizens who played no role in the Pearl Harbor attack.

"In resisting the onslaughts of those who would have the War Relocation Authority imitate the savageries of the ruling factions in the nations with which we are a war," Ickes said, "I am sure that we have the support of virtually all Americans." Ickes was "particularly grateful to those groups and individuals on the West Coast who have been brave enough and Christian enough to speak out against the vindictive, bloodthirsty onslaughts of professional race mongers."[262]

Ickes's biggest problem was that he still lacked the support of the one person who mattered most: Roosevelt.

"The more I think of this problem of suddenly ending the orders excluding Japanese Americans from the West Coast the more I think it would be a mistake to do anything drastic or sudden," FDR wrote Ickes and Acting Secretary of State Edward Stettinius, Jr. on June 12, who had taken over at State after Hull's retirement. Roosevelt wanted to determine "how many Japanese families would be acceptable to public opinion" for relocation back to the West Coast and to "extend greatly the distribution of other families" to other parts of the United States—"one or two families to each county as a start. Dissemination and distribution constitute a great method of avoiding public outcry."[263]

200   CHAPTER 4

For FDR, the fate of Japanese Americans remained primarily a political problem, not a humanitarian one. He clearly wanted the issue kept out of the papers, and thus off the public radar, as the 1944 election approached.

Ickes got belated official War Department support for his position in a July 3, 1944, memo from WDC commander MG C.H. Bonesteel to Assistant Secretary of War John McCloy, in which Bonesteel stated categorically that "there is no longer a military necessity for the mass exclusion of the Japanese from the West Coast as a whole."[264] For the next four months, Bonesteel would wage his own bureaucratic guerilla battle within the War Department in an effort to end the internment and exclusion policy. Just before Halloween, Bonesteel threatened to issue his own order to end exclusion and internment, only to be overruled by McCloy, who stated "we shall have a greater opportunity for constructive plans at a date later than November 6th."[265]

The presidential and congressional elections were on Tuesday, November 7.

In the weeks that followed, FDR finally greenlighted planning for ending internment and exclusion for most persons of Japanese ancestry. At the same time, the Korematsu and Endo cases were heading for decisions by the Supreme Court. Knowing they were almost certainly facing defeat in the Endo habeas case, War Department officials on December 17 officially rescinded the exclusion and internment orders.[266] The next day, the Supreme Court upheld Korematsu's conviction for violating the now-rescinded orders but also upheld Endo's habeas action and ruled unconstitutional the indefinite detention of "admittedly loyal" citizens.[267] But it was WDC, not the Supreme Court, that would have the last word about which Japanese Americans could be released and when.

Between December 17, 1944, and March 31, 1945, there was a running, internal bureaucratic war between WRA at Interior and WDC in the War Department over the level of additional "loyalty" screenings of Japanese persons prior to their release and what kind of restrictions on their movements in or near military zones on the West Coast should remain in effect. In a March 31, 1945, memo to Ickes, WRA Director Dillon Myer blasted WDC officials for their conduct in processing and dealing with Japanese American detainees.

Noting that the original agreement with WDC called for "not more than 5000 individuals" to be "designated either for exclusion from the West Coast or for continued detention," by March 1945 WDC had "designated a total of nearly 10,000 for exclusion ... and has continued to add new people to its lists from week to week."[268] The effect, Myer told Ickes, would be that between "18,000 to 20,000 individuals will be tied up in centers of some type and not free to move at all."[269]

"DEVELOPING A GESTAPO IN THIS COUNTRY" 201

Of special concerns to Myer that among a subgroup of 1,150 targeted for continued detention,

> The great majority of this latter group are American citizens and more than half of them were given leave clearance by the War Relocation Authority prior to the [exclusion order] revocation announcement. Most of them are youngsters between 18 and 25 who originally answered "no" to the loyalty question and who later changed their answers. We are convinced that their original answers were motivated largely by disillusionment over the evacuation, the confusion that surrounded the registration program, and the pressures exerted by their parents. I believe they have since had time to think the matter of their loyalties through more calmly and that it would be a serious injustice and a mistake to restrict their liberties because of answers made under such circumstances.[270]

"Continuation of these endless investigations and discriminatory restrictions is having a profound adverse effect," Myer wrote Ickes, "particularly on many of the younger evacuees and may result in their permanent embitterment." Myer urged transferring the processing and release function from WDC to the Justice Department.[271]

Myer's prediction was borne out by the number of applications for expatriation to Japan. By the end of 1942 only 2,255 such applications had been filed by Japanese internees, and less than 500 were citizens over the age of 18. Before the end of 1945, over 20,000 internees would request repatriation. Only around 8,000 would actually follow through and leave the United States, but as the authors of *Personal Justice Denied* note, "No other statistics chronicle so clearly as these the decline of evacuees' faith in the United States."[272]

Franklin Delano Roosevelt would not live to see most of the backlash that released Japanese Americans faced from their fellow Caucasian citizens. On June 18, just over two months after FDR's death, an Army Service Forces intelligence report told the tale:

> Individual acts of violence upon Japanese returning from the relocation centers to the West Coast are increasing. Homes have been burned. Some white organizations openly advocate hatred. One group proposes that all persons of Japanese ancestry be expelled from the United States. Part of this feeling stems from racial hatred. Part of it comes from whites who do not want to resume business competition with returning Japanese.[273]

202   CHAPTER 4

The ASF intelligence report expected that the "problems of relocated Japanese can be handled by local civil authorities unless the unlikely need for martial law arises," but it was expected that the end of the war would lead "such organizations as the [American] Civil Liberties Union to reclaim property or to sue the government for damages but these will result in legal action only."[274]

Decades would pass before the US government would even acknowledge, much less apologize for, the race-based, unconstitutional detention of over 100,000 of its own citizens.

CONCLUSION

In terms of assaults on the very foundations of the Bill of Rights, the first half of the 1940s ranks as one of the most consequential periods in American history.

The country's chief executive, as early as 1936, directed the American national security establishment to prepare to imprison—without charge—groups of Americans based strictly on the commonality of their racial heritage with a potential wartime opponent. He also directed his attorney general to engage in wiretapping in direct violation of both the law at the time and a relevant Supreme Court decision affirming that law's constitutionality. Finally, FDR created his own private, taxpayer-funded political intelligence operation via John Franklin Carter and his network of spies and investigators. And he did all of these things while proclaiming, throughout his presidency, his fealty to the Bill of Rights.

In the case of Congress, the creation of dedicated, temporary committees to investigate domestic civil society organizations for undefined subversive activities went from being an occasional public outrage to a de facto permanent one with the creation of the House Select Committee on Un-American Activities. Renewed every Congress throughout FDR's tenure, HUAC terrorized not only domestic organizations it deemed populated with Soviet fellow travelers, but the entire federal workforce as well. Chairman Martin Dies's willingness to utilize raids and even wiretapping—despite the Constitution giving Congress no police powers—was made possible by FDR's unwillingness, and that of Attorney General Robert Jackson, to take direct, decisive legal action against Dies. Instead, FDR tried to placate Dies by giving him access to the tax returns of individuals and organizations, a move that only subjected more innocent Americans to Dies's public histrionics.

Most civil society organizations dedicated to defending or advancing individual rights spent this period much as they had in the previous decade—on the defensive.

The National Negro Congress and the NAACP were able to accomplish some of their objectives via the March on Washington movement. But relentless FBI, MID, and ONI surveillance and informant penetration of Black political groups for signs of Soviet infiltration or control, combined with the pervasive, systemic racism in multiple sectors of American society, kept those and other groups on the political margins. Their broader goals of desegregation and full voting rights remained beyond reach. The racial tinderbox exploded in Detroit in 1943, with Hoover (predictably) claiming Soviet-inspired agitation as the cause while downplaying or even dismissing the reality of racism in American society as the true driver of rage and despair in the Black community.

The nation's highest court also acquitted itself execrably during this era. The willingness of the Supreme Court to take at face value executive branch pronouncements about the potential threat posed by Japanese Americans, and thus the military necessity for their internment, was an abdication of judicial oversight responsibility that has had lasting consequences to this day. To be sure, Justice and War Department lawyers who deliberately withheld evidence from MID and ONI files that contradicted the official rationale for internment bear the brunt of the blame for the outcomes in the Yasui, Hirabayashi, and Korematsu cases. Yet nothing stopped the justices from asking for specific proof as to why every single Japanese American needed to be locked up for the duration of the war. Instead, the Supreme Court showed an unseemly, and decidedly unwarranted, deference to the claims of executive branch officials in those cases. That pattern of federal court deference to presidential claims of harms to national security should the Court rule against the executive branch have become a systemic pathology enabling ever greater power grabs by successive administrations. Many more such precedents would be set under FDR's immediate successor, Harry Truman.

NOTES

1. Letter from H.M. Gallagher to Secretary of War Henry Stimson, January 22, 1941. NARA RG 165, Records of the Military Intelligence Division, Box 566, File number 1766-Z-714.
2. Letter from Senator Guy Gillette to Secretary of State Hull, January 3, 1941. NARA RG 59, Department of State Records, Central Decimal Files, 1930–39, File number 894.2222/4, Box 5909.

204   CHAPTER 4

3. Letter from Senator Guy Gillette to Secretary of State Hull, January 3, 1941.
4. Biographical profile of Kilsoo Haan, Densho Encyclopedia, accessed at https://encyclopedia.densho.org/Kilsoo_Haan/.
5. Letter from Secretary of State Hull to Senator Guy Gillette, January 8, 1941, 2. NARA RG 59, Department of State Records, Central Decimal Files, 1930–1939, File number 894.2222/4, Box 5909.
6. Letter from J. Edgar Hoover to Assistant Secretary of State Adolph Berle, Jr. January 14, 1941. NARA RG 59, Department of State Records, Central Decimal Files, 1930–1939, File number 894.2222/8, Box 5909.
7. Letter from Secretary of the Navy Frank Knox to Secretary of State Cordell Hull, January 24, 1941. NARA RG 59, Department of State Records, Central Decimal Files, 1930–1939, File number 894.2222/11, Box 5909.
8. Letter from Secretary of War Henry Stimson to Secretary of State Cordell Hull, January 18, 1941, 2. NARA RG 59, Department of State Records, Central Decimal Files, 1930–1939, File number 894.2222/10, Box 5909.
9. Memo of COL C.H. Mason, Chief/Intelligence Branch to Chief/Counterintelligence Branch, War Department G-2, February 12, 1941, 1. NARA RG 165, Records of the Military Intelligence Division, File number 1766-Z-699 (30), Box 566.
10. Memo of COL C.H. Mason, Chief/Intelligence Branch to Chief/Counterintelligence Branch, War Department G-2, February 12, 1941, 2.
11. "Summary of Intelligence Activity of the Honolulu Field Office Leading Up to, during and following the Japanese Air Attack of December 7, 1941," FBI File 100-HO-2550, 214. NARA RG 65, Records of the FBI, FBI HQ: Investigative Records—Classified Subject Files Released Under the Nazi & Japanese War Crimes Disclosure Acts, Classification 100: Domestic Security, Folder 100-97-1 (Sections 6 and 7), Box 92.
12. Cole, *Roosevelt and the Isolationists*, 413–414.
13. Cole, *Roosevelt and the Isolationists*, 415.
14. Theoharis and Stuart Cox, *The FBI and American Democracy*, 31–33.
15. Douglas M. Charles, *J. Edgar Hoover and the Anti-Interventionists: FBI Political Surveillance and the Rise of the Domestic Security State, 1939–1945* (Columbus: The Ohio State University Press, 2007), 42–54.
16. Memo from L.B. Nichols/FBI to FBI Assistant Director Clyde Tolson, December 16, 1940. FBI File 100-4712-3, Pt. 1 of 19 FOIA release on AFC.
17. Memo from Lawrence Smith, Chief, Neutrality Laws Unit, Department of Justice to Hoover, December 19, 1940. FBI File 100-4712-5, Pt. 1 of 19 FOIA release on AFC.
18. Referral routing slip, February 21, 1941, from Secretary to the President Stephen Early to Hoover. FDRL, OF 4330—America First Committee, 1938–1945.
19. Memo from Hoover to Presidential Secretary Edwin Watson, February 26, 1941. FDRL, OF 10B, FBI Investigative Reports, File 658, Box 13.
20. Hoover to Early memo, March 1, 1941, FBI File 100-4712-18 and FBI memo on AFC, March 3, 1941, FBI File 100-4712-17X, both from Pt. 1 of 19 FOIA release on AFC.
21. Hoover memo to Edwin Watson, February 21, 1941. FDRL, OF 10B, FBI Investigative Reports, File 655A, Box 13.
22. Hoover memo to Edwin Watson, March 19, 1941, 2. FDRL, OF 10B, FBI Investigative reports, File 690, Box 13.
23. Hoover memo to Edwin Watson, March 19, 1941, 2.

"DEVELOPING A GESTAPO IN THIS COUNTRY" 205

24. From the text of H.R. 2266, introduced in the House of Representatives by Rep Samuel Hobbs (D-AL) on January 16, 1941, 1. Text retrieved via ProQuest Congressional.
25. Memo from James Rowe, Jr., Administrative Assistant to the President, to Attorney General Robert Jackson, February 21, 1941. FDRL, OF 4326-Wire Tapping, 1940–1941.
26. FDR letter to Rep Thomas Eliot, February 21, 1941. FDRL, OF 4326-Wire Tapping, 1940–1941.
27. Memo from J. Edgar Hoover to Attorney General Robert Jackson, February 27, 1941, 1. LOC, Papers of Robert Jackson, Box 89.
28. Memo from J. Edgar Hoover to Attorney General Robert Jackson, May 12, 1941. LOC, Papers of Robert Jackson, Box 94.
29. Memo from J. Edgar Hoover to Attorney General Robert Jackson, May 12, 1941.
30. Memo and Attachments from J. Edgar Hoover to Attorney General Robert Jackson Regarding ONI Wiretapping, May 12, 1941. LOC, Papers of Robert Jackson, Box 94.
31. Memo and Attachments from J. Edgar Hoover to Attorney General Robert Jackson Regarding ONI Wiretapping, May 12, 1941.
32. Strictly Personal and Confidential Memo from J. Edgar Hoover to Attorney General Robert Jackson, May 17, 1941. LOC, Papers of Robert Jackson, Box 94.
33. Strictly Personal and Confidential Memo from J. Edgar Hoover to Attorney General Robert Jackson, May 17, 1941.
34. Strictly Personal and Confidential Memo from J. Edgar Hoover to Attorney General Robert Jackson, May 17, 1941.
35. Layton et al., *And I Was There*, 104–111.
36. Strictly Personal and Confidential Memo from J. Edgar Hoover to Attorney General Robert Jackson, April 26, 1941, 1–2. LOC, Papers of Robert Jackson, Box 94.
37. Memo from Attorney General Robert Jackson to FDR, April 29, 1941, 1. LOC, Papers of Robert Jackson, Box 94.
38. Memo from Attorney General Robert Jackson to FDR, April 29, 1941, 1.
39. Memo from Attorney General Robert Jackson to FDR, April 29, 1941, 1.
40. Memo from Attorney General Robert Jackson to FDR, April 29, 1941, 2.
41. Memo from Attorney General Robert Jackson to FDR, April 29, 1941, 2.
42. Memo from Attorney General Robert Jackson to FDR, April 29, 1941, 2.
43. Confidential letter from J. Edgar Hoover to Assistant Secretary of State Adolph Berle, Jr. regarding a National Negro Congress demonstration in Brooklyn, NY, March 6, 1941. NARA RG 165, Correspondence of MID Relating to "Negro Subversion," 1917–1941, M1440, File number 10218-458-1.
44. Confidential letter from J. Edgar Hoover to Assistant Secretary of State Adolph Berle, Jr. regarding a National Negro Congress demonstration in Brooklyn, NY, March 6, 1941.
45. See Erik S. Gellman, *Death Blow to Jim Crow: The National Negro Congress and the Rise of Militant Civil Rights* (Chapel Hill: University of North Carolina Press, 2012), 4 (Kindle edition).
46. Gellman, *Death Blow to Jim Crow*, 134.
47. Memo from M.H. Crump to Colonel Crump, Office of the Chief of Ordnance, War Department, April 3, 1941. NARA RH 165, Correspondence of MID Relating to "Negro Subversion," 1917–1941, M1440, File number 10218-459-1.
48. Memo from Major Howard Engler, Lowry Field S-2 to the Assistant Chief of Staff, G-2, Eighth Corps Area, "Subject: National Negro Congress," April 18, 1941, with

206   CHAPTER 4

enclosure. NARA RG 165, Correspondence of MID Relating to "Negro Subversion," 1917–1941, M1440, File number 10218-460-1.

49. FBI Washington Field Office report on NAACP, 100–893, March 11, 1941, 1. Available on the FBI's Vault website at https://vault.fbi.gov/.

50. FBI Washington Field Office report on NAACP, 100–893, March 11, 1941, 1.

51. FBI Washington Field Office report on NAACP, 100–893, March 11, 1941, 11–12.

52. J. Edgar Hoover to BG Sherman Miles, Assistant Chief of Staff/G-2, War Department, March 20, 1941. NARA RH 165, Military Intelligence Division, File number 2801-445-88, Box 1854.

53. J. Edgar Hoover to BG Sherman Miles, Assistant Chief of Staff/G-2, War Department, March 20, 1941. See specifically File numbers 2801-445-89 through 2801-445-93 for the names. Pelley is listed in 2801-445-90 and Laughland in 2801-445-93. For details on Laughland's leftist political activities, see Peter Catterall, *Labour and the Free Churches, 1918–1939: Radicalism, Righteousness and Religion* (Bloomsbury Academic: London, 2016).

54. Cross reference memo for the File, "Memorandum for the Attorney General," April 9, 1941. FDRL, OF-10B, Department of Justice, Box 11.

55. Cross reference memo for the File, "Memorandum for the Attorney General," April 9, 1941.

56. Memo of Attorney General Robert Jackson to Edwin Watson, Secretary to the President, April 15, 1941. FDRL, PSF, Series 4-Departmental Correspondence-Department of Justice, 1940–1944, Box 56.

57. FBI memorandum on Joseph E. Camp, President of the Constitutional Education League, March 10, 1941, 3. FDRL, PSF, Series 4-Departmental Correspondence-Department of Justice, 1940–44, Box 56.

58. FBI memorandum on Joseph E. Camp, President of the Constitutional Education League, March 10, 1941, 2.

59. FBI memorandum on Joseph E. Camp, President of the Constitutional Education League, March 10, 1941, 2.

60. Memo of Attorney General Robert Jackson to Edwin Watson, Secretary to the President, April 15, 1941. FDRL, PSF, Series 4-Departmental Correspondence-Department of Justice, 1940–1944, Box 56.

61. Telegram from Robert Stripling to Rep Martin Dies, April 23, 1941, 1. NARA RG 233, Records of the U.S. House of Representatives, Special Committee on Un-American Activities, Member and Staff Correspondence (1938–1944), folder "Dies, 1941," Box 1.

62. American Peace Mobilization, FBI File 100–32736. Available via FOIA.

63. Telegram from Robert Stripling to Rep Martin Dies, April 23, 1941, 1. NARA RG 233, Records of the U.S. House of Representatives, Special Committee on Un-American Activities, Member and Staff Correspondence (1938–1944), folder "Dies, 1941," Box 1.

64. Telegram from Robert Stripling to Rep Martin Dies, April 23, 1941, 1.

65. Confidential memo from J. Edgar Hoover/FBI to Captain Alan G. Kirk, Director/Office of Naval Intelligence, May 24, 1941. NARA RG 165, M1440, Correspondence of MID Relating to "Negro Subversion," 1917–1941, Reel 6, File number 10218-461-1, 1.

66. Confidential memo from J. Edgar Hoover/FBI to Captain Alan G. Kirk, Director/Office of Naval Intelligence, May 24, 1941, 2.

"DEVELOPING A GESTAPO IN THIS COUNTRY" 207

67. Confidential memo from J. Edgar Hoover/FBI to Captain Alan G. Kirk, Director/ Office of Naval Intelligence, May 24, 1941. NARA RG 165, M1440, Correspondence of MID Relating to "Negro Subversion," 1917–41, Reel 6, File number 10218-463-2.

68. FDR memo to White House Secretary Marvin McIntyre, June 7, 1941. FDRL, OF 93-Colored Matters, Folder "Colored Matters, June–July 1941," Box 4.

69. See Jean Edward Smith, *FDR* (New York: Random House, 2007), 493–494.

70. Confidential memo from J. Edgar Hoover/FBI to Edwin Watson/Secretary to the President, June 19, 1941, 2. FDRL, OF 10B, FBI Investigative Reports, File number 835, Box 14.

71. MID memo, "Statement of Captain Walker, I.O., Fort Meyer, VA to G-3 at 11:15 a.m.," June 24, 1941. NARA RG 165, M1440, Correspondence of MID Relating to "Negro Subversion," 1917–1941, Reel 6, File number 10218-465-3, 1.

72. MID memo, "Statement of Captain Walker, I.O., Fort Meyer, VA to G-3 at 11:15 a.m.," June 24, 1941.

73. Memo of J. Edgar Hoover, FBI to Edwin Watson, Secretary to the President, May 12, 1941, 1. FDRL, PSF, Series 4-Departmental Correspondence, Justice-Hoover, Pt. 5, Box 57.

74. Memo of J. Edgar Hoover, FBI to Edwin Watson, Secretary to the President, May 12, 1941, 2.

75. Confidential memo of Secretary of War Henry Stimson and Secretary of the Navy Frank Knox to FDR, June 21, 1941. FDRL, OF 4695-Office of Censorship, Box 1.

76. Memo of Bureau of the Budget Director Harold Smith to FDR, July 5, 1941. FDRL, OF 4695-Office of Censorship, Box 1.

77. Confidential memo from LTC M.S. Eddy, G-2, HQ III Corps Area to Assistant Chief of Staff/G-2, War Department, June 4, 1941. NARA RG 165, Military Intelligence Division, Reports and Correspondence, 1917–41, File number 2801-447-4, Box 1855.

78. Confidential memo from LTC M.S. Eddy, G-2, HQ III Corps Area to Assistant Chief of Staff/G-2, War Department, June 4, 1941. See also the May 22, 1940, memo from J. Edgar Hoover/FBI to BG Sherman Miles/MID, G-2 regarding fencing clubs. NARA RG 165, Military Intelligence Division, Reports and Correspondence, 1917–41, File number 2801-447-1, Box 1855.

79. MID memo, May 23, 1941, "German Bund support for America First Committee." NARA RG 165, Military Intelligence Division, Reports and Correspondence, 1917– 1941, File number 2801-1600-2, Box 1870.

80. The MID file on the investigation into Heinz Schultze can be found in NARA RG 165, Military Intelligence Division, Reports and Correspondence, 1917–1941, File number 2801-1612-3, Box 1870.

81. Memo of 1st Lt. William Slayden to Major N. S. Beckett, May 27, 1941, 2. NARA RG 165, Military Intelligence Division, Reports and Correspondence, 1917–1941, File number 2801-1612-3, Box 1870.

82. Memo of 1st Lt. William Slayden to Major N. S. Beckett, May 27, 1941, 2.

83. Transcript of interview with Heinz Ernest Schultze by 1st LT William Slayden, MID, May 21, 1941, 2. NARA RH 165, Military Intelligence Division, Reports and Correspondence, 1917–1941, File number 2801-1612-3, Box 1870.

84. War Department/G-2 memo to II Corps Area G-2, "Investigation of Individuals," June 12, 1941. NARA RG 165, Military Intelligence Division, Reports and Correspondence, 1917–1941, File number 2801-1612-8, Box 1870.

208   CHAPTER 4

85. ONI card on Max Hirth, July 8, 1941. NARA RG 165, Correspondence and Records of the Military Intelligence Division, 1917–1941, File number 2801-2152-1, Box 1872.

86. See Bradley F. Smith, *The Shadow Warriors* (New York: Basic Books Publishing, 1983), 63–64.

87. Smith, *The Shadow Warriors*, 64.

88. Memo of John Franklin Carter to FDR, March 1, 1941, along with FDR note of March 3, 1941, directing Carter to share with War, Navy, State, and the British ambassador. FDRL, PSF, Series 5-Subject File, John F Carter, March–October 1941, Box 97.

89. See John Franklin Carter memo to FDR, "Report on Developments at CIO Convention, Detroit (as of November 16)," November 17, 1941, as well as November 18, 1941, Follow up Report. FDRL, PSF, Series 5-Subject File, John Franklin Carter, March–October 1941, Box 97.

90. July 1941 correspondence between FDR and Assistant Secretary of State Adolph Berle, Jr. FDRL, PSF, Series 5-Subject File, John F Carter, March–October 1941, Box 97.

91. Department of Justice bio on William J. Donovan, https://www.justice.gov/criminal/history/assistant-attorneys-general/william-j-donovan Accessed on June 24, 2020.

92. See James MacGregor Burns, *Roosevelt: Soldier of Freedom* (New York: Open Road Media, 2012), 74.

93. "Memorandum of Establishment of Service of Strategic Information," FDRL, PSF, Series 5-Subject File, Coordinator of Information, 1941, Box 128.

94. Memo of John Franklin Carter to FDR, "Memorandum Concerning Chief of ONI Kirk," July 30, 1941. FDRL, PSF, Series 5-Subject File, John F. Carter, March–October 1941, Box 97.

95. "Proposed Troops Use Outside Hemisphere Draws Congress' Fire," *Washington Morning Star*, July 4, 1941, 1. Retrieved via LOCCA.

96. "Proposed Troops Use Outside Hemisphere Draws Congress' Fire."

97. Ickes, *The Lowering Clouds*, 571.

98. John Franklin Carter memo to FDR, "Memorandum on Senator Wheeler's Iceland Information," July 11, 1941, Cover Note. FDRL, PSF, Series 5-Subject File, John F. Carter, March–October, 1941-Box 97.

99. John Franklin Carter memo to FDR, "Memorandum on Senator Wheeler's Iceland Information," July 11, 1941, Cover Note.

100. John Franklin Carter memo to FDR, "Memorandum on Senator Wheeler and the Great Northern Railway," July 16, 1941. FDRL, PSF, Series 5-Subject File, John F. Carter, March–October, 1941-Box 97.

101. John Franklin Carter memo to FDR, "Memorandum on the Chicago Situation and the 'America First" Set-up," July 22, 1941, 1. FDR Library, President's Secretary's File, Series 5-Subject File, John F. Carter, March–October, 1941-Box 97.

102. John Franklin Carter memo to FDR, "Memorandum on the Chicago Situation and the 'America First' Set-up," July 22, 1941, 8.

103. Cross Reference Note of July 24, 1941, Regarding Letter from LTC R. B. Lord, G.S.C., Deputy Director, Bureau of Public Relations, War Department. FDRL, PPF 723.

104. Cable from BG Sherman Miles, G-2/War Department to II Corps Area G-2, Governors Island, New York, July 24, 1941. NARA RG 319-Army Staff, Office of the Assistant Chief of Staff for Intelligence, G-2, Records of the Investigative Records Repository, Intelligence, and Investigative Dossiers-Personal Name File, 1939–76, Box 854.

"DEVELOPING A GESTAPO IN THIS COUNTRY" 209

105. "Wheeler Accuses Roosevelt, Stimson of 'Smear Campaign'," *Washington Evening Star*, July 25, 1941, A2. Retrieved via LOCCA.
106. "Wheeler Accuses Roosevelt, Stimson of 'Smear Campaign.'"
107. Senate Manual Containing the Standing Rules and Orders of The United States Senate, Senate Document No. 187, 69th Congress (Second Session), Section 37, 152–153.
108. Cable from BG Sherman Miles, G-2/War Department to II Corps Area G-2, Governors Island, New York, July 28, 1941. NARA RG 319-Army Staff, Office of the Assistant Chief of Staff for Intelligence, G-2, Records of the Investigative Records Repository, Intelligence, and Investigative Dossiers-Personal Name File, 1939–76, Box 854.
109. FDRL, OF 4453-Propaganda, Senator Wheeler, 1933–45, Box 1.
110. Cole, *Roosevelt and the Isolationists*, 440.
111. ONI memo to FBI, "Japanese Intelligence Network in the United States," May 26, 1941. NARA RG 38.4, Records of the Office of Naval Intelligence, Sabotage, Espionage and Counterespionage Section, Oriental Desk, 1936–46, Box 1.
112. ONI memo to FBI, "Japanese Intelligence Network in the United States," May 26, 1941, 2.
113. ONI memo, "Japanese Espionage System in the United States and Suggested Counter Policy," June 11, 1941, 1–2. NARA RG 38.4, Records of the Office of Naval Intelligence, Sabotage, Espionage and Counterespionage Section, Oriental Desk, 1936–1946, Box 1.
114. 14th Naval District Investigation Report, "Japanese Undercover Organization-14th Naval District," May 15, 1942. NARA RG 38.4, Records of the Office of Naval Intelligence, Sabotage, Espionage and Counterespionage Section, Oriental Desk, 1936–46, Box 1.
115. 14th Naval District Investigation Report, "Japanese Undercover Organization-14th Naval District," May 15, 1942, 3–4.
116. 14th Naval District Investigation Report, "Japanese Undercover Organization-14th Naval District," May 15, 1942, 3.
117. See Peter Irons, *Justice at War: The Story of Japanese American Internment Cases* (New York: Oxford University Press, 1983), 79.
118. FBI San Francisco Field Office Report "Japanese American Citizens League" of July 11, 1941, File number 100-SF-4272, 1. NARA RG 165, Correspondence and Records of the Military Intelligence Division, 1917–41, File number 1766-Z-775, Box 566.
119. FBI San Francisco Field Office Report "Japanese American Citizens League" of July 11, 1941, File number 100-SF-4272, 1.
120. FBI San Francisco Field Office Report "Japanese American Citizens League" of July 11, 1941, File number 100-SF-4272, 2.
121. FBI San Francisco Field Office Report "Japanese American Citizens League" of July 11, 1941, File number 100-SF-4272, 17.
122. J. Edgar Hoover memo to Edwin Watson, Secretary to the President, October 29, 1941. FDRL, OF 10B-Justice Files, FBI Investigative Reports, File 956, Box 15.
123. J. Edgar Hoover memo to Edwin Watson, Secretary to the President, November 13, 1941, 2. FDRL, OF 10B-Justice Files, FBI Investigative Reports, File 980, Box 15.
124. J. Edgar Hoover memo to Edwin Watson, Secretary to the President, November 13, 1941, 2.

210   CHAPTER 4

125. John Franklin Carter memo to FDR, "Memorandum Concerning Japanese Situation on the West Coast," October 22, 1941. FDRL, PSF, Series 5-Subject File, John Franklin Carter, March to October 1941, Box 97.

126. John Franklin Carter memo to FDR, "Memorandum Concerning Japanese Situation on the West Coast," October 22, 1941, 4.

127. Memo of John Franklin Carter to FDR, "Memorandum on Japanese Problem (West Coast, Mexican Border)," December 8, 1941, 17. FDRL, PSF, Series 5-Subject File, John Franklin Carter, November–December 1941, Box 97.

128. See Pamela Rotner Sakamoto, *Midnight in Broad Daylight: A Japanese American Family Caught Between Two Worlds* (New York: HarperCollins, 2016), 1–2.

129. Cabinet Meeting Minutes of AG Francis Biddle, December 7, 1941, 2. FDRL, Papers of Attorney General Francis Biddle, Folder "Cabinet Meetings, 1941," Box 1.

130. Cabinet Meeting Minutes of AG Francis Biddle, December 7, 1941, 2.

131. Cabinet Meeting Minutes of AG Francis Biddle, December 7, 1941, 2.

132. Cabinet Meeting Minutes of AG Francis Biddle, December 7, 1941, 2.

133. For an overview, see the National Archives webpage "World War II Enemy Alien Control Program Overview" at https://www.archives.gov/research/immigration/enemy -aliens-overview.

134. See William C. Sullivan and Bill Brown, *The Bureau: My Thirty Years in Hoover's FBI* (New York: W.W. Norton & Company, 1979), 23.

135. Sullivan, *The Bureau,* 23.

136. Memo of J. Edgar Hoover/FBI to Edwin Watson/Secretary to the President, December 11, 1941, 2. FDRL, OF-10B, Justice Files, Box 15, Folder DoJ/FBI Reports, 1941, File number 1045.

137. Letter of Edward Ross and John Haynes Holmes/ACLU to FDR, December 12, 1941, 1. FDRL, OF 2111-American Civil Liberties Union, 1933–1945.

138. Letter of Edward Ross and John Haynes Holmes/ACLU to FDR, December 12, 1941, 1–2.

139. "Censorship Clamped," *Wilmington Morning Star,* December 8, 1941, 3. Accessed via LOCCA.

140. "18 Are Arrested Here as F.B.I. Rounds Up 'Dangerous Aliens,'" *Washington Evening Star,* December 9, 1941, A4. Accessed via LOCCA.

141. Presidential statement of December 16, 1941. FDRL, OF 4695, Office of Censorship, Box 1, Folder "Office of Censorship, 1941–42."

142. 55 Stat 593, December 18, 1941, Sec. 303.

143. "Jap Pilot Is Stoned to Death by Woman on Hawaiian Isle," *Washington Evening Star,* December 17, 1941, A11. Accessed via LOCCA.

144. John Franklin Carter cover memo to FDR, "Summary of Report on Program for Loyal West Coast Japanese," December 19, 1941. FDRL, PSF, Series 5-Subject File, John Franklin Carter, November–December 1941, Box 97.

145. Curtis B. Munson, "Report and Suggestions Regarding Handling Japanese Question on the Coast," December 20, 1941, 1–2. FDRL, PSF, Series 5-Subject File, John Franklin Carter, November–December 1941, Box 97.

146. Memo of Colonel Kendall Fielder, Assistant Chief of Staff/G-2 to Captain Irving Mayfield, 14th Naval District Intelligence Officer, January 8, 1942. NARA RG 181, 14th ND Staff HQ Records, Box 27, folder AF-2(3) Censorship, May 1941-Se 1942.

"DEVELOPING A GESTAPO IN THIS COUNTRY" 211

147. Memo of MG E. S. Adams, Adjutant General, War Department to Commanding Generals, Field Forces; Eastern Theatre of Operations; Western Defense Command; Armies; Corps Areas; Replacement Training Centers, "Training and Assignment of Soldiers of Japanese Descent," January 23, 1942. NARA RH 494, Records of U.S. Army Forces in the Middle Pacific, 1942–1946, Correspondence pertaining to soldiers of Japanese Extraction, Box 5.

148. *Attack upon Pearl Harbor by Japanese Armed Forces. Report of the Commission Appointed by the President of the United States to Investigate and Report the Facts Relating to the Attack Made by Japanese Armed Forces upon Pearl Harbor in the Territory of Hawaii on December 7, 1941.* Senate Document no. 159, 77th Congress (2nd Session), 12.

149. Frank, *Tower of Skulls*, 490–491.

150. *Personal Justice Denied: Report of the Commission on Wartime Relocation and Internment of Civilians.* Seattle: University of Washington Press, 2000, 67–72.

151. *Personal Justice Denied*, 74–75.

152. Executive Order 9066, February 19, 1942. Retrieved from the FDRL website at http://www.fdrlibrary.marist.edu/archives/pdfs/internment.pdf.

153. WH cross reference memo on letter of Hoshi Arimoto, March 12, 1942. FDRL, OF10B-Justice Department, FBI X-refs, Folder 2, Box 11.

154. The text of EO 9102 can be found on the website of the American Presidency Project at https://www.presidency.ucsb.edu/documents/executive-order-9102-establishing -the-war-relocation-authority.

155. FDR to Secretary of War Stimson, May 5, 1942. FDRL, PSF, Series 2-Confidential File, War Department, January–August 1942, part 2, Box 10.

156. See Robert V. Nightingale, *Camp Letters: 1942–1945* (Scotts Valley: CreateSpace Publishing, 2011), 1–2.

157. Nightingale, *Camp Letters: 1942–1945*, 5.

158. See Arthur D. Jacobs, *The Prison Called Hohenasperg: An American Boy Betrayed by His Government during World War II* (Boca Raton: Universal Publishers, 1999), Chronology section, Kindle edition.

159. Jacobs, *The Prison Called Hohenasperg*.

160. Jacobs, *The Prison Called Hohenasperg*.

161. See Mary Elizabeth Basile Chopas, *Searching for Subversives: The Story of Italian Internment in Wartime America* (Chapel Hill: University of North Carolina Presss, 2017), 43–46.

162. Chopas, *Searching for Subversives*, 55.

163. Chopas, *Searching for Subversives*, 45.

164. Memo of J. Edgar Hoover, FBI to Edwin Watson, Secretary to the President, February 13, 1942. FDRL, OF 10B, Justice Files, FBI Investigative Reports, File number 1158, Box 15.

165. See Ruth Sarles, *A Story of America First: The Men and Women Who Opposed U.S. Intervention in World War II* (Westport: Praeger, 2003), 170–171.

166. Memo of J. Edgar Hoover, FBI to Edwin Watson, Secretary to the President, February 23, 1942. FDRL, OF 10B, Justice Files, FBI Investigative Reports, File number 1178, Box 15.

167. White House–FBI correspondence on Senator Rufus Holman, May 2–13, 1942. FDRL, OF-10B, Justice Files, FBI Investigative Reports, folder "FBI Reports, 1942, File 2129, Box 16.

212   CHAPTER 4

168. White House–FBI correspondence on Senator Rufus Holman, May 30, 1942. FDRL, OF-10B, Justice Files, FBI Investigative Reports, folder "FBI Reports, 1942," File 2129, Box 16.

169. See John Earl Haynes and Harvey Klehr, *Venona: Decoding Soviet Espionage in America* (New Haven: Yale University Press, 1999), 254–255.

170. May 11, 1942, memo from FDR to Attorney General Biddle Regarding the May 2, 1942, edition of *The Hour* newsletter. FDRL, OF-419-Congress, Box 4.

171. Memo of J. Edgar Hoover, FBI to Edwin Watson, Secretary to the President, June 30, 1942, 1. FDRL, OF-10B, Justice Files, folder "FBI Reports, 1942," File 2197, Box 16.

172. Memo of J. Edgar Hoover, FBI to Edwin Watson, Secretary to the President, June 30, 1942, 3.

173. Memo of J. Edgar Hoover, FBI to Edwin Watson, Secretary to the President, March 27, 1942. FDRL, OF 10B, Justice Files, FBI Investigative Reports, File number 2056, Box 16.

174. Memo of J. Edgar Hoover, FBI to Edwin Watson, Secretary to the President, July 18, 1942. FDRL, OF 10B, Justice Files, FBI Investigative Reports, File number 2216A, Box 16.

175. Memo of John Franklin Carter to FDR, April 10, 1942. FDRL, PSF, Series 5-Subject File, John. F. Carter, March–May 1942, Box 98.

176. Memo of John Franklin Carter to FDR, May 14, 1942. FDRL, PSF, Series 5-Subject File, John. F. Carter, March–May 1942, Box 98.

177. For an unequaled insider's account of the role of signals intelligence in both battles, see Layton et. al., *And I Was There*, 393–448.

178. Memo of CWO W. H. Purdin to the Adjutant General, War Department, September 25, 1942. NARA RG 319—Army Staff (G-2), Army Intelligence Decimal File, 1941–1948, File number AG 326.21, folder "291.2 Japanese, 81/43 to 10/26/42," Box 390.

179. Memo of CWO W. H. Purdin to the Adjutant General, War Department, September 25, 1942.

180. Memo of Colonel E. C. Lynch, War Department G-1 Executive, October 21, 1942. NARA RG 319—Army Staff (G-2), Army Intelligence Decimal File, 1941–48, File number WDGAP 291.2, folder "291.2 Japanese, 81/43 to 10/26/42," Box 390.

181. Memo of Army CIC Agent Thornton Green, May 8, 1942, 1. NARA RG 319, Army Staff (G-2), Army Intelligence Decimal File, 1941–1948, folder 291.2 (1/32/43) to 291.2 (Chinese), Box 381.

182. Memo of Army CIC Agent Thornton Green, May 8, 1942, 3.

183. 4th Army G-2 memo, "Negro Situation at Ft. Huachuca," May 15, 1942, 1. NARA RG 319, Army Staff (G-2), Army Intelligence Decimal File, 1941–1948, folder 291.2 (1/32/43) to 291.2 (Chinese), Box 381.

184. 4th Army G-2 memo, "Negro Situation at Ft. Huachuca," May 15, 1942, 1.

185. 14th ND Counterintelligence Summary, October 31, 1942, 21. NARA RG 181, 14th ND Staff HQ Records, folder A8–2 (11), January–February 1943 (1 of 2), Box 36.

186. 14th ND Counterintelligence Summary, November 30, 1942, 21. NARA RG 181, 14th ND Staff HQ Records, folder A8–2 (11), January–February 1943 (1 of 2), Box 36.

187. FBI General Intelligence Survey, December 1942. FDR Library, Official File, OF-10 Justice Files, OF-10B, FBI Investigative Reports, File number 2294, Box 17.

188. Irons, *Justice at War*, 81.

189. As quoted in Irons, *Justice at War*, 84.

190. Irons, *Justice at War*, 82–83.

191. Irons, *Justice at War*, 82–83.

192. Irons, *Justice at War*, 87–88.

193. Irons, *Justice at War*, 93.

194. Irons, *Justice at War*, 92.

195. Irons, *Justice at War*, 93–96.

196. Irons, *Justice at War*, 99–103.

197. Letter with draft executive order from Attorney General Francis Biddle to FDR, October 26, 1942. FDRL, OF-10L.

198. Executive Order: Establishing the Interdepartmental Committee to Consider Cases of Subversive Activity on the Part of Federal Employees, February 5, 1943. FDRL, OF-10L.

199. Rep Martin Dies House floor speech, February 1, 1943. *Congressional Record*, 474–486.

200. H. Res. 105, 78th Congress (1st Session), February 9, 1943, 1–2.

201. Letter of Interior Secretary Harold Ickes, Jr. to Re Martin Dies, February 6, 1943. NARA RG 233, Dies Committee, Agency/Department Correspondence, 1938–44, folder "Kerr Committee (1)," Box 2.

202. FDRL, OF 5308—Veterans of the Abraham Lincoln Brigade, 1937–1943.

203. Robert De Vore, "Biddle Seen as 'Brake" as Subversives Stay On," *Washington Post*, April 8, 1943, 11. National Archives Record Group 233, Dies Committee, Agency/ Department Correspondence, 1938–1944, folder "Kerr Committee (2)," Box 2.

204. *Report of the Committee on Appropriations Acting Pursuant to House Resolution 105 of the Seventy-Eighth Congress, on the Fitness for Continuance in Federal Employment of Goodwin B. Watson and William E. Dodd, Jr., Employees of the Federal Communication Commission, and Robert Morss Lovett, Arthur E. Goldschmidt, and Jack Bradley Fahy, Employees of the Department of the Interior,* House of Representatives, Union Calendar No. 158, Report No. 448, 78th Congress (1st Session), 4–5.

205. U.S. Constitution, Article I, Sec. 9.

206. See Clinton Rossiter and Charles R. Kesler, ed., *The Federalist Papers* (New York: Signet Classic, 1999), 279.

207. *Fletcher v. Peck*, 10 U.S. (6 Cranch) 87, 138 (1810).

208. See L. 78–132; 57 Stat. 431; 78 H.R. 2714, Sec. 304.

209. Message from the President of the United States transmitting Statement with Regard to His Reluctance to the Signing of H.R. 2714, the Urgent Deficiency Act of 1943, House of Representative Document no. 264, 78th Congress (1st Session), 1.

210. Message from the President of the United States transmitting Statement with Regard to His Reluctance to the Signing of H.R. 2714, 2.

211. Message from the President of the United States transmitting Statement with Regard to His Reluctance to the Signing of H.R. 2714, 2.

212. "U.S. Invites Congress to Hire Own Lawyer in Ouster of Trio," *Washington Evening Star*, December 6, 1943, A7. Retrieved via LOCCA.

213. U.S. Reports: *United States v. Lovett*, 328 U.S. 303 (1946).

214 CHAPTER 4

214. FDR letter to Secretary of War Henry Stimson, February 1, 1943. NARA RG 38.4, Records of ONI, CI Branch—Sabotage, Espionage, and Counterespionage Section, Oriental Desk, Folder 1, Box 5.

215. Memo for the files of Ensign Don Gorham, U.S.N.R., March 14, 1943, 1. NARA RG 38.4, Records of ONI, CI Branch—Sabotage, Espionage, and Counterespionage Section, Oriental Desk, Folder 1, Box 5.

216. Memo for the files of Ensign Don Gorham, U.S.N.R., March 14, 1943, 1.

217. Memo for the files of Ensign Don Gorham, U.S.N.R., March 14, 1943, 2.

218. Memo for the files of Ensign Don Gorham, U.S.N.R., March 14, 1943, 2.

219. Memo for the files of Ensign Don Gorham, U.S.N.R., March 14, 1943, 2.

220. FBI San Francisco field office letter to Assistant Chief of Staff, G-2, Headquarters, Fourth Army, Presidio of San Francisco, October 15, 1942. Contained in FBI file 100-HQ-200845, Section 1. Released by NARA via FOIA.

221. FBI file 100-HQ-200845 on Seeger, released by NARA via FOIA.

222. Letter of Interior Secretary Harold Ickes to FDR, April 13, 1943. FDRL, OF 4849, War Relocation Authority, Box 1.

223. FDR letter to Interior Secretary Harold Ickes, April 24, 1943. FDRL, OF 4849, War Relocation Authority, Box 1.

224. Letter from Milton Eisenhower, Office of War Information to FDR, April 22, 1943, 1–2. FDRL, OF 4849, War Relocation Authority, Box 1.

225. Irons, *Justice at War*, 227.

226. United States Reports, *Hirabayashi v. United States*, 320 U.S. 81 (1943).

227. United States Reports, *Hirabayashi v. United States*.

228. Irons, *Justice at War*, 204.

229. Memo of Assistant Secretary of War John McCloy to LTG Joseph McNarney, Army Deputy Chief of Staff, October 2, 1943, 1–2. NARA RG 319—Army Staff (G-2), Army Intelligence Decimal File, 1941–48, folder "291.2 Japanese 10/6/43 through 11/30/43, Box 390.

230. Memo from Attorney General Biddle to FDR, "Re: War Relocation Authority Supervision of Persons of Japanese Ancestry Evacuated from Western Military Areas," December 30, 1943, 1. FDRL, PSF Series 4, Departmental Correspondence—Justice—Biddle, Francis, 1941–1943, pt. 2, Box 56.

231. Memo from Attorney General Biddle to FDR, "Re: War Relocation Authority Supervision of Persons of Japanese Ancestry Evacuated from Western Military Areas," December 30, 1943, 2.

232. Memo from Attorney General Biddle to FDR, "Re: War Relocation Authority Supervision of Persons of Japanese Ancestry Evacuated from Western Military Areas," December 30, 1943, 3.

233. J. Edgar Hoover, FBI to Marvin McIntyer, Secretary to the President, June 29, 1943, 1. FDRL, OF 10B, FBI Investigative Reports, file 2373, Box 18.

234. Telegram of Walter White, NAACP Secretary to FDR, June 21, 1943. FDRL, OF 93, Colored Matters, folder "Detroit Race Riots, 1943–45," Box 8.

235. Telegram of Walter White, NAACP Secretary to FDR, June 21, 1943.

236. Telegram of Walter White, NAACP Secretary to FDR, June 21, 1943, 6–7.

237. Telegram of Walter White, NAACP Secretary to FDR, June 21, 1943, 12–13.

238. Memo of C.E. Rhetts to AG Biddle, July 12, 1943, 7. FDRL, OF 93, Colored Matters, folder "Detroit Race Riots, 1943–45, Box 8.

"DEVELOPING A GESTAPO IN THIS COUNTRY" 215

239. Memo of C.E. Rhetts to AG Biddle, July 12, 1943, 7.
240. Memo of C.E. Rhetts to AG Biddle, July 12, 1943, 12.
241. Memo of Attorney General Francis Biddle to FDR, July 15, 1943, 3. FDRL, OF 93, Colored Matters, folder "Detroit Race Riots, 1943–1945," Box 8.
242. *United States v. Wheeler*, 254 U.S. 281 (1920).
243. Memo of Elmer Davis, Bureau of the Budget to William Hassett, September 6, 1943. FDRL, PPF 902 (FBI Report on Urban League).
244. FBI Report on the National Urban League, August 27, 1943, 2. FDRL, PPF 902 (FBI Report on Urban League).
245. FBI Report on the National Urban League, August 27, 1943, 3.
246. FDR letter to William Granger, Urban League Executive Secretary, September 7, 1943. FDRL, PPF 902 (FBI Report on Urban League).
247. Edwin Watson cover note to William Hassett (undated). FDRL, PPF 902 (FBI report on Urban League).
248. John F. Carter memo to FDR, July 9, 1943. FDRL, PSF Series 5-Subject File: John Franklin Carter, June–July 1943, Box 99.
249. John F. Carter memo to FDR, September 9, 1943, 2. FDRL, PSF Series 5-Subject File: John Franklin Carter, August–December 1943, Box 99.
250. John F. Carter memo to FDR, September 9, 1943, 2.
251. John F. Carter memo to FDR, October 13, 1943, 1. FDRL, PSF Series 5-Subject File: John Franklin Carter, August–December 1943, Box 99.
252. John F. Carter memo to FDR, November 3, 1943. FDRL, PSF Series 5-Subject File: John Franklin Carter, August–December 1943, Box 99.
253. Memo of W. T. Smith, DIO, 4th Naval District to ONI, February 15, 1944, 1. NARA RG 38.4: Records of the Office of Naval Intelligence, Records of the CNO, ONI Formerly Classified Administrative Correspondence, 1921–46, Box 245.
254. Memo of W. T. Smith, DIO, 4th Naval District to ONI, February 15, 1944, 2–19.
255. Memo of COL J. M. Roamer, Director of Intelligence/Army Service Forces to Jonathan Daniels, Office of the Commanding General, Army Service Forces/War Department, April 19, 1944, 1. FDRL, OF 4245g-War Department Materials concerning Minorities, 1943–1945, folder "Office of Production Management, Commission on Fair Employment Practices, War Dept., Matters Concerning Minority, March–April 1944," Box 9.
256. Second Service Command Report, "Negro Candidates May Seek Election in Jamaica-Rockaway Community," May 12, 1944. FDR Library, Official File—OF 4245g-War Department Materials concerning Minorities, 1943–1945, folder "Office of Production Management, Commission on Fair Employment Practices, War Dept., Matters Concerning Minority, May–June 1944," Box 9.
257. See Charles V. Hamilton, *Adam Clayton Powell, Jr.: The Political Biography of an American Dilemma* (New York: Atheneum, 1991), 119 on the newspaper and 175–178 for the FBI initial investigations into Powell.
258. Hamilton, *Adam Clayton Powell, Jr.*, 176–177.
259. EO 9423, *Transfer of the War Relocation Authority to the Department of the Interior*, February 16, 1944.
260. Department of Interior press release, April 13, 1944. NARA RG 220—Commission on Wartime Relocation and Internment of Civilians, Box 119.
261. *Personal Justice Denied*, 178–179.

216 **CHAPTER 4**

262. Department of Interior press release, April 13, 1944. NARA RG 220—Commission on Wartime Relocation and Internment of Civilians, Box 119.

263. FDR memo to Interior Secretary Harold Ickes and Acting Secretary of State Edward Stettinius, Jr., June 12, 1944, 1–2. NARA RG 220—Commission on Wartime Relocation and Internment of Civilians, Box 119.

264. Memo of MG C.H. Bonesteel, WDC to Assistant Secretary of War John McCloy, July 3, 1944, 1. NARA RG 220—Commission on Wartime Relocation and Internment of Civilians, Box 119.

265. Irons, *Justice at War*, 274–276.

266. Irons, *Justice at War*, 345.

267. See *Korematsu v. U.S.*, 323 U.S. 214 (1944) and *Ex parte Endo*, 323 U.S. 383 (1944).

268. Memo of Dillon Myer, WRA Director to Interior Secretary Harold Ickes, March 31, 1945, 1. NARA RG 220—Commission on Wartime Relocation and Internment of Civilians, Box 119.

269. Memo of Dillon Myer, WRA Director to Interior Secretary Harold Ickes, March 31, 1945, 1.

270. Memo of Dillon Myer, WRA Director to Interior Secretary Harold Ickes, March 31, 1945, 1–2.

271. Memo of Dillon Myer, WRA Director to Interior Secretary Harold Ickes, March 31, 1945, 3–4

272. *Personal Justice Denied*, 251–252.

273. Extract from Army Service Forces SECRET report, "Estimate of the Domestic Intelligence Situation," June 18, 1945. NARA RG 38.4, Records of the Office of Naval Intelligence, CI Branch—Sabotage, Espionage, and Counterespionage Section, Box 1.

274. Extract from Army Service Forces SECRET report, "Estimate of the Domestic Intelligence Situation," June 18, 1945.

CHAPTER 5

"One Nation Divided, with Fear and Insecurity for All"

1945–1952

During his more than 12 years in office Franklin Roosevelt created the largest, most powerful domestic surveillance apparatus in American history. His successor, Harry Truman, would do nothing to dismantle it. Even though Truman did not believe the domestic threat of subversion from the Soviets posed a genuine threat to American democracy, he also knew his view was not shared—not only by his Republican opponents, but by many in his own party.

Rep. John Rankin's (D-MS) legislative power play at the beginning of the new Congress to make HUAC a permanent standing committee meant that congressional witch hunts for alleged Soviet sympathizers and fronts would continue in the postwar era. It also meant that scrutiny of federal employees through a permanent employee loyalty program, which Truman countenanced via an executive order, also continued.

As the Cold War with the Soviets intensified and a real war with North Korea broke out in the summer of 1950, Truman was confronted at home with an intensification of the domestic security crackdown via the Internal Security Act (known also by its sponsor's name, the McCarran Act), which Truman vetoed and which the House and Senate promptly overrode. The McCarran Act also engendered HUAC a Senate counterpart: the Senate Internal Security Subcommittee. It was during Truman's tenure that the congressional witch hunt committee phenomenon approached its zenith, leading to, among other things, the infamous Hollywood blacklists in the wake of HUAC hearings on alleged Reds in the entertainment industry.

218   CHAPTER 5

Truman's tenure, however, began much as FDR's had more than a decade earlier, with the American intelligence and law enforcement establishment trying to figure out how to take the hunt for subversives and spies to the next level and J. Edgar Hoover trying to curry favor with his new boss.

BUREAUCRATIC TURF BATTLES AND ELECTRONIC SURVEILLANCE

Truman's first act as president was to confirm that the scheduled April 25, 1945, San Francisco Conference on the United Nations would go ahead as FDR would have wished.[1] The new chief executive wanted to move forward with his predecessors' vision for rebuilding the international order once hostilities ended. Months before FDR's passing and Truman's ascension to the presidency, American intelligence officials were also busy planning for the postwar world and how they would spy on many of those same countries that would comprise the membership of the United Nations. Their prime focus was on how to keep the enterprise secret, even at the expense of traditional constitutional liberties, if necessary.

Less than a year before FDR's death, Navy Lieutenant (JG) John Connorton and Army Lieutenant Floyd Tomkins, Jr. prepared a more than 100-page Top Secret/ULTRA report for the US Army-Navy Communication Intelligence Coordinating Committee that chronicled communications intelligence leaks over the last several decades, the damage they had allegedly caused, and the need for radical legislative remedies to prevent future leaks.[2] In justifying their case, Connorton and Tomkins used a formulation that would become embedded in every speech, every Capitol Hill presentation, and every major national security–related court case involving intelligence matters from the post–World War II era to the present day.

"It is recognized that a satisfactory solution of this problem will probably encroach upon the freedom of the press and freedom of speech," they wrote. "The issues at stake are so important, however, that some action must be taken in the interest of national safety."[3]

Claiming the Espionage Act's provisions were insufficient to disincentivize and punish those who exposed America's codebreaking capabilities, the two military officers wanted legislation that would prevent "disclosures by civilians, journalists, war correspondents, etc. who may have acquired knowledge of cryptographic or cryptanalytical activities either through their official position or by any other means."[4]

"ONE NATION DIVIDED" 219

This was not an encroachment on the First Amendment—it was a proposal to destroy it in the name of national security.

Connorton and Tomkins also wanted a statutory prepublication review gag law for current and former US government intelligence personnel who had ideas about following in the footsteps of *American Black Chamber* author Herbert Yardley.[5]

Connorton and Tomkins made no allowance for the deliberate, concerted misuse of the classification system to conceal waste, fraud, abuse, mismanagement, or even criminal conduct. Yardley had certainly alleged as much in his book, which, under the Connorton–Tomkins proposal, would never have seen the light of day.

Roosevelt had ignored the Supreme Court ruling in the *Nardone* case expressly prohibiting wiretapping to order his then–Attorney General Robert Jackson to go ahead with wiretapping in the name of national security. What if a future chief executive did something similar, and someone on the White House staff or at the Justice Department objected and decided to write a book about the incident but was blocked from publishing it by a White House claim of national security or executive privilege?

An even more basic issue being debated within the American intelligence establishment in the last year of the war was whether or not communications eavesdropping in peacetime would be considered lawful for national security purposes.

Army and Navy lawyers both worked up justifications for the continued interception of foreign diplomatic electronic communications that at best amounted to an exercise in legal contortionism. The Army opinion noted that:

> The question is whether Section 605 [of the Communications Act] prohibits the Executive Branch of the Government from investigating the communications of foreign Governments in the manner described in the statement of facts. . . . Section 605 does not prohibit any such investigations, which are essential for the national defense and the development of an enlightened foreign policy in time of peace, and of great tactical and strategic value in time of war.[6]

On March 2 Vice Chief of Naval Operations Admiral F. J. Horne, acting on behalf of CNO Admiral Ernest J. King, recommended to Navy Secretary James Forrestal that the Navy Judge Advocate General be asked to give his opinion as to the legality of such communications intercepts. Rear Admiral Thomas Leigh Gatch responded on March 26 in a confidential opinion, and he was as categorical as his Army counterparts.

220   CHAPTER 5

He dismissed the applicability of the *Nardone* case, which Gatch described as "a private crime" involving "the mere administration of the internal criminal law" and "distinguished from potential offenses against and dangers to the sovereign interest, which the activities of the Navy Department here under consideration are intended to forestall."[7] Gatch then declared:

> It is the definite opinion of this Office that the activities of military intelligence, acting under the authority of the Executive, including the interception, acquisition, and use of telecommunications, are legitimate activities not prohibited by any provision of law so long as they are directed to the protection of the national defense and security of the national interests in the international field.[8]

The Communications Act's language was clear: "no person not being authorized by the sender shall intercept any communication and divulge or publish the existence, contents, substance, purport, effect, or meaning of such intercepted communication to any person."[9] For Navy and Army lawyers, the plain language of the law was no barrier to intercepting foreign communications because, in their view, Congress had not expressly forbidden it with explicit language to that effect.

While the need for such intelligence had clearly been demonstrated both in peace and war over the prior quarter century, the fact remained that American citizens routinely used international communications to conduct business, including with foreign governments. The Army–Navy approach guaranteed that those communications would get swept up in such intelligence efforts, a fact both services, and Navy Secretary Forrestal, chose to ignore.

When Admiral Horne recommended to Forrestal on May 14 that he approve Gatch's opinion, he also offered the view that "it will be necessary to obtain a similar opinion, more general in its application, from the Attorney General" and that "the War and Navy Departments jointly request the Attorney General to render such an opinion."[10]

Because only the attorney general had the authority to set legal policy for the entire executive branch, Horne knew the Navy and Army couldn't go it alone, particularly on something so sensitive and, in some quarters of the government, controversial. Forrestal concurred, approving Gatch's opinion on June 8.[11] On June 22 he sent a memo to his War Department counterpart, Henry Stimson, asking for a united approach to incoming Attorney General Tom Clark.[12] By the fall, the issue remained unresolved.

Clark had not acted on the request, and by late October 1945, it was clear that some in the private sector, specifically telecom giant RCA, were

"ONE NATION DIVIDED" 221

prepared to assist the Navy and War departments without a formal, written opinion by the attorney general. VADM Joseph Redman, chief of naval communications, was not at all keen on the idea.

In an October 19 memo to Forrestal, Redman noted that RCA's willingness to accept "oral assurances" of the legality of the intercepts from the attorney general was "not acceptable" for multiple reasons, not the least of which was that "changing personalities in either the Department of Justice or an affected company subject oral commitments to nullification at any moment."[13] Redman also characterized oral commitments as "elusive, uncertain, and provocative of misunderstanding" and that "Cooperation could be expected to fail in the very instance when it is most needed, since the critical instances are generally the controversial instances."[14]

Redman's frustration with Clark was also palpable.

"If the Attorney General considers the activities of communications intelligence illegal," Redman wrote, "then certainly it is his duty to so advise the Navy Department, and it should be equally the concern of the Navy Department to know of their illegality and undertake corrective procedure. If, however, the activities are lawful, there appears no valid reason why the Attorney General should not so state."[15]

Even as the internal bureaucratic war over the legality and future of electronic surveillance unfolded as the country transitioned from war to peace, some in the president's inner circle had no compunction about using the FBI's existing surveillance capabilities against his actual or suspected political enemies.

HOOVER AND TRUMAN:
UNCOMFORTABLE PARTNERS

Roosevelt's death put J. Edgar Hoover in the position of trying to curry favor with his replacement. As former FBI Assistant Director William Sullivan would later note, "the word went out to the entire bureau that anyone related to, friendly with, or personally known by the new president should step forward to become Hoover's personal emissary to the White House."[16] It didn't go well.

Hoover dispatched a Special Agent Chiles—born in the president's hometown of Independence, Missouri—to let the president know the FBI was happy to be of service. Truman indeed knew Special Agent Chiles's father, but he also knew when he was being played by America's longest serving government bureaucrat. The president thanked the young man for coming but added "any time I need the services of the FBI, I will ask for it through my attorney general." Sullivan noted, "from that time on, Hoover's hatred of Truman knew no bounds."[17]

Historian David McCullough has claimed that "Truman had little use for the FBI" and that "Truman considered Hoover and the FBI a direct threat to civil liberties."[18] But if Truman actually had those concerns, his Senate record didn't reflect it; he never introduced any civil liberty–related bills and conducted no investigations into FBI practices while in the Senate. Moreover, whatever his personal feelings about Hoover and the Bureau, it didn't stop his most senior advisors from using the Bureau to spy on Truman's enemies within the Democratic party. Among the targets were FDR political appointee Ed Pritchard and Democratic lobbyist and "super lawyer" Tom "Tommy the Cork" Corcoran.

A Kentuckian, Pritchard had been an early and enthusiastic supporter of FDR and during the war had held senior positions in the Office of Economic Stabilization and the Office of War Mobilization and Reconversion (OWMR). His time at the senior legal levels of the Roosevelt administration had allowed him to become friends with no less a figure than Supreme Court Justice Felix Frankfurter.[19] The two had first met years earlier when Pritchard was a student at Princeton, and their friendship had only deepened during the war. The problem for Pritchard, besides his own outsized ego, was that Truman was suspicious of New Dealers like Pritchard and Corcoran, who he believed were working, in McCullough's words, "against [him] by leaking denigrating material to influential liberals and the press."[20]

At the time of FDR's death Pritchard was working in OWMR out of an office in the White House, putting him in the perfect place to keep political tabs on the new chief executive. Sensing the threat, White House Secretary Harry Vaughan decided to take Hoover up on his offer of assistance, and by April 23 Hoover had delivered the first installment of what would become known as the White House Survey—an FBI examination of the political activities of several White House staffers, including Pritchard.[21] The first wiretap on Pritchard started sometime between April 23 and May 7, as the first transcript on Pritchard—a conversation with Frankfurter about the reaction to Germany's surrender, the various memorial speeches on FDR's passing by various senior administration officials, key political developments on Capitol Hill, and more—had been generated on May 8.[22]

The name of columnist Drew Pearson came up repeatedly in the conversation, only fueling the belief among Truman and his senior advisors that Pritchard and other FDR holdovers were the source of unhelpful media leaks to the columnist. A subsequent June 12, 1945, Pearson column, which

"ONE NATION DIVIDED" 223

contained details about meetings between presidential advisor Harry Hopkins and Soviet leader Joseph Stalin, triggered a White House request for a search for the leaker. On August 17 Hoover gave his nine-page investigative summary to the White House.

Hoover reported that nearly 300 people could have had access to some or all of the cables and related messages Hopkins sent back to the White House between May 26 and June 6, making it "impossible to definitively fix responsibility as to the actual source of Pearson's information, although the investigation suggests several possibilities."[23] Of the 12 named individuals of greatest interest, Pritchard and Corcoran figured most prominently in the assessment, though Hoover could provide no proof either man was the source of the leak.[24] Pritchard would be out of government and Washington by October 1945, bringing his wiretap to an end, but the tap on Corcoran continued until at least May 9, 1948.[25]

Exactly how many other individuals on the White House staff were targeted for wiretaps, mail covers, or physical surveillance during this period is unknown. However, we do know Truman received domestic political intelligence from the FBI on a former cabinet secretary: Harold Ickes.

Ickes and Truman had parted company—publicly and bitterly—over Truman's nomination of California oil man Edwin Pauley to be Navy undersecretary. Ickes had been called to testify at Pauley's Senate confirmation hearing about rumors Pauley had tried to pressure Ickes into keeping the Interior Department out of the offshore oil exploration leasing controversy. The infamous Teapot Dome scandal had occurred only two decades before, and many Senators clearly felt Pauley had a conflict of interest.

Ickes confirmed the rumors, essentially linking Pauley to a de facto pay-to-play scheme (i.e., no federal interference with leases leading to major campaign contributions to the DNC) and thus effectively dooming Pauley's nomination. Truman was livid, particularly after Ickes told the press that he was "unable to commit perjury for the sake of the party" and that Truman was "neither an absolute monarch nor a descendant of a putative Sun Goddess."[26]

On December 6 Hoover, in response to a direct request from Vaughn, conducted a search of Bureau files "with respect to a possible connection between Mr. Harold L. Ickes, former Secretary of the Interior, and any gas company interested in acquiring the Big Inch Pipe Line."[27] The pipeline in question was one of two championed by Ickes prior to and during World War II as a way to cross-country ship oil from Texas so as to avoid the German U-boat menace.[28]

Hoover told Vaughn there was nothing in FBI files currently connecting Ickes to a gas company but that a Bureau "confidential source" claimed

Ickes had been "proposed for consideration as a director" of a gas company Tommy Corcoran was supposedly creating for the purpose of bidding on the surplus pipelines.[29] Corcoran's efforts came to naught, the Texas Eastern Transmission Corporation winning the competition.[30]

Whether Truman or Vaughn told the War Assets Administration (which oversaw the bidding) that any Ickes-connected bid was to be rejected is unknown. However, in his letter accepting Ickes's resignation, Truman had added, "I also consider that this terminates all your other government activities."[31] Vaughn had tasked Hoover to uncover any connections between Ickes and the Big Inch auction. The surveillance—which had no legal predicate, as Ickes and Vaughn were both private citizens engaged in legal commerce—and the bid outcome appear more than coincidental.

RACISM, SURVEILLANCE, AND CIVIL RIGHTS: POWELL VERSUS RANKIN, FBI, AND MID

It wasn't just White House officials or other executive-branch employees that were targets of Hoover's wiretaps or other forms of surveillance. As had been the case in previous decades, certain members of Congress were subjected to such politically tinged surveillance as well. One of them was the newly elected House member from New York's 22nd Congressional District, the Reverend Adam Clayton Powell, Jr.

Powell came to prominence in Harlem not only because of his oratorical gifts but because of his newspaper, *The People's Voice*, one of the few Black-owned and operated newspapers in the country. Powell and his paper had been targeted for Bureau investigation for years for alleged communist connections or sympathies.[32] The paper had been the subject of a wiretap at least as early as December 1944 as part of an effort to monitor Powell's attempts to organize support for wartime aid to Russia.[33] The irony was that Powell had actually been a cooperative source and interlocutor with the Bureau during the first two years of the war, answering Bureau questions about at least three individuals under investigation for potential Hatch Act violations or alleged sedition.[34]

None of that prior cooperation shielded Powell or his activities—on or off Capitol Hill—from scrutiny and surveillance, which was not confined to the FBI.

On April 26, 1945, Secret Service Special Agent Harry Anheir forwarded to his White House counterpart Special Agent Michael Reilly an April 21 Army Service Forces report on a speech Powell made in Philadelphia the day after FDR's death. His "questionable statements" in the eyes of Army intelligence analysts were, among others, that "We are going to lift F.D.R's spirits in America, and when we find an ally we are going with him—if America doesn't lead, Russia will" and "Today we face the danger of the enemies who have been waiting in the shadows to push Russia back."[35]

For its part, the Bureau maintained surveillance of Powell and his newspaper throughout 1945, including the use of technical surveillance—either phone taps or microphone surveillance—that captured Powell in conversations with supporters, *People's Voice* staff or supporters, and his mistress and future second wife, pianist Hazel Scott. A regular theme of the reports was that Powell was close to known or suspected Soviet sympathizers, the implication being Powell himself was Red—something Powell's own actions and statements clearly refuted.[36]

Powell also had powerful enemies in Congress. Among the most prominent was unrepentant antisemite and racist Rep. John Rankin (D-MS). Elected to Congress in November 1920, Rankin rarely passed up the chance to expound on his view of the racial superiority of whites, particularly those from his home state.

At a May 9, 1924, Mississippi Society event in Washington, Rankin extolled "the immortal Jefferson Davis" as well as "L.Q.C. Lamar and James Z. George, who, with the assistance of other great leaders of the South, wrested that section from negro rule, and placed forever the standard of white supremacy above the capitol of every Southern state."[37] Lamar and George had both been key officials in the Confederacy, and Davis of course the one and only president of the Confederate states.

Rankin's racism and antisemitism often found expression through his actions and speeches as a long-standing member of HUAC. Powell's arrival in the House ushered in a new era of very public confrontation between civil rights advocates like himself and defenders of the existing racist power structure in Washington like Rankin. Powell relished Rankin's refusal to sit near him in the House chamber. "I am happy that Rankin will not sit by me because that makes it mutual," he said in the *People's Voice*. "The only people with whom he is qualified to sit are Hitler and Mussolini."[38]

And even as Powell and other House members were preparing for the start of the 79th Congress, Rankin scored the biggest and most enduring legislative victory of his career, one that would ensure Rankin had a platform to continue attacking Powell, other civil rights advocates, and anyone else deemed subversive or un-American.

Martin Dies's departure from the House in 1944 coincided with the looming expiration of the committee that had (informally) borne his name.

Figure 5.1. Representative John Rankin (D-MS) singlehandedly saved from extinction the discredited House Select Committee on Un-American Activities in January 1945, which as a permanent House committee for thirty more years would destroy the career and lives of thousands of Americans. *Library of Congress*

Years of bombastic, unsubstantiated attacks by Dies, Rankin, and their colleagues on the House Select Committee on Un-American Activities had, by late 1944, so eroded public and institutional support for the committee that it seemed destined to die. Rankin had other ideas, and he got support for them from a key constituency: the American Legion.

On December 29, 1944, Rankin received a letter from the California chapter of the Legion, passing along a copy of a resolution adopted at their state convention in August, calling for HUAC's continuation. In offering the Legion's support, James Fisk, speaking for the California chapter, told Rankin "we trust that the Congress will see fit not to discontinue the splendid, loyal Americanism work of such a group."[39]

The day before the new Congress was to convene and as Rankin prepared to make his legislative move, he thanked Fisk for "your splendid resolution" and made his intentions clear. "If I can have my way," Rankin wrote, "this Committee for Investigation of Un-American Activities will be continued,

"ONE NATION DIVIDED" 227

and these records saved for future reference, in order to protect this country against all subversive influences."[40]

Rankin got his way.

When the new Congress convened, Rep. Adolph Sabath rose to offer the resolution on the rules that would govern the operation of the House during the 79th Congress. After the clerk had read the resolution and before Sabath could speak, Rankin rose to offer his amendment to make HUAC permanent.

Declaring that HUAC had done "marvelous work" and that "Today, when our boys are fighting to preserve American institutions, I submit it is no time to destroy the records of that committee, it is no time to relax our vigilance. We should carry on in the regular way and keep this committee intact, and above all things, save those records."[41]

Rankin immediately got support from fellow HUAC member Rep. Karl Mundt (R-SD), who praised Rankin for his efforts and asserted that making HUAC permanent would "render a great public service."[42] The assist from Mundt, an influential political hawk in the GOP conference, made Rankin's amendment a legitimately bipartisan effort and vastly strengthened the Mississippi lawmaker's hand during the debate.

Sabath himself had supported creation of the McCormack–Dickstein Committee and ultimately the Dies Committee itself. Indeed, just before 4 p.m. on December 7, 1941, he had telephoned Hoover's office and told a Hoover aide that the FBI director should immediately "pick up all the God-damned Japanese and all the God-damned Nazis" in the wake of the attack on Pearl Harbor. In his note to Hoover, his aide said he had informed the State Department of Sabath's request and that the congressman "sounded inebriated at the time."[43]

Sabath's real objection to HUAC is that it had focused nearly all of its efforts on individuals or groups on the political left, rather than going after the individuals Sabath wanted investigated—those he deemed fascists or Nazi sympathizers, a fact he subsequently reiterated on the House floor.[44] On the opening day of Congress, Sabath tried to block Rankin's effort to ram through a permanent extension via the House rules. Sabath failed due to a procedural ruling by the speaker.[45]

The remainder of the debate involved additional attempts by several members to defer action on the amendment, to question how it would be funded, and to object overall to using the House rules resolution as a vehicle for making HUAC permanent. All failed, including an attempt to table (i.e., kill) Rankin's resolution (the vote was 146–134 in Rankin's favor).[46] The final vote on the Rankin amendment was 208–186, with 40 members not voting.[47]

228   CHAPTER 5

Rankin's mastery of the legislative process, as well as support from key House GOP leaders and the American Legion, gave HUAC supporters the victory. Over the next 30 years, Rankin's revived HUAC would do massive professional, personal, and political damage to thousands of individual Americans and domestic civil society organizations. Among the targets would be Rankin's new House colleague, Adam Clayton Powell, Jr.

THE FEDERAL EMPLOYEE LOYALTY PROGRAM

If the president was worried about political insider threats at the White House like Ed Pritchard, he was, at least initially, less concerned about the loyalty of the entire federal workforce. In deciding how to approach the issue, Truman had to contend with the hand his predecessor had dealt him.

In February 1943 FDR issued Executive Order 9300, creating in the Department of Justice an Interdepartmental Committee to Consider Cases of Subversive Activity on the Part of Federal Employees.[48] That program, like the FBI's war production plant surveillance program, had been established in response to fears that American citizens with family ties to or recent immigrants from Axis nations represented a potentially serious security threat. Those fears had proven almost totally groundless. The assault on their constitutionally protected free association rights, and the damage to the professional and personal lives of those dismissed from either government or industry jobs on the basis of hearsay or innuendo, had been real. Accordingly, in his first year in office, Truman saw no need to continue those programs, much less make them permanent through formalized executive orders or legislation.

Others inside and outside the administration felt very differently.

In June 1945 the FBI arrested six people with ties to an Asia-focused, leftist magazine called *Amerasia*. Among those arrested was State Department China specialist John Stewart Service, who was accused of providing the magazine with classified Office of Strategic Services (OSS) reports on China. The case played out over the balance of 1945 and into mid-1946, and ultimately a grand jury refused to indict Service, who was allowed to return to work at the State Department.[49] Even so, those involved in the *Amerasia* episode would face continued persecution in the years that followed, particularly John Service. More broadly, as the first major de facto postwar alleged espionage case, the Service investigation helped set the stage for many of the repressive government measures that became features of Cold War American political life.

"ONE NATION DIVIDED" 229

For his part Hoover was making sure that Truman and his most senior aides were aware of alleged Soviet attempts to infiltrate or otherwise undermine the American military. On February 6, 1946, he sent a confidential memo to Truman and his chief military aide, Brigadier General Harry Vaughn, "a summary of available information concerning Communist infiltration of and agitation in the Armed Forces."[50] Hoover alleged, credibly, that the "Communist Party of the United States of America, through the activity of individual members, is seeking to urge the servicemen to further demonstrate against the alleged slow-down in the demobilization program."[51] Hoover further noted that "this tactic is not new" and that "instructions were originally issued in this regard by the Comintern."[52]

Even as Hoover continued to send a steady flow of "personal and confidential" missives to Truman and Vaughn about alleged Soviet-directed CP USA agitation in the armed forces and among recently demobilized veterans, by the fall of 1946, Truman was facing pressure from his own party to take action on the federal civilian employee loyalty question.

On October 1, 1946, Rep. Jennings Randolph (D-WV), chairman of the House Civil Service Committee, phoned the White House to complain that Truman "has not yet acted on setting up of the Interdepartmental Commission in connection with subversive influences . . . that the President said he would appoint this commission two weeks ago."[53]

Randolph's impatience was understandable. In July 1946 his committee had issued a short but informative report that made it clear the pressure to create a permanent federal employee loyalty program was real and growing. In the words of the report's authors:

> It is obvious to this committee that the only way to afford complete protection to our Government is to require all persons who apply for positions to be thoroughly investigated and fingerprinted in advance of employment, This, of course during the war period was not possible. It is not now possible due to lack of personnel and funds.[54]

Randolph's committee recommended that Truman appoint a commission consisting of representatives from the Departments of Justice, War, Navy, State, Treasury, and the Civil Service Commission to "make a thorough study of existing laws and the adequacy of existing legislation . . . standards, procedures, techniques, needed funds and personnel necessary" to uncover disloyal employees or federal job applicants and to report their recommendations by the beginning of the 80th Congress in January 1947.[55]

230   CHAPTER 5

Not long after Randolph's committee report had been filed, Congress adjourned for the summer recess and fall campaigning for the midterm elections. Randolph's call to Truman was a reminder that the president was running out of time. Because of John Rankin's success in making HUAC permanent, further investigations by HUAC of alleged ties to Soviet agents or fronts among federal employees was inevitable. If Truman didn't act before HUAC began its own witch hunt, the administration would be on the defensive on the government employee loyalty issue. Three weeks after the GOP landslide win in the 1946 election, Truman issued Executive Order 9806, creating the very interdepartmental commission Randolph's committee had recommended.[56] He gave it until February 1947 to provide its findings and recommendations.

Having spent more than two months studying the issue, the five commissioners conceded that "the employment of disloyal or subversive persons represents more than a speculative threat" but they were "unable, based on the facts presented . . . to state with any degree of certainty how far reaching that threat is."[57] The Commission acknowledged that "the vast majority of federal employees are loyal" but viewed the potential threat of ideologically or financially motivated disloyal federal workers as such a threat as requiring "continuous screening, scrutiny and surveillance of present and prospective employees."[58]

The core commission proposal involved the creation of a Loyalty Review Board (LRB) within the Civil Service Commission (CSC), with clones of the Board to be established in each federal department or agency and responsible for sending their disloyalty investigation results to the main CSC LRB for final action. All agencies and departments were directed to send to the FBI the names of federal employee on the rolls for name checks for any derogatory information, which was to be forwarded to the CSC LRB for potential action.

Employees accused of disloyalty and recommended for dismissal could request an administrative hearing before the CSC LRB, but unlike a civil court proceeding, the process lacked a true adversarial component; the accused were denied documentary discovery or the ability to confront those who had made allegations of disloyalty against them. Worse, one of the acceptable channels of information for loyalty review boards to rely on was none other than HUAC, a committee well known for accepting hearsay or otherwise unverified claims of disloyalty or subversive associations.

After the Commission delivered its report to Truman in March 1947, he accepted its findings and codified them in Executive Order 9835 on

"ONE NATION DIVIDED" 231

March 21, 1947.[59] For the balance of Truman's presidency, opposition to the loyalty program would become a rallying point for many Americans. Not surprisingly, organized labor—which represented many federal workers— reacted with outrage.

Among the first to object was Abram Flaxer, president of the United Public Workers of America, who wrote Truman in early April 1947 that EO 9835 laid "the basis for nationwide intimidation without redress" for federal workers and asked that the EO be revoked.[60] CIO President Phil Murray weighed in on April 14, assailing the lack of "clear guarantees of due process" and expressing his alarm "at the prospect that any organization of citizens, gathered together to express their ideas on matters of mutual interest, may be declared 'subversive' without any specification, definition or limitation of the meaning of that term."[61]

Truman's response on April 15 asserted that Murray was "unduly alarmed about the Order. The Order was most carefully drawn with the idea in view that the Civil Rights of none would be infringed upon and its administration will be carried out in that spirit. Of course, I am glad to have your views on it."[62]

In Congress a running battle had been underway since the beginning of 1946 between two Senate Democrats over the issue of federal employee loyalty. On one side was Senator Sheridan Downey (D-CA), who advocated for legislation authorizing judicial review of CSC loyalty-related dismissal decisions.[63] On the other side was Senator Pat McCarran (D-NV), who in July 1946 pushed through a rider to the State Department appropriations bill that gave plenary powers to the Secretary of State to

> in his absolute discretion, on or before June 30, 1947, terminate the employment of any officer or employee of the Department of State or of the Foreign Service of the United States whenever he shall deem such termination necessary or advisable in the interests of the United States, but such termination shall not affect the right of such officer or employee to seek or accept employment in any other department or agency of the Government if declared eligible by the United States Civil Service Commission.[64]

The legislation was rife for abuse and obliterated the concept of due process, but Truman signed it anyway. State Department employees soon paid the price.

On June 27, 1947, State Department officials announced that ten employees had been fired over disloyalty allegations utilizing the McCarran rider authority, with Secretary of State George Marshall having personally reviewed some of the cases. Another seventy State employees had also been fired earlier in the year for alleged disloyalty, though without invoking the McCarran rider provision.[65]

The uproar in the press and among many on Capitol Hill led Marshall to announce on July 9 that he was moving forward with the creation of a department-level loyalty review board per EO 9835, insisting "we are not engaged in a witch hunt and I will not permit unfounded charges based on prejudice to force our hand."[66]

But as *Washington Evening Star* reporter Garnett Horner noted in his story, Marshall "said at the same time that he had adopted for his guidance the policy of dismissing any employee against whom there is enough evidence to create a decided suspicion of disloyalty, pointing out that conclusive evidence rarely could be developed."[67]

In August syndicated columnists Joe and Stewart Alsop had taken up the case of "The Ten" (as they called them). The duo noted that one of the dismissed State employees simply admitted to having "attended a few left-wing meetings in his college days, out of curiosity" while another "was the friend of a friend of a man who had fought with the Loyalists in the Spanish Civil war." The Alsop brothers' view was that "certain subordinate officials of the State Department, harking to congressional cries for communist blood, decided that a respectable number of heads must be served up on a platter," which resulted in "the harshest kind of injustice" on those affected and that struck "very close to the heart of American civil liberties."[68] But it was not just "certain subordinate officials" at Foggy Bottom who targeted the Ten (and subsequently others) for termination on the basis of alleged associations. It was the Secretary of State himself.

By early October, Marshall's standard of a "decided suspicion of disloyalty" was being applied to those who had alleged "habitual or close association" with individuals simply "believed to be" communists—not simply those accused of actually engaging in espionage on behalf of the Soviets.[69] For former First Lady and Democratic Party political powerhouse Eleanor Roosevelt, it was all too much.

Writing to Truman on November 13, Roosevelt told her late husband's successor that, "I feel we have capitulated to our fear of Communism, and instead of fighting to improve Democracy, we are doing what the Soviets would do in trying to repress anything which we are afraid might not command public support, in order to insure acceptance of our own actions." Her thanks to Truman for appointing her to the newly created United Nations Human Rights Commission likely took little of the sting out of her critique of his civil liberties failures on the loyalty issue.[70] The next day, Truman issued a press release announcing the CSC LRB had begun operations.[71]

In his official statement on the program, Truman claimed he didn't want federal employees "to fear they are the objects of any 'witch hunt.' They are not being spied upon; they are not being restricted in their activities . . . Rumor, gossip, or suspicion will not be sufficient to lead to the dismissal of an employee for disloyalty."[72]

The president's claims were, of course, false. Federal employees *were* being spied upon by Hoover's agents as well as their counterparts in the War and Navy departments. Innuendo and false allegations had already led to the termination of a number of State employees, and more would meet the same fate in the years ahead.

Decades later, close Truman advisor and consummate Washington insider Clark Clifford would admit to journalist Carl Bernstein that the allegations of communists in the federal workforce "was a political problem" since "Truman was going to run in '48" for reelection. Clifford went even further, telling Bernstein that "the President didn't attach fundamental importance to the so-called Communist scare. He thought it was a lot of baloney. But political pressures were such that he had to recognize it."[73]

The federal employee loyalty program was the primary focus of EO 9835, but another key provision would have even more far-reaching implications for American society at large.

Part V, Section 2 of the order stated that "Activities and associations of an applicant or employees" could be considered as grounds for denial of employment or dismissal from government service, including

> Membership in, affiliation with or sympathetic association with any foreign or domestic organization, association, movement, group or combination of persons, designated by the Attorney General as totalitarian, fascist, communist, or subversive, or as having adopted a policy of advocating or approving the commission of acts of force or violence to deny persons their rights under the Constitution of the United States, or as seeking to alter the form of government of the United States by unconstitutional means.[74]

The 1939 Hatch Act had been the first attempt to create a de facto government-run enemies list of civil society organizations by targeting federal employees alleged or proven to have been members of or associated with communist, fascist, or other so-called subversive organizations. Subsequent wartime appropriations bills had directed the attorney general to continue the practice.[75] Truman's EO 9835 now effectively made permanent and formalized the policy. It would become known as the Attorney General's List of Subversive Organizations (AGLOSO).

If Truman and his advisors thought they had politically inoculated themselves on the loyalty issue, they were mistaken.

HUAC RAMPAGES

On December 4 Attorney General Tom Clark released to the press the names of eighty organizations and eleven schools deemed Soviet fronts or otherwise subversive. Not surprisingly, the CP USA was on the list, as was the Ku Klux Klan. Recognized civil rights organizations such as the Civil Rights Congress and the National Negro Congress were also listed among others.[76] Also listed were groups that no longer existed, including the German American Bund.

The next day, HUAC Chairman J. Parnell Thomas (R-NJ) proclaimed, "If the Attorney General can't do any better than this, the Committee on Un-American Activities will supply a list that will just put his to shame. There are hundreds of Communist and Communist-front organizations alone."[77]

Indeed, all during 1947 as the administration slowly formulated its response to the loyalty controversy surrounding the federal work force, HUAC had been busy hunting for communists in multiple sectors of American society.

It started in earnest with a February 1947 hearing on alleged communist infiltration or control of labor unions. One of the witnesses, Floyd Lucia, spoke about his former union, Local 248 of the United Automobile Workers, at the Allis-Chalmers plant in West Allis, Wisconsin. The Allis-Chalmers plant had been involved with various military production projects before and during the war, including the Manhattan Project, and had been the scene of multiple strikes over the years—strikes HUAC believed were communist inspired or even led.

The three union workers who appeared before the committee on February 27 gave accounts that seemingly validated the committee's contention, with Floyd Lucia telling new HUAC member Rep. Richard Nixon (R-CA) that he and other rank-and-file union members feared for their safety if they went against the union leadership, which they charged was being run by communists. Nixon's questioning was, in contrast to most other HUAC members, precise and cogent:

"ONE NATION DIVIDED" 235

NIXON: Policemen are beaten, company representatives are beaten, but I think the committee is interested also in what would happen to the rank-and-file members of the same union in the event they cross their leaders.

LUCIA: We will know more about that after we get back to town. I imagine it will be pretty rough.

NIXON: Would you say, then, that the great majority of the members of the union who are not in the inner circle are afraid to come out and say anything against the leaders?

LUCIA: Emphatically, yes.

NIXON: Physically afraid?

LUCIA: Yes. They fear violence to themselves or their families.

NIXON: They fear violence to themselves or families?

LUCIA: Yes.

NIXON: That is all.[78]

It made for great headlines in national newspapers, and the fact that Lucia and hundreds of other workers had left UAW Local 248 in order to form their own union certainly buttressed the committee's case that Local 248 had been hijacked by Soviet sympathizers. But what Nixon and his fellow HUAC members failed to show was that any alleged communists among Local 248 members had actually passed along military secrets to known Soviet agents.

In March the committee went further, offering bills to actually outlaw the Communist Party of the United States and related alleged or actual communist organizations. They invited their favorite anticommunist, J. Edgar Hoover, to report on the threat and give his thoughts on the legislation.

Hoover began by noting that the FBI and HUAC had the same goal, "the protection of the internal security of this nation," and he lavished praise on HUAC for rendering "a distinct service" every time "it publicly reveals the diabolic machinations of sinister figures engaged in un-American activities."[79] Hoover professed concern about loosely labeling someone as a communist, arguing that the CP USA "capitalize upon ill-founded charges associating known honest progressive liberals with left-wing causes. I have always entertained the view that there are few appellations more degrading than 'Communist' and hence it should be reserved for those justly deserving the degradation."[80]

Given the number of times Hoover and his organization had falsely accused or insinuated that a given American or civil society organization was communist or a communist front, it was an amazing display of disingenuousness.

236   CHAPTER 5

Unfortunately for the committee, Hoover would not give HUAC Chairman J. Parnell Thomas and his colleagues what they most wanted: an endorsement of their bills to outlaw a political party. When asked directly by Rep. Richard Vail (R-IL) whether or not he supported the legislation, Hoover reminded Vail that "the question as to the desirability or the undesirability of legislation is strictly a function for the Attorney General." As a matter of Department of Justice policy, practice, and tradition, Hoover was right—the call was not his.

But Hoover was no ordinary federal bureaucrat; when he spoke on a matter, the entire country took note. He was also mindful of the need to stay in the good graces of both his nominal boss, the attorney general, and his biggest Capitol Hill fan club, HUAC. Hoover tried to let Vail and his colleagues down gently:

> I do think that before any such action is taken it ought to be given very, very serious consideration and study, because I would hate to see a group that does not deserve to be in the category of martyrs have the self-pity that they would at once invoke if they were made martyrs, by some restrictive legislation that might later be declared unconstitutional. . . . I think the activity of this committee to expose and to bring out into the spotlight the activity of these individuals can do far more good, at least at the present time, than any very restrictive legislation. I wouldn't want to say that I am unalterably opposed to it, but I have my grave doubts as to its wisdom.[81]

The subsequent *Washington Evening Star* story headline summed up the effect of Hoover's testimony: "House Unit to Press Red Probe, but Party Ban Seems Unlikely."[82]

Hoover did, however, help the committee pick its next target.

When asked by Nixon whether "there is any one area which should deserve the attention of this committee more than [any] other area?" Hoover said no but offered the suggestion "that this committee would approach the inquiry into those field which mold public opinion and in which Communists have been successful in effecting infiltration, such as the radio, the motion pictures."[83]

It was all the encouragement the committee needed, as the day after Hoover testified, it was Motion Picture Association of America (MPAA) President Eric Johnston's turn in the witness chair.

In his opening statement, Johnston encouraged Congress to "outline a policy definitely fixing the status of Communists and the Communist Party in the United States" but made clear he was "not concerned about the legitimate political activities of Communists or any other minority group. . . . The Socialists advocate a form of economic collectivism, but no one accuses them of disloyalty or conspiracy. They are loyal Americans who operate within the framework of our constitutional system."[84]

Johnston had either forgotten or chose to ignore the persecution of Socialist presidential candidate Eugene V. Debs.

The MPAA chief did draw a distinction between speech and action, much as Roger Baldwin of the ACLU had done before the notorious Fish Committee in 1930. "Conspiratorial activities do not constitute legitimate political activities and they should not be tolerated under that guise," Johnston said. "There is no constitutional immunity for sedition, subversion, or treason."[85]

But he offered a seemingly full-throated, eloquent defense of the First Amendment, telling Nixon, Rankin, and the rest:

> I would rather have the Communists on the ballot than risk the danger of undermining the right of franchise. I'd prefer to extend the Communists every right to propagate their beliefs by means of the written or spoken word than to risk the danger of undermining the right of free speech. The Bill of Rights is not selective. It is not to be extended or withdrawn by whim, caprice, or arbitrary choice. It is a sacred part of the fundamental law of the land. It expresses the very essence of American belief.[86]

And yet, Johnston did not believe the Constitution's guarantee of freedom of association extended to communists.

Directly referencing Truman's loyalty program EO as model for the private sector, Johnston said of communists, "They should not be allowed, by law, to hold office in a corporation, a cooperative, or a union where they are in position to pursue their disruptive tactics. They have no loyalties to these associations just as they have no loyalty to America."[87]

The very entities that Johnston wanted to keep communists out of were entities that were directly engaged in the political process—specifically political speech and action—that Johnston claimed he wanted to protect. It was form of political pretzel logic.

HUAC VERSUS HOLLYWOOD

In May Thomas and his HUAC colleague Rep. John McDowell (R-PA) made the trip to Hollywood to conduct executive session (i.e., secret) interviews and hearings with entertainment industry figures who were sympathetic to the committee's position and were prepared to "name names."[88] Thomas, Rankin, Nixon, and other HUAC members were especially focused on what Nixon, in the March hearing, had termed the threat of Hollywood communist screenwriters using "their positions in some subtle manner to affect the film or affect a script" by injecting the communist "party line" into films, plays, and so forth.[89] Thomas and McDowell got exactly what they were looking for during their trip: a lengthy list of alleged communists in the Screen Writers Guild (SWG) and elsewhere in the entertainment industry, courtesy of some of their colleagues.

Despite the interviews and hearings allegedly being secret, Thomas and his cohorts let many details leak, including a list of films allegedly suffused with communist propaganda. The left-leaning press responded with derision, the Montana-based *The People's Voice* editorializing about "the movies Gauleiter Thomas . . . would have you shun."[90] The term "Gauleiter" was a reference to a Nazi political officer in charge of a conquered territory or jurisdiction. Among the films allegedly conveying Soviet propaganda was the Academy Award, Golden Globe, and British Academy of Film and Television Arts (BAFTA) winner *The Best Years of Our Lives*.

After the two HUAC members left town, key senior HUAC staffers stayed in Los Angeles, conducting a pressure campaign against the studios to fire screenwriters with alleged communist connections or sympathies, threatening to subpoena studio officials who refused to cave to the pressure.[91]

The month after Thomas and McDowell left Hollywood, the MPAA's Johnston—who already supported a legislative bar on alleged or actual communists holding leadership positions in organizations like the SWG— tried to convince movie studio executives to go further. Johnston proposed that the studios bar "proven Communists" from holding jobs that touched in any way on film content. The studio heads refused to have their hiring and firing decisions dictated by anybody—Johnston, HUAC, the press, or others.[92]

Indeed, in late June Congress passed, over Truman's veto, legislation requiring a de facto loyalty affidavit of officers in any union. The bill, called the Labor Management Relations Act (P.L. 80–101), was better known as the Taft–Hartley Act after its two lead sponsors—Senator Robert A. Taft (R-OH) and Representative Fred Hartley, Jr. (R-NJ).

The provision in question prohibited any investigation of a union claim of unfair labor practices unless there was one on file with the National Labor Relations Board:

an affidavit executed contemporaneously or within the preceding twelve month period by each officer of such labor organization and the officers of any national or international labor organization of which it is an affiliate or constituent unit that he is not a member of the Communist Party or affiliated with such party, and that he does not believe in, and is not a member of or supports any organization that believes in or teaches, the overthrow of the United States Government by force or by any illegal or unconstitutional methods.[93]

While the bill's scope encompassed all of labor, its timing had clear ramifications for the Screen Writers Guild and related entertainment industry unions who employed people in leadership positions who were targets of HUAC. The long congressional summer recess simply postponed the inevitable confrontation.

Thomas had wanted the hearings on communists in Hollywood to start before the end of September, but Nixon and Rep. Karl Mundt (R-SD) were on a European congressional delegation trip, and other committee members were also unavailable, so the hearings were rescheduled to begin on October 20. The witness list was a veritable who's who of the entertainment industry at the time: Charlie Chaplin, Ronald Reagan, Walt Disney, Robert Taylor, Louis Mayer, Sam Goldwyn, Jack Warner, Eric Johnston, and a number of prominent screenwriters who, if not household names before the hearings, were afterward.[94]

Thomas's hearing playbook and strategy were little different than that of his predecessor, Martin Dies: force the witnesses to either admit their guilt by confirming their subversive (in this case, communist) connections or status, or find them in contempt should they refuse to answer questions or otherwise behave in ways Thomas deemed uncooperative.

Like every single HUAC or Dies Committee hearing since 1938, the October 1947 entertainment industry hearings were not designed to find facts but to confirm the committee's biases; sharpen the "us vs. them" dynamic between those Americans deemed loyal and those deemed not; and effectively coerce Hollywood studio executives into creating a private sector equivalent to the federal employee loyalty program. As with all HUAC productions, this too would be a political show trial, capitalizing on more than six months' worth of public and private attacks and threats aimed not just at the screenwriters, producers, directors, and actors but at their employers— the studio heads. The HUAC approach succeeded, almost certainly beyond Thomas's wildest expectations.

To be sure, most of the committee's targets *were* either communists, sympathetic to extreme leftist causes, or actively involved in such causes. Most had been supporters of the 1930s-era Popular Front, and one, screenwriter Alvah Bessie, had served with the Abraham Lincoln Brigade alongside the Loyalists in during the Spanish Civil War.[95] But HUAC had no evidence any of the nearly four dozen people they had subpoenaed to appear before the committee were KGB or GRU (Soviet military intelligence) assets, or that any of them had taken any action to try to overthrow the US government by force. Simply stated, HUAC was going after these individuals strictly because of their disfavored political beliefs and activities, past and present. And early on the first day of hearings, they got help from Warner Brothers Vice President Jack Warner.

In his prepared statement, Warner railed that "Ideological termites have burrowed into many American industries" but assured the committee that the studio "will be happy to subscribe generously to a pest removal fund . . . to ship to Russia the people who don't like our American system of government and prefer the communistic system to ours."[96]

Warner reaffirmed what he had told the committee in secret in Los Angeles in May, that he had not rehired a number of writers and others he believed to be communists "or read in the papers" that a given person was allegedly a communist.[97] Warner's testimony showed HUAC's coercive tactics and political pressure had made the charge of communist sympathies enough to render someone unemployable in Hollywood.

Over the next week and one by one, the screenwriters fingered as communists were called before the committee. Every time one of the accused tried to read a prepared statement, they were prevented from doing so by Thomas—a complete departure from how pro-HUAC witnesses had been treated and a total break with normal House custom, courtesy, and decorum.

Screenwriter John Howard Lawson, who like the others refused to confirm or deny his political affiliation or beliefs, became so enraged at Thomas's refusal to let him give anything more than "yes" or "no" answers to questions that he began shouting over Thomas as he banged his gavel. After Lawson again refused to discuss his political beliefs or affiliations, Thomas again pounded his gavel and declared "Excuse the witness," to which Lawson replied, "I have written Americanism for many years, and I shall continue to fight for the Bill of Rights, which you are trying to destroy."

At Thomas's direction, US Capitol Police forcibly ejected Lawson from the hearing room.[98] He was the first to be charged with contempt of Congress but was soon joined by nine of his colleagues who, although they did not engage in the kind of heated exchanges with Thomas as Lawson did, likewise refused to discuss their political affiliations or beliefs.

"ONE NATION DIVIDED" 241

In an unpublished letter in November 1947, "Hollywood Ten" screen-writer Lester Cole expressed his feelings by rewriting a key line from the Pledge of Allegiance: "I pledge allegiance to the Thomas-Rankin Commit-tee, and to the anti-democratic forces for which it fronts; one nation divided, with fear and insecurity for all."[99]

Over the next two-and-a-half years, the Hollywood Ten would lose their jobs and their subsequent contempt of Congress court cases, resulting in jail time for each. Some, such as legendary screenwriter Dalton Trumbo, only managed to work in films when friends in Hollywood fronted their material. Others never worked in the industry again.[100]

The chilling effect on speech was real, with one studio executive telling *New Yorker* writer Lillian Ross that when it came to reading new scripts, "I'm scared to death, and nobody can tell me it isn't because I'm afraid of being investigated."[101] The battle also ultimately extended beyond the entertain-ment industry to encompass radio and television broadcasting and the music sectors and involve more than HUAC's relative "old timers" like Thomas and Rankin. In the years after the Hollywood Ten episode, two of the commit-tee's newcomers, Nixon and Mundt, became key congressional players in the new Red Scare, and other established committees joined in the hunt for communists—real or imagined—inside and outside of government.

LOYALTY PROGRAM DISSIDENTS

Not everyone in the Truman administration embraced the loyalty program as promulgated in EO 9835. One political appointee at the Department of Interior was so appalled by its lack of due process protections for federal employees that he mounted a campaign to get the order changed. His name was Crowe Girard "Jebby" Davidson.

A Louisiana native with law degrees from Tulane and Yale, Davidson had served in FDR's administration at the Tennessee Valley Authority and later at the War Production Board.[102] He joined Interior as an assistant secretary in 1946 because Davidson was one of the few people the incoming Secretary of Interior, Julius Krug, knew at the department, based on Davidson's prior background in power generation issues.[103]

From its inception Truman's loyalty program order had rubbed Davidson the wrong way, and he was not the only one. Davidson's network of loyalty program dissidents included FCC Commissioner Clifford Durr, President's Council of Economic Advisors Vice Chairman Leon Keyserling, former Undersecretary of the Interior (and future Supreme Court Justice) Abe

242   CHAPTER 5

Fortas, and Commerce Department Solicitor Isaac N.P. Stokes.[104] Many, but not all, were part of Special Counsel to the President Clark Clifford's "Monday Night Group" that met weekly to strategize about how to move Truman's overall agenda forward while trying to correct policy decisions with which they disagreed.[105]

In the months immediately following the HUAC Hollywood Ten congressional show trial, Davidson became increasingly concerned about the number of federal employees who were being effectively smeared by the CSC's LRB and the FBI, which was charged with doing the actual investigations. Durr of the FCC had directly, and publicly, questioned the quality of FBI investigations in October, causing Hoover to direct that no further loyalty-related investigative reports be sent to the FCC.[106] In early December Indiana Republican Senator Homer Capehart's response was to call for Congress to investigate Durr for a "brazen effort" to "sabotage the Federal Bureau of Investigation."[107] The majority of FCC commissioners subsequently issued a statement of support for Hoover and the Bureau, and as a result the flow of unsubstantiated allegations of communist connections among FCC employees or license applicants resumed.[108]

Less than two weeks after the Capehart–Durr episode, Davidson decided to make his own public statement on the consequences of EO 9835 for federal employees at a panel discussion sponsored by the Radio Press Section of the American Veterans Committee. Sharing the stage with Davidson was FBI Assistant Director Louis Nichols.[109] As Davidson would later recount for Jerry Hess of the Truman Presidential Library:

> The FBI was not happy about my public speeches, and I had debated one of their assistant directors on this issue. I remember I was horrified when he said during this debate that one of the criteria the FBI used in a loyalty investigation was whether the Government employee associated with a person of a different color. Just because one was walking down the street with a black was enough to put this whole machinery of an FBI investigation into gear to determine whether he was a subversive. I said that if they had any respect for the Bill of Rights of our Constitution such a criterion should be abandoned immediately.[110]

Just before the end of 1947, Davidson took the case for reform directly to Clifford, hoping Truman's confidant could persuade the president to change course on the loyalty program.

Davidson argued that the existing program's due process–free nature was stifling federal employees' "imagination, ingenuity and independent judgment" and thus harming the "efficiency and effectiveness" of the government overall. Conceding that "eliminating from government service individuals who are disloyal" was necessary, Davidson told Clark that it could be done "without sacrificing the basic civil rights of government employees and without creating an atmosphere of fear and intimidation that will undermine the effectiveness of the Government as a dynamic, progressive institution." If the FBI could get a 96 percent conviction rate (as it had in criminal cases in 1946) using constitutional standards for due process, Davidson maintained, "I see no reason why the FBI cannot do the same in loyalty cases."[111]

Hoover subsequently surreptitiously sought a copy of Davidson's remarks to the American Veterans Committee, prompting Davis to send a copy to Hoover unsolicited.

"I have learned that a member of your staff has been seeking elsewhere to obtain a copy of the statement. . . . In view of your apparent desire to obtain a copy," Davidson wrote Hoover, "I am transmitting one herewith."[112]

Decades later, Davidson would tell the Truman Presidential Library's Benedict Zobrist that he viewed Hoover's inquiry as a clear indicator that he himself was now effectively on the FBI director's personal enemies list and likely a surveillance target.

Commenting on the fallout from his public confrontation over EO 9835 with Hoover's deputy Louis Nichols in December 1947, Davidson told Zobrist:

> It is interesting to note the flurry of activity by the F.B.I. following this debate, and J. Edgar Hoover himself seemed to take a particular interest in my loyalty since I had the audacity to criticize the F.B.I. I have always felt that the F.B.I. may have been responsible for the leak of the letter to Clark Clifford, hoping that the repercussions would be such that I would be fired. (See the editorial in the *Times Herald* and the *Evening Star*.)[113]

As he learned years later by filing a Freedom of Information Act (FOIA) request with the FBI, he was right about being a Hoover target.

"I obtained the files covering the investigation of my loyalty by the FBI under the Freedom of Information Act," he wrote Zobrist, "and although there are numerous names and passages blocked out, it makes interesting reading and causes one to wonder why so much money is spent on exercises of this kind."[114]

Davidson spent nearly all of 1948 lobbying Clark, and subsequently CSC Chairman Seth Richardson, to modify the loyalty program to ensure that those investigated and cleared got notice of the fact not more than sixty days after their case was closed, and that the Bureau should be required to

244   CHAPTER 5

recontact all witnesses interviewed in cleared cases that the subjects had in fact been cleared. Davidson eventually won enactment of the first change on October 15, 1948, with Richardson informing him by letter that "I see no reason why a sixty-day period should not be established, after which in the absence of notification to the contrary, the employee may be notified, as you suggest in your letter."[115]

Richardson tried to convince Hoover to have his agents notify witnesses that had accused an employee of disloyalty who was subsequently cleared be notified of the fact, as a way to further dispel suspicion, but Hoover refused.[116]

Despite Hoover's intransigence Davidson's allies recognized the significance of his accomplishment in the face of enormous resistance and at great personal and professional peril to himself. Writing from his post at the White House, Leon Keyserling told Davidson on November 3:

> Among the higher officials of the Government, so far as I know, you have been practically alone in your courageous and persistent efforts to inject the common principles of fair play into the loyalty procedure. The results of yesterday should convince more people of the feasibility of being guided by the light of what is right.[117]

Clifford Durr, who had ultimately resigned from the FCC in protest over the loyalty program, wrote Davidson on November 4 that Truman's reelection and imminent Democratic control of Congress might make this "a good time to make a pitch in the direction of the abandonment of the whole loyalty program."[118] Durr also asserted that "From the standpoint of clearing out dangerous people it hasn't worked and it can't work. . . . The sum total of the program to date has been to hurt and terrorize a lot of people to no good purpose."[119]

Davidson no doubt agreed with Durr, but Truman's upset win over Republican Thomas Dewey in the presidential contest, which also returned the House and Senate to Democratic control, had come in no small part because he had maintained a relatively hard line on the Soviet threat, including standing by EO 9835. As Clark Clifford noted in his memoir:

> After the 1948 election, he [Truman] indicated to me his growing dissatisfaction with both Hoover and the developing atmosphere. Never once, though, did he indicate that he thought the Loyalty Program had either contributed to the problem or was a mistake; in his eyes, the program had been designed to prevent the excesses which

"ONE NATION DIVIDED" 245

were taking place, and would not have become a problem if Hoover had not perverted it. He felt that without the Loyalty Program, the political pressures would have been much greater, and more difficult to resist.[120]

Having invested himself so politically and publicly in the program, Truman was not about to abandon it.

Truman's posture was also driven by an attack that came from his political left flank prior to and during the 1948 election in the form of former Democratic vice president and ex-Truman Commerce Secretary, Henry Wallace. As he had with Ed Pritchard, Tom Corcoran, and Harold Ickes, the president and his senior White House aide, Harry Vaughn, availed themselves of J. Edgar Hoover's services in thwarting Wallace's political threat.

Between September 12, 1947, and at least as late as January 27, 1948, Hoover sent over a dozen reports, some to Allen but most to Vaughn.[121] Throughout the same period and well into the fall of 1948, FBI field offices were forwarding to Hoover press clips, informant gossip, and related material on Wallace, his campaign, or groups connected to him.[122] On May 20, 1948, Attorney General Tom Clark asked Hoover to determine the source of some 20,000 pro-Wallace flyers being distributed in New York City through FBI informants but that "we should be most discreet as this inquiry should not get back to Wallace."[123]

Wallace was not wanted for any federal crime. He was a presidential candidate running a legitimate, lawful political campaign. Some media outlets claimed—without any hard evidence—that the leadership of Wallace's new political party, the Progressive Party, was dominated by communists or communist sympathizers.[124] The FBI itself, despite putting Wallace under an investigative microscope since at least as early as 1943, had developed no evidence that Wallace was a communist.[125] The surveillance of him and his supporters was based on no legal predicate, only a political one. And it did not end with the 1948 election.

NIXON AND MUNDT TARGET CP USA

One reason key anti-Soviet hardliners like Nixon and Mundt had coasted to reelection was their continued exploitation of the loyalty issue, the public hunt for those deemed subversive, and related Red Scare tactics. The first vehicle they created to achieve the goal was a series of HUAC hearings in February 1948 to examine potential additional legislation to meet the

246   CHAPTER 5

alleged communist and/or subversive threat. As Nixon chaired HUAC's legislative subcommittee, the hearings put him in the limelight.

His fellow HUAC colleague Karl Mundt was the lead witness and author of a bill to require all CP USA and related organizations to register with the attorney general. Mundt said his purpose in offering the bill was to "devise a legislative formula whereby Congress can enact a law which will strip the dark mantle of secrecy from the nefarious activities of Communists in this country."[126] When another HUAC colleague, Illinois's Richard Vail, asked Mundt why his bill didn't simply outlaw the Communist Party—as the American Legion, the Veterans of Foreign Wars (VFW), and other patriotic organizations had called for—Mundt argued that "if we simply make the party illegal they will continue their activities under some other name or through some other organization or individually."[127]

Mundt's proposal was designed to create a trap for American communists: register and be publicly identified, and thus politically neutralized, or fail to register and face prosecution. In essence, it was an anticommunist sibling of the 1940 anti-Nazi Foreign Agents Registration Act. It was also, by the standards of the day, the least controversial proposal before HUAC.

H.R. 5821, offered by Rep. Gordon McDonough (R-CA), would have made "the practice of communism a treasonable act in the United States."[128] In his statement on the two bills, Attorney General Tom Clark gave HUAC members a refresher course in the First Amendment and due process, citing multiple prior and relatively recent Supreme Court decisions and the plain language of the Constitution itself, telling the committee that "an organized group, whether you call it political or not, could hardly be barred from the ballot without jeopardizing the constitutional guarantees of all other political groups and parties."[129]

Over the seven days of hearings in February, Nixon and his fellow HUAC members heard from dozens of witnesses regarding the bills, pro and con—including CP USA national committeeman Benjamin J. Davis, an African American city councilman from New York.[130] Davis's statement was generally long on CP USA rhetoric, and he wasted no opportunity citing Attorney General Clark's concerns about the bills.

The CP USA got a platform to denounce the legislation. But letting Davis testify was a political masterstroke by Nixon, who got extremely favorable publicity in the *New York Times* story on the hearings for his "fairness to witnesses" and from Arthur Garfield Hays of the ACLU for the opportunity to express his opposition to the bills "without earning personal ill will."[131]

By late April, HUAC had sidelined McDonough's "communism is treason" bill for a revamped and expanded version of Mundt's legislation, which

"ONE NATION DIVIDED" 247

also got a name change from the passive-sounding Communist-front Organization Registration Act to the more forceful sounding Subversive Activities Control Act of 1948.[132]

The bill criminalized any attempts "to establish in the United States a totalitarian dictatorship" under foreign control (something already covered under sedition statutes), stripped American citizenship for those who attempted to do it should they subsequently leave the United States, barred communists from US government employment (Truman's loyalty program EO 9835 already did this), denied passports to members of communist political organizations, required communist organizations to register with the attorney general (also covered by EO 9835), made it a crime for any individual to become or remain a member of an organization designated as communist by the attorney general, criminalized the sending of mail sponsored by communist organizations, and denied tax exempt status to the same.[133]

Hoover reported to Vaughn on May 8 that the Mundt–Nixon bill "has caused considerable consternation with the Communist Party-USA," with the CP USA DC office having dispatched an urgent message to affiliates and allies on May 3 that "opinion Mundt bill will be acted upon at end of this week or beginning of next week, serious threat of passage. Bill of Rights, Trade Unions, Third Party, and all Progressives seriously threatened and life of Party at stake."[134]

It was one prediction the CP USA got right.

On May 20 the House voted 319 to 58 for the Mundt–Nixon bill, sending it to the Senate. That same day, Senate Judiciary Chairman Alexander Wiley (R-WI) told the *Washington Evening Star* that there "certainly" would be hearings, but the controversy surrounding the bill in the Senate—including among Wiley's fellow Republicans—made its future uncertain.[135]

The bill also became a lightning rod issue in the contentious 1948 presidential campaign. On June 1 former Vice President Henry Wallace asked the leader of his presidential campaign in Washington state, former Rep. Jerry J. O'Connell, to head up a new national "Committee to Defeat the Mundt Bill" to try to kill the measure in the Senate.[136] Two months later, it was effectively sidelined by a spectacular series of events, starting with the July 20 federal grand jury indictments of 12 CP USA members on charges of conspiracy under the Smith Act to overthrow the government.[137] The fact that the Truman administration was able to bring charges against the CP USA members under existing law undermined the case for the Mundt–Nixon bill.

Another Associated Press (AP) story just one day later, however, would set in motion a series of events that would, before the summer was out, give

248   CHAPTER 5

HUAC, and especially Nixon, the committee's greatest public victory ever and ultimately paved the way for even more repressive legislation in the years ahead.

RICHARD NIXON:
CONGRESSIONAL SPY HUNTER

On July 21 the AP reported than an unidentified woman and former CP USA member had undergone a change of heart and contacted the FBI about an alleged large Soviet spy ring operating inside the US government.[138] The Senate Committee on Expenditures in the Executive Branch was the first committee to follow up on the news. On the afternoon of July 28 in a secret, closed session chaired by Senator Homer Ferguson (R-MI), it conducted the initial hearing with the woman in question: Elizabeth Terrill Bentley.

Over nearly two hours, she told a rapt committee audience about taking over a Soviet spy ring after her American-born Soviet agent and lover, Jacob Golos, died in November 1943. Bentley had dabbled in socialist organizations up to that point, but her foray in leading two Soviet front companies—one a tourist agency, the other a shipping concern—brought her into contact with multiple government officials in FDR's administration who had previously been recruited by Golos.

Among those she named as having passed government secrets along to her were Lauchlin Currie, a senior economist and diplomatic troubleshooter for FDR during the war; and Gregory Silvermaster, a former Farm Security Administration official and head of the American group of spies.[139] She had passed all of this information to the FBI in August 1945, yet only now were most House and Senate members learning of this particular spy ring. Three days later, she told her story in even greater detail in open session with HUAC. The effect was politically explosive.

The *Washington Evening Star*'s page-one headline read "High Officials Named in Spy Ring Probe" and listed not only Currie and Silvermaster but Assistant Treasury Secretary Harry Dexter White and William Remington of the Commerce Department as being Soviet agents, among others.[140] Currie, Silvermaster, and White all publicly denied the allegations even as they were subpoenaed to appear before the committee. In the interim, HUAC's staff director, Robert Stripling, decided to play a hunch that Bentley had only revealed one part of the Soviet spy network in America. He wanted to put former avowed communist Whittaker Chambers in the witness chair to see how much of Bentley's story he could confirm, and

"ONE NATION DIVIDED" 249

who else he might be able to name as alleged traitors.[141] Chambers did not disappoint.

Chambers had joined the CP USA in 1924 but left in 1938 after realizing that the Soviet Union was, in fact, a ruthless totalitarian dictatorship and not the utopian panacea it portrayed in its propaganda efforts. When he appeared before HUAC, he was senior editor at *Time* magazine and a vocal anticommunist.

Chambers confirmed Bentley's account of how the Soviets ran their undercover espionage operations, how they illegally obtained valid passports, and so on, as well as the fact that he had passed along that information to then-State Department official Adolph Berle in August 1939. He then named names for the committee, including White, Currie, and some others Bentley had not. The most prominent of those who Chambers accused of being a Soviet agent was former State Department official Alger Hiss, who by the time of the hearings was the chief executive at the Carnegie Endowment for International Peace.

Those two facts—Chambers's 1939 missive to Berle and the first-time public allegation that Hiss was a Soviet agent—are what Nixon zeroed in on in his questioning of Chambers:

MR. NIXON:	Mr. Chambers, were you informed of any action that was taken as a result of your report to the Government at that time?
MR. CHAMBERS:	No; I was not. I assumed that action would be taken right away which was, of course, rather naive of me; and it wasn't until a great deal later that I discovered apparently nothing had been done.
MR. NIXON:	It is significant, I think, that the report was made 2 days after the Stalin-Hitler pact at the time, in other words, when we could not say by any stretch of the imagination that the Russians were our allies; and yet apparently, no action was taken.[142]

Truman administration officials may not have known about Hiss, but Truman's senior-most aide had definitely known about the Silvermaster ring since at least November 8, 1945. On that date, Hoover had sent Vaughn a TOP SECRET three-page memo that named Silvermaster, Harry Dexter White, Lauchlin Currie, and ten other current or former federal officials as

250 CHAPTER 5

Soviet agents, based on a "highly confidential source" whose name Hoover did not include in the memo: Elizabeth Terrill Bentley.[143]

During the summer congressional hearings into Bentley's allegations, and later those of Chambers, the committee would call many witnesses. But Hoover was not one of them. Had he been called and asked about whether he had communicated Bentley's Silvermaster ring allegations to the White House, Hoover likely would have been forced to either admit that he had or declined to answer on the basis of related ongoing investigations, which would have triggered a further political uproar for Truman. Ferguson's document request was another potential political landmine.

Accordingly, Clark Clifford chaired an emergency, off-the-record interdepartmental meeting on August 4 to devise a response to Ferguson, the consensus of which was that Truman should refuse to turn over personnel records having to do with loyalty or related investigations.[144]

The next day, Truman issued a public statement effectively declaring Bentley's revelations old news, stating that Bentley's allegations "had long been known to the FBI" and "long since been presented to a Federal grand jury" which declined to indict anyone she named. Truman refused to release any loyalty or investigative records to any congressional committee, declaring the ongoing hearings as "serving no useful purpose" by "doing irreparable harm to certain persons, seriously impairing the morale of Federal employees, and undermining public confidence in the Government."[145] House and Senate members denounced Truman's action but had little recourse. Existing legal precedents regarding executive power, particularly in personnel matters, were clearly on his side. Ferguson, Nixon and their like-minded colleagues pushed on with the hearings.

The same day Truman issued his statement, Hiss appeared before HUAC. He not only categorically denied Chambers' allegations, but he also denied even knowing him. While Hiss did verbally fence with Nixon somewhat during the questioning, the *Washington Evening Star*'s Miriam Ottenberg noted that Hiss "answered questions promptly and showed every wish to cooperate" with the committee.[146]

At this point, it was simply the word of one man against another, and Nixon and the committee seemed on course to repeat a blunder that had cost both credibility during the late winter of 1948.

Earlier in the year, the committee had burned itself by falsely accusing National Bureau of Standards scientist Dr. Edward U. Condon of being a Soviet agent; the public backlash was severe when it came out HUAC had left out the fact that the FBI had found no evidence Condon was a spy.[147] It looked like a hit job, and Hiss was clearly trying to convince the public that he was simply HUAC's latest victim. He got his chance on August 25, when he and Chambers appeared together publicly before HUAC in a hearing that lasted over ten hours and that led Hiss to file a libel suit against Chambers.

The 1948 election season resulted in a lull in HUAC's public schedule of events, but the discovery phase of the Hiss libel suit against Chambers led the *Time* editor to turn over some, but not all, of the documentary evidence he had of Hiss's treason—classified government documents with Hiss's handwritten notes on many.[148] Chamber's lawyers had no choice but to turn the material over to the Justice Department, but one of his attorneys gave Nixon and Stripling a tip that they should further interview Chambers.

What Nixon needed was incontestable documentary evidence that Hiss was, in fact, a Soviet agent. While Chambers had been subpoenaed to *testify*, he had never been subpoenaed for *documents*. Stripling now corrected that oversight, and the investigators he dispatched to Chambers's house in Maryland were rewarded when the former Soviet spy handed over three rolls of microfilm of classified documents directly linking Hiss to the espionage ring. Nixon used his influence to ensure Chambers was not charged with perjury; Hiss was indicted for perjury on December 15.[149]

Nixon, who had claimed the Truman administration had covered up the entire espionage episode, was called before a federal grand jury and forced to admit he had no evidence to that effect and apologized.[150]

Even so, Nixon's success in proving Hiss was a spy solidified his reputation as a serious, successful congressional investigator, seemingly validated HUAC's reason for existing, and positioned Nixon for a Senate run in 1950—a place his colleague Karl Mundt had already reached, thanks in no small part to the political capital he gained from his Subversive Activities Control Act bill.

HOOVER'S MAN ON THE NSC: J. PATRICK COYNE

As the debate over Soviet subversion and espionage publicly raged during the spring and summer of 1948, inside the administration a directly related battle was being waged. Davidson's campaign for due process rights for those accused of disloyalty took place against the backdrop of a larger struggle over exactly how great the Soviet threat really was to America and how best to confront it. A key trigger for the evaluation was the passage of the National Security Act in July 1947.[151]

Enacted based on the lessons learned prior to and during World War II, the law was meant to centralize the national security command and control

252   CHAPTER 5

functions of the government, and specifically the armed forces, through the creation of a White House–based policy coordinating body known as the National Security Council; establishment of the position of Secretary of Defense with line-of-control authority over all military forces; and the transition of earlier intelligence and covert action bodies such as the Office of Strategic Services and the Office of the Coordinator of Information into a unified Central Intelligence Agency.[152]

The legislation and the institutions it created were, by definition, *outward* facing—designed to deal with external military threats to the United States, its allies and interests overseas. But by the time the legislation was enacted, the major debate being fueled by Mundt, Nixon, Thomas, Rankin, Ferguson, and others in Congress and by conservative media outlets and commentators was about the *internal* threat being created by a foreign actor—Soviet Russia. In many respects, it was a replay of the kinds of debates that took place in the late 1930s and early 1940s regarding Nazi and Imperial Japanese efforts to subvert the United States internally through American-based agents or proxies. By the early summer of 1948, the NSC was tackling the problem via a confidential 36-page report on "The Internal Security of the United States" prepared by Hoover deputy and FBI Internal Security Division Director J. Patrick Coyne.[153]

Declaring "World-wide Communism" to be "a far greater threat to our existence than any other,"[154] Coyne spent much of the report describing the size, ideology, and actions of the CP USA and its Soviet benefactor. Communism was "organized deception and violence directed specifically at the United States" whose destruction was essential to Moscow's plans for "the conquest and enslavement of the world."[155]

In Coyne's view, the US national security establishment was not properly configured and coordinated to blunt the threat. Various internal security functions and activities were spread among six different cabinet-level departments and several additional independent boards, commissions, or interdepartmental committees. No single person or entity was in charge of coordinating or otherwise managing the internal security effort.[156] Among Coyne's recommendations was the creation of a special assistant to the NSC for internal security to solve that problem.[157] One of Coyne's ideas was demonstrably unconstitutional:

> It is, therefore, an absolute necessity that a detailed program be worked out, including preparation of policies and procedures to be followed with regard to the arrest, detention, parole, and release of United States citizens who are deemed to constitute a danger in time of emergency

to the internal security of this country. Communists, Trotskyites, and other subversives should be included in the aforementioned category.[158]

In its 1944 *ex parte Endo* decision, the Supreme Court had made it clear that "When the power to detain is derived from the power to protect the war effort against espionage and sabotage, detention which has no relationship to that objective is unauthorized."[159] For Coyne, simply being a American communist was enough to warrant detention without trial in the event of an unspecified national emergency, even in the absence of evidence of involvement in espionage, sabotage, or violation of any other federal law.

The NSC approved his report and recommendations on August 8, and as it had prior to and during World War II, the FBI began compiling lists of individuals to be arrested and detained in the event of a national emergency. By November Coyne would report to the NSC that the attorney general and FBI had developed the new wartime detention program, including drafts of appropriate "proclamations, and joint Congressional Resolutions, as well as the necessary Executive Orders" and the "this plan has been cleared on the Cabinet level."[160]

Coyne by now was the NSC special assistant for internal security—the very post he said should be created. Hoover got something critical as well: a trusted former FBI official deep inside the Truman administration.

It was another bureaucratic victory for Hoover, ensuring the Bureau's access to Truman administration deliberations on security issues and buttressing Hoover's power in internal battles over intelligence policy. And it came at a critical time, as publicly Hoover was taking a beating over an espionage case that had become a national embarrassment for the FBI and the administration.

FBI WIRETAPPING: THE COPLON FIASCO

FDR's May 1940 authorization to then-Attorney General Robert Jackson to wiretap in national security cases, if necessary, was something that clearly violated the Supreme Court's decision in the *Nardone* case. For years Hoover had gotten away with it because it was among the best kept secrets in Washington—and also because Hoover and the Justice Department had never been forced to try to make an espionage case with wiretap evidence in court. That changed when one of the department's own employees was discovered to be a Soviet agent.

Barnard College graduate Judith Coplon had been hired by Justice in 1944 despite having known CP USA affiliations.[161] By 1945 Coplon had been recruited by Soviet intelligence and was supplying classified information to her handlers. She might have been able to go on spying for the Soviets for many years were it not for the limited but critical success of an Army Signal Intelligence Service (SIS) codebreaking operation codenamed VENONA, started in 1943. It was the Army's SIS VENONA team that tipped off the FBI that the Justice Department had one or more Soviet moles in their midst.

On Christmas Eve 1948 the FBI's Washington Field Office (WFO) notified Hoover that "a series of messages dated July 20, 1944 to January 8, 1945" had been received at Justice that indicated that a person codenamed "Sima" had, on December 31, 1944, "been transferred to the Foreign Agents Registration Section" of Justice. WFO, via Justice personnel records checks, led the agents to conclude that "Sima is without doubt identical with Judith Coplon" of the FARA Section of Justice.[162]

It took no convincing by Hoover to get Attorney General Tom Clark not only to authorize wiretaps on any phone used by Coplon, but to conduct physical surveillance to see if they could catch her with a Soviet courier or even her handler.[163] The FBI's New York field office's agents followed her and her suspected handler, Valentin Gubitchev, around the city the afternoon of March 4 and arrested her for trying to pass FBI reports on Soviet espionage activity in America to Gubitchev.[164] A federal grand jury returned a two-count indictment against Coplon on March 16. It seemed the FBI had a sure winner of a case.

They didn't.

In the subsequent trials and appeals that played out over the next year, Hoover fought efforts by the judges and Coplon's lawyers to force the FBI to produce originals of the 28 reports on Soviet espionage efforts she had purloined and intended to pass to Gubitchev.[165] The even larger problem for the Bureau was the wiretaps themselves, which clearly flew in the face of the *Nardone* decision. There was also evidence that Bureau wiretaps had collected conversations between Coplon and her attorney—a flagrant Sixth Amendment violation.[166] In the midst of Coplon's first trial, former FCC Commissioner Clifford Durr, now the president of the National Lawyers Guild (NLG), wrote to Truman on June 20 to protest the outrages Hoover and his agents had perpetrated.

Durr characterized the revelations as revealing "a menacing situation, one fraught with the gravest danger to political freedom in America" involving "practices and policies of the FBI that strike at the very roots of our civil liberties."[167] Further arguing that the "growing volume of dossiers on Americans suspected of no criminal activity marks a dangerous tendency toward

"ONE NATION DIVIDED" 255

a police state," Durr blasted the Bureau's practice of prying "into the family and social lives of American citizens."[168]

After going through a catalogue of FBI abuses revealed thus far in the Coplon case, Durr ended his letter by calling on Truman "to appoint a Committee of outstanding citizens, including representatives of the national bar associations and civil liberties organizations, to undertake a comprehensive investigation into the operations and methods of the Federal Bureau of Investigation."[169]

Truman replied on June 23 that he would take Durr's suggestion "under consideration."[170]

What Durr did not know was that the FBI had been monitoring the NLG itself since at least 1940, and that as of May 1941, the FBI's WFO had obtained detailed information on the "officers, members, minutes, conventions, and miscellaneous correspondence of Guild" through "a highly confidential source."[171] The material ran to more than 800 pages and could only have been supplied by an NLG source in the Guild, a fact that would not be revealed for nearly four decades.

That source is likely the "confidential source" Hoover referenced in a January 14, 1950, letter to Vaughn, with the claim that the Guild "was preparing a report attacking the Administration, and the Department of Justice in particular, on the basis of the reports of this Bureau" that had come out in the 1949 Coplon trial. Hoover's source went on to claim that NLG Executive Secretary Robert Silberstein was seeking a meeting with Truman prior to the NLG report critical of the FBI, but if Truman declined to meet, Silberstein would hold "a press conference . . . on January 20, 1950, at which time the National Lawyers Guild report will be released."[172]

Hoover's information was accurate. Truman declined to meet with NLG representatives, and on January 19, Durr sent another letter to Truman, with the final version of their report attacking the FBI, as a courtesy before the Guild made the report public.[173] With the second Coplon trial data in hand, Durr told Truman that the latest revelations:

> demonstrate beyond any reasonable doubt extensive illegal practices by the FBI . . . that the FBI has long been conducting a vast "loyalty" program of compiling "dossiers" or making investigations of private persons who are not government employees or applicants for government employment. . . . The disclosures issuing from the second Coplon trial strengthen our conviction that the liberties of the American people are not safe so long as the FBI continues on its present path.[174]

256   CHAPTER 5

Durr ended by urging Truman to appoint an independent body to investigate the FBI. His letter went unanswered.

That Coplon was a Soviet spy was beyond all doubt. Even so, her convictions were overturned on appeal, for many of the reasons Durr had cited. In that sense, the federal appeals court ruling was a victory, albeit a largely empty one. None of the FBI practices exposed in the Coplon case were ended as a result of the court's ruling.

The reality is that the Bureau never needed to violate the Communications Act of 1934 to secure Coplon's conviction.

The *Nardone* decision only applied to *wiretaps*. If the FBI had used hidden microphones in her office and secured warrants to get permission to place microphones in her home, they likely could have captured some useable recordings. More importantly, they apparently never attempted to get microphone coverage of Gubitchev's office at the UN (where he masqueraded as a Soviet diplomat).

The Bureau also failed to enlist other Justice employees who worked with or supervised Coplon to try to convince her that they were sympathetic to the Soviets or opposed to US policy toward the USSR and wanted to do something about it. Such an approach might have taken a little more time to gather non-wiretap-derived evidence to convict her, but all were proven—and legal—counterintelligence methods that would have been unassailable in federal court.

Instead, despite the massive embarrassment of the domestic surveillance operations and the Justice Department's botching of the Coplon case, Hoover kept his job. He got help via a massive Red-baiting campaign waged by the new junior senator from Wisconsin: Joseph Raymond McCarthy.

THE MCCARTHY ERA BEGINS

Lee Overman. Hamilton Fish. John McCormack and Samuel Dickstein. Martin Dies. J. Parnell Thomas. These leaders of congressional witch hunt committees between 1919 and 1950 made McCarthy's rise possible. They set the tone and example that McCarthy would take to a whole new level of intensity.

It began with the Alger Hiss espionage case.

On January 22, 1950, the federal jury in Manhattan had found Hiss guilty on two counts of perjury for lying to Congress about knowing Whittaker Chambers; the statute of limitations had passed for Hiss to be charged under the Espionage Act.[175] His friend, Secretary of State Dean Acheson, was appalled at the outcome, and on Monday, January 25, at a scheduled press conference he was asked about the verdict.

"I should like to make clear to you," America's top diplomat said, "that whatever the outcome of any appeal which Mr. Hiss or his lawyers may take in this case I do not intend to turn my back on Alger Hiss."[176]

Acheson's loyalty to Hiss would be used as a weapon against not just the Secretary of State but also his boss, Truman. Indeed, GOP House and Senate members blamed Truman and Acheson for the "loss" of China in 1949— the victory of Mao Zedong's communist forces over Nationalist Chiang Kai-Shek's troops in the Chinese civil war—and Acheson's friendship with and defense of Hiss reinforced the image of the administration as being "soft" on communism, abroad and at home.

That same afternoon, McCarthy joined Mundt on the Senate floor as the latter was in the midst of a multihour attack on the administration's foreign policy. After reading Acheson's defense of Hiss from the press conference, the junior senator from Wisconsin asked his South Dakota colleague if he was aware of Acheson's "most fantastic statement . . . on the conviction of Alger Hiss." Mundt replied that he was "not greatly concerned about what influence Alger Hiss has on the position of Dean Acheson's back" but "about the degree of influence Hiss may have had upon the position of Dean Acheson's mind."[177]

Soon Mundt's Senate colleague was moving beyond Alger Hiss and Secretary Acheson. McCarthy's target became the entire State Department.

In a Lincoln Day speech in Wheeling, West Virginia, McCarthy smeared ousted State China expert John Stewart Service as having helped "torpedo our ally Chiang Kai-shek and stating, in effect, that communism was the best hope of China." Going on to claim that the State Department was "infested with communists," McCarthy claimed, "I have in my hand 57 cases of individuals who would appear to be either card-carrying members or certainly loyal to the Communist Party, but who nevertheless are still helping to shape our foreign policy."[178]

Two days later McCarthy sent a telegram to Truman directly quoting his speech, reiterating his accusations, and demanding that Truman turn over CSC LRB records on the individual government employees McCarthy accused of being Soviet agents. "Failure on your part will label the Democratic party of being the bedfellow of international communism."[179] A week later at the annual Democratic Jefferson-Jackson Day dinner in Washington, Truman returned fire, denouncing GOP tactics as simply more baseless scaremongering.[180]

Truman's claim was true but irrelevant. McCarthy, Mundt, and other Senate and House Republicans sensed they had a winning political issue, and no real restraining or moderating forces within their own party preventing them from exploiting it.

The *Amerasia*, Silvermaster, Hiss, and Coplon episodes, along with the Truman administration's loss of China, had been woven into a simplistic, toxic, and frequently fact-free narrative that nonetheless gained real political traction from the fall of 1949 onward. Truman's creation of the loyalty program via EO 9835, intended to forestall such political attacks, was painted by McCarthy as hopelessly ineffectual against a seemingly relentless Soviet subversion and espionage campaign. McCarthy became the GOP spear carrier on the issue.

On the Senate floor on February 20, he resumed his attack. Referencing his Wheeling, West Virginia, speech in which he charged nearly sixty communists were on the State Department payroll, McCarthy now revised his figure upward, and claimed that "the State Department refused to discharge approximately 200" alleged communists.[181] His Senate colleague, Senator Scott Lucas (D-IL), challenged him on his numbers and specific cases and names, causing McCarthy to refuse to yield the floor to Lucas and turning the Senate chamber into his own personal circus.

Even after his fellow Senate Foreign Relations Committee (SFRC) member Senator Henry Cabot Lodge, Jr. (R-MA) offered to introduce a resolution creating a special subcommittee to investigate McCarthy's charges, McCarthy thanked him and simply kept up his antics, going so far as to force quorum calls to drag his colleagues to the floor to hear his rambling rant.[182] After two days of relatively minor wrangling over the language, McCarthy got his SFRC investigation into alleged State Department employee disloyalty via Senate Resolution 231.[183]

Between the passage of S. Res. 231 and the start of the SFRC hearings, McCarthy would not be the only Senate Republican taking aim at the Truman State Department. Senator William Knowland (R-CA) would do what McCarthy had not, as yet, done: Knowland would name names at the State Department. The first target on his list was an academic expert on China and Central Asia and former State Department consultant, Owen Lattimore.

In a March 2 Senate floor speech, Knowland asserted Lattimore had "played a considerable part in our policy toward China, which resulted in the debacle" of the Red Chinese victory over Chiang Kai-Shek's Nationalists.[184] He attacked Lattimore for a January 19 article in the *Atlantic* magazine in which Lattimore characterized South Korea as "an American liability" and urged American recognition of the new Chinese Communist regime. Knowland denounced Lattimore's views as "a policy of appeasement" that would "result in the domination not only of the entire Asiatic land mass by communism but will lead to all of the island nations going into the Communist orbit as well."[185]

"ONE NATION DIVIDED" 259

Eleven days later McCarthy joined the attack on Lattimore during the third day of SFRC subcommittee hearings into State Department employee loyalty. He attacked Lattimore over his writings and policy prescriptions regarding China and his association with the Institute of Pacific Relations (IPR) and other left-leaning civil society organizations, some branded as communist fronts by HUAC or the attorney general.

McCarthy ended his lengthy attack on Lattimore by stating that his "close collaboration and affiliation with numerous Communist organizations; his friendship and close cooperation with pro-Communist individuals" left "absolutely no doubt that he is an extremely bad security risk" and his "affinity for the Soviet cause . . . might well have already done this Nation incalculable and irreparable harm."[186]

In none of his statements, exhibits, or documents was McCarthy able to actually show that Lattimore was a member of the CP USA or a Soviet agent. His attack was strictly based on innuendo, the selective and misleading use of quotes from Lattimore's published work, and McCarthy's own clear bias against Lattimore and other long-time China academic or government experts.

During the initial hearings in March, Lattimore was in Afghanistan working for the United Nations Technical Assistance Mission in Kabul, where he began getting inquiries from journalists by March 14.[187] As of March 24, McCarthy was telling journalists—off the record—that Lattimore was the top Soviet agent at the State Department.[188] Lattimore was neither a communist nor a pushover. He retained Washington super lawyer (and future Supreme Court justice) Abe Fortas to help him mount a defense and counterattack—the latter coming in the form of a letter to McCarthy telling him to retract his charges or face a possible libel suit.[189]

While McCarthy and Knowland were busy targeting Lattimore and several other prominent State Department personnel, SFRC investigative subcommittee chairman Millard Tydings (D-MD) was trying to get State Department, CSC, and FBI files on the eighty-plus people McCarthy had claimed were Soviet agents or sympathizers. Tydings, facing reelection that fall, knew perfectly well that if he didn't push Truman on the issue the Maryland GOP would have a field day with it.

It was Attorney General J. Howard McGrath who first got wind that Tydings was going to request the documents, and he was horrified to learn that State Department officials were asking Truman to consider surrendering them.

In a SECRET five-page cable to Truman on March 17, McGrath urged Truman to "withhold permission to make the files available to the

260   CHAPTER 5

subcommittee." The attorney general reminded Truman that just two years earlier when he started the loyalty program, he had directed that "all reports, records, and files in connection with the program be preserved in strict confidence." McGrath also argued that disclosing FBI confidential sources might damage the Bureau's ability to get anyone to cooperate with a loyalty investigation, and that he feared "the use of particular or selected reports" could "constitute the grossest injustice, and we all know that a correction never catches up with an accusation."[190]

When Tydings's formal request for the records arrived on March 22, Truman took nearly a week to respond with a categorical "no."

His four-page March 28 letter made clear his reasons for refusing to turn over the files, drawing verbatim some of the language in McGrath's March 17 cable and adding in dire warnings from Hoover about the disclosure of FBI investigative techniques would aid "criminals, foreign agents, subversives, and others" in evading FBI detection. Truman finished by telling Tydings that the CSC would be directed to open investigations on all those of concern to the committee.[191]

Tydings wasted no time issuing subpoenas, demanding that Acheson, McGrath, and CSC Chairman Seth Richardson appear before his subcommittee, with the documents in hand, on April 4. On April 3 Truman informed Tydings he had told State, Justice, and CSC "not to comply with your subpoenas."[192]

Three days later, Lattimore made his appearance before Tydings's subcommittee. His testimony was lucid, focused, and withering.

Calling McCarthy's charges against him "unworthy of a Senator or an American" and "base and contemptible lies," Lattimore asserted that McCarthy had violated his responsibilities as a legislator "by impairing the effectiveness of the United States Government in its relations with its friends and allies" and "by instituting a reign of terror among officials and employees in the United States Government" through disclosure "without authorization . . . secret documents obtained from official Government files."[193] Lattimore made clear that McCarthy wasn't simply a bully. He was a coward:

> Twice on the floor of the Senate he stated that any charges that he made under the cloak of immunity, he would repeat in another place so that their falseness could be tested in a court of the United States. He said that if he should fail to do this he would resign. He has been called to repeat his charges so that they could be tested in a court action. He has failed to do so. And he has not resigned.[194]

"ONE NATION DIVIDED"   261

Lattimore spent the rest of his statement refuting McCarthy's allegations one by one, demonstrating their obvious falsehood with existing records (including some McCarthy himself had referenced) dating back to 1936.[195]

Lattimore spent hours in the witness chair, answering question after question, primarily from McCarthy's de facto stand in, Senator Bourke Hickenlooper (R-IA). It was Tydings who finally put an end to the charade.

Tydings informed Lattimore, the subcommittee, the press, and the crowd in the hearing room that he and a select group of other senators had, at the agreement of the administration, had the FBI's record on Lattimore read to them.

"It was quite lengthy," Tydings told Lattimore. "And at the conclusion of the reading of that summary in great detail, it was the universal opinion of all of the members of the committee present, and all others in the room, of which there were two more, that there was nothing in that file to show that you were a Communist or had ever been a Communist, or that you were in any way connected with any espionage information or charges, so that the FBI file puts you completely, up to this moment, at least, in the clear."[196] After a few more exchanges between Lattimore, Tydings, and one other member, Tydings gaveled the hearing to a close shortly before 5 p.m.

While it appeared that Lattimore had eviscerated McCarthy and his charges—despite McCarthy's nonattendance at the hearing—the junior senator from Wisconsin was not done with Lattimore or the more than eighty other current or former federal employees he claimed were Reds.

McCarthy turned up the heat on Tydings, publicly and privately, and Tydings in turn leaned on the administration. On May 5 Truman capitulated, granting Tydings's subcommittee access to the State Department files on the 81 persons in question, but access to FBI reports was denied.[197] A month after Truman granted access, Tydings wrote the president that "they are the same cases and person that have previously been investigated by four separate committees of Congress" and that "none of the 81 persons accused was stated by any of the committees to be either a disloyal employee or a Communist."[198]

Even so, Tydings asked Truman to have the CSC LRB investigate each to ensure "the ultimate findings will be accepted without question."[199] The notion that McCarthy or any of his supporters would accept any exoneration of the 81 accused by a Truman administration CSC was nonsensical.

On June 1 seven of McCarthy's own GOP Senate colleagues abandoned him. Senator Margaret Chase Smith (R-ME), without needing to name McCarthy, attacked his tactics as an attempt to "see the Republican Party ride to political victory on the Four Horsemen of Calumny—fear, ignorance, bigotry, and smear." She got six GOP colleagues to cosign a declaration condemning "Certain elements of the Republican Party" for trying to achieve political victory "through the selfish political exploitation of fear, bigotry, ignorance, and intolerance."[200]

The Tydings subcommittee report was published on July 20. It labeled every single one of McCarthy's allegations false and denounced his tactics as "perhaps the most nefarious campaign of untruth in the history of our Republic."[201] As events would show, it would take far more than harsh language to deter Joe McCarthy.

SENATOR PAT MCCARRAN AND THE INTERNAL SECURITY ACT

Even as the political drama involving McCarthy's baseless accusations against hundreds of current or former State Department officials unfolded during the first half of 1950, others were pushing legislation that would have a similar chilling effect on civil society organizations and foreign nationals residing in the United States.

Nixon and Mundt had never abandoned their belief in the need for an overarching subversive activities control legislative regime. In the first months of the 81st Congress, Nixon had introduced his Subversive Activities Control Act (H.R. 3342), which was essentially the same bill he and Mundt had pushed the year before.[202] For his part Mundt—joined by his Senate colleagues Homer Ferguson (R-MI) and Olin Johnston (D-SC)— had introduced S. 2311, the Senate companion to Nixon's House bill.[203] By the spring of 1950 a number of their colleagues began working on their own versions. On a related issue, Rep. Sam Hobbs (D-AL) had introduced H.R. 10, which gave the attorney general plenary power to detain allegedly deportable foreign nationals without trial or other due process.[204]

Throughout the spring and summer of 1950 Truman and his team tried to figure out how to limit the damage, both to the Constitution and to Democrats' political prospects in the upcoming mid-terms, should any of the bills pass. On May 16 senior White House aides Stephen Spingarn and Charles Murphy gave Truman a memo warning of the looming dangers posed by the Hobbs and Mundt bills.

Noting the "prevailing impetus . . . toward ever stiffer internal security measures," Spingarn and Murphy noted the "tendency . . . to draft these measure in very broad, loose terms—to paint the whole barn in order to cover the knothole."[205] The price, they told Truman, was to bring "normal administrative operations to a stand-still," which prevents "the interchange of ideas necessary to scientific progress, and—most important of all—encroaches on the individual rights and freedoms which distinguish a democracy from a totalitarian country."[206]

The duo also noted that the administration had not been speaking with a single unified voice on the issue.

When Tom Clark had been attorney general, he had testified *in favor* of Hobbs's H.R. 10, despite its clearly unconstitutional indefinite detention provision opposed by Truman and others in the administration.[207] It didn't take much reading between the lines to know they were indirectly referring to Hoover's outsized influence on all internal security policy issues and legislation.

Spingarn and Murphy noted that the FBI and the Immigration and Naturalization Service "are inclined to resolve all doubts in favor of security." For Spingarn and Murphy, things were out of balance. They urged Truman to direct the current attorney general, Jim McGrath, to have DoJ's Civil Rights Section weigh in on the civil liberties impacts of any internal security legislation and that Truman charge McGrath with ensuring that "a proper balance has been struck between internal security and individual rights" before DoJ backed any internal security bills.[208]

It was too little, too late. The administration failed to get friendly House or Senate members to introduce less radical alternatives that spring or summer, leaving the existing draconian but bipartisan Mundt and Nixon bills unopposed.

Another reason the administration was losing ground on the issue was the revelation of the most successful Soviet espionage operation to date: the theft and provision of US atomic weapon design secrets to the Soviets by a number of American citizens.

Once again, VENONA decrypts provided the initial evidence, though the often years-long lag between the intercept of Soviet VENONA traffic and even the partial decryption of the messages meant federal authorities only learned about the technology thefts long after the fact.[209] The public got the bad news initially on June 16, with the *Washington Evening Star* giving front-page coverage to the arrest of Harry Gold in Philadelphia, Alfred Dean Slack in Syracuse, and former Army Sergeant David Greenglass in Albuquerque.[210] During July and August, more arrests followed, specifically Morton Sobell and a married couple, Julius and Ethel Rosenberg.[211]

The Soviet nuclear program itself existed long before the Fuchs–Rosenberg spy ring was established, but historians generally credit the espionage with advancing the Soviets' first nuclear test by one to two years.[212] Compared to the total number of Americans on the federal payroll involved in foreign affairs or national security work in the period, the number of actual

264 CHAPTER 5

Soviet agents uncovered was relatively small. Moreover, the press coverage surrounding these episodes inevitably failed to mention US efforts to steal Soviet secrets. The Soviets and Americans, like all great powers for centuries, were always after the secrets of their actual or potential opponents.

However, the political, bureaucratic, and legislative fallout from the subsequent trials was immediate and extended beyond Truman's presidency. The political effect of having even a relatively small number of current or former federal employees implicated as Soviet spies seemed to validate the views of House and Senate internal security hawks, who stepped up their campaign for even greater internal security measures.

Sensing the situation slipping out of his control, Truman sent a six-page missive to Congress on August 8, outlining his objections to the existing bills and offering his own alternatives, including extending the statute of limitations on espionage-related crimes, strengthening the Foreign Agents Registration Act, and requiring deportable aliens to report their whereabouts regularly—but he opposed any legislation that would criminalize speech.

"Once a government is committed to the principle of silencing the voice of opposition . . . it becomes a source of terror to all its citizens and creates a country where everyone lives in fear," Truman told the House and Senate. "We must not be swept away by a wave of hysteria."[213]

Truman's letter did nothing to stop the momentum for passage of some version of the Mundt–Nixon–McCarran proposal. In a despairing August 24 memo to White House colleague Robert Landry, Spingarn noted that multiple internal security bills opposed by the administration were up for debate the week of August 28.

"The outlook is very gloomy," Spingarn told Landry. "It looks as if the President's recommendations will be badly licked and we are in for a 1950 version of the Alien and Sedition laws of 1798."[214]

Spingarn's prediction was spot on. It would be McCarran's legislation, repackaged as H.R. 9490, that would make it through both chambers less than three weeks after Labor Day 1950.

Truman issued a blistering veto statement on September 22, stating pointedly that the bill would "aid potential enemies by requiring the publication of a complete list of vital defense plants, laboratories, and other installations" and "require the Department of Justice . . . to waste immense amounts of time and energy attempting to carry out its unworkable registration provisions," all the while "antagonizing friendly governments" as well as putting "the Government of the United States in the thought-control business."

The very kind of smear campaign and victimization of innocent Americans that the president predicted would happen was in fact underway the

"ONE NATION DIVIDED" 265

day he vetoed the McCarran bill. The target was the wife of Rep. Adam Clayton Powell, Jr.—Hazel Scott Powell, who had decided to voluntarily respond to HUAC charges that she was a communist or Soviet sympathizer.

A publication called *Red Channels* had claimed Powell was connected to or had supported multiple communist front organizations, a charge she categorically denied in an amusing exchange with Rep. Burr Harrison (D-VA):

> MRS. POWELL: May I ask you a question? If any committee, an official committee, lists me as having two heads, does that make me have two heads, and does that give *Red Channels* a right to publish I have two heads?
>
> MR. HARRISON: Would you deny the right to reprint from official records without comment?
>
> MRS. POWELL: They say they want to protect innocents.
>
> MR. HARRISON: They make no bones of the fact they do not evaluate the listings.
>
> MRS. POWELL: They simply prepare a blacklist.
>
> MR. HARRISON: I don't agree with you.[215]

When asked if she was a communist, Powell replied, "I am not now, never have been, have never entertained the idea, and never will become a member, which is something nobody has ever asked me."[216] Chairman Wood thereupon hurriedly adjourned the hearing. To the best of the author's knowledge, no wife of a White House or Senate member was ever hauled before HUAC and questioned about their alleged or actual political affiliations as Hazel Scott Powell was that day.

The next day, both chambers overrode Truman's veto of H.R. 9490 by overwhelming margins. With the passage of the McCarran Act, the Subversive Activities Control Board (SACB) became a reality, with Truman on October 23 appointing former CSC head Seth Richardson to be its first chairman.[217] To ensure that the McCarran Act was carried out by Truman and his successors, the Senate on December 21 passed S. Res. 366, creating within the SJC what would become known as the Senate Internal Security Subcommittee (SISS). HUAC now had a Senate clone, and in a gesture of solidarity with McCarran, Mundt, and others who had worked to pass the Internal Security Act and create the SISS, HUAC's final report of 1950 labeled the National Committee to Defeat the Mundt Act "A Communist Lobby."[218]

266   CHAPTER 5

EXPANDING THE INTERNAL SECURITY STATE

The backlash against the McCarran Act from civil society organizations and, in a limited sense, the administration was swift and vocal but ineffective. The internal security state Truman himself had helped create via EO 9835, along with the machinations of HUAC, SISS, McCarthy, and Hoover, drove American society deeper into spiral of fear and repression.

At the April 18 NSC meeting Coyne briefed the members on his March 26 report on progress toward meeting the internal security goals established in the summer 1948. Among the initiatives was a "study of the problem of controlling the procurement, possession, and use of firearm and explosives by persons who are actually or potentially dangerous to the United States."[219] It was a revival of an idea surfaced by Hoover and others prior to World War II, which had been dropped out of fears of potential political blowback by American gun owners.

Also recommended "at the appropriate time" was a pitch to Congress to formally give the FBI, via attorney general authorization, formal wiretapping authority in civilian cases and for the G-2, ONI, and the Air Force Office of Special Investigations (OSI) to get wiretap authority from their respective service secretaries.[220] Left unaddressed was exactly why the military services would need domestic wiretap authority at all.

The FBI reported to the NSC that it had "identified approximately 14,500 individuals as dangerous or potentially dangerous" for possible apprehension and detention and that the number in that category "is increasing as additional derogatory information is received and investigations are conducted." According to Hoover, 95 percent were CP USA affiliated, while the other 5 percent were linked to "other Marxist-revolutionary groups or are engaged in other types of subversive activities."[221] No actual criminal predicate was indicated for inclusion on the list, much less arrest and detention.

As for the arrest and detention criteria themselves (which were defined by the executive branch, not Congress), "The determination as to the question of potential or actual danger to the security of the country is made in each individual case only after the investigation indicates present subversive activities and sympathies."[222] Again, simply having alleged or actual associations with subversive elements—not legally defined—was all that was required for potential arrest and detention of indefinite length.

Another breathtaking achievement was the FBI's informant penetration of defense-related manufacturing facilities designated as "vital" by the

Secretary of Defense. As of December 20, 1950, "over 13,000 informants had been developed by the FBI" to cover some 5,300 defense plants—nearly three informants per facility.[223] And on the informant recruiting front, the FBI was just getting started.

HUAC AND SISS: CONGRESSIONAL SHOW TRIAL ROADSHOWS

The McCarran Act also fundamentally altered the congressional oversight landscape; there were now two Un-American Activities committees in Congress. Both were busy throughout 1951, in open and closed hearings, acting on the same kind of gossip, innuendo, and rumor about alleged communist affiliations of Americans in the entertainment, telecommunications, defense, legal, agricultural, and academic fields. The two most high-profile investigations were HUAC's multihearing attacks on the entertainment industry and SISS's first official investigation targeting the Institute of Pacific Relations.

HUAC's post–Hollywood Ten public hearings in 1951 stretched from March through September and followed the usual "congressional theater" pattern of patient elucidation of names of alleged communists from friendly—or intimidated—witnesses or through badgering and confrontation with those who refused to answer or, more commonly, invoked their Fifth Amendment rights.

At an April 10 hearing that lasted more than three hours, HUAC chief counsel Frank Tavenner got Hollywood leading man and former decorated OSS agent Sterling Hayden to acknowledge his brief membership in the CP USA and to provide names of other alleged members.[224] Years after that day Hayden would recall in his memoir, *Wanderer*, his feelings leading up to his testimony:

> They know I was a Party member—they don't want information, they want to put on a show, and I'm the star. They've already agreed to go over the questions with me in advance. It's a rigged show: radio and TV and the papers. I'm damned no matter what I do. Co-operate and I'm a stool pigeon. Shut my mouth and I'm a pariah.[225]

Others simply refused to play HUAC's game.

At the April 24 HUAC hearing Tavenner verbally fenced with entertainment industry agent George Willner over his representation of the leftist magazine *New Masses*. After Willner invoked his Fifth Amendment rights and accused the committee of "trying to link me with one of those organizations which you list as subversive," HUAC Chairman John Wood (D-GA) disingenuously said, "But bear in mind, sir, that this committee isn't endeavoring to link you anywhere." Willner replied, "I feel that they are. I have given my reasons, and I stand on them." Wood responded, "If you don't want to answer that question, then cloak yourself under the protection of the Fifth Amendment of the Constitution of the United States. That is your privilege."[226]

Wood used the verb "cloak" as a smear, just one of the many tactics he and his fellow HUAC members and staff would use throughout the balance of the year against uncooperative witnesses.

Over in the Senate, the new Internal Security Subcommittee continued mining the "Truman lost China" political narrative by having the committee staff seize and pore over the records of the Institute of Pacific Relations.[227] During hearings spanning from July to October 1951, Owen Lattimore's name was invoked over 560 times, with McCarran and his SISS colleagues dredging up decades-old correspondence between Lattimore and current and former IPR officials, still trying to prove—despite the FBI's prior clearance of Lattimore the year before—that the China policy expert was a communist and at least partly to blame for the loss of China to Mao. Despite all the sound and fury, nothing stuck. Even so, it was hard to escape the conclusion that McCarran wasn't finished with Lattimore; the scholar had not been invited or compelled to answer the fresh charges made by the committee yet.

While HUAC and SISS were dragging still more innocent Americans through their Star Chamber–like hearings, Justice Department officials had far more luck in federal court against the twelve CP USA members who had been indicted in July 1948.

If federal prosecutors had been forced to demonstrate that any of the twelve CP USA defendants were actual Soviet agents engaged in espionage, they would have failed; the evidence wasn't there. Instead, the men had been charged under the vaguely worded Smith Act's conspiracy provisions. It was a far lower legal bar to get over, and the prosecution had succeeded in the initial trial and on appeal. The defendant's lawyers had tried twice to get federal courts to declare the Smith Act's provisions unconstitutional and lost. In the fall of 1950 the Supreme Court agreed to hear arguments.

The two sides made their cases to the justices on December 4. Six months later, America's highest court would render a 6–2 decision in favor of the Justice Department's position.[228] The Court's majority ruled that the Smith Act did not

"ONE NATION DIVIDED" 269

inherently, or as construed or applied in the instant case, violate the First Amendment and other provisions of the Bill of Rights, or the First and Fifth Amendments because of indefiniteness. Petitioners intended to overthrow the Government of the United States as speedily as the circumstances would permit. Their conspiracy to organize the Communist Party and to teach and advocate the overthrow of the Government of the United States by force and violence created a "clear and present danger" of an attempt to overthrow the Government by force and violence. They were properly and constitutionally convicted for violation of the Smith Act.[229]

It was the second major executive branch victory for the use of the Smith Act against leftist organizations, the first being the 1941 prosecution of Socialist Workers Party members.[230] It would remain a potent weapon in the Justice Department's hands well into the 1950s. The case had another effect: it galvanized further vocal, public opposition to the Smith Act and related repressive laws and measures.

It didn't take long for the October 8 piece in the *Daily Worker* to catch the attention of the FBI Washington Field Office, which subsequently informed Hoover via a memo titled, "150 Notables Form Emergency Civil Rights Committee."[231] Founders Dr. Paul Lehman of Princeton Theological Seminary and retired investment banker James Imbrie openly called for the repeal of the Smith Act and attacked it and similar measures as blatantly unconstitutional.[232] While the FBI's Newark Field Office would remain the lead in investigating the Emergency Civil Rights Committee (ECRC), multiple FBI offices around the country would be enlisted in following up leads about those Americans in any way connected with the committee.[233]

The FBI, unsurprisingly, had informants close to members of ECRC. What was truly astonishing was how vast FBI informant recruitment had become by the close of 1951.

When Coyne submitted his internal security progress report to the NSC on December 20, 1951, he was able to relay that "the FBI has developed 52,791 informants" to cover the 5,300 plants designated as vital by the Secretary of Defense—a 400 percent increase from the previous year.[234] The Bureau had also "continued its program of regularly contacting 62,688 members of the American Legion" for any internal security–related tips or leads.[235] On average, the Bureau now had at least ten informants in every defense business of concern to the Pentagon.

There were no breakout figures in Coyne's report regarding overlap between FBI informants who were or were not Legion members, but it's

270   CHAPTER 5

highly unlikely all of the nearly 53,000 in military production plants were Legionnaires. What it did mean is that in a nation of nearly 155 million at the time, just the defense plant informant coverage alone meant that there was an average of one FBI informant for every 292 Americans.

OWEN LATTIMORE FIGHTS BACK

By early November 1951 Lattimore had had enough. McCarran's subcommittee had spent the summer and fall using public hearings to further smear him as an alleged communist without offering him a chance to respond. On November 6 from his office at the Walter Hines Page School of International Relations at Johns Hopkins University in Baltimore, Lattimore wrote McCarran that the committee had "promised that I will be given an opportunity to refute publicly the false and slanderous allegations that have been made about me," and he asked to be notified "at an early date" when he could appear publicly before the committee.[236]

Beginning on February 26, 1952, and running for nearly a week, Lattimore was subjected to a SISS-orchestrated public campaign of intimidation, interruption, and badgering as he attempted to simply give his opening statement regarding his relationship with the IPR, the nominal subject of the SISS hearings.

His exchanges with Senator Herbert O'Conor (D-MD), Homer Ferguson (R-MI), and Willis Smith (D-NC) were typical of the bipartisan attacks Lattimore endured. Referring to earlier witnesses who had accused him of being a communist, Lattimore attempted to continue reading his statement:

> MR. LATTIMORE: Senator, I am not legally trained myself. I am trying to read a statement that I have made in as simple English as I can, and I have been interrupted repeatedly. I don't want to give an impression of evasiveness or hairsplitting or anything of that kind, but I cannot help but be conscious of what I believe is one difference between the grand jury procedure which you yourself mentioned not long ago and this kind of procedure, namely, that I believe that a grand jury is not usually composed exclusively of trained lawyers.

| SENATOR SMITH: | I do not know of any grand jury— |
| MR. LATTIMORE: | When on the other hand I am perhaps unwarrantedly aware of the fact that I am sitting here under conditions in which my own lawyer is not allowed to tender advice to me while I am asked rather complicated questions involving legal points which might be pitfalls for me, to which I have to try to reply to the best of my ability.[237] |

And so it went for six days, Lattimore reading a sentence or perhaps at most a paragraph of his statement, and SISS members or their chief counsel, J.G. Sourwine, interrupting Lattimore about his every word—either from his prepared statement or from the multitude of past articles and correspondence involving him, IPR, or State Department officials.

When it was all over, *Washington Evening Star* columnist Robert K. Walsh would observe:

> Thus, when subcommittee members seemed to put some of his past activities in a Red Trojan horse pasture, he protested that the charge was about as pertinent as "whether Trojan horses have horse feathers." And, on another occasion, there was dead silence when he asked a Senator: "Is your argument post hoc or propter hoc?"[238]

Lattimore had made SISS members look like the fools they were, but it would be no deterrent to SISS persecuting other innocent Americans.

CONCLUSION

By Truman's last year in office the organizational and programmatic machinery of federal surveillance and political repression had matured and become virtually routinized, encompassing all three branches of the government. New civil society organizations like the Emergency Civil Rights Committee, opposed to state-sponsored surveillance and political repression, were able to grab some headlines but had no real impact on either the administration or Congress. Government insiders like Jebby Davidson tried but failed to get the federal employee loyalty program ended or at least modified to include true due process protections. The existing political climate made it all but impossible to

272   CHAPTER 5

blunt the federal government's march toward ever greater surveillance, investigations, and in some cases, prosecutions on the basis of political beliefs.

Without question, Congress remained a key driver and enabler of the climate of fear that now permeated virtually every sector of American life.

HUAC alone held over forty days of hearings in search of Soviet sympathizers in Los Angeles, Detroit, Chicago, Dayton, the District of Columbia, and Philadelphia, as well as still more hearings on "Reds in Hollywood" and testimony from another HUAC target previously cleared by the FBI: Dr. Edward U. Condon.[239]

The House Select Committee on Tax-Exempt Foundations held seventeen days of hearings in November and December 1952 seeking to learn whether organizations like the Ford or Rockefeller Foundations were "using their resources for un-American and subversive activities or for purposes not in the interest or tradition of the United States."[240]

For its part, the SISS expanded beyond its inquisition against IPR and Lattimore to include examinations of potential Soviet-inspired or directed activities in the telecommunications field, the education sector, and unions.[241] Not to be outdone, the Senate Committee on Labor and Public Welfare devoted ten days of hearings on the topic of "Communist Domination of Unions and National Security."[242]

If the public tone was being largely set by Congress, executive branch elements were not far behind.

The FBI's massive, ever-growing informant network helped provide grist for FBI field office reporting on alleged or actual communist or other subversive activities—material that made its way to FBI HQ and subsequently to the White House via FBI Current Intelligence Summaries (CISs), almost always sent by courier.[243]

The relatively short (usually two to five pages) CISs were sent to the White House virtually daily, keeping the Bureau's internal security work in front of Truman and his senior aides and thus maintaining a constant sense of threat, whether from specific individuals or organizations. But ongoing controversies involving the accuracy of derogatory information about alleged or actual associations with communists, or nebulously defined subversive organizations, by prospective or current federal employees persisted throughout the spring and summer of 1952. The SISS–Lattimore confrontation had received enormous press coverage, as had other congressional hearings questioning federal employee loyalty.

In fact, program duplication, as well as the accuracy or misuse of information of alleged disloyalty, suitability, or status as a security risk for existing federal employees or aspirants, led Truman on August 7 to direct executive

"ONE NATION DIVIDED" 273

branch elements to cooperate with the CSC in the creation "of a plan for a single general program covering eligibility for employment in the Federal service, whether on grounds of loyalty, security, or suitability."[244] The initiative, one of Truman's last to try to protect the federal workforce from further congressional witch hunts, would not come to fruition before he left office.

What was progressing was the NSC-approved internal security program.

In what would be the last major NSC Internal Security Progress Report submitted to Truman before he left office, Coyne on December 17 informed NSC members that with respect to efforts at identifying those deemed "dangerous or potentially dangerous" to American internal security to be rounded up and detained without formal charges in the event of a national emergency or general war, "As of October 10, 1952, 19,436 individuals have been so identified, as compared with approximately 17,000 a year ago."[245]

Coyne also had good news regarding Smith Act prosecutions.

"Based on FBI-developed evidence," he noted, "85 leading functionaries of the Communist Party have been indicted, and thus far 31 have been convicted for conspiracy to advocate overthrow of the U.S. Government by force and violence."[246]

Coyne noted that the trials, convictions, and attendant negative publicity for the CP USA had been crippling, "impairing substantially the membership, organizational operations, financial condition and general effectiveness of the party apparatus . . . with membership decreasing to approximately 24,674 as compared with 35,310 as of June 30, 1951."[247]

It was quite an accomplishment against an organization that never represented a serious threat to either the integrity of the federal government or the political and social fabric of the nation. The tools and the mentality that made it possible now passed from an outgoing Democratic administration to the first Republican to reclaim the Oval Office since Herbert Hoover. In all the ways that mattered, the worst was yet to come.

NOTES

1. See David McCullough, *Truman* (New York: Simon and Schuster, 1992), 348–352.
2. LT (JG) John Connorton, USNR and LT Floyd Tomkins, Jr., USA, "The Need for New Legislation Against Unauthorized Disclosures of Communication Intelligence Activities," Report for U.S. Army-Naval Communication Intelligence Coordinating Committee, June 9, 1944. NARA RG 38, Records of the CNO, Crane Naval Security Group Library Collection, Box 142. ULTRA was the codename given to the most sensitive communications intercept and decryption program involving Japanese codes.
3. Connorton and Tomkins, "The Need for New Legislation," 5.
4. Connorton and Tomkins, "The Need for New Legislation," 56–57.

274   CHAPTER 5

5. Connorton and Tomkins, "The Need for New Legislation," 69–70.
6. Memorandum of February 20, 1945, from LTC Harmon Duncomee to LCDR Braun, Military Intelligence Service legal opinion, "Legality of Obtaining Intelligence by Interception of Communications of Foreign Countries," 1–3. NARA RG 38, Records of the CNO, Crane Naval Security Group Library Collection, Box 142.
7. Confidential legal opinion of RADM Thomas Leigh Gatch, March 26, 1945, 7. NARA RG 38, Records of the CNO, Crane Naval Security Group Library Collection, Box 142.
8. Confidential legal opinion of RADM Thomas Leigh Gatch, March 26, 1945, 7.
9. Communications Act of 1934, 47 U.S.C. § 605.
10. Memorandum from ADM F. J. Horne to Navy Secretary James Forestall, May 14, 1945, 2. NARA RG 38, Records of the CNO, Crane Naval Security Group Library Collection, Box 142.
11. Confidential legal opinion of RADM Thomas Leigh Gatch, March 26, 1945, 11. NARA RG 38, Records of the CNO, Crane Naval Security Group Library Collection, Box 142.
12. Memo of Navy Secretary James Forestall to War Secretary Henry Stimson, June 22, 1945. NARA RG 38, Records of the CNO, Crane Naval Security Group Library Collection, Box 142.
13. Memo of VADM Joseph R. Redman to Navy Secretary James Forrestal, October 19, 1945, 1. NARA RG 38, Records of the CNO, Crane Naval Security Group Library Collection, Box 142.
14. Memo of VADM Joseph R. Redman to Navy Secretary James Forrestal, October 19, 1945, 1.
15. Memo of VADM Joseph R. Redman to Navy Secretary James Forrestal, October 19, 1945, 2.
16. Sullivan and Brown, *The Bureau*, 38.
17. Sullivan and Brown, *The Bureau*, 38.
18. McCullough, *Truman*, 367.
19. See Tracy Campbell, *Short of the Glory: The Fall and Redemption of Edward F. Pritchard* (Lexington: University Press of Kentucky, 1998), 94–98.
20. McCullough, *Truman*, 367.
21. Campbell, *Short of the Glory*, 98.
22. Transcript of FBI wiretap of Edward Pritchard and Justice Felix Frankfurter, May 8, 1945. HSTL, PSF, Box 277.
23. FBI memo, "Re: Possible sources of information contained in Drew Pearson's column of June 12, 1945, relating to the Hopkins-Stalin Conferences," August 17, 1945, 1. HSTL, PSF, Box 277.
24. FBI memo, "Re: Possible sources of information," 6–7.
25. HSTL, PSF, Box 281.
26. See Robert J. Donovan, *Conflict and Crisis: The Presidency of Harry S. Truman, 1945–1948* (New York: W.W. Norton & Company, 1977), 178–184.
27. Memo of J. Edgar Hoover to MG Harry Vaughn, December 6, 1946. HSTL, PSF, Box 143, folder 3.
28. Jerrell Dean Palmer and John G. Johnson, "Big Inch and Little Inch," *Handbook of Texas*, Texas State Historical Association. Accessed at https://www.tshaonline.org /handbook/entries/big-inch-and-little-big-inch.

"ONE NATION DIVIDED" 275

29. Memo of J. Edgar Hoover to MG Harry Vaughn, December 6, 1946. HSTL, PSF, Box 143, folder 3.
30. Palmer and Johnson, "Big Inch and Little Inch."
31. Donovan, *Conflict and Crisis*, 182.
32. FBI New York Field Office file 100–42735, February 26, 1945. Released via the Freedom of Information Act.
33. FBI New York Field Office file 100–22684, January 4, 1945. Released via the Freedom of Information Act.
34. FBI New York Field Office file 100–22684, January 20, 1945. Released via the Freedom of Information Act.
35. Army Service Forces, Headquarters, Third Service Command confidential memo, April 21, 1945. Truman Presidential Library, CF, Box 37.
36. See FBI file 100-HQ-51230, previously released by the FBI via FOIA.
37. Rankin speech to the Mississippi Society D.C. Chapter, May 9, 1924, 1–2. Papers of John E. Rankin, J.D. Williams Library Special Collections, University of Mississippi, Box 139, folder "Women, 1924."
38. Hamilton, *Adam Clayton Powell, Jr.*, 178.
39. Letter of James Fisk to Rep John Rankin, December 29, 1944. Papers of John E. Rankin, J.D. Williams Library Special Collections, University of Mississippi, Box 20, folder "Committee on Un-American Activities (1 of 8)."
40. Letter of Rep John Rankin to James Fisk, January 2, 1945. Papers of John E. Rankin, J.D. Williams Library Special Collections, University of Mississippi, Box 20, folder "Committee on Un-American Activities (1 of 8)."
41. *Congressional Record*, Proceedings of the 79th Congress (First Session), House, January 3, 1945, 10.
42. *Congressional Record*, Proceedings of the 79th Congress (First Session), House, January 3, 1945, 10.
43. A. Rosen to J. Edgar Hoover memo of 12/7/41 regarding Rep Adolph Sabath's Japanese-Nazi round up request. FBI case file 94-HQ-4-5249 on Rep Adolph Sabath, declassified by NARA on September 25, 2019, pursuant to author's FOIA request RD 63222.
44. See remarks Rep Adolph Sabath, *Congressional Record*, Proceedings of the 79th Congress (First Session), House, January 6, 1945, 90.
45. Rep Adolph Sabath, *Congressional Record*, Proceedings of the 79th Congress (First Session), House, January 6, 1945, 11.
46. Rep Adolph Sabath, *Congressional Record*, Proceedings of the 79th Congress (First Session), House, January 6, 1945, 14.
47. Rep Adolph Sabath, *Congressional Record*, Proceedings of the 79th Congress (First Session), House, January 6, 1945, 15.
48. Executive Order 9300, February 5, 1943. HSTL, OF 252-H, Interdepartmental Committee to Consider Cases of Subversive Activity on the Part of Federal Employees, Box 923.
49. Donovan, *Conflict and Crisis*, 62–64.
50. Personal and confidential memo from J. Edgar Hoover, FBI to Brigadier General Harry Hawkins Vaughn, Military Aide to the President, February 6, 1946, 1. HSTL, PSF, Box 142.
51. Personal and confidential memo from J. Edgar Hoover, FBI to Brigadier General Harry Hawkins Vaughn, Military Aide to the President, February 6, 1946, 1.

276   CHAPTER 5

52. Personal and confidential memo from J. Edgar Hoover, FBI to Brigadier General Harry Hawkins Vaughn, Military Aide to the President, February 6, 1946, 1.
53. White House inter-office memo, October 1, 1946. HSTL, OF 252-H, Interdepartmental Committee to Consider Cases of Subversive Activity on the Part of Federal Employees, Box 923.
54. *Report of Investigation with Respect to Employee Loyalty and Employment Policies and Practices in the Government of the United States, Committee on the Civil Service,* House of Representatives, 79th Congress (Second Session), 5.
55. *Report of Investigation with Respect to Employee Loyalty,* 7.
56. Executive Order 9806, Establishing the President's Temporary Commission on Employee Loyalty, November 25, 1946. Viewable on the HSTL website at https://www.trumanlibrary.gov/library/executive-orders/9806/executive-order-9806.
57. Report of the President's Temporary Commission on Employee Loyalty March 1947, 25. HSTL, OF 252-I, President's Tem Commission on Employee Loyalty (1 of 2), Box 923.
58. Report of the President's Temporary Commission on Employee Loyalty March 1947, 27.
59. Executive Order 9835, Proscribing Procedures for the Administration of an Employees Loyalty Program in the Executive Branch of the Government, March 21, 1947. Viewable on the HSTL website at https://www.trumanlibrary.gov/library/executive-orders/9835/executive-order-9835.
60. White House cross reference memo on letter from Abram Flaxer, President of the United Public Workers of America to Truman regarding EO 9835. April 2, 1947. HSTL, OF 252-I, President's Tem Commission on Employee Loyalty (2 of 2), Box 923.
61. Letter of Phil Murrary, President, CIO to Truman, April 14, 1947, 1. HSTL, OF 252-K, Government Employees Loyalty Program (1945–1947), Box 923.
62. Truman note to Phil Murray, CIO, April 15, 1947. HSTL, OF 252-K, Government Employees Loyalty Program (1945–1947), Box 923.
63. Joseph Young, "Many Bills Vital to U.S. Workers Face Congress," *Washington Evening Star,* January 13, 1946, B1. Retrieved via LOCCA.
64. United States Statutes at Large, 60 Stat. 458, July 5, 1946.
65. "Ten in State Department Fired on Suspicion of Disloyalty," *Washington Evening Star,* June 27, 1947, A-1. Retrieved via LOCCA.
66. Garnett D. Horner, "3-Man Board Planned at State Department to Screen Loyalty Cases," *Washington Evening Star,* July 9, 1947, A-6. Retrieved via LOCCA.
67. Horner, "3-Man Board Planned," A-6.
68. Joseph and Stewart Alsop, "The Case of the Ten," *The Wilmington Morning Star,* August 16, 1947, 4. Retrieved via LOCCA.
69. Garnett D. Horner, "Associates of Suspected Reds Will Lose State Department Jobs," *Washington Evening Star,* October 7, 1947, A-1. Retrieved via LOCCA.
70. Note from Eleanor Roosevelt to President Truman, November 13, 1947. HSTL, OF 2-E, Loyalty Review Board, Box 14.
71. White House press release on the Civil Service Commission's Loyalty Review Board, November 14, 1947. HSTL, OF 2-E, Loyalty Review Board, Box 14.
72. White House press release on the Civil Service Commission's Loyalty Review Board, November 14, 1947.
73. McCullough, *Truman,* 553.

"ONE NATION DIVIDED" 277

74. EO 9835, Part V, Section 2(f).
75. For details on the FDR-era program, see Robert Justin Goldstein, *American Blacklist: The Attorney Generals' List of Subversive Organizations* (Lawrence: University of Kansas Press, 2008), 18–43.
76. "Clark Subversive List Farcical, Thomas Says, Offering Another," *Washington Evening Star*, December 5, 1947, 1, 6. Retrieved via LOCCA.
77. "Clark Subversive List Farcical," 1.
78. *Hearings Regarding Communism in Labor Unions, Hearings before the Committee on Un-American Activities*, House of Representatives, 80th Congress (First Session), February 27, 1947, 25.
79. *Investigation of Un-American Propaganda Activities in the United States, Hearings before the Committee on Un-American Activities*, House of Representatives, 80th Congress (First Session) on H.R. 1884 and H.R. 2122, Bills to Curb or Outlaw the Communist Party of the United States, Part 2: Testimony of J. Edgar Hoover, Director, Federal Bureau of Investigation, March 26, 1947, 33.
80. *Investigation of Un-American Propaganda Activities*, 38.
81. *Investigation of Un-American Propaganda Activities*, 48–49.
82. Robert K. Walsh, "House Unit to Press Red Probe, but Party Ban Seems Unlikely," *Washington Evening Star*, March 27, 1947, A-1. Retrieved via LOCCA.
83. *Investigation of Un-American Propaganda Activities in the United States, Hearings before the Committee on Un-American Activities*, House of Representatives, 80th Congress (First Session) on H.R. 1884 and H.R. 2122, Bills to Curb or Outlaw the Communist Party of the United States, Part 2: Testimony of J. Edgar Hoover, Director, Federal Bureau of Investigation, March 26, 1947, 45–46.
84. *Investigation of Un-American Propaganda Activities in the United States, Hearings before the Committee on Un-American Activities*, House of Representatives, 80th Congress (First Session) on H.R. 1884 and H.R. 2122, Bills to Curb or Outlaw the Communist Party of the United States, March 24–28, 1947, 288.
85. *Investigation of Un-American Propaganda Activities*, 288.
86. *Investigation of Un-American Propaganda Activities*, 289.
87. *Investigation of Un-American Propaganda Activities*, 289.
88. See Larry Ceplair and Steven Englund, *The Inquisition in Hollywood: Politics in the Film Community, 1930–1960* (Chicago: University of Illinois Press, 2003), 258–259.
89. *Investigation of Un-American Propaganda Activities in the United States, Hearings before the Committee on Un-American Activities*, House of Representatives, 80th Congress (First Session) on H.R. 1884 and H.R. 2122, Bills to Curb or Outlaw the Communist Party of the United States, March 24–28, 1947, 293.
90. "Shades of Shirley Temple," editorial by *The People's Voice*, May 16, 1947, 4. Retrieved via LOCCA.
91. Ceplair and Englund, *The Inquisition in Hollywood*, 260.
92. Ceplair and Englund, *The Inquisition in Hollywood*, 259.
93. Public Law 80–101, Sec. 9(h).
94. "Hollywood Red Probe Postponed by Thomas; Will Open October 20," Associated Press as carried by the *Washington Evening Star*, September 21, 1947, A-8. Retrieved via LOCCA.
95. Ceplair and Englund, *The Inquisition in Hollywood*, 287.

278   CHAPTER 5

96. *Hearings Regarding the Communist Infiltration of the Motion Picture Industry, Hearings before the Committee on Un-American Activities,* House of Representatives, 80th Congress (First Session), Public Law 601, October 20–30, 1947, 10.

97. *Hearings Regarding the Communist Infiltration of the Motion Picture Industry,* 13.

98. *Hearings Regarding the Communist Infiltration of the Motion Picture Industry,* 294–295.

99. *Hearings Regarding the Communist Infiltration of the Motion Picture Industry,* 327.

100. David L. Dunbar, "The Hollywood Ten: The Men Who Refused to Name Names," *The Hollywood Reporter,* November 16, 2015 (online version). Accessed at https://www.hollywoodreporter.com/lists/hollywood-ten-men-who-refused-839762.

101. Ceplair and Englund, *The Inquisition in Hollywood,* 340.

102. "C.G. Davidson, 86, Member of Truman Advisory Group," *New York Times* obituary, September 26, 1996, D-23.

103. HSTL, Oral History Interviews, C. Girard Davidson Oral History Interview, July 1, 1972.

104. Correspondence between Davidson, Durr, Keyserling, Fortas, and Stokes can be found at the HSTL, Papers of C. Girard Davidson, Box 31.

105. "C.G. Davidson, 86, Member of Truman Advisory Group," *New York Times* obituary, September 26, 1996, D-23.

106. "FBI vs. FCC," *Washington Evening Star,* December 3, 1947, A-8. Retrieved via LOCCA.

107. "Capehart Hits Durr for 'Brazen Attempt to Sabotage' FBI," Associated Press as carried by the *Washington Evening Star,* December 5, 1947, A-7. Retrieved via LOCCA.

108. "Capehart Hits Durr," A-7.

109. Memo of Assistant Secretary of the Interior C. Girard Davidson to White House Special Counsel Clark Clifford, December 22, 1947. HSTL, Papers of C. Girard Davidson, Box 31.

110. HSTL, Oral History Interviews, Oral History Interview of C. Girard Davidson, July 17, 1972. Accessed via https://www.trumanlibrary.gov/library/oral-histories/davidsn1.

111. Letter from Assistant Secretary of Interior C. Girard Davidson to White House Special Counsel Clark Clifford, December 29, 1947, 1–2. HSTL, Papers of C. Girard Davidson, Box 31.

112. Letter from Assistant Secretary of Interior C. Girard Davidson to J. Edgar Hoover, January 13, 1948. HSTL, Papers of C. Girard Davidson, Box 31.

113. Letter from Assistant Secretary of Interior C. Girard Davidson to Benedict K. Zobrist, Director, HSTL, September 17, 1985, 1. HSTL, Papers of C. Girard Davidson, Box 31.

114. Letter from Assistant Secretary of Interior C. Girard Davidson to Benedict K. Zobrist, Director, HSTL, September 17, 1985, 1.

115. Letter to Assistant Secretary of Interior C. Girard Davidson from Seth Richardson, Chairman, Civil Service Commission, October 15, 1948. HSTL, Papers of C. Girard Davidson, Box 31.

116. Letter to Assistant Secretary of Interior C. Girard Davidson from Seth Richardson, Chairman, Civil Service Commission, November 19, 1948. HSTL, Papers of C. Girard Davidson, Box 31.

117. Letter to Assistant Secretary of Interior C. Girard Davidson from Leon Keyserling, Vice Chairman, President's Council of Economic Advisors, November 3, 1948. HSTL, Papers of C. Girard Davidson, Box 31.

"ONE NATION DIVIDED" 279

118. Letter to Assistant Secretary of Interior C. Girard Davidson from Clifford Durr, November 4, 1948. HSTL, Papers of C. Girard Davidson, Box 31.

119. Letter to Assistant Secretary of Interior C. Girard Davidson from Clifford Durr, November 4, 1948.

120. Clark Clifford with Richard Holbrooke, *Counsel to the President: A Memoir* (New York: Random House, 1991), 182.

121. HSTL, PSF, Box 144.

122. Several hundred pages of largely declassified FBI reports on Wallace can be found on the FBI's Vault website at vault.fbi.gov/.

123. Memo from J. Edgar Hoover to Assistant FBI Directors Clyde Tolson, D. Milton Ladd, and Edward Tamm, May 20, 1948. FBI File 62-HQ-71788-103. Available via the FBI Vault website at vault.fbi.gov/.

124. Raymond Brandt, "Platform and Rules of Progressive Party Show Red Tinge Extent," *Washington Evening Star*, July 26, 1948, A-3. LOCCA.

125. Based on the authors examination of declassified FBI records on Wallace available on the FBI's Vault website.

126. *Hearings on Proposed Legislation to Curb or Control the Communist Party of the United States, Hearings before the Subcommittee on Legislation of the Committee on Un-American Activities,* House of Representatives, 80th Congress (Second Session), on H.R. 4422 and H.R. 4581, February 5, 1948, 3.

127. *Hearings on Proposed Legislation to Curb or Control the Communist Party,* 12–13.

128. From the description of H.R. 5281, 80th Congress (First Session).

129. Statement of Attorney General Tom Clark in *Hearings on Proposed Legislation to Curb or Control the Communist Party of the United States, Hearings before the Subcommittee on Legislation of the Committee on Un-American Activities,* House of Representatives, 80th Congress (Second Session), on H.R. 4422 and H.R. 4581, February 5, 1948, 20.

130. See the statement of Benjamin J. Davis in *Hearings on Proposed Legislation to Curb or Control the Communist Party of the United States, Hearings before the Subcommittee on Legislation of the Committee on Un-American Activities,* House of Representatives, 80th Congress (Second Session), on H.R. 4422 and H.R. 4581, February 20, 1948, 449–459.

131. See John A. Farrell, *Richard Nixon: The Life* (New York: Vintage Books, 2017), 101.

132. H.R. 5852, the Subversive Activities Control Act, 1948, 80th Congress (Second Session).

133. H.R. 5852, the Subversive Activities Control Act, 1948, 80th Congress (Second Session), Sections 4 through 12.

134. Memo from J. Edgar Hoover to MG Harry Vaughn, May 8, 1948, 1. HSTL, PSF, Box 143.

135. "Senate Hearings on Mundt Bill, but No Early Action, Promised," Associated Press as carried in the *Washington Evening Star*, May 20, 1948, 1, 5. Retrieved via LOCCA.

136. William S. White, "Wallace Forces Take Lead of Anti-Mundt Bill March," *New York Times*, June 2, 1948, 1, 6. Retrieved via https://www.nytimes.com/search/?srchst=.

137. "Federal Grand Jury Probing Reds Makes Sealed Indictments: Bench Warrant Ordered by Judge after Year of Inquiry in New York," Associated Press as carried by the *Washington Evening Star*, July 20, 1948, 1. Retrieved via LOCCA.

138. "American-Born Blonde Is Reported Key in Probe of Red Ring," Associated Press as carried in the *Washington Evening Star*, July 21, 1948, A-5. Retrieved via LOCCA.

280   CHAPTER 5

139. For details, see Testimony of Elizabeth Terrill Bentely before the Committee on Expenditures in the Executive Departments, Investigations Subcommittee, United States Senate. Executive Session hearing transcript, July 28, 1948.

140. Miriam Ottenberg, "High Officials Named in Spy Ring Probe," *Washington Event Star*, July 31, 1948, A-1. Retrieved via LOCCA.

141. Farrell, *Richard Nixon*, 106.

142. *Hearings Regarding Communist Espionage in the United States, Hearings before the Committee on Un-American Activities,* House of Representatives, 80th Congress (Second Session), August 3, 1948, 581.

143. Memo of J. Edgar Hoover to MG Harry Vaughn, November 8, 1945. HSTL, PSF, Box 143.

144. Memo of Clark Clifford to President Truman, August 4, 1948. HSTL, OF-252K—Loyalty 1948 (1 of 2), Box 924.

145. Statement of President Harry S. Truman, August 5, 1948. HSTL, OF-252K—Loyalty 1948 (1 of 2), Box 924.

146. Miriam Ottenberg, "Hiss Testifies He Has Never Been Communist," *Washington Evening Star*, August 5, 1948, A-5. via LOCCA.

147. Farrell, *Richard Nixon*, 102–103.

148. Farrell, *Richard Nixon*, 120.

149. Farrell, *Richard Nixon*, 122–124.

150. Farrell, *Richard Nixon*, 124.

151. Public Law 80-253, signed by President Truman on July 26, 1947, with an effective date of September 18, 1947.

152. For an excellent one-volume history of the creation of the NCS, JCS and CIA, see Amy Zegart, *Flawed by Design: The Evolution of the CIA, JCS, and NSC* (Stanford: Stanford University Press, 1999).

153. J. Patrick Coyne, "A Brief Study Concerning he Internal Security of the United States," June 28, 1948. HSTL, PSFs, Box 171. Hereinafter cited as Coyne.

154. Coyne, "A Brief Study," 6.

155. Coyne, "A Brief Study," 21.

156. Coyne, "A Brief Study," 22–26.

157. Coyne, "A Brief Study," 34–36.

158. Coyne, "A Brief Study," 30.

159. *ex parte Endo*, 323 U.S. 302.

160. National Security Council Progress Report by NSC Representative on Internal Security on the Implementation of Internal Security (NSC 17/4; 17/6), November 7, 1949, 3. HSTL, PSFs, Box 173.

161. John Earl Haynes and Harvey Klehr, *Venona: Decoding Soviet Espionage in America* (New London: Yale University Press, 1999), 158.

162. FBI Washington Field Office message to Director, FBI, December 31, 1948, FBI file 65-HQ-58365-1. Available on the FBI Vault website at vault.fbi.gov/.

163. Athan Theoharis, *Chasing Spies: How the FBI Failed in Counterintelligence but Promoted the Politics of McCarthyism in The Cold War Years* (Chicago: Ivan R. Dee, 2002), 84–85. Hereinafter, *Chasing Spies*.

164. *Coplon v. United States* (two Cases), 191 F.2d 749 (D.C. Cir. 1951).

165. Theoharis, *Chasing Spies*, 86–87.

166. Theoharis, *Chasing Spies*, 86–87.

"ONE NATION DIVIDED" 281

167. Letter from Clifford Durr, National Lawyers Guild to President Truman, June 20, 1949, 1. HSTL, OF 10, Box 87.
168. Letter from Clifford Durr, National Lawyers Guild to President Truman, June 20, 1949, 1.
169. Letter from Clifford Durr, National Lawyers Guild to President Truman, June 20, 1949, 2.
170. Letter from President Truman to Clifford Durr, National Lawyers Guild, June 23, 1949. HSTL, OF 10, Box 87.
171. FBI records on the NLG can be found at New York University's Tamiment Library. The FBI WFO May 1941 report is FBI file 100–7321, obtained via litigation in *NLG v. Attorney General*.
172. Letter from J. Edgar Hoover to MG Harry Vaughn, Military Aide to the President, January 14, 1950. HSTL, PSF, Box 143.
173. Letter from Clifford Durr, National Lawyers Guild to President Truman, January 19, 1950. HSTL, OF 10, Box 87.
174. Letter from Clifford Durr, National Lawyers Guild to President Truman, January 19, 1950, 1–2.
175. Robert J. Donovan, *Tumultuous Years: The Presidency of Harry S. Truman, 1949–1953* (New York: W. W. Norton & Company, 1982), 134. Hereinafter cited as *Tumultuous Years*.
176. Donovan, *Tumultuous Years*, 135.
177. *Congressional Record—Senate*, January 25, 1950, 895.
178. Lincoln Day speech of Senator Joseph R. McCarthy, February 9, 1950, Wheeling, WV. Retrieved via the Digital History Project, University of Houston at http://www .digitalhistory.uh.edu/disp_textbook.cfm?smtID=3&psid=3633.
179. Donovan, *Tumultuous Years*, 162–163.
180. Donovan, *Tumultuous Years*, 163.
181. *Congressional Record—Senate*, February 20, 1950, 1952.
182. *Congressional Record—Senate*, February 20, 1950, 1955–1964.
183. *Congressional Record—Senate*, February 22, 1950, 2129–2150.
184. *Congressional Record—Senate*, March 2, 1950, 2642.
185. *Congressional Record—Senate*, March 2, 1950, 2642–2643.
186. *State Department Employee Loyalty Investigation, Hearings before a Subcommittee of the Committee on Foreign Relations,* United States Senate, 81st Congress (Second Session), Pursuant to S. Res. 231, Testimony of Senator Joseph R. McCarthy, March 13, 1950, 104.
187. Owen Lattimore, *Ordeal by Slander* (New York: Carol & Graf Publishers, 2004), 3–4.
188. Lattimore, *Ordeal by Slander*, 1–2.
189. "Libel Suit Threat Sent McCarthy in Lattimore Case: Paul Porter's Firm Warns Senator to Retract Charge," *Washington Evening Star*, March 27, 1950, A-1. Retrieved via LOCCA.
190. Cable of Attorney General J. Howard McGrath to President Truman, March 17, 1950, 1–2. HSTL, OF 419K (Congress), Box 1322.
191. Letter of President Truman to Senator Millard Tydings, March 28, 1950, 1–4. HSTL, OF 419K (Congress), Box 1322.
192. Letter of President Truman to Senator Millard Tydings, April 3, 1950, 2. HSTL, OF 419K (Congress), Box 1322.

282 CHAPTER 5

193. *State Department Employee Loyalty Investigation, Hearings before a Subcommittee of the Committee on Foreign Relations*, United States Senate, 81st Congress (Second Session), Pursuant to S. Res. 231, Testimony of Owen Lattimore, April 6, 1950, 418.
194. *State Department Employee Loyalty Investigation.*
195. *State Department Employee Loyalty Investigation*, 424.
196. *State Department Employee Loyalty Investigation*, 486.
197. Cecil Holland, "Contempt Action Asked on Field and Browder: Senate Probers Plan to Begin Examining Loyalty Files Monday," *Washington Evening Star*, May 6, 1950, A-1, 2. Retrieved via LOCCA.
198. Letter of Senator Millard Tydings to President Truman, June 5, 1950, 1. HSTL, OF 419K (Congress), Box 1322.
199. Letter of Senator Millard Tydings to President Truman, June 5, 1950, 2.
200. *Congressional Record—Senate*, June 1, 1950, 7894–7895.
201. *State Department Loyalty Investigation.* Report of the Committee on Foreign Relations pursuant to S. Res. 231, Senate Report No. 2108, 81st Congress (Second Session), July 20, 1950, 151.
202. H.R. 3342, Subversive Activities Control Act of 1949, March 8, 1949.
203. S. 2311, Subversive Activities Control Act of 1949, June 2, 1949.
204. H.R. 10, January 3, 1949.
205. Memo of White House Administrative Assistants Stephen Spingarn and Charles Murphy to President Truman, May 16, 1950, 1. HSTL, OF 2750 (Internal Security Legislation), Box 1776.
206. Memo of White House Administrative Assistants Stephen Spingarn and Charles Murphy to President Truman, May 16, 1950, 1.
207. Memo of White House Administrative Assistants Stephen Spingarn and Charles Murphy to President Truman, May 16, 1950, 2.
208. Memo of White House Administrative Assistants Stephen Spingarn and Charles Murphy to President Truman, May 16, 1950.
209. Haynes and Klehr, *Venona*, 34–39.
210. "Former Army Enlisted Man Seized in Klaus Fuchs Atomic Spy Ring; Jet Expert Accused of Being Red," Associated Press as carried by *The Washington Evening Star*, June 16, 1950, 1. Retrieved via LOCCA.
211. See the FBI's "Famous Cases & Criminals: Atom Spy Case/Rosenbergs" website at https://www.fbi.gov/history/famous-cases/atom-spy-caserosenbergs.
212. See the Atomic Heritage Foundation entry on the Fuchs case at https://www.atomicheritage.org/profile/klaus-fuchs.
213. Message of President Truman to the House and Senate, August 8, 1950, 4–5. HSTL, OF-2750 (Internal Security Legislation), Box 1776.
214. Memo of Stephen Spingarn to MG Robert Landry, August 24, 1950, 1. HSTL, OF-2750 (Internal Security Legislation), Box 1776.
215. *Hearing before the Committee on Un-American Activities*, House of Representatives, 81st Congress (Second Session), September 22, 1950. Testimony of Hazel Scott Powell, 3617.
216. *Hearing before the Committee on Un-American Activities*, House of Representatives, 81st Congress (Second Session), September 22, 1950, 3619.

"ONE NATION DIVIDED" 283

217. Order of President Harry Truman appointing Seth Richardson chairman of the Subversive Activities Control Board, October 23, 1950. HSTL, OF-2750-D (Subversive Activities Control Board), Box 1788.

218. *Report on the National Committee to Defeat the Mundt Bill: A Communist Lobby. House Committee on Un-American Activities*, House Report No. 3248, December 7, 1950.

219. NSC Progress Report on Internal Security, March 26, 1951, 6. HSTL, PSF, Box 177.

220. NSC Progress Report on Internal Security, March 26, 1951, 8.

221. NSC Progress Report on Internal Security, March 26, 1951, 9.

222. NSC Progress Report on Internal Security, March 26, 1951, 9.

223. NSC Progress Report on Internal Security, March 26, 1951, 10.

224. *Communist Infiltration of Hollywood Motion-Picture Industry, Part 1. Hearings before the Committee on Un-American Activities*, House of Representatives, 82nd Congress (First Session), April 10, 1951, Testimony of Sterling Hayden, 128–171.

225. Sterling Hayden, *Wanderer* (Pickle Partners Publishing: Auckland, 2014, Kindle Edition).

226. *Communist Infiltration of Hollywood Motion-Picture Industry, Part 2. Hearings before the Committee on Un-American Activities*, House of Representatives, 82nd Congress (First Session), April 24, 1951, Testimony of George Willner, 377–378.

227. *Institute of Pacific Relations. Hearings before the Subcommittee to Investigate the Administration of the Internal Security Act and Other Internal Security Laws of the Committee on the Judiciary*, United States Senate, 82nd Congress (First Session), on the Institute of Pacific Relations, Part 1, July 25, 1951, 3.

228. *Dennis v. United States*, 341 U.S. 394 (1951).

229. *Dennis v. United States*, at 341 U.S. 517.

230. Stone, *Perilous Times*, 255.

231. FBI Washington Field Office memo to FBI Director Hoover, "Emergency Civil Liberties Committee—Information Concerning," October 19, 1951, FBI file 100-HQ-384660, released to the Cato Institute via FOIA on February 12, 2021.

232. "150 Notables Form Emergency Civil Rights Committee," *Daily Worker*, October 8, 1951, 1. Contained in FBI file 100-HQ-384660, released to the Cato Institute via FOIA on February 12, 2021.

233. FBI file 100-NK-35610, Newark Field Office Report of August 6, 1952, "Emergency Civil Liberties Committee—Internal Security-C," released to the Cato Institute via FOIA on February 12, 2021.

234. NSC Progress Report on Internal Security, December 20, 1951, 17. HSTL, PSF, Box 179.

235. NSC Progress Report on Internal Security, December 20, 1951, 17.

236. *Institute of Pacific Relations, Hearings before the Subcommittee to Investigate the Administration of the Internal Security Act and Other Internal Security Laws of the Committee on the Judiciary*, United States Senate, 82nd Congress (Second Session) on the Institute of Pacific Relations, Part 9, February 26, 1952, 2899–2900.

237. *Institute of Pacific Relations, Hearings before the Subcommittee*, 2933.

238. Robert K. Walsh, "The Professor's Vocabulary Is Colorful," *Washington Evening Star*, March 10, 1952, A-8. Retrieved via LOCCA.

239. Based on the author's review of HUAC hearings obtained via ProQuest Congressional, March 2021.

240. *Tax-Exempt Foundations, Hearings before the Select Committee to Investigate Tax-Exempt Foundations and Comparable Organizations*, House of Representatives, 82nd Congress

284   CHAPTER 5

(Second Session) on H. Res. 561, November 18, 19, 20, 21, 24, 25 and December 2, 3, 5, 8, 9, 10, 11, 15, 22, 23, and 30, 1952.

241. Based on the author's review of SISS hearings obtained via ProQuest Congressional, March 2021.

242. *Communist Domination of Unions and National Security. Hearings before a Subcommittee of the Committee on Labor and Public Welfare,* United States Senate, 82nd Congress (Second Session) on Communist Domination of Unions and National Security, March 17, 18, 19, June 6, 11, 13, 17, 19, 27, and July 8, 1952.

243. Dozens of such domestic intelligence summaries for the June–July 1952 period alone can be found at the HSTL, CF, Department of Justice, Box 18.

244. Memo President Truman to all executive branch agencies and departments, August 7, 1952. HSTL, OF 252-K, Loyalty, 1952–53, Bo 925.

245. NSC Internal Security Progress Report, November 24, 1952, 3 as contained in NSC 127th Meeting Minutes, December 17, 1952. HSTL, PSFs, Box 181.

246. NSC Internal Security Progress Report, November 24, 1952, 3.

247. NSC Internal Security Progress Report, November 24, 1952, 3.

CHAPTER 6

"Is This Idolatry of Security?"
1953–1961

As president, Dwight Eisenhower's internal security policies intensified the federal government's surveillance efforts, as well as its direct assault on the CP USA and others deemed in league with Soviet political subversion or espionage efforts.

Eisenhower's executive order on federal employee loyalty, even harsher than Truman's, formalized the targeting of homosexuals for exclusion or expulsion from the federal workforce. Eisenhower's embrace of the Communist Control Act, passed by Congress in August 1954, made him the first president to sign a law outlawing a political party.

In 1958 he would be briefed on and not object to J. Edgar Hoover's most controversial anticommunist initiative to date: the Counterintelligence Program (COINTELPRO). An officially sanctioned infiltration and disruption operation, COINTELPRO would ultimately be employed against a range of groups and individuals, including the Southern Christian Leadership Conference, Students for a Democratic Society, and thousands of others. Army and naval domestic intelligence operations also continued in this era, and the formal creation of the National Security Agency (NSA) in 1959 would add another centralized, electronic communications capability to internal security operations via the SHAMROCK program.

During most of the Eisenhower era, resistance to existing internal security policies and congressional investigations by civil society groups would prove just as ineffectual as they had with his predecessor. But by the last year of his presidency, a new group—the National Committee to Abolish

286   CHAPTER 6

the House Un-American Activities Committee—would begin to change that dynamic. And new, more politically aggressive liberals like Rep. John Moss (D-CA) would openly and relentlessly mount public attacks on the ever-growing federal national security establishment, and particularly government secrecy.

INTERNAL SECURITY INTENSIFIED

The 1952 presidential campaign had, toward the end, turned nasty. Senator Joseph McCarthy's year-long relentless attacks on Eisenhower's mentor and wartime commander, General George Marshall, over the "loss" of China had produced only a tepid statement of support from Eisenhower in August. His subsequent embrace of McCarthy on the campaign trail prompted Truman to blast Eisenhower for coddling "moral pygmies" such as McCarthy. In response Eisenhower claimed that if he prevailed in the election he would not ride in the same car as Truman on Inauguration Day 1953.[1]

In fact the two men would ride in the same car to Eisenhower's swearing-in ceremony. Perhaps conscious of the need to bring the nation back together after the campaign, Eisenhower's opening prayer included two sentences designed to serve that purpose:

> Give us, we pray, the power to discern clearly right from wrong, and allow all our words and actions to be governed thereby, and by the laws of this land. Especially we pray that our concern shall be for all the people regardless of station, race or calling.[2]

Regarding confronting the communist threat, Eisenhower told his fellow citizens that "we view our Nation's strength and security as a trust upon which rests the hope of free men everywhere."[3] As events would show, Eisenhower's promise to be guided by fairness and racial colorblindness would take a back seat to security measures targeting alleged Reds in government, business, academia, Hollywood, and virtually every other segment of American society.

Even before he took office, key aides to Eisenhower sought to kill a proposal to have the entire federal government loyalty program subjected to an independent investigation.

On January 12, 1953, Milton Hill sent a five-page SECRET memo to General Wilton "Jerry" Persons outlining objections to the proposed commission.[4] Hill claimed that such a commission would be "a direct affront to Congress"

Figure 6.1. President Eisenhower's Executive Order 10450 on the federal employee loyalty program led to mass firings or resignations among thousands of Americans who had no actual ties to Soviet espionage. His reluctant support for the Civil Rights Act of 1957 was more than offset by his allowing the FBI to spy on the NAACP and other civil rights organizations. *Eisenhower Presidential Library*

and cited the failed Nimitz Commission as an example.[5] Hill went on to claim that "The basic idea behind the commission, undoubtedly obscured in the good faith of its present supporters, seems to be to limit the effectiveness of the Federal Bureau of Investigation." Hoover, Hill told Persons, was "diametrically opposed to the idea of a Presidential commission."[6] The idea was quietly shelved. Instead, the new administration chose to take a much more aggressive posture toward finding and ejecting alleged Soviet sympathizers not only from the federal government but from the country itself.

At the March 27, 1953, cabinet meeting, Attorney General Herbert Brownell announced that the program to identify, denaturalize, and deport alleged US communists was ongoing, with some 10,000 naturalized US citizens under investigation for "engaging in subversive activities."[7] Twelve thousand foreign nationals living in the United States were also under investigation for potential Soviet or CP USA connections.[8] Like anarchists in the early twentieth century, immigrants with favorable views toward aspects of socialism or communism were very much in the administration's crosshairs.

Natural-born federal employees were not much better off. While they could not be deported, they could be run out of government service on the basis of unverified innuendo that they were Soviet fellow travelers. And under the new administration, sexual orientation was added to the list of reasons a person with an otherwise stellar service record could be fired from a federal job.

The leadership of the nation's national security establishment had long been hostile to homosexuality in the ranks.

At a March 7, 1949, House Armed Service Committee hearings on the Uniform Code of Military Justice (UCMJ), military witnesses made it clear that homosexuality in the ranks was considered a "morals" offense and that even if a servicemember had been "tried for something else, such as robbery, and it was thrown out, then we do not want to keep him if we know he is a homosexual."[9] The policy was formally codified by the new Defense Department Personnel Policy Board in an October 11, 1949, memo.[10]

Hoover's interest in "sex deviates" (his term) as an investigative target went back to at least the late 1930s.[11] As the confrontation with the Soviets intensified and the hunt for Soviet spies with it, the issue of homosexuality as a security risk (to blackmail, coercion, etc.) arose. Hoover made finding and rooting out homosexuals in the federal government a major FBI focus. One of his first targets, Charles Thayer, worked for the newly created Voice of America (VOA).

The head of VOA's operation in New York, Thayer had in May 1948 complained to the media that the FBI's slow pace in closing background investigations of VOA job applicants was harming VOA's mission as it was understaffed. Hoover and his chief aides immediately viewed Thayer as hostile to the Bureau. When they realized he had managed to evade a loyalty investigation due his status as an FDR political appointee, they went looking for "derogatory information" on Thayer to justify an investigation. The Bureau would spend four years accumulating allegations of Thayer's homosexuality, culminating in his resignation from the State Department in March 1953.[12]

It was against this backdrop that Eisenhower and his senior advisors developed Executive Order 10450, which replaced Truman's EO 9835 and acted as the regulatory implementation of a government employee loyalty law, Public Law 81–733 of August 26, 1950.[13] Even as administration officials worked out the details of the new order, three days before its official unveiling Attorney General Brownell warned his cabinet colleagues that abuse of the new authority "as a means of eliminating incompetent personnel would destroy the program's effectiveness."[14]

Eisenhower's new loyalty program order mandated a complete review of all prior cases where "there has been conducted a full field investigation under Executive Order No. 9835" and that each agency or department head should "as may be appropriate, shall re-adjudicate, or cause to be re-adjudicated, in accordance with the said act of August 26, 1950, such of those cases as have not been adjudicated under a security standard commensurate with that established under this order."[15]

Eisenhower was telling the federal bureaucracy to "reinvent the wheel" vis-à-vis prior security investigations. It was also a gratuitous political slap at his former predecessor and a requirement that had no apparent justification on the basis of any new, concrete derogatory information on those previously investigated. For federal employees who had previously been the targets of such scrutiny, it also meant they were to undergo the same humiliating and fear-inducing process yet again.

The order also included vague, broad criteria for launching investigations, including, "Any behavior, activities, or associations which tend to show that the individual is not reliable or trustworthy."[16] Would support for the NAACP—a continual FBI surveillance target—constitute an untrustworthy association? A group opposed to the McCarran Act, such as the relatively recently formed Emergency Civil Liberties Committee? The sweeping nature of the language invited the very kind of abuse Brownell had warned against.

The president's new directive also got the executive branch squarely into the public morals business, with the order justifying an investigation on the basis of "Any criminal, infamous, dishonest, immoral, or notoriously disgraceful conduct, habitual use of intoxicants to excess, drug addiction, sexual perversion."[17]

Without a doubt, alcoholism and drug addiction were vulnerabilities from a counterintelligence standpoint. But what constituted "infamous" or "notoriously disgraceful" conduct? The order provided no boundaries, guidance, or examples. And although "sexual perversion" was likewise left undefined, everyone in 1950s America knew the phrase was a euphemism for homosexuality.

During Truman's first term, the State Department had fired nearly 100 individuals it deemed or who had admitted to being gay.[18] And throughout 1950, Senator Clyde Hoey (D-NC) had chaired a Senate investigation into the alleged threat homosexuals in government represented.[19] In making the claim that having homosexuals or other "sex perverts" in government service represented a counterintelligence risk, Hoey's subcommittee provided no examples of it actually happening since the start of the Cold War. Also left unsaid was the fact that effectively criminalizing private behavior itself created the very blackmail risk that Hoey and his colleagues decried. Thus, the groundwork for a purge of gay and lesbian federal employees was laid by both the executive and legislative branches of the federal government.

Through EO 10450, Hoover and every other head of an executive branch agency or department had official sanction to investigate and run out of government any federal employee deemed homosexual, regardless of whether they had engaged in espionage.

EO 10450 would also prove a boon to HUAC, SISS, and any other congressional committee investigating alleged subversives in the government. The order allowed investigation of any federal employee for "Refusal by the individual, upon the ground of constitutional privilege against self-incrimination, to testify before a congressional committee regarding charges of his alleged disloyalty or other misconduct."[20] A federal employee who invoked their constitutional right not to answer a question under Fifth Amendment protection could be fired, and a prospective federal job seeker who did so would be barred from federal service.

The order did charge the Office of Personnel Management (OPM) with monitoring implementation of EO 10450 for any "Tendencies in such programs to deny to individual employees fair, impartial, and equitable treatment at the hands of the Government, or rights under the Constitution and laws of the United States or this order."[21] But given that the order itself considered the invocation of a constitutional right against self-incrimination to be grounds for investigation or a bar to federal employment, the OPM oversight provision was largely meaningless, particularly since the new order, like its predecessor, denied employees accused of disloyalty the opportunity to directly confront their accusers and the evidence being used against them.

On October 23, White House Press Secretary James Hagerty issued a press release touting the new program's accomplishments at the four-month mark. Since it had went into effect, EO 10450 had resulted in nearly 1,500 federal employees leaving the government through dismissal or resignation.

"Of the 1456 employees, 863 were dismissed from Federal service by their various agencies and departments and 593 resigned," Hagerty noted. "In all of the resignation cases, the agencies and departments had unfavorable reports on these employees, based on the criteria outlined in Section 8 of the Executive Order."[22] Between the start of the program under Truman and the end of Eisenhower's first term, federal employs separated under the two orders (through dismissal or resignation) would number nearly 15,000.[23]

While the administration relied on the various executive branch agencies and departments to carry out the mandate contained in EO 10450 to cleanse the federal work force of alleged Soviet sympathizers and other undesirable elements, it called upon another federal entity—the Subversive Activities Control Board (SACB)—to help it find, expose, and neutralize communists in civil society organizations. Interestingly, it would be one of Eisenhower's first appointments to SACB that would cause him the most opposition—privately and publicly—to the revised government employee loyalty program.

JUDICIAL ACTIVISM:
THE STATE SECRETS PRIVILEGE

Eisenhower's first year in office would also see the Supreme Court hand the executive branch a sweeping mandate to use claims of secrecy to conceal government activities alleged to be vital to protecting the nation. In reality, and in a replay of the kind of Army Department lies and omissions to the Supreme Court that were the hallmark of the *Korematsu* and *ex parte Endo* cases, the Air Force would win the case by concealing from the high court and the victims' families the real reason for the crash of a B-29 bomber in 1948.

On October 6, 1948, a B-29 Stratofortress lifted off from Robins Air Force Base in Georgia just shy of 1:30 p.m. to test electronics associated with

292   CHAPTER 6

the Air Force's Project Banshee, an effort to develop an unmanned, nuclear armed version of the B-29 for use in a potential war with the Soviet Union.[24] The flight ended in disaster forty minutes later, with an engine fire triggering a series of events that led to the plane exploding at about 15,000 feet. Of the thirteen men onboard, only four survived.[25]

Three widows of civilian engineers killed in the crash subsequently sued the federal government for damages in 1949, and the Air Force began a legal battle to deny the claims and, more tellingly, to keep the investigation report on the crash out of the public domain.[26] With the help of Philadelphia lawyer Charles Biddle—a former World War I flying ace—Phyllis Brauner, Elizabeth Palya, and Pat Reynolds beat the Air Force in the opening round. Eastern District of Pennsylvania Judge William H. Kirkpatrick ordered the Air Force to release the accident report and related records they had denied Biddle during the discovery phase of the case. The Air Force appealed, lost again at the appellate level, and finally appealed to the Supreme Court to review the decisions of the lower courts. The case was argued in October 1952, with the Supreme Court finally handing down its decision on March 9, 1953.

Unlike at the district court stage, during the appeals phase and before America's highest court, Air Force and Justice Department officials made the fantastical claim that records about the crash could not be released "without seriously hampering national security."[27] The widows did not seek any information on the still-classified Project Banshee; they wanted to know whether the Air Force had been negligent with maintenance on the plane in which their husbands had perished.

For the 6–3 majority that ruled in the Air Force's favor, even that narrow request represented a risk too great to take.

"In the instant case, we cannot escape judicial notice that this is a time of vigorous preparation for national defense," Chief Justice Fredrick Moore Vinson wrote for the majority. "Experience in the past war has made it common knowledge that air power is one of the most potent weapons in our scheme of defense, and that newly developing electronic devices have greatly enhanced the effective use of air power. . . . Certainly there was a reasonable danger that the accident investigation report would contain references to the secret electronic equipment which was the primary concern of the mission."[28]

Vinson went on to argue that once the Air Force had invoked "a Claim of Privilege," judges at all levels should proceed with extreme caution. Acknowledging that "Judicial control over the evidence in a case cannot be abdicated to the caprice of executive officers," Vinson also said the Court would not "go so far as to say that the court may automatically require a

"IS THIS IDOLATRY OF SECURITY?" 293

complete disclosure to the judge before the claim of privilege will be accepted in any case."[29]

The standard federal judges should use, Vinson wrote, was that in cases where "there is a reasonable danger that compulsion of the evidence will expose military matters which, in the interest of national security, should not be divulged. When this is the case . . . the court should not jeopardize the security which the privilege is meant to protect by insisting upon an examination of the evidence, even by the judge alone, in chambers."[30]

What Vinson and his five colleagues who sided with the Air Force had, in fact, done was abdicate the federal judiciary's responsibility to act as a check on executive branch overreach. This court-created doctrine would become known as the state secrets privilege.

There was absolutely nothing from stopping Vinson and his colleagues from demanding to review all relevant Air Force records in the case. Appropriate security measures could easily have been instituted to allow each justice and their respective clerks (where needed) to review the records. Had they done so, they would have realized that it was not only perfectly possible to segregate or redact the Project Banshee information from the actual accident report, but they would also have seen that the report itself was not classified. It would be over 50 years before that fact would become public. In the meantime, the nation's highest court had given Eisenhower and those who would follow him a nearly impenetrable legal shield behind which to hide any activity deemed related to national security, including waste, fraud, abuse, mismanagement, and even criminal conduct.

LOYALTY PROGRAM NEMESIS: SENATOR HARRY CAIN

When Washington Republican Senator Harry Pulliam Cain lost his reelection bid in 1952, he became one of many Eisenhower supporters hoping for a spot in the new administration. By April, he was on the short list to fill a vacancy on SACB and was ultimately nominated by Eisenhower for the position.

At his April 23 Senate confirmation hearing, his wartime service and interactions with Russian military personnel were the subject of much of the questioning. In form, those questions were similar to those hurled at "hostile" witnesses called before HUAC or SISS, but Cain's former Senate colleagues were far more respectful of him. His military service, and his time in the Senate, helped him evade any charge of being pro-Soviet.

Interestingly, his opposition to the internment of Japanese Americans after Pearl Harbor—he was one of only two West Coast politicians to publicly oppose the policy—was not raised by any of his Senate questioners.[31] The fact that he'd voted for the McCarran Act (which created SACB), and to override Truman's veto of it, probably allayed their concerns about Cain "going rogue" on civil liberties questions.[32]

The day before Cain's confirmation hearing, his soon-to-be colleagues on SACB received from Attorney General Brownell petitions on twelve organizations, seeking their designation as communist front groups.[33] Among the targets were the Civil Rights Congress, the Veterans of the Abraham Lincoln Brigade, the International Workers Order, and the Labor Youth League.[34]

In what would become a standard pattern throughout the 1950s, organizations accused by the Justice Department of being communist fronts challenged not only the constitutionality of the McCarran Act and the Board itself but filed dozens of motions with the Board seeking to delay or extend proceedings, challenging Justice Department evidence and claims, and otherwise seeking to delegitimize SACB and the law that created it. Additional confusion was created by the occasionally updated AGLOSO.

On April 29, 1953, Attorney General Brownell issued an updated AGLOSO that listed 190 organizations designated as subversive in connection with the federal employee loyalty program per EO 10450.[35] Among the repeat offenders were the three organizations that had won the first anti–Red

Figure 6.2. Attorney General Herbert Brownell championed Eisenhower's executive order on the federal employee loyalty program and Hoover's sweeping domestic surveillance and informant recruitment programs. *Library of Congress*

Scare Supreme Court case via the anti-AGLOSO McGrath Supreme Court ruling. Despite the victory at the high court, the Joint Anti-Fascist Refugee Committee and the International Workers Order would cease to exist as a result of continuing federal government pressure (in the case of the former) or liquidation proceedings by a state government (in the case of the latter).[36] The National Council on American-Soviet Friendship survived and remained a Justice Department target via AGLOSO and SACB.

SCIENTIST SMEARED AND EXILED: J. ROBERT OPPENHEIMER

The Rosenberg nuclear espionage affair had laid bare the fact that Soviet intelligence operatives had managed to penetrate the American nuclear research enterprise. One of the men most responsible for the success of the US nuclear program had, as an indirect result of the Rosenberg case, also become an investigative target: J. Robert Oppenheimer.

Years before his fellow Americans would come to know him as "the father of the atomic bomb," Oppenheimer had definitely circulated comfortably in leftist political circles. During the Spanish Civil War, Oppenheimer had made generous financial contributions in support of the anti-Franco forces, with some of that cash given directly to San Francisco area CP USA officials.[37] By 1941 the FBI had opened a file on Oppenheimer, monitoring his movements and contacts, some of which were either suspected or avowed CP USA members.[38]

Despite the clandestine surveillance and working of informants, the Bureau turned up no hard evidence that Oppenheimer himself was a CP USA member, much less a Soviet spy. His wartime work on the Manhattan Project was credited by US officials as having helped end the war in the Pacific, and his status in the scientific community was, by this point, akin to demigod status. Oppenheimer himself repeatedly denied being a party member. But in the new era of the federal employee loyalty program (and as a paid government consultant, Oppenheimer fell under the executive order), old suspicions and past associations were enough to trigger renewed scrutiny.

Oppenheimer was summoned before HUAC in closed session in early June 1949, ostensibly to answer questions about his knowledge of an alleged communist cell at the University of California at Berkley Radiation Laboratory. The physicist was extremely cooperative with the committee until he was asked about his brother's CP USA involvement. On those questions, he declined to answer and told the committee they should ask his brother

296   CHAPTER 6

those questions. HUAC did exactly that, summoning Frank Oppenheimer to appear just days after Robert's closed-door session.

Oppenheimer's younger sibling had been a CP USA member from 1937 to 1940 but left it after becoming disillusioned by its true character. Frank concealed his party membership from his subsequent employer, the University of Minnesota, but on the eve of his appearance before HUAC in mid-June 1949, he finally came clean, though it cost him his academic career.

Hoover's agents made regular visits to the remote Colorado town where Frank and his wife had retreated after the HUAC testimony debacle. The effect, as Frank would later observe, was to "poison the atmosphere" and turn "my friends, my neighbors, my colleagues against me."[39] Frank Oppenheimer would not work in academia again for another decade.

Like his brother, Robert Oppenheimer's own career would also become a casualty of the Eisenhower administration's destructive and dysfunctional loyalty program.

Less than a year after his closed-door appearance before HUAC, the California state senate equivalent of the infamous House committee heard testimony from two former CP USA members who claimed Oppenheimer hosted a CP USA party at his home the month after Hitler's invasion of the Soviet Union.[40] Oppenheimer vehemently denied the allegations and restated he had never been a CP USA member.

Rivals in his own field also sought to bring down Oppenheimer.

Oppenheimer's former subordinate-turned-rival Edward Teller went to the FBI in 1951 and claimed Oppenheimer's opposition to the creation and fielding of an American hydrogen bomb was the result of direction from Kremlin officials.[41] It was a lie, but the damage, and thus doubts about Oppenheimer's loyalty, mounted. By the fall of 1953, Oppenheimer was given a choice by Atomic Energy Commission (AEC) head Lewis Strauss: resign or face investigation by a panel appointed by Strauss. Ultimately, Oppenheimer chose to fight his security clearance suspension and the attacks on his integrity.

During April and May 1954, Oppenheimer would be grilled for hours by Strauss's hand-picked security clearance review panel. It was a de facto show trial, with Strauss having employed FBI wiretapping of Oppenheimer's lawyers, allowing the panel to use hearsay evidence and generally stacking the deck against the scientist from the outset.[42]

On May 23, 1954, the panel voted 2–1 to recommend Oppenheimer's clearance not be reinstated. He'd broken no law and was not a Soviet spy, but his opposition to the H-bomb program was "sufficiently disturbing as to raise a doubt" as to whether he should be allowed to continue working in

"IS THIS IDOLATRY OF SECURITY?"   297

the field on behalf of the federal government.[43] Oppenheimer was effectively barred from federal service, as an employee or contractor.

A CONGRESSIONAL "REDS IN AMERICA" TOUR

While the executive branch's machinery of surveillance and political repression rolled on with increasing intensity, multiple congressional committees—and some key individual House and Senate members—continued to stoke the Red Scare from Capitol Hill and in the press in a series of hearings best characterized as the "Reds in America" tour.

On April 7 and 8, 1953, HUAC convened in Los Angeles for the fourth installment of its Investigations of Communist Activities in the Los Angeles Area, where twenty-one witnesses were questioned about their alleged association with the American Federation of Teachers or other education-related unions, as well as the Jefferson School of Social Science, an alleged communist front. The sloppiness of HUAC's work was on clear display when Dr. Charles Albert Page was questioned on April 7.

When HUAC chief counsel Frank Tavenner claimed that a December 3, 1946, *Daily Worker* article listed Page as participating in a Jefferson School event, Page stated categorically that he had never been associated with the Jefferson School and that he never went by his middle name.

"I might explain, Mr. Counsel, that I was subpoenaed 15 months ago under my correct name as Charles Albert Page. . . . During those notifications the 'Charles' seems to have gotten lost. . . . I think it is useless to pursue any further questions identifying me as an Albert Page."[44]

After again denying any connection with the Jefferson School, Tavenner asked Page, "In other words, the Albert Page referred to here is not you, Charles Albert Page?"

"Obviously no," Page replied.[45]

Tavenner got in additional shots at Page during the balance of the questioning over Page's refusal to discuss his employment status between 1936 and 1941 by invoking the Fifth Amendment, with Tanner doing his best to paint the former State Department employee as a Soviet sympathizer.[46] The other twenty witnesses got similar treatment over the two days HUAC was in Los Angeles.

In May, HUAC's Red-hunting road show took to New York City to grill renowned band leader and musician Artic Shaw about his involvement with the Hollywood Independent Citizens Committee of the Arts, Sciences, and Professions.[47] In June HUAC held two days of field hearings billed as

298   CHAPTER 6

Investigation of Communist Activities in the Columbus, Ohio, Area.[48] In July the committee spent two days in Albany, New York, hearing testimony from friendly, ex-communist witnesses such as Canadian Patrick Walsh, who testified at length about alleged communist infiltration of Canadian government and civil society organizations.[49]

After the August recess, HUAC returned to Washington for a post–Labor Day hearing at which James McNamara testified that the subpoena he had received from HUAC induced him to resign his position as a commissioner in the US Conciliation Service in Cincinnati.[50] McNamara had received CP USA help with union organizing but had never acted as an espionage agent or taken any action to undermine the federal government. HUAC hearings during 1953 achieved headlines but produced little in the way of new, original revelations about Soviet tactics or intentions. They did continue to cause personal and professional calamity for people like McNamara.

HUAC's Senate counterpart spent the last part of 1952 and nearly all of 1953 focusing much of its attention on American citizens employed by the United Nations.

Exactly how a committee of the US Congress had any authority to investigate American citizens who were, by definition, employed by a non–US government entity with no direct access to US government secrets was a question neither posed nor addressed by the committee. What was clear was that a federal grand jury in the Southern District of New York had, between June 1951 and December 1952, been convened "to investigate violations of laws of the United States including those directed against subversive activities and espionage" and that the same grand jury had informed the court "that startling evidence has disclosed infiltration into the United Nations of an overwhelmingly large group of disloyal United States citizens, many of whom are closely associated with the international Communist movement" and who "have long records of Federal employment, and at the same time have been connected with persons and organizations subversive to this country."[51]

Yet despite a lengthy investigation, the grand jury returned no legal indictments, only a political one. The remorseless hunt for alleged Soviet sympathizers at the UN didn't just wreck careers. It led one distinguished former American diplomat to kill himself.

Acting Assistant Secretary General of the UN Abraham Feller, a former official in FDR's administration and one of the key drivers behind the creation of the United Nations, had been dealing with a multitude of challenging issues at the time of his death. A chief proponent of the UN intervention in Korea, Feller and his UN colleagues were struggling to find a way to end the war. On November 10 Feller's boss and friend, UN Secretary General

"IS THIS IDOLATRY OF SECURITY?"   299

Trygve Lie, had resigned as a result of ongoing pressure from the McCarran Committee and the negative publicity about alleged American communists working for the UN.

For Feller it proved too much. On November 13 he leapt twelve stories to his death from his Manhattan apartment.[52] Just hours after Feller's death, Lie issued a statement praising his former aid and blaming his death on the communist witch hunt being carried out by McCarran's subcommittee and the federal grand jury.[53]

McCarran remained unfazed. And despite the GOP taking control of the Senate in 1953, he remained a key player on SISS until his death in September 1954. The law and the subcommittee that bore his name would, like HUAC, go on to ruin the professional and personal lives of a number of his fellow citizens. But one of McCarran's Senate colleagues was on course to eclipse him and every other Red-baiting member of the House and Senate.

Senator Joseph McCarthy's increasingly strident and fact-free attacks on federal employees and others had, by the late spring of 1953, created a growing sense of alarm among some in the business community and other Eisenhower allies. A few began approaching Eisenhower privately about what they viewed as the urgent need for the president to put the demagogue in his place. One was long-time Eisenhower friend and chairman of General Mills Harry Bullis.

On May 9, Bullis wrote to Eisenhower with the suggestion that the president tell McCarthy that "you have allowed him to obtain a large amount of publicity but that when he reaches the point where he really embarrasses you, you will crack down on him." Describing McCarthy as a man with "unlimited personal ambitions, unmitigated gall, and unbounded selfishness," Bullis cautioned the president that "it is a fallacy to assume that McCarthy will kill himself. That can only be accomplished by too much liquor and women. It is our belief that McCarthy should be stopped soon."[54]

Eisenhower replied to Bullis on May 18, telling him "I continue to believe that the President of the United States cannot afford to name names. . . . This applies with special force when the individual concerned enjoys the immunity of a United States Senator."

He also pointed out what Bullis himself understood: McCarthy's pathological need to be in the public limelight.

"Nothing would probably please him more," Eisenhower wrote, "than to get the publicity that would be generated by public repudiation by the President."[55]

The President tried to reassure Bullis that he recognized the threat McCarthy posed and that he had a game plan for dealing with him.

Eisenhower told Bullis, "I do not mean that there is no possibility that I shall ever change my mind" on going after McCarthy publicly, but "that as of this moment, I consider that the wisest course of action is to continue to pursue a steady, positive policy in foreign relations, in legal procedures in cleaning out the insecure and the disloyal, and in all other areas where McCarthy seems to take such a specific and personal interest."

Eisenhower also got in a dig on McCarthy.

"My friends on the Hill tell me that of course, among other things, he wants to increase his appeal as an after-dinner speaker and so raise the fees he charges."[56]

INTERNAL SECURITY OPERATIONS AND PLANNING: DETENTION, WIRETAPPING, AND MORE

As for the administrative machinery of the growing American internal security apparatus, the administration continued and refined the procedures for tracking alleged or actual subversives or Soviet sympathizers developed under Truman.

By August 1953 Coyne was able to report to the NSC that wartime plans for the detention of various categories of individuals had been worked out. Coyne noted that "As of July 3, 1953 (nearest date), the FBI through its investigations identified 21,968 individuals who are being considered for apprehension and detention should circumstances require such action." The "individuals of nonmilitary status" were American citizens; separate plans were in place for the detention of Soviet diplomatic personnel and others designated as enemy aliens.[57]

The American intelligence community had also vastly expanded its domestic informant network across the country, "including key facilities designated by the Secretary of Defense, the Atomic Energy Commission, Air Force installations, strategic air command bases particularly, and other facilities having classified contracts with the Department of Defense."[58] Coyne noted that the expanded informant program was "designed to circumvent or to control and prosecute acts of sabotage, espionage, and other subversive activities and to collect domestic intelligence."[59]

Vice President Nixon, who usually attended NSC meetings, wanted to go much further.

At the September 17, 1953, NSC meeting, Nixon pressed the NSC staff and Deputy Attorney General William Rogers to follow the example of some other countries and develop legislation to ban the CP USA. Rogers indicated that a complete internal security legislative review was underway

"is this idolatry of security?" 301

but resisted Nixon's call for legislation to outlaw the CP USA.[60] There was also a push by Brownell, strongly supported by other NSC members, that the administration seek legislation to modify the rules of evidence to allow wiretap-derived material to be used in espionage prosecutions.

Brownell testified before SISS on November 17 that "There are cases of espionage presently in the Department of Justice, but since some of the important evidence was obtained by wiretapping, the cases cannot be proved in court and therefore there will be no prosecution so long as the law remains in its present state." He explicitly cited the Coplon episode as an example, though bringing up an overt act of DoJ and FBI illegality (the wiretaps on Coplon and her attorney) was hardly a credible way to make his case. Even so, the attorney general only got a handful of questions on the topic, and no senator raised constitutional objections to Brownell's proposal.[61]

Two days later the *Wall Street Journal* editorial board had a very different reaction.

In criticizing Brownell's proposal to grant immunity from prosecution to compel testimony from individuals who invoke their Fifth Amendment rights before the courts, a grand jury, or Congress, the *Journal* said Brownell's idea represented "an undermining of a basic American safeguard" that "could lead to serious abuses."[62] But the paper's editorial board spent most of their time condemning the wiretap evidence proposal.

"The wrong principle," the *Journal* observed, "is the abrogation of the security of the individual."

Noting that the wiretap provision might not violate the letter of the First Amendment, it "could easily violate the First Amendment's spirit. It could create an atmosphere in which people would be afraid to talk on the telephone about anything."[63]

The *Journal*'s editorial staff then offered an observation that no doubt resonated with anyone who had been called before HUAC, SISS, or any other investigative body engaged in the hunt for alleged Soviet spies or sympathizers.

"Telephone conversations can be misconstrued, innocent remarks interpreted as evil. Who would feel wholly secure knowing that any conversation could be recorded to use against him?"[64]

Reminding its readers that "Constitutional safeguards were written precisely to protect the people from such dangers to their freedom from the state," the *Journal* noted that the lack of such authority had not prevented the government from finding and exposing spies and removing them from the government when found there. Indeed, it would be decades before the role of VENONA in finding the Rosenberg atomic secrets spy ring would

302   CHAPTER 6

become public, yet it was a perfect example of how such cases could be managed: an alternative method of getting evidence needed for conviction was often possible. The *Journal* finished its pronouncement by expressing confidence that finding and eliminating espionage threats could "successfully be made without infringing the Bill of Rights."[65]

It was remarkable that the paper of record for Wall Street and the entire American business community—a reliable, conservative voice generally highly supportive of Eisenhower's policies—took such a principled, high-profile stand against a key administration internal security priority.

The *Washington Post* editorial board took a different approach, supporting a bill offered by Rep. Kenneth Keating (R-NY) that would "permit wiretapping in national security cases under rules to be laid down by the Attorney General" that would also "require any officer operating under those rules to go before a Federal judge" to get wiretap authorization.[66] The *Post* suggested Brownell's appearance before SISS showed the administration would likely find a receptive audience for some kind of change in wiretapping authority on Capitol Hill in 1954.

Meanwhile, at the December 15 cabinet meeting, Nixon renewed his push for legislation that would ban the CP USA. Brownell pointed to the pending Supreme Court case involving the CP USA and SACB as possibly being just as good, with one meeting participant saying a decision in SACB's favor forcing the CP USA to register as a Soviet front "might have the desired effect of making Communists 'marked men.'" US Ambassador to the UN Henry Cabot Lodge, Jr. "noted in passing the merit of a country considering itself sufficiently strong to allow the existence of the Communist Party."[67] The administration elected to wait to offer or support legislation outlawing the CP USA pending action by the Supreme Court.

On the wiretap evidence change he sought, Brownell expressed the concern that pursuing legislation "would open up discussion which might lead to requiring court permission for initiating wire taps" and if that happened "the Justice Department would prefer no legislation at all."[68] It was a clear sign that contrary to the *Post*'s editorial board's take, Brownell—no doubt under pressure from Hoover—would not readily accept Keating's bill mandating federal court approval for wiretaps in order to use evidence obtained in criminal cases.

The detailed study on potential new, even more draconian internal security legislation that Nixon sought, and which was formally presented to the NSC on December 28, mirrored the top priority of Rogers, Hoover, and the military intelligence establishment: getting legislation approved authorizing the use of wiretap evidence in federal court, at least in espionage cases.

The Supreme Court's ruling in the *Nardone* case during FDR's administration had been explicit: Section 605 of the Communications Act of 1934

"IS THIS IDOLATRY OF SECURITY?" 303

expressly prohibited the disclosure of communications obtained via wiretap. So while the Bureau, MID, and ONI had been able to use wiretaps or other forms of communications interception for *intelligence gathering* purposes, the material was not useable in court for prosecutions. Yet as the report noted, the Court allowed state law enforcement organizations to use wiretap-obtained evidence in criminal procedures.

"The anomaly is striking: wiretap evidence is admissible in evidence for punishment of common crimes committed by otherwise loyal citizens of the United States, but not for punishment of crimes against the national security committed by the disloyal citizen or the hostile alien," the report noted.[69]

Other items on the NSC's internal security legislation wish list included adding the death penalty for peacetime breaches of the Espionage Act; a statute compelling people to testify before Congress, grand juries, and the courts if they have been given immunity from prosecution by the attorney general, a change in law to apply wartime penalties for sabotage to peacetime as well, and increased penalties for violations of the Foreign Agents Registration Act, among others.[70]

There were some proposals by Nixon and others that Brownell and Rogers at Justice felt were demonstrably unconstitutional.

Regarding the suggestion that the administration seek passage of an American version of the British Official Secrets Act, the report noted:

> with reference to British statutory presumptions which aid the prosecution in cases not involving transmittal to a foreign nation, it is concluded that grave doubts as to the constitutionality of any such legislation are raised. An American counterpart of the British Acts is not, therefore, recommended at this time. It is recommended that the Department of Justice prepare such legislation of this nature as may be possible under our Constitution, for possible enactment as wartime legislation.[71]

The mentality behind the recommendation was clear: pushing through even more draconian measures that eviscerated the Bill of Rights would be more easily achieved in the heightened state of fear that accompanied a "hot war" rather than the present Cold War. The proposed American version of the Official Secrets Act remained on the shelf for the duration of Eisenhower's presidency.

After the new Congress convened in January 1954, four wiretapping bills were introduced in Congress, three in the Senate and one in the House. Pat McCarran's bill would have given Brownell what he wanted and what he didn't: wiretap authority to get evidence in national security cases, but only with a level of judicial approval.[72] But it would be Keating's bill in the House, H.R. 8649, that nearly became law that year.

Introduced on March 31, Keating's bill would have made wiretap information obtained prior to the bill becoming law admissible as evidence in cases involving treason, sabotage, espionage, sedition, seditious conspiracy, or violations of the McCarran Act and the Atomic Energy Act. The bill also cleared the way for all future wiretap evidence to be admissible if the wiretap was approved by a federal judge in advance, provided that "the judge is satisfied that there is reasonable cause to believe that such crime or crimes have been or about to be committed and that the communications may contain information which would assist in the conduct of such investigation."[73] After a little over a week of debate, Keating's bill passed the House on April 8 by an overwhelming 379 to 10 margin, with 45 House members not voting.[74]

Despite the massive support shown by the House for H.R. 8649, Keating's bill, like the wiretap issue itself, went nowhere that year in the Senate.

Even as the Senate Judiciary Committee held hearings in late April and early May on all four surveillance bills, like so many other legislative issues, the debate over wiretapping authority was pushed into the background by news involving McCarthy's latest hearings on alleged subversion and espionage in the Army.

The fresh confrontation between McCarthy and the administration made the Senator's prior attacks on State Department employees and the Civil Service Commission pale in comparison. But in the spring of 1954, things would end very differently. His relentless public assault on the US Army and some of its key leaders, civilian and military, would be McCarthy's undoing.

MCCARTHY IMPLODES; CP USA IS BANNED

In October 1953 McCarthy held a series of hearings targeting the Army Signal Corps at Fort Monmouth, New Jersey. Julius Rosenberg had worked there at one point, and not surprisingly McCarthy and his staff wanted to interrogate every person they could find who knew, much less interacted with, Rosenberg. Because a number of former federal employees had invoked their Fifth Amendment privilege against self-incrimination before HUAC, SISS, and McCarthy's Senate Government Oversight Committee, the senator was getting political mileage out of the issue. Eisenhower, at Brownell's urging, had subsequently amended EO 10450 to make invoking

"IS THIS IDOLATRY OF SECURITY?" 305

the Fifth Amendment before a congressional committee a cause for a loyalty investigation.[75]

The move played into McCarthy's hands. By late October, the Army had suspended or fired nearly three dozen Fort Monmouth employees, including at least one man who, it became clear later, was the victim of mistaken identity.[76]

Eisenhower's de facto cave-in to McCarthy on the Fifth Amendment invocation issue by federal employees was hardly the only way administration officials were trying to placate McCarthy in the vain hope he would go away.

Army Secretary Robert Stevens had, since August 1953, been giving preferential treatment to McCarthy Committee staffer and new Army draftee G. David Schine, the close personal friend of McCarthy Committee counsel Roy Cohn. Cohn had for months relentlessly worked Stevens to get Schine a commission—something Stevens believed he was clearly unqualified to receive—and postings that kept him close to Cohn and the committee's work. When in mid-January 1954 Cohn was informed that Schine would be sent to Georgia for at least five months of training before a possible overseas posting, Cohn persuaded McCarthy to take the loyalty investigations to the next level: subpoenas to loyalty board members.[77]

On January 21, key White House advisors, including Brownell, gathered to develop a plan to thwart McCarthy. The first involved Brownell concluding that Eisenhower could refuse to honor any congressional subpoenas seeking personnel or security files on government employees. The second involved getting the Army to chronicle every improper request by McCarthy (via Cohn) for special treatment for David Schine. The first step was defensive in nature, the second a weapon to be used against McCarthy.[78]

When McCarthy learned in January that an Army officer and dentist, Major Irving Peress, had written "Federal Constitutional Privilege" on a form asking about any relationship to any so-called subversive organizations, he pounced, hauling Peress in front of his committee on January 30. Peress repeatedly invoked the Fifth Amendment every time McCarthy tried to get him to answer whether or not he was a communist, knew of other communists in the Army, and so on.

In reality, for McCarthy, Peress was simply a means to an end. The Army general who commanded the installation where Peress had been based was his real target.

That commander, Brigadier General Ralph Zwicker, was among the thousands of American GIs who went ashore at Omaha Beach on D-Day during World War II. His awards for gallantry under fire—Silver Star, three Bronze Stars, and the Legion of Merit, among others—spoke to his physical courage and commitment to his country. His 45 minutes before the McCarthy Committee in executive session on February 18 marked a turning point in the confrontation between the senator and the Army.

Prior to the hearing, Zwicker had been instructed by Army Counsel John Adams to not reveal names or any security-related information to McCarthy. His legal shield was a Truman-era executive order barring the provision of executive branch personnel records to Congress.[79] When Zwicker refused to try to speculate on whether Peress invoked the Fifth Amendment before the committee because he was a communist, McCarthy went after him:

THE CHAIRMAN:	What do you think he was called down here for?
GENERAL ZWICKER:	For that specific purpose.
THE CHAIRMAN:	Then you knew that those were the questions he was asked, did you not, General, let's try and be truthful. I am going to keep you here as long as you keep hedging and hemming.
GENERAL ZWICKER:	I am not hedging.
THE CHAIRMAN:	Or hawing.
GENERAL ZWICKER:	I am not hawing, and I don't like to have anyone impugn my honesty, which you just about did.
THE CHAIRMAN:	Either your honesty or your intelligence; I can't help impugning one or the other, when you tell us that a Major in your command who was known to you to have been before a Senate committee, and of whom you read the press releases very carefully—to now have you sit here and tell us that you did not know whether he refused to answer questions about Communist activities. I had seen all the press releases, and they all dealt with that. So when you do that, General, if you will pardon me, I cannot help but question either your honesty or your intelligence, one or the other. I want to be frank with you on that.[80]

"IS THIS IDOLATRY OF SECURITY?" 307

Despite the fact that Peress's promotion to major prior to his separation occurred due to an act of Congress, McCarthy tried to get Zwicker to agree that Peress was a communist and should never have been in the Army, much less promoted; Zwicker refused. McCarthy exploded.

"Then, General, you should be removed from any command. Any man who has been given the honor of being promoted to general and who says, 'I will protect another general who protected Communists,' is not fit to wear that uniform, General."[81] Zwicker had said no such thing; it was another example of McCarthy's pathological dishonesty.

Once the hearing transcript was made public on February 22, McCarthy experienced blowback from the administration, the press, and his Senate colleagues.

After Secretary Stevens subsequently announced he would bar any Army officer from appearing before the McCarthy committee again, the *Washington Post* editorialized that "Mr. Stevens intervened to challenge an outrageous manifestation of McCarthyism."[82]

Just two days later in a private meeting with McCarthy, Mundt, and Senator Everett Dirksen (R-IL), Stevens backtracked and agreed to provide the names of Army officers involved in the Peress incident.[83] That prompted a 24-hour whirlwind of White House damage control that culminated in Stevens reading a statement from the executive mansion the next day vowing to "never accede to the abuse of Army personnel under any circumstances, including committee hearings." White House Press Secretary Jim Hagerty told the assembled reporters that regarding Stevens's statement, Eisenhower "approves and endorses it 100 percent."[84]

From this point forward, Eisenhower and his team had one goal: destroy McCarthy.

They got their first assist from members of the Senate GOP conference, who, with Senator Homer Ferguson (R-MI) in the lead, began the process of prohibiting one-man committee investigations like McCarthy's. Via the *New York Times*'s Arthur Krock, they also slipped the knife into McCarthy's chief counsel Roy Cohn, letting Krock leak the fact that "there is a record of Cohn's interventions with the Army with respect to [G. David] Schine that will become public and will certainly be no asset to them."[85]

The implication was clear: Cohn could not have sought and got special treatment for Schine without at least McCarthy's blessing, if not outright support. And the "record" that Krock referenced was a 30-plus page chronology of the Cohn–Schine affair prepared at Stevens direction, which the administration provided to key Senate allies and McCarthy himself late on March 11; it was subsequently leaked in full to the press and became a

308 CHAPTER 6

national story the next day.[86] McCarthy declared release of the report "blackmail" and vowed to continue fighting.[87] But his fate was sealed.

Within a month the Senate voted to hold public hearings on what became known as the Army–McCarthy hearings, which began on April 22 and where the charges and countercharges were examined in detail over the course of two months with nearly three dozen witnesses called. The Army came off as inept in the Peress case, but as historian William Hitchkock noted, the televised hearings—the first of their kind—showed "on national television the brutish, hostile, sneering, and demagogic style of Joe McCarthy."[88]

By mid-June McCarthy was subject to a resolution stripping him of his chairmanship; on July 20 a censure resolution against him was introduced. The resolution's author, 73-year-old Vermont Republican Ralph Flanders, said in his speech offering the bill that the Wisconsin senator's "anti-communism so completely parallels that of Adolph Hitler as to strike fear into the hearts of any defenseless minority."[89] Because of the civil war it caused within the GOP, as well as the intervening 1954 midterm elections, the actual vote didn't take place until December 2. The censure resolution passed 67–22.[90] The Democrats' November mid-term election Senate victories ensured McCarthy would never again chair any committee. He died in 1957 of acute hepatitis.[91]

Ironically, even as McCarthy's congressional colleagues turned against him, they gave him and his supporters a major legislative victory: an outright ban on the Communist Party.

McCarthy's charges of "twenty years of treason" by Democrats had clearly put the party on the defensive, with his "soft on communism" line frequently echoed by other GOP hardliners like Nixon and Mundt. Sensing his colleagues were ready to make a major play on the issue, Senator John Butler (R-MD) introduced the Communist Control Act (S. 3706) two weeks before the McCarthy censure resolution was offered by Flanders. Joining Butler as original cosponsors were Senators Barry Goldwater (R-AZ), Herman Welker (R-ID), Homer Ferguson (R-MI), and Pat McCarran (D-NV).

In its original form, Butler's bill would have not only outlawed the CP USA but also made party membership a felony. That provision was dropped in the House-Senate conference version that eventually became law.[92] Instead the version adopted ensured that any labor union determined by SACB to be "Communist infiltrated" would be deprived "of its legal standing under the National Labor Relations Act as a labor organization for the purpose of representing employees in any bargaining unit."[93]

"IS THIS IDOLATRY OF SECURITY?"   309

There was virtually no meaningful debate in the Senate or House on a measure that would, for the first time in US history, ban a political party. On August 19 the Senate voted 79–0 in favor; the House vote was a lopsided 265–2.

Democrat Abraham J. Multer of Brooklyn told the *New York Times* that he voted against the bill because "putting any group out of business in this [way] is basically wrong in principle; it is the way a Fascist would use, the totalitarian way." Republican Usher Burdick of North Dakota inveighed, "I am against any form of tyranny over the mind of man. I am for freedom of speech, freedom of the press. I am opposed to silence from fear, instead of reason."[94]

Five days after the bill passed, Eisenhower signed it into law and claimed that Americans "are determined to protect themselves and their institutions against any organization in their midst which . . . is actually a conspiracy dedicated to the violent overthrow of our entire form of government" but that they were "determined to accomplish this in strict conformity with the requirements of justice, fair play and the Constitution of the United States."[95]

In official Washington in August 1954, Usher Burdick and Abe Multer seemed to be the only two voices speaking in defense of the Bill of Rights.

CIVIL RIGHTS AND SURVEILLANCE

Even as the administration pushed for more domestic spying authority and as multiple congressional committees continued to perpetuate a climate of fear in the country through seemingly endless Red-hunting investigations, other long-simmering issues involving fundamental liberties and rights were beginning to take center stage. In the post–World War II era, civil rights leaders inside and outside of government had been pushing for an end to federal policies that helped maintain a segregated America.

In the House, Adam Clayton Powell, Jr. was a driving force for change, having called out Eisenhower in June 1953 for allowing officials at multiple federal agencies and departments to effectively ignore his own policy against the use of federal funds in support of segregation.[96]

During Eisenhower's first year in office, key white Senate liberals— led by Senator Hubert Humphrey (D-MN)—had introduced legislation to create a commission on civil rights in the executive branch. In a January 16, 1953, Senate floor speech discussing his bill, Humphrey made

310   CHAPTER 6

clear the proposal was the bare minimum Congress should be doing given the magnitude of the problem. "I can see no reason why the Senate of the United States cannot unanimously pass this legislation and help us take the civil-rights question out of partisan or sectional controversy and off dead center."[97]

Neither Humphrey's bill nor a competing version by Senator Everett Dirksen (R-IL) moved in the Senate during the 83rd Congress, but the Senate Judiciary Committee hearings on the bills in late January 1954 helped build momentum for—and create political pressure on Eisenhower to act on—civil rights reform.

After dispensing with the pleasantries, NAACP Washington office director Clarence Mitchell was blunt with the all-white Senate panel.

"I think that today the Negroes of the United States are in the position of asking for bread, and the Congress is in the position of offering them a stone."[98] Mitchell's critique of the two bills was short and pointed.

"The chief concern of our organization . . . is that neither of these bills would effectively remedy basic problems in the field of civil rights," Mitchell said. "They emphasize the study aspect of problems in human relations rather than an action program. In fairness to the members of this subcommittee, I must tell you that the colored people of the United States are tired of being studied."[99]

As had been the case for decades prior to Mitchell's testimony, Hoover was most definitely not tired of studying the NAACP for signs of communist infiltration or control, despite the lack of any real evidence that even a fraction of the Black community was showing an affinity for the Soviet system.

A little over six months after Mitchell's appearance before Dirksen's committee, and just two months after the NAACP's landmark legal victory at the Supreme Court in the *Brown v Board of Education* case, the FBI New York field office sent a report to Hoover noting that "Informant reports NAACP operates approximately 1000 branches throughout 40 of the 48 states. Reported total membership of about 200,000. NAACP leaders denounce Communism and reveal awareness of the CP to infiltrate and 'Push' the CP line. . . . Indications of CP to infiltrate and dominate the NAACP branches throughout the United States and its territories set forth."[100]

A December 13, 1954, follow-up report from the New York field office explicitly described NAACP efforts to thwart CP USA infiltration efforts dating from the Truman administration. The FBI agent writing the report quoted from a copy of the NAACP's flagship publication, *The Crisis*, from March 1949:

There is in progress a campaign of misrepresentation of the NAACP currently running in the "Daily Worker," the Communist newspaper. All the old phrases are there. The name-calling has started all over again. The slanted and angled "news" stories appear. Half-truths and whole lies see print. The object is to discredit NAACP leadership, local and national; to tear the Association apart through suspicion and strife; to take it over, if not obviously, then deviously, so as to control its elections, meetings, speakers, program, policy conventions, resolutions, and other public statements.[101]

Before the start of Eisenhower's second term, the FBI would go far beyond simply surveilling groups it believed were under Soviet control or influence.

THE FEDERAL EMPLOYEE LOYALTY PROGRAM: CAIN VERSUS EISENHOWER

Even as Harry Cain did his best to make an inherently biased SACB process seem as fair as possible, he began to hear from federal employees about how the loyalty program under EO 10450 was ruining their lives. Those stories, along with several high-profile federal employee loyalty cases in 1953 and 1954, caused him to begin questioning whether the program could possibly work without destroying the professional and personal lives of those subjected to it.[102] Even though concerns about the loyalty program were technically outside of the mandate of SACB, the reality was that the two issues were inextricably intertwined.

Setting aside the CP USA, many other organizations targeted by the attorney general via AGLOSO were either no longer in existence—in which case prior membership of a federal employee or applicant should have been a moot question—or genuinely legitimate civil society organizations very publicly at odds with the existing political and legal status quo on key issues, the Civil Rights Congress and the National Lawyers Guild among them.

During the fall and winter of 1954–1955, Cain conveyed his concerns to Eisenhower advisor Max Rabb, who apparently told Cain privately that a change in administration policy was unlikely given the "soft on Communism" political allegation that had worked so well for so long for McCarthy until the Army–McCarthy hearings.[103]

By early 1955 Cain was on a collision course with the administration over the effects of EO 10450, though publicly he appeared to be fully behind SACB and the administration's anticommunist internal security measures.

312   CHAPTER 6

Cain chose a local Republican party event in Spokane on January 15 to make public his growing disquiet with the loyalty program.

His speech was titled, "Can Freedom Live with Internal Security?" and Cain opened by noting approvingly that CP USA officials had said that if the constitutionality of SACB and its processes were upheld by the Supreme Court, the communist organization would be "required to commit suicide."[104] He went on to briefly defend SACB's work and asserted that "No one among us denies that the present is an age of peril," but he expressed confidence that if it came to it, America would "prevail and survive through any war which may be forced on civilization" by the Soviets.[105]

Having provided his Republican audience with the rhetorical red meat they were undoubtedly expecting, Cain shifted his focus. Commenting on the loyalty program, Cain observed:

> My own considered view is that our security system has worked well and fairly on the average but that conspicuous and inexcusable examples to the contrary have occurred much too often. It isn't persuasive that we should be complimented because we seldom err. Our Nation can't long tolerate a system which doesn't soon eliminate the possibility for errors which are disastrous to anyone like you or me when they arise. As I see it, some changes in both attitudes and procedures must be agreed to or the system will never work as the President intends that it shall operate.[106]

Cain went on to talk at length about the cases of Wolf Ladejinsky at the Department of Agriculture, Air Force Master Sergeant Victor Havris, and Air Force 1st LT Milo Radulovich, whose case had become a sensation after a *CBS News* story, spearheaded by legendary journalist Edward R. Murrow, attacked McCarthy over his demonstrably false charges of Soviet sympathies against Radulovich.[107]

For Cain, there was a key lesson and clear thread running through each of their cases.

"Above all else, the Nation's need is for security personnel who can tell the difference between disloyalty and non-conformity; between treason and heresy."[108] Cain then got very pointed, telling his audience that too many federal security bureaucrats "are the people who indict the innocent without reason and overlook the guilty for lack of knowledge, training, and experience."[109]

The SACB member then took a direct rhetorical head shot at Eisenhower's executive order on the loyalty program: "The basic criterion in Executive

Order 10450 ought, I think, to be reexamined in the light of every development in the last twenty months."[110]

A key pet peeve of Cain's was the administration's failure to tightly define the concept of security risk and who, exactly, constituted one. "A person who drinks too much can often recover from that indiscretion and build a new life—if given a chance," Cain said. "The risk dismissed for being disloyal will remain disgraced for life. Here again we should be trying to strengthen our Federal structure without unnecessarily destroying individuals in the process."[111]

Cain also drew a clear distinction from actual espionage agents—like the Rosenbergs—and others who might be viewed as unconventional in their thinking by the standards of day but whose loyalty to the Republic was clear.

"Espionage agents will be found among the disloyal," Cain observed. "These are the ones we ought to try the hardest to discover. When we do, we ought to execute them. Risks who are otherwise loyal will not often be found in this category. We ought to treat them accordingly—without needless embarrassment or harassment."[112]

Cain closed with words that could only be fairly construed as a direct and very pointed attack on the administration he ostensibly served, declaring that:

> A whole clique of spies could hardly do as much damage to us as could our failure as a government to have confidence in our people. Any government, to deserve to survive, must deserve the respect of its citizenry. A government is under no compulsion to be less than severe in punishing crimes against the state, but that government is under every compulsion to extend consideration and just treatment to every citizen. He or she must be treated as what they actually are— the fiber and substance from which a free nation derives its strength and purpose.[113]

Five days after the speech, Cain was summoned to the White House for a meeting with Eisenhower's chief of staff, Sherman Adams, who read Cain the riot act for "rocking the boat" and failing to clear his remarks in advance.[114]

Although somewhat apologetic, Cain was undeterred. He remained convinced the administration's internal security approach was fatally flawed and, at base, unconstitutional as far as due process rights for federal workers were concerned.

Cain would give additional speeches on the topic during the balance of 1955, and he did provide copies to the White House in advance of his

Figure 6.3. Senator Harry Cain (R-WA) was a relentless, outspoken critic of Eisenhower's loyalty program executive order, a stance that ultimately cost him his seat on the Subversive Activities Control Board. *Truman Presidential Library*

appearances—but never so far in advance so as to give Adams, Rabb, or anyone else in the administration time to talk him out of giving an address criticizing the loyalty program.

The former Washington senator's most devastating remarks were not made before a rotary club or other civic organization. Cain saved some of his most savage attacks on EO 10450 for an appearance before a Senate Post Office and Civil Service subcommittee hearing on June 2, 1955, where the implementation and effects of the loyalty program on federal workers was the focus.

Cain noted for his former Senate colleagues that Public Law 83-176 stated that "No housing unit constructed under this act shall be occupied by any person who is a member of any organization designated as subversive by the Attorney General."[115] The SACB member noted that anyone seeking public housing had to sign an affidavit that certified that "no person who is to occupy the housing accommodations in connection with which this certificate is furnished (that is, the accommodations for which I am making, or have made, application) is a member of any of said organizations."[116]

"IS THIS IDOLATRY OF SECURITY?"   315

"Not only is a person required to say that he does not belong to any organization on the list, which has never been adjudicated," Cain said, "but he is required under that determination of the law to be his brother's keeper, a subject of concern, I take it, to all of us."[117] Cain reminded his colleagues that:

> A free society, which the United States has been and prides itself on being, is certain to lose its strength, prostitute its purpose, and then die, unless its national climate permits and encourages dissent and debate; assumes that the other person is innocent of wrongdoing except as supportable facts prove otherwise; moves with intelligent relentlessness against those whose overt conduct represents conspiratorial or rebellious activity against the state; and maintains a mutual feeling of trust, confidence, and respect between citizens and those who speak and act in their name—the Government.[118]

Cain noted that "you have no less than 10 million persons covered directly by our present security screen"—about 1 in 17 Americans in 1955.[119] The sheer scope and impact of the program was staggering, but the mentality behind it is what concerned Cain the most.

Noting that the actual number of hard-core, irreconcilable communists in their midst "were not the mass target" of the loyalty and related government security programs, Cain asserted that:

> Carry the test too far into the past, make the test arbitrary, unreasonable, and mechanical, and you expose millions and millions to the danger of being branded disloyal or security risks. When state and city governments take up the practice, and the contagion is caught by well-intentioned civic bodies, hatemongers, plain racketeers, and superpatriots, freedom is indeed imperiled. . . . An overbuilt security system yields no confidence but misgivings; not unity but division; not strength but festering internal suspicions from which dictatorships erupt.[120]

Appealing to their own self-interest, Cain also cautioned his former colleagues that they and their House counterparts were not immune from being swept up in the program, using the origins of the Civil Rights Congress—a major administration target under AGLOSO—as a case study.

"I looked this morning, just before I came to you, at the testimony itself and the information by the Government's witnesses was that 10 or 12 Congressmen were the sponsors of the parent body, which was taken over by the Civil Rights Congress."[121]

316   CHAPTER 6

Cain also noted that state legislatures had seized on AGLOSO to pass their own version of it or legislation criminalizing membership in AGLOSO-designated organizations.

"Is this idolatry of security? I think so," Cain told his Senate audience.[122]

The SACB member noted that "this security program—which directly affects 2,300,000 employees, and all their relatives and family, and so on—did not benefit from any to be expected refinements or improvements until March 4, 1955, when the Attorney General advocated seven steps through which the program would retain its desired firmness while providing fairer treatment to every employee."[123] But Cain cautioned that Brownell's actions didn't constitute real reform of the program, just a "more careful and cautious administration" of it.[124] His testimony made clear his dissatisfaction with Brownell's approach, and by extension, Eisenhower's.

For Cain, real reform meant implementing at least five major changes to the loyalty program: revising the law to ensure federal employees continued to get paid while investigations were ongoing; that they be able to cross-examine witnesses against them; that they have access to legal counsel at government expense; that security hearing boards be given subpoena power; and that allegedly derogatory information on a federal employee be subjected to thorough, probing examination.[125]

While the ex-Washington senator got a number of questions from his former colleagues, none really challenged his basic arguments. Had he been before SISS or HUAC, his reception would have been frosty at best. But those committees were populated with political opportunists like Mundt; they were not interested in an efficient, fair federal employee screening program but in finding evidence—even flimsy, circumstantial evidence—of Reds infesting the federal workforce.

Cain was a man of contradictions. His support for the potential forced registration of a domestic political party with the government, namely, CP USA—something seemingly irreconcilable with the First Amendment—versus his forcefully stated opposition to a disjointed, duplicative, and largely arbitrary government employee loyalty program was a prime example. But unlike the vast majority of his contemporaries, Cain was usually able to keep core constitutional issues and concerns in focus.

He was also willing to change his mind on the basis of evidence and experience. Cain initially supported Joe McCarthy's anticommunist crusade until it became clear that McCarthy's operation was based on fear, suspicion, inuendo, and gossip—traits that Cain believed were hallmarks of the EO 10450 program.[126]

"IS THIS IDOLATRY OF SECURITY?" 317

He did get the satisfaction of seeing the Supreme Court in June 1956 rule that EO 10450's failure to define the term "national security" had led to the improper dismissal of a military veteran from the Department of Health, Education, and Welfare in the case *Cole v. Young*.[127] However, Cain's crusade against the loyalty program guaranteed that when his SACB term expired in August 1956, he would not be reappointed. Like former FCC commissioner and NLG leader Clifford Durr, who helped lead the first public revolt against the loyalty program Truman started, Cain would spend the rest of his public life fighting government assaults on the Bill of Rights from outside the system.

WIRETAPPING OVERSIGHT: HOOVER VERSUS CONGRESS

As Cain and other civil libertarians campaigned for dramatic changes to the federal employee loyalty program, others inside and outside of government debated the legitimacy of the tactics and techniques underpinning the American internal security system.

Between March 1955 and the summer of 1956, as SISS and HUAC continued their quests to find communists anywhere in American society, the HJC once again tackled a controversy-generating issue: wiretapping.

In twelve days of hearings taking place between March 23 and June 1, HJC took testimony on no less than five House wiretapping-related bills that had been introduced since the start of the 84th Congress.

The bills all sought to address the issue in roughly similar ways, with the exception of the one-page Curtis bill, which simply sought to impose severe fines and up to three years in prison for illegal wiretaps. None of the bills invoked the Fourth Amendment's probable cause standard for judicial orders authorizing wiretaps; the more nebulous "reasonable cause" formulation was used by Forrester and Keating, "reasonable ground" by Celler. But all four bills that would actually authorize federal wiretaps mandated the issuance of a warrant by a federal judge for the taps to be placed. That notional safeguard was itself insufficient for several key civil society groups.

At the April 26 hearing, ACLU Executive Director Irving Ferman told the committee that, "In essence, the very nature of wiretapping is violative of the Fourth Amendment, because any order to tap, in effect, becomes a general warrant. The very dragnet feature of wiretapping makes it impossible to prescribe beforehand the limits of personal invasion."[128] Ferman made it

318   CHAPTER 6

clear the ACLU disagreed with FDR's interpretation of the *Nardone* decision and his subsequent memo to then-Attorney General Robert Jackson authorizing wiretapping in alleged national security–related cases.

But Ferman also said something extraordinary for the representative of a civil liberties–focused organization—a willingness to at least tolerate wiretapping authority in extremely limited circumstances.

Perhaps concerned that the political winds were shifting in favor of federal domestic electronic surveillance, Ferman suggested that if the committee ultimately decided to allow federal wiretapping, it "should be prohibited except by Federal officials in cases involving treason, sabotage, espionage, and kidnapping. In the latter type of case, parents' wires should be tapped only with their prior consent."[129]

Ferman also argued that any judicial wiretapping approvals "should be vested in one Federal judge assigned by the Justices of the Supreme Court for 10-year periods for each district."[130] He went on to outline additional requirements for wiretaps, such as authorization by the attorney general only, with rigorous record keeping and taps authorized for 90 days with 90-day renewals possible.[131]

Ferman, perhaps without even realizing it, had just made a very plausible case for the feasibility of federal wiretapping.

It was an interesting position given that a month earlier, Assistant Attorney General Warren Olney had come before the committee and reiterated the previous DoJ view that all the administration required was a change in Section 605 of the Communications Act of 1934 to allow for the introduction of wiretap evidence in criminal, and primarily security-related, cases. Olney placed in the record Attorney General Brownell's statement to the SJC in April 1954 that reiterated that request—and the Department's opposition to judicial court orders for wiretaps.[132]

The committee would hear from many other witnesses during the course of the hearings into early June, but the administration's refusal to back off its opposition to judicial authorization for wiretaps ensured the stalemate over wiretapping authority continued. A key reason was Hoover's vehement opposition to any judicial involvement in wiretap authorizations.

Just over six weeks after the HJC wiretapping hearings concluded, Hoover, in his capacity as chairman of the Interdepartmental Intelligence Conference (IIC), sent a classified two-page memo to NSC Advisor Dillon Anderson, regarding the five wiretap bills considered by HJC. Of particular concern to Hoover was HJC Chairman Celler's bill.

Regarding H.R. 4513, Hoover asserted that if enacted it "would seriously restrict the IIC agencies in the carrying out of our responsibilities in connection with the investigation of espionage, counterespionage, sabotage, subversion, and related intelligence matters."[133] A portion of the memo remained classified as of June 2021, but Hoover's key argument was unredacted.

"A law which would require a court order from a Federal Judge before any wiretap could be placed," Hoover said, "would mean that this country would not have the protection it has heretofore had from foreign agents, spies, and potential subversive elements."[134]

It was at best a specious claim, particularly in light of the fact that the Bureau had multiple, court-sanctioned tools for running down Soviet spies, including informants, microphone surveillance, and the like—a point Brownell had made to SJC the year before when asking for legislation to allow the use of wiretap evidence.

What Hoover likely feared was discovery of wiretaps that should never have been authorized, like the ones on Adam Clayton Powell, Jr., among others. But Hoover also gave away another reason in the next to last paragraph of his letter to Dillon.

"We feel very strongly that the authority to authorize the placing of wiretaps by Federal agencies within the Executive branch of the Government should be retained within the Executive Branch."[135]

It was, for Hoover, about control—first, last and always—and he clearly felt neither Congress nor federal courts should have a meaningful oversight role over wiretapping carried out by his agents.

COMINFIL AND CIVIL RIGHTS

Ever since the post-Reconstruction era, Black Americans had been fighting a seemingly endless political battle against a racist, southern Democrat–dominated political hierarchy in the former Confederate states. The system, designed to perpetuate Black people as second-class citizens, involved restrictions running the gamut from poll taxes designed to suppress Black votes to segregated schools, public restrooms, and more. In 1955, the Jim Crow segregated South had shown both its resistance and vulnerability to change.

Just over a year after the Supreme Court's May 1954 ruling in *Brown v. Board of Education*, the country received a reminder that southern white racists remained a lethal threat to young Black men.

320   CHAPTER 6

Emmett Till, born in Chicago in 1941, was vacationing in Money, Mississippi, visiting family members in late August 1955. After Till allegedly flirted with or whistled at Bryant's wife while in the Bryants' grocery store, Till was kidnapped and murdered by Roy Bryant and J. W. Milam. Once photographs of the lynched Till circulated—his mother had an open-casket funeral in Chicago so the entire world could see the brutality visited upon her teenage son—it had a galvanizing effect on the Black community and those whites working with them to end racial discrimination and racially motivated murders.[136]

Hoover's reaction was quite different. He attempted to blame the CP USA for the rage sweeping through the African American community in the wake of Till's murder.

Between September 6, 1955, and January 18, 1956, Hoover would send at least five memos to the White House about ongoing protests and organizing efforts among civil rights activists in the aftermath of Till's lynching. In every memo, Hoover cited confidential informants claiming a CP USA role in keeping the Till murder in the press and effectively manipulating the Black community's response to the crisis.

In his September 6 memo to Eisenhower's special assistant Dillon Anderson, Hoover claimed that the CP USA was working in tandem with the Civil Rights Congress "and other Communist front groups" to work the press, and that the CP USA would "also use its influence in the National Association for the Advancement of Colored People, which has already been aroused over this slaying."[137]

Not among the memos sent to Anderson during this period was an October 21, 1955, FBI memo written by Hoover protégé Alan Belmont. Titled "Communist Infiltration into the National Association for the Advancement of Colored People," Belmont noted that the "Communist Party (CP) has had measure of success in controlling isolated chapters but unable to dominate the organization on a state or national level."[138] And even Belmont's assertion that the CP USA had succeeded "in controlling isolated chapters" was open to question, based on reporting from FBI field offices across the country that found little or no CP USA activity targeting NAACP chapters for penetration.[139]

Hoover's selective feeding of information to Eisenhower and his key aides created a distorted, if not outright false, impression of the driving factors behind the growing civil rights movement. It also guaranteed that Hoover and his federal intelligence community colleagues would continue to misread and misrepresent the underlying motivations of those involved in that movement.

"IS THIS IDOLATRY OF SECURITY?"   321

In December 1955, motivated in part as a response to Till's murder, a single Black woman would put the country on the path of confronting another form of discrimination—racially segregated public transportation.

Rosa Parks's mistreatment on a Montgomery, Alabama, public bus and her subsequent arrest and imprisonment on December 1, 1955, for violating Alabama's segregation laws became another catalyzing moment in the history of the American civil rights movement. Parks's ordeal led directly to the Montgomery bus boycott later that same month, organized by a young Baptist minister from Atlanta named Martin Luther King, Jr.

As the boycott went on into the spring and summer of 1956 and civil rights protests multiplied, between April 24 and July 13, 1956, the Senate Judiciary Committee held 10 days of hearings on 16 civil rights-related bills, including S. 902, offered by Senator Hubert Humphrey (D-MN), which called for the creation of a Civil Rights Division within the Justice Department. Several legislators from southern states described Humphrey's bill and related proposals as calling for the creation of a "Gestapo" in the United States.[140] And those same southern Democrats continued to claim—on the basis of Hoover's assurances—that it was the CP USA who were stirring up America's Black citizens.

Indeed, Hoover continued to believe, despite all evidence to the contrary, that the CP USA was behind America's racial unrest. The reality was that the CP USA was in a shambles.

Cain and his SACB colleagues and supporters scored a major victory in the Supreme Court in April 1956, when in *Communist Party v. SACB* the justices ruled that despite the use of tainted evidence in the SACB finding that the CP USA was a "Communist action" organization and must register under the McCarran Act, the underlying legislation was, in fact, constitutional.[141] Combined with the 1954 passage of the Communist Control Act, ongoing HUAC and SISS hearings and investigations, and the Justice Department's anti-CP USA prosecutions under the Smith Act, the CP USA was effectively reduced to political impotence.

But for Hoover, his most trusted deputies, the leaders of Army and Navy intelligence, and those running the federal employee loyalty program, it was not enough.

At least as early as 1955, the FBI initiated the "Communist Infiltration" or COMINFIL program. Any known or suspected CP USA member remained a target, as were those non–CP USA members who had regular contact with CP USA types or seemed to engage in political activity that allegedly aligned with the CP USA's positions. As an intelligence collection activity, COMINFIL was sweeping in scope, covering at least twelve distinct categories involving racial, political, legislative, gender, religious, educational, agricultural, industrial, youth, and other activities. It also included the press.[142]

An FBI source, almost certainly on the staff of the *New York Times*, told the Bureau's New York field office (NYC FO) in early 1955 that Penn Townsend Kimball was "recognized as one of the leaders of the pro-Communist faction in the Newspaper Guild." The NYC FO report went on to note that "the above information consists of the opinions of [the source] alone. When recontacted concerning these opinions, [source] stated that he was unable to furnish any additional details or any corroborating information."[143]

And it was likely the same NYC FO mole at the *Times* who also claimed that then-Sunday editor Lester Markel "ranked as the 'Number one pro-Communist' on the 'New York Times' with the ability to pick reporters, foreign and Washington correspondents, News Department executives, and people in all key positions at the newspaper."[144] Both claims had been provided without foundation or corroboration. Kimball would be a federal surveillance target for years.

THE BIRTH OF COINTELPRO

Even as the COMINFIL intelligence collection program accelerated, Hoover and his key subordinates were thinking beyond surveillance and prosecutions in the Bureau's war against alleged or suspected American communists.

At Hoover's direction, the Bureau developed a secret initiative using many of the same tactics employed the Soviet intelligence operatives and turned them on the CP USA and other domestic US civil society groups and leaders deemed a threat to internal security—including Black civil rights leaders and organizations. It would become the most infamous domestic surveillance and political repression operation in American history: the Counterintelligence Program, or COINTELPRO, for short.

Decades after COINTELPRO was exposed, Hoover loyalist and FBI Assistant Director Cartha "Deke" DeLoach would defend the program as a tit-for-tat response to Soviet efforts to destabilize American society. The FBI, via COINTELPRO-CP USA, would "Do unto others as they are doing unto you," in DeLoach's words.[145] He also claimed his rival and future FBI Assistant Director William C. Sullivan was the originator of the program and criticized him for occasional "reckless abandon" in running COINTELPRO.

For his part, Sullivan later made clear that, "Actually, these counterintelligence programs were nothing new. I remember sending out anonymous letters and phone calls back in 1941, and we'd been using most of the same disruptive techniques sporadically from field office to field office as long as I'd been an FBI man." Sullivan noted that it was Alan Belmont who, in 1956, moved "to incorporate all counterintelligence operations into one program directed at the Communist party." The available record supports Sullivan's account on this latter point.[146]

The initial COINTELPRO memo was authored by Belmont on August 28, 1956, less than a week after Eisenhower accepted his party's nomination for a second term. Capitalizing on the increasing factionalism of the CP USA and elsewhere on the socialist/communist left, Belmont succinctly described how FBI operations against CP USA and similar organizations would evolve.

"In other words," Belmont wrote, "the Bureau is in a position to initiate, on a broader scale than heretofore attempted, a counterintelligence program against the CP, not by harassment from the outside, which might only serve to bring the various factions together, but by feeding and fostering from within the internal fight currently raging."[147]

The initial four-step plan called for utilizing informants with membership in the relevant organizations to increase the political animosity between the CP USA and the Socialist Workers Party (SWP); cause dissension within the CP USA itself by criticizing CP USA leadership actions and initiatives; identify and prosecute CP USA underground members who had evaded taxes or filed under aliases; and be alert to CP USA efforts to work in coalition with the Fellowship of Reconciliation and be prepared to exploit or disrupt depending upon events. Over a dozen FBI field offices were initially tasked with carrying out the initial COINTELPRO operation.[148]

The deliberate targeting of political parties by an element of the executive branch had only one precedent in American history: the infamous Alien and Sedition Acts of 1798. But the debate, and ultimately the terrible consequences, of those laws played out in public. Hoover's unilateral decision to try to destroy one or more political parties he deemed nothing more than Soviet proxies was conducted behind a wall of secrecy. For the balance of Eisenhower's presidency, the Bureau would refine and expand COINTELPRO-CP USA to every FBI field office. It would become a template for use against other allegedly subversive domestic threats in the years that followed.

324   CHAPTER 6

LOOKING FOR RELIGIOUS REDS

Even as Hoover and his agents stepped up their communist hunting efforts after neutering the CP USA, his congressional counterparts in the anticommunist crusade continued their own investigations. Neither HUAC or SISS shied away from going after religious figures or organizations they claimed were communist fronts or otherwise communist influenced. One such organization targeted by SISS resulted in the Senate subcommittee being sued in federal court.

Originally known as the Methodist Federation for Social Service, the Methodist Federation for Social Action had been in existence since at least 1907. The organization's ties to and support for organized labor and social justice causes was well established by World War I.[149] The group became a focus of FBI interest at least as early as 1923.[150] During Eisenhower's first term, MFSA's support for domestic groups viewed as communist or subversive had made it a target of HUAC.

The Reverend Jack McMichael had served as executive secretary of MFSA from 1945 to June 1953, just a month before being subpoenaed by HUAC. Now the new pastor of the Community Methodist Church in Upper Lake, California, McMichael was subjected to HUAC member questioning for two days at the very end of July 1953 about his long association with MFSA.

To his credit, McMichael engaged in a very gentle, indirect form of verbal guerilla warfare throughout the hearing—asking to be able to consult his own copies of documents to compare to what the committee counsel was reading, objecting when the committee counsel departed from asking questions to simply reading affidavits into the record, and insisting upon consulting his personal diary when asked about where he was on a given date, and so on.[151] After seven grueling hours, McMichael was reminded he was under subpoena to appear the next day as well. When he told acting HUAC chairman Rep. Donald L. Jackson (R-CA) that the committee had "taken me away from my pastoral calling and visiting the bereaved and the sick," Jackson responded he was sure "they will probably find it possible to get along for a couple of days."[152]

When HUAC's interrogation of McMichael resumed the next morning, committee counsel Robert Kunzig began by asking McMichael about a pro–campus free speech event at Columbia University in October 1940 at which McMichael spoke. Kunzig's angle was that the sponsoring organization, the American Student Union, had been designed by the attorney general as a subversive organization.

"IS THIS IDOLATRY OF SECURITY?" 325

In response to Kunzig's question, McMichael said he had indeed spoken at the meeting.

> "In the same way Jesus spoke at meetings of Pharisees and publicans and sinners," McMichael noted, clearly referring to Columbia University officials who attempted to suppress campus speech with which they disagreed.
>
> Rep. Gordon Scherer (R-OH) interrupted McMichael.
>
> "Can't we leave Jesus out—"
>
> "It's a little hard for me to leave Jesus out," McMichael responded. "You may be able to do it—"
>
> "In a situation like this?" Scherer replied.
>
> "But I can't. In a situation like this, where guilt by association seems to be the principle upon which you are operating rather than by an analysis of the activities itself, I am sure He would have long ago been haled by the committee," McMichael responded.
>
> Kunzig jumped back into the fray, saying to McMichael, "A man is also known by the company he keeps."
>
> "Then Jesus was a wine drinker, glutton, and sinner," McMichael responded, "according to the people who have said that and what you have said today—you know men by the company they keep."[153]

And so it went for over six hours for the pastor from California.

The MFSA would get the same kind of scrutiny and treatment by HUAC and SISS over the next two years, the latter publishing a booklet at the end of April 1956 that labeled MFSA a communist "religious front group" with no connection to the Methodist church—both blatant falsehoods.[154] While MFSA had never been an official Methodist Church organization, its staff and supporters were most definitely Methodist in their faith profession, and the organization's interaction with the national Methodist Church and Methodist churches across the country was on a daily basis.

In the wake of the SISS attack, the MFSA appealed to a different kind of higher power: the federal courts.

The organization sued SISS for defamation and, in a rather ironic twist, sought an injunction against SISS members, the Public Printer, and the Superintendent of Documents from further publishing or distributing the SISS booklet. On May 3 Judge Robert Wilkin of the D.C. Circuit issued a temporary restraining order preventing further publishing or distribution of the document pending a review of the matter by a three-judge panel.

326   CHAPTER 6

"Because a man is a legislator or a judge doesn't give him the right to slander any one or commit any other crime unless the acts are within the grant of power the constitution gives," Wilkin said at the time of his ruling.[155]

Wilkin was careful to say he was not ruling on the merits, simply giving his trio of colleagues on the federal D.C. bench the chance to get up to speed on the case so they could rule on the merits. When they did, their opinion should have surprised no one.

Noting that the Constitution contained no provision allowing anyone to stop the president or the Supreme Court from publishing anything, the three judges stated, "We think it equally clear that nothing authorizes anyone to prevent Congress from publishing any statement."[156] The judges dismissed the case. The Constitution's Speech and Debate clause, as MFSA and every other individual and group targeted by HUAC and SISS learned, was very much a double-edged sword.

Even so, the larger problem with the existence and conduct of HUAC and SISS was not legal but political. The Senate's belated censure action against McCarthy showed that in the most extreme cases, the upper chamber was willing to act against one of its own when a majority of their colleagues believed they'd gone too far. But HUAC and SISS represented systemic threats to civil society organizations. Only their abolition would end the threat they posed to individuals and organizations. Before Eisenhower's presidency concluded, a new organization with that very mission would be born.

FBI VERSUS MLK, JR.: THE OPENING ROUND

Rosa Parks's stand against segregated buses in her hometown of Montgomery inspired others to follow her example, leading ultimately to the November 1956 landmark Supreme Court decision in *Gayle v Browder*, which held that such segregation violated the Constitution's equal protection clause.[157] For the young Reverend Martin Luther King, Jr. and his allies, the victory was an enormous one in their campaign for equal rights for African Americans. But King wanted more. He knew full political emancipation for Black people would only come through further, far more sweeping legislative action by Congress.

As King and his allies prepared for the resumption of congressional hearings on a proposed civil rights bill in 1957, Hoover and his agents were keeping the White House informed about the political organizing and lobbying activities of key King allies.

"IS THIS IDOLATRY OF SECURITY?" 327

On January 25, 1957, Hoover sent a four-page confidential memo to White House Cabinet Secretary and Eisenhower civil rights political troubleshooter Max Rabb. Hoover's letter to Rabb cited a "confidential informant" as claiming that King advisors and collaborators Bayard Rustin, Ella Baker, and Stanley Levison intended to ask Eisenhower to "place his influence behind the integration movement" by touring southern states. The letter to Eisenhower was to be signed by several prominent white civil rights leaders, including theologian Reinhold Niehbur, who Hoover claimed was being used as a de facto stalking horse by Rustin, Baker, and Levison.[158] Hoover then went on to cite Rustin's and Levison's alleged or known ties to the CP USA or other alleged Soviet front organizations.[159]

While acknowledging that Rustin was, by his own public declaration, no longer a communist, the inference he wanted Rabb to draw was clear: Eisenhower should steer clear of Rustin, the others, and their activities.

On February 14 the Senate Judiciary Committee began thirteen days of hearings on various civil rights bill proposals. The administration's more than year-long push for Congress to create a Civil Rights Division within the Justice Department and give it civil enforcement powers to combat voter suppression efforts by so-called White Citizen Councils had stalled. The first witness that day was Attorney General Brownell, who reiterated Eisenhower's call for passage of the administration's civil rights program.[160]

As Brownell made the administration's case before the committee, 1,100 miles away in New Orleans, King and nearly a hundred civil rights leaders ended a two-day meeting by announcing their intent to conduct a "pilgrimage of prayer" to the nation's capital "unless President Eisenhower speaks out to the South on segregation violence."[161]

Responding to the administration's request, on March 19 House Judiciary Committee Chairman Emanuel Celler introduced H.R. 6127, a bill designed to implement Eisenhower's four-point civil rights program, including the creation of a civil rights commission, the establishment of the Civil Rights Division within the Justice Department, the creation of civil penalties for civil rights violations, and a bar on attempts to intimidate or otherwise prevent any person from voting.[162] Celler's move began the battle in the House to pass the legislation.

While King and his allies prepared for the march, Hoover had his agents and their sources monitor the civil rights leader and those around him. On April 26 Hoover sent Eisenhower aide Robert Cutler a four-page confidential memo passing along what the Bureau had learned about the upcoming march.

Hoover told Cutler that King and his associates had selected May 17 as the day for the demonstration—the third anniversary of the Supreme Court's

Brown v Board of Education decision.[163] Hoover noted that the NAACP was helping coordinate the event and that the only three Black members of Congress—Adam Clayton Powell, Jr. of New York, William Dawson of Illinois, and Charles Diggs, Jr. of Michigan—"will support this mobilization."[164]

Hoover spent the rest of the memo discussing how the virtually defunct CP USA was allegedly supporting the march as well.

"This was to be done by having Party members work within the NAACP, trade unions, and similar organizations so that it will appear that this support is coming from those organizations and not from the CP," Hoover told Cutler.[165]

Hoover's own agents had previously given him reports that CP USA penetration of NAACP elements was negligible at best and only in isolated cases. Even so, the FBI director continued to imply that the civil rights movement was being infiltrated and manipulated by an organization that Congress had outlawed, that the FBI and Justice Department had decimated with prosecutions, and that HUAC and SISS continued to hound.[166] It was not the CP USA that was driving the civil rights movement, a fact Hoover would never acknowledge.

Although the May 17 Prayer Pilgrimage drew only half of the NAACP-promised 50,000 attendees, it had a galvanizing effect, with King's "Give Us the Ballot" speech helping to place him firmly in the national spotlight and providing political momentum in Congress. Celler's civil rights bill passed the House by a comfortable 286–126 on June 18, and in a somewhat watered-down form in the Senate on August 7 by a vote of 72–18.[167]

King credited Vice President Nixon for helping secure passage of the legislation. The two had met in June when King and the Reverend Ralph Abernathy had been in D.C. Just over three weeks after Senate passage of the legislation, King thanked Nixon for his support but made clear his organizing and advocacy for his fellow Blacks was just beginning.

"This is why I am initiating in the south a crusade for citizenship in which we will seek to get at least two million negroes registered in the south for the 1960 elections," King told Nixon.[168]

The vehicle King would use to accomplish that goal had been founded by him, Abernathy, and several other close colleagues just two weeks before in Montgomery, Alabama: the Southern Christian Leadership Conference.[169]

On September 20 Hoover sent a message to the Atlanta field office, alerting them to SCLC's creation. Initially, Hoover told his agents to take a cautious approach to SCLC.

"In the absence of any indication that the Communist Party has attempted, or is attempting, to penetrate this organization you should conduct no investigation of this matter," Hoover wrote. "However, in view of the

"IS THIS IDOLATRY OF SECURITY?" 329

stated purpose of the organization you should remain alert for public source information concerning it in connection with the racial situation."[170]

By the summer of 1958 and in the years that followed, Hoover would take a very different approach to SCLC.

CHALLENGING EXECUTIVE BRANCH SECRECY: JOHN MOSS AND THOMAS HENNINGS

By mid-1955, California Democrat John Moss, elected to the House in 1952, had been waiting over two years for his chance.

During his first House term, Eisenhower's Civil Service Commission had stiff-armed Moss when he requested that the agency turn over records on federal employee terminations under the executive branch's loyalty program.[171] During 1953–1954, the GOP still controlled both chambers, which meant Moss had no real leverage to force CSC to turn over the documents. After Democrats retook both congressional chambers after the 1954 midterm elections, Moss intended to turn the tables on the administration.

By late March 1955, the Defense Department had also entered the information denial business, telling its own employees and contractors that the release of information would be governed not only by the burgeoning government secrecy regime, but by a "constructive contribution" test vis-à-vis the Pentagon.[172]

Widespread public criticism of the policy, particularly from the press, subsequently helped keep the issue alive in Congress. Moss, despite his relatively junior status in the House, secured the position of chairman of the newly created Special Subcommittee on Government Information within the House Government Operations Committee.[173] For the duration of Eisenhower's presidency, Moss's subcommittee would become the executive branch's new nemesis—the first real congressional challenge to government secrecy and information control in the twentieth century.

Beginning in November 1955 and stretching through 1959, Moss would hold over two dozen hearings and issue multiple reports on executive branch refusals to turn over to Congress requested information clearly relevant to the oversight of the agencies or departments in question. One of his first targets was the aforementioned DoD information control policy.

At a July 9, 1956, hearing with Defense Department officials, Moss questioned DoD Assistant Secretary for Public Affairs Robert Ross on exactly what criteria the Department was using to potentially withhold information, especially information that originated outside of DoD.

330   CHAPTER 6

Ross responded that any such review would be focused on whether the data in question "would have intelligence value to a potential enemy."

"Have intelligence value?" Moss asked.

"Or which would be harmful to the national security," Ross responded. "It is synonymous."

But the two were not at all necessarily synonymous, as Moss pointed out. The slipperiness, the shifting definition from person to person inside the executive branch, is what Moss zeroed in on.

"Then in these guidelines used for review procedure there is no attempt to define policy," Moss observed. "It becomes a matter of individual definition by the person who undertakes the review."[174]

Throughout the course of the hearings Moss conducted during Eisenhower's second term, he and his subcommittee colleagues would encounter the same evasiveness or lack of precision in the definition of what constituted national security-related information. Moss sought to change that by changing the law. In the effort, he would have a Senate partner—Thomas Hennings of Missouri.

Together, Moss and Hennings would push through Congress H.R. 2767, an amendment to existing federal department and agency recording keeping law that explicitly stated, "This section does not authorize withholding information from the public or limiting the availability of records to the public."[175] But Eisenhower's signing statement on the law effectively neutered it.

"In its consideration of this legislation the Congress has recognized that the decision-making and investigative processes must be protected," Eisenhower wrote. "It is also clear from the legislative history of the bill that it is not intended to, and indeed could not, alter the existing power of the head of an Executive department to keep appropriate information or papers confidential in the public interest. This power in the Executive Branch is inherent under the Constitution."[176]

The word "secret" or "secrecy" appears only once in the Constitution—Section I, Article 5, which grants Congress the power to keep its proceedings secret if necessary. Nothing in the text of the Constitution explicitly grants any chief executive the power to classify a single piece of paper. It was an assertion of raw executive power and privilege on Eisenhower's part, something the federal courts had, unfortunately, upheld via its prior decisions, such as the *Reynolds* case.

While Moss continued to investigate and make the case for legal limits on what the executive branch could withhold in the name of national security, Hennings continued his focus on another largely secret government activity posing real risks to the rights of Americans: wiretapping.

Via hearings in 1958 and 1959, Hennings examined the implications of the December 1957 Supreme Court decision in *Benanti v. United States*, which ruled that state-originated wiretap evidence could not be used in federal courts because of Sec. 605 of the 1934 Communications Act.[177] Not surprisingly, civil liberties advocates were elated by the decision. State and local law enforcement officials complained it would allow criminal organizations to run amok.

At the July 9, 1959, hearing Hennings chaired, Kings County, New York District Attorney Edward Silver was blunt.

"If, for any reason, the Senate or the Congress doesn't do something to correct the *Benanti* decision," Silver claimed, "we just will not be able to use wiretapping in our law enforcement, and it simply means that a lot of people are going to have carte blanche in their criminal operations. You will not be depriving me but the people who elected me to fight crime in our county. If I am compelled to hunt lions with a peashooter, so be it. I think the Congress has a serious responsibility in this matter."[178]

Silver overstated the problem and failed to mention that other forms of electronic surveillance—microphones, for example—were still available to state and local law enforcement officials. There was also no ban on the use of confidential informants. What Silver and other prosecutors across the country understood was that going to the phone company to get taps was a lot easier than trying to get an electronic bug planted in a mobster's office or home. The *Benanti* decision, and Congress's lack of action to address it, represented a tangible setback for prosecutors like Silver, but neither he nor his colleagues were without means to monitor and penetrate organized crime operations.

Yet even as Hennings and his colleagues grappled with how or even whether to respond to the *Benanti* decision, the Eisenhower administration pushed ahead with an aggressive expansion and normalization of the collection of electronic communications.

ELECTRONIC SURVEILLANCE: WARTIME LESSONS AND DOMESTIC PERILS

If World War II had taught America's senior most political and military leaders anything, it was that signals intelligence (SIGINT, in Defense Department and Intelligence Community lingo) was absolutely vital not just in the conduct of military operations, but in diplomacy and counterespionage as well.

332   CHAPTER 6

The failure of ONI leaders in Washington to decrypt, analyze, and disseminate the "bomb plot" messages being sent from the Imperial Japanese consulate in Honolulu to Japanese naval planners in Tokyo was a key reason Japan's attack on Pearl Harbor had succeeded. Now that the world was in the Nuclear Age, a failure to detect hostile Soviet intentions via SIGINT was simply not an option. Moreover, the job Army cryptographers did in cracking at least portions of the Soviet VENONA code was the key reason why the Rosenberg nuclear spy ring had been uncovered, underscoring SIGINT's counterintelligence value.

Concerns over the military service–centric nature of America's SIGINT operations—the Army and Navy operating separate, and to some degree, rival, cryptography bureaucracies—led in 1952 to the promulgation of the TOP SECRET National Security Council Intelligence Directive No. 9, Communications Intelligence (NSCID 9) on October 24, 1952, creating the National Security Agency (NSA).[179] However, the document also made clear that the FBI retained full authority to engage in wiretapping as it had been since FDR's second term, with NSCID 9 stating that nothing in the Directive "shall be construed to encroach upon or interfere with" the FBI's "unique responsibilities . . . in the field of internal security."[180]

While NSA's primary daily mission was trying to crack the codes of potential adversaries like the Soviets, NSCID 9 defined "communications intelligence" (COMINT) in broad terms, including "all procedures and methods used in the interception of communications . . . and the obtaining of information from such communications by other than the intended recipients."[181] In practical terms, it meant that while NSA was to conduct COMINT operations "against foreign governments," the language was broad enough to encompass COMINT involving individuals or organizations known or suspected to be operating on behalf of a foreign government.

It was language that also effectively formalized an arrangement that NSA's Army predecessor organization, the Army Security Agency, had maintained with RCA Global, ITT World Communications, and Western Union International on a verbal or "hand shake" basis since at least 1947, in which the three international telecommunications providers turned over cable traffic of interest to NSA.[182] Under this program, subsequently codenamed SHAMROCK, the private communications of Americans receiving or sending telegrams to certain foreign countries were given to NSA.[183]

In that respect, SHAMROCK was a de facto evasion of Section 605 of the 1934 Communications Act, which explicitly prohibited federal government wiretapping. In this case, NSA wasn't tapping the telecommunications companies themselves; the companies were voluntarily turning over the

"IS THIS IDOLATRY OF SECURITY?" 333

private messages of their American customers to NSA. And there was no requirement in NSCID 9 or any other document dealing with NSA's activities that its operations be conducted strictly in compliance with the Fourth Amendment rights of Americans.

By early 1957, Eisenhower's key intelligence advisors were convinced that NSCID 9's authorities and structure were simply not sufficient to give NSA's director the ability to manage his own workforce, protect NSA personnel from public exposure, and make the still-secret agency as efficient in its mission as it could be. As of late July 1957, Secretary of Defense Charles Wilson was lobbying Bureau of the Budget Director Percival Brundage to send legislation to Congress formally authorizing NSA in statute and providing its director with broad powers to keep the agency's operations and information secret.[184] The process would take two years, and Wilson would be long gone from the administration by the time it happened. But in the end, Defense Department advocates got the bill they wanted.

The NSA Act of 1959 passed both congressional chambers without debate and by unanimous consent, with Eisenhower signing the bill into law on May 29, 1959.[185] Section 6 of the new law allowed NSA's director to bar "the disclosure of the organization or any function of the National Security Agency"—sweeping language which ensured that constitutionally dubious programs like SHAMROCK would remain hidden from public or judicial review.

The executive branch's level of control over information about intelligence activities with clear implications for the constitutional rights of Americans had a direct, negative impact on congressional oversight of such issues. But it was also true that even well-known civil liberties advocates in Congress at the time did not probe deeply enough to ferret out information about administration actions like those authorized under NSCID 9.

Even as the NSA Act quietly made its way through both congressional chambers during the late winter and spring of 1959, there were no hearings held by Senator Hennings of Missouri in the Senate Judiciary Committee's Constitutional Rights Subcommittee that he chaired, or in its House counterpart. The omission was astonishing in light of the testimony less than 15 years earlier before the joint Congressional Pearl Harbor investigative committee about the Navy's failure to decode and circulate the Imperial Japanese government's Honolulu consulate's cable traffic about ship-in-harbor reports.

If the Navy had access to commercial cable traffic between Honolulu and Tokyo, it meant it had access to both foreign government cable traffic and those of American citizens. It would have been easy for Hennings, and his

334   CHAPTER 6

House Judiciary Committee colleague, Emanuel Celler, to have had oversight hearings for the purpose of determining what safeguards, if any, were in place to ensure that only foreign government communications were the targets of NSA's activities, unless those foreign government communications clearly implicated American citizens in espionage. And virtually all of the key Navy personnel who testified before the Pearl Harbor Committee about that commercial cable traffic were still very much alive and available to testify as the NSA Act moved toward passage.

But no such oversight hearings on the NSA Act took place. Instead, Hennings held hearings in April on the chilling effect of the loyalty program on scientific inquiry and in and July on the Supreme Court decision in *Greene v. McElroy* case that ruled unconstitutional the administration's implementation of a security clearance program that lacked an appeal or adversarial/challenge process.[186] Hennings's only other foray into government electronic surveillance practices took place in July and December 1959 on existing, relatively well-publicized wiretapping controversies.[187] While useful in laying out the existing public record on the controversies in question, the hearings broke no new ground and produced no fresh legislative limits on the loyalty program or federal electronic surveillance practices.

OPPONENTS OF OPPRESSION: NCAHUAC AND JAMES ROOSEVELT

Eisenhower's last year in office would see the emergence of new domestic opponents of the burgeoning American security state. One of those adversaries was also to become HUAC's greatest public critic, and ultimately, responsible for its demise.

Frank Wilkinson was the son of a Methodist doctor and American Legion member who, during Herbert Hoover's presidency, was active in the antivice and temperance movements.[188] Initially inclined to follow his father's example and enter the Methodist ministry and conservative politics, his subsequent travels at home and abroad during the Depression caused him to gravitate toward liberal politics and public service. He eventually secured a job with the Los Angeles Housing Authority.[189] It was his time at the L.A. Housing Authority, combined with the political leftist company he kept, that came to the attention of the California Committee on Un-American Activities. Wilkinson and his wife Jean, a social studies teacher, were subpoenaed to appear before the California legislature's version of HUAC in 1952. Wilkinson had previously refused to answer questions about his

"IS THIS IDOLATRY OF SECURITY?" 335

political affiliations at a housing condemnation proceeding, which triggered a backlash from his Los Angeles government employer. At the California state HUAC hearing, Wilkinson and his wife refused to answer questions about the political beliefs and associations, and as a result were fired from their jobs.[190]

By this point, Wilkinson's activities had become of interest to the Los Angeles FBI field office, a development that would ultimately result in Wilkinson becoming such a focus of the Bureau in the ensuing years that his FBI file would grow to more than 130,000 pages.[191] Wilkinson also became a target of the congressional HUAC, being subpoenaed to testify on December 7, 1956.

Since being fired from his Housing Authority post, Wilkinson had become secretary of the newly created Citizens Committee to Preserve American Freedoms (CCPAF), an organization dedicated to opposing HUAC.[192] Getting CCPAF off the ground and functioning had clearly been cathartic for Wilkinson, as his completely defiant appearance before HUAC showed.

At the outset, Wilkinson declined to even give his address in response to a question from HUAC counsel and staff director Richard Arens, leading to a rancorous, circular exchange—Arens asking for Wilkinson's occupation, addressing him as "Witness," and Wilkinson responding in kind.

"I am answering no questions of this committee," Wilkinson told the HUAC members, "because the House Committee on Un-American Activities stands in direct violation, both by its mandate, by its existence and by its practices, of the First Amendment to the United States Constitution. The committee should be abolished, and the question is none of your business."

After some further back-and-forth, the HUAC subcommittee voted to hold Wilkinson in contempt.[193] The full committee elected not to move the contempt citation in 1956, but less than two years later when Wilkinson was again hauled before HUAC, he once more refused to answer any questions. This time, the full committee did cite him, and he was found guilty on January 22, 1959.[194] Wilkinson was undeterred.

In the aftermath of an infamous and spectacularly failed HUAC hearing in San Francisco in May 1960—which witnessed the first major student protest against the House committee—Wilkinson intensified his organizing efforts, both at the national and local level. On October 10, 1960, Wilkinson and other key civil liberties activists met in New York to formally launch the National Committee to Abolish the House Un-American Activities Committee (NCAHUAC).[195] Hoover had advance warning of the move, and for the next fifteen years the FBI would work closely with HUAC to try to discredit, and even destroy, NCAHUAC.[196]

336   CHAPTER 6

However, Wilkinson and his organization were not without allies, both in and out of Congress.

On April 24, the ACLU had called for a "maximum effort" to abolish HUAC at its biennial conference. Historian and *New York Herald Tribune* columnist Walter Millis noted that the "great heresy hunt" had abated somewhat but that "too much of its spirit survives."[197] The ACLU coordinated its action with a House member prepared to take on his colleagues over HUAC.

FDR's son James had been elected to the House in the 1954 midterms. The Pacific War veteran—he left the Marine Corps as a brigadier general—had both the name recognition and the wartime service credibility to take on HUAC, and in the last year of Eisenhower's tenure, he did just that. On April 25, 1960, in an hour-long House floor speech, Roosevelt rhetorically incinerated HUAC's practices, record, and rationale for existing.

Titling his address "The Dragon Slayers," Roosevelt said that like him, an increasing number of his House colleagues "are reaching the conclusion that if the committee ever did have any usefulness, it has now completely outlived it." Noting that some of the civil society groups that had also called for HUAC's abolition had been attacked by the committee for their support of food programs for the poor, Roosevelt observed, "Presumably just by their coming out for three square meals a day, that would stamp eating as a Communist doctrine and persuade us all to starve to death."[198]

To illustrate how thin-skinned HUAC's leadership was vis-à-vis criticism, Roosevelt referenced the November 1957 HUAC report titled "Operation Abolition," a fifteen-page screed that smeared civil society groups calling for an end to HUAC.

"Out of the 15 pages," Roosevelt said, "14 are devoted to alleged dossiers of the critics as if to say that this alone destroys their credibility."[199]

Roosevelt readily conceded that "we are living in a hostile world in which communism poses a threat," but he warned against the reflexive, unthinking attitude fostered by HUAC.

"Do we decide the farm program, the budget, school bills, foreign aid, conservation, or social security merely by reading the *Daily Worker* and then voting the opposite?" he asked.[200]

Roosevelt laid out how HUAC had the largest individual committee appropriation in the House and that its defenders claimed the expense was justified "on the ground that the committee is protecting the security of their country." The California Democrat disposed of that argument as well.

"But of course it must be recognized that the basic responsibility for protection of this country against treason or espionage is not in the hands of the

"IS THIS IDOLATRY OF SECURITY?"   337

committee and never has been," Roosevelt said, "but is in the hands of the FBI, and other counterespionage agencies of the Federal Government. The committee does not catch spies or saboteurs."[201]

After detailing several more prominent HUAC gaffes and errors, Roosevelt drove home his central argument.

"My conviction," he told the House, "is that the committee is closer to being dangerous to America in its conception than most of what it investigates. My conviction is that it is a continuing discredit to the country, and more immediately, to this House. My conviction is that so long as we continue its existence, we must equally share the guilt for the evil which it does."[202]

Roosevelt had started a political civil war in the House over HUAC. The committee and its supporters responded predictably.

HUAC subcommittee chairman Gordon Sherer (R-OH) slammed Roosevelt on June 2 for adopting the CP USA line in attacking the committee, attempting to blame Roosevelt for the student protests at HUAC's May 1960 hearing in San Francisco.

"Only two weeks before the incident," Scherer told the New York Times, Roosevelt had made his "shocking, unjustified, scurrilous" House floor speech attacking HUAC, claiming that Roosevelt's speech had been used by anti-HUAC protestors in the Bay City.[203]

During an August 17 speech in Houston before the National Congress of Petroleum Retailers, pro-HUAC demonstrators hung Roosevelt in effigy and displayed a banner reading "Go Home Red Roosevelt." The California Democrat was unfazed, telling reporters that HUAC was "doing the very things the Communists want to see done," namely the curtailment of First Amendment rights.[204]

Just over two months after NCAHUAC's creation, Roosevelt sent a four-page New Year's Eve "Dear Colleague" to all House members summing up his anti-HUAC campaign to date. Roosevelt catalogued the damage HUAC had done.

"It has helped to poison the invigorating atmosphere which once encouraged the flourishing of democratic dissent," Roosevelt wrote his colleagues. "It has blackened our reputation abroad, and at home it has frightened into silence citizens who may have something important to say. Its methods have been reprehensible."[205]

Yet Roosevelt himself knew that the votes were simply not there—yet—to get rid of HUAC. Fear was the reason why.

He recognized that "it is still politically dangerous for many members of Congress to express by means of a direct vote their innermost feelings about the Committee," Roosevelt conceded. "I know, because they have told me." He called upon the press and civil society organizations to step up the pressure to help create a political climate in which voting to abolish HUAC would not become a career-ending move for a House member.

"Until that day," Roosevelt said, "I do not plan to move formally again for the abolition of the Committee, lest the resulting vote mislead the public into thinking that this Committee really has the backing of the House. I will also not prejudice adoption of the liberal legislative program pledged in the Democratic platform by putting my colleagues on the spot at this time."[206] He ended his missive to his House colleagues by calling for real scrutiny of HUAC's budget.

The battle to eliminate HUAC would be a long one.

HOOVER AND EISENHOWER: A FOND FAREWELL

Early in Eisenhower's tenure, Hoover had worked hard to re-create the kind of trust and close working relationship with Ike that the FBI head had enjoyed with FDR. He succeeded from the outset.

At the end of Eisenhower's first year in office, Deputy Attorney General Rogers sent Hoover a note of gratitude for the FBI's work investigating a slew of potential Eisenhower nominees.

Commenting on some thirty-three persons recommended by congressional GOP members and party officials, Rogers noted that "The Attorney General refused in each instance to recommend the nomination solely on the basis of information resulting from the character investigation conducted by agents of the FBI."[207] Rogers went on to note that if the nominations had gone forward, they might have potentially resulted in "serious prejudice to the best interest of the United States" and "acute embarrassment to the President. There could be no more convincing proof of the value of the FBI investigations than this list of cases."[208]

Whether any alleged derogatory information on each of the thirty-three persons in question was, in fact, accurate, was beside the point as far as Rogers and the White House were concerned. Hoover helped protect Ike politically, and for the duration of his two terms in office, Eisenhower returned the favor several times over the years, publicly praising and defending Hoover whenever he was attacked.

On his last full day in office, Eisenhower responded to a recent letter from Hoover in glowing terms, addressing Hoover as "Dear Edgar."

Noting that "the 'voice' of the FBI is an important one to me, both officially and personally," Eisenhower expressed his admiration for "the splendid performance of the whole organization which you head" and his gratitude "for the prompt and thoughtful responses" to his inquiries and taskings to Hoover personally over the years.

"I repeat that my admiration of the work of the FBI is great. And I wish there were about a thousand J. Edgar Hoovers in key spots in the government!"[209]

Hoover would find Eisenhower's replacement, and the new attorney general, to be less to his liking.

CONCLUSION

Truman's departure from the presidency brought to the Oval Office America's wartime European theater commander, Dwight Eisenhower—a change in leadership and attitude on all things internal security–related that ushered in a golden age for Hoover and the FBI. Eisenhower's modification of Truman's executive order on the federal employee loyalty program making sexual orientation fair game for dismissal from service or denying a gay person a federal job meshed perfectly with Hoover's world view about homosexuals. Men like Voice of America's Charles Thayer paid the price.

Early in Eisenhower's first term, the Supreme Court would hand him and every one of his successors one of the most powerful legal instruments for keeping the Congress, the press, and the public in the dark about the government's hidden conduct via the *Reynolds* case: the state secrets privilege. What made the *Reynolds* decision so outrageous was not just that the nation's highest court set a precedent of showing unjustified deference to the executive branch on matters of national security. It was also the fact that Air Force and Defense Department lawyers *knowingly lied* to the Supreme Court about the true facts of the case. Had the justices demanded to see the full documentation surrounding the crash of the B-29, they would have realized quickly that the Air Force was using claims of secrecy to hide its aircraft maintenance failures, not protect real secrets. In multiple cases over subsequent decades, those seeking redress in cases of alleged wiretapping or other forms of surveillance would have their claims die at the hands of federal courts taking executive branch invocations of the state secrets privilege at face value.

By Eisenhower's second term Hoover and his lieutenants had moved beyond simply surveilling and trying to prosecute CP USA members or others they believed were Soviet fellow travelers. The FBI leadership formally

340 CHAPTER 6

adopted some of the very tactics their Soviet counterparts used to infiltrate and destroy organizations deemed a threat to the prevailing order. As the Church Committee would note in its report on the program two decades later, the Justice Department claimed that Eisenhower was personally briefed on COINTELPRO CP USA by Hoover on November 6, 1958.[210] The author found no evidence in Eisenhower's papers that the president expressed any reservations about COINTELPRO CP USA at the time. This was yet another example of a presidential precedent on domestic surveillance, and in this case outright political repression, that would have explosive political consequences decades later.

NOTES

1. See William I. Hitchcock, *The Age of Eisenhower: America and the World in the 1950s* (New York: Simon & Schuster, 2018), 76–82.
2. First Inaugural Address of President Dwight D. Eisenhower, January 20, 1953. Retrieved from The American Presidency Project at https://www.presidency.ucsb.edu /documents/inaugural-address-3.
3. First Inaugural Address of President Dwight D. Eisenhower, January 20, 1953.
4. Memo of Milton D. Hill to General Wilton Persons, "Analysis of Rockefeller Committee Proposal for a Citizens Commission to Investigate Subversives," January 12, 1953. DDEL, WHCF, OF 104-J, Security and Loyalty Program of Government Employees, Box 413.
5. Memo of Milton D. Hill to General Wilton Persons, 2.
6. Memo of Milton D. Hill to General Wilton Persons, 4.
7. Minutes of Cabinet Meeting, March 27, 1953, 4. DDEL, Papers as President, 1953– 1961 (Ann Whitman File), Cabinet Series, Box 2.
8. Minutes of Cabinet Meeting, March 27, 1953, 4.
9. *Uniform Code of Military Justice, Hearings before a Subcommittee of the Committee on Armed Services,* House of Representatives, 81st Congress (First Session) on H.R. 2498, March 7, 1949, testimony of COL John Curry, USMC, 1221–1222.
10. Memo of Defense Personnel Policy Board Chairman Hubert Howard to the Service Secretary's, October 11, 1949. HSTL, CF, Box 26.
11. Douglas M. Charles, *Hoover's War on Gays: Exposing the FBI's "Sex Deviates" Program* (Lawrence: University Press of Kansas, 2015), 22–35.
12. Charles, *Hoover's War on Gays,* 77–79, 127–130.
13. Executive Order 10450—Security Requirements for Government Employment, April 27, 1950. Retrieved via the NARA website at https://www.archives.gov/federal -register/codification/executive-order/10450.html. See also 64 Stat. 476, retrieved via the LOC Statutes at Large website at https://www.loc.gov/law/help/statutes-at -large/81st-congress.ph.
14. Minutes of Cabinet Meeting, April 24, 1953, 3. DDEL, Papers as President, 1953– 1961 (Ann Whitman File), Cabinet Series, Box 2.

"IS THIS IDOLATRY OF SECURITY?"   341

15. EO 10450, Sec. 4.
16. EO 10450, Sec. 8(a)(1)(i).
17. EO 10450, Sec. 8(a)(1)(iii).
18. See David K. Johnson, *The Lavender Scare: The Cold War Persecution of Gays and Lesbians in the Federal Government* (Chicago: University of Chicago Press, 2006), 1–2.
19. *Employment of Homosexuals and Other Sex Perverts in Government. Interim Report Submitted to the Committee on Expenditures in the Executive Departments by Its Subcommittee on Investigations Pursuant to S. Res. 280.* Senate Document 241, 81st Congress (Second Session), December 15, 1950.
20. EO 10450, Sec. 8(a)(8).
21. EO 10450, Sec. 14(a)(2).
22. White House press release of October 23, 1953. DDEL, WHCF, OF 104-J, Security and Loyalty Program of Government Employees, Box 413.
23. Stone *Perilous Times*, 351.
24. Aviation Safety Network report, accessed via https://aviation-safety.net/wikibase /148092.
25. Barry Siegel, "How the Death of Judy's Father Made America More Secretive," *Los Angeles Times*, April 18, 2004 (digital edition).
26. Barry Siegel, "How the Death of Judy's Father Made America More Secretive."
27. *United States v. Reynolds*, 345 U.S. 1 (1953).
28. *United States v. Reynolds*, at 345 U.S. 10.
29. *United States v. Reynolds*, at 345 U.S. 10.
30. *United States v. Reynolds*, at 345 U.S. 10.
31. Stone, *Perilous Times*, 296.
32. See C. Mark Smith, *Raising Cain: The Life and Politics of Senator Harry Cain* (Bothel: Book Publishers Network, 2011), 208. Hereinafter cited as Smith.
33. *Third Annual Report of the Subversive Activities Control Board*, Fiscal Year Ended June 30, 1953 (Washington: Government Printing Office, 1953), 6–7.
34. *Third Annual Report of the Subversive Activities Control Board.*
35. Department of Justice Order No. 12–53, Designation of Organizations in Connection with the Federal Employee Security Program, April 29, 1953. DDEL, Papers of William Rogers (1938–62), Papers—Attorney General (1), Box 51.
36. Goldstein, *Political Repression in Modern America*, 161.
37. See Kai Bird and Martin J. Sherwin, *American Prometheus: The Triumph and Tragedy of J. Robert Oppenheimer* (New York: Alfred A. Knopf, 2005), 121–123.
38. Bird and Sherwin, *American Prometheus*, 137–138.
39. Bird and Sherwin, *American Prometheus*, 402–405.
40. Bird and Sherwin, *American Prometheus*, 438–439.
41. Bird and Sherwin, *American Prometheus*, 443–444.
42. Bird and Sherwin, *American Prometheus*, 539.
43. Bird and Sherwin, *American Prometheus*, 541.
44. *Investigation of Communist Activities in the Los Angeles Area—Part 4. Hearings before the Committee on Un-American Activities,* House of Representatives, 83rd Congress (First Session), April 7, 1953, 763–764.
45. *Investigation of Communist Activities in the Los Angeles Area—Part 4.*
46. *Investigation of Communist Activities in the Los Angeles Area—Part 4*, 765–770.

342   CHAPTER 6

47. *Investigation of Communist Activities in the New York City Area—Part 1. Hearings before the Committee on Un-American Activities,* House of Representatives, 83rd Congress (First Session), May 4, 1953, 1156–1171.

48. *Investigation of Communist Activities in the Columbus, Ohio, Area. Hearings before the Committee on Un-American Activities,* House of Representatives, 83rd Congress (First Session), June 17–18, 1953.

49. *Investigation of Communist Activities in the Albany, New York, Area—Part 1. Hearings before the Committee on Un-American Activities,* House of Representatives, 83rd Congress (First Session), July 13–14, 1953, 2363–2416.

50. *Communist Methods of Infiltration (Government-Labor, Part 3). Hearings before the Committee on Un-American Activities,* House of Representatives, 83rd Congress (First Session), September 15, 1953, 3028–3032.

51. *Activities of United States Citizens Employed by the United Nations. Hearings before the Subcommittee to Investigate the Administration of the Internal Security Act and Other Internal Security Laws of the Committee on the Judiciary,* United States Senate, 82nd Congress (Second Session), December 17, 1952, Appendix B, 407.

52. "United Nations: Death of an Idealist," *Time*, November 14, 1952. Accessed online at http://content.time.com/time/subscriber/article/0,33009,817355,00.html.

53. Paul W. Ward, "U.N. Counsel Ends Life in 12-Story Leap," *The Baltimore Sun*, November 14, 1952, 1.

54. Letter from Harry Bullis to President Eisenhower, May 9, 1953, 1. DDEL, WHCF, OF 99-R, McCarthy, Box 317.

55. Letter from President Eisenhower to Harry Bullis, May 18, 1953, 1. DDEL, WHCF, OF 99-R, McCarthy, Box 317.

56. Letter from President Eisenhower to Harry Bullis, May 18, 1953, 1.

57. NSC 161, Part 10: Internal Security Program, 10–6. DDEL, White House Office, National Security Council Staff: Papers, 1948–61, Disaster File, Box 11.

58. NSC 161, Part 10: Internal Security Program, 10–6, 10–4.

59. NSC 161, Part 10: Internal Security Program, 10–6, 10–4.

60. Minutes for the 162nd Meeting of the NSC, September 17, 1953, 10. DDEL, Papers as President, 1953–61 (Ann Whitman File)—NSC Series, Box 4.

61. *Interlocking Subversion in Government Departments, Part 16. Hearings before the Subcommittee to Investigate the Administration of the Internal Security Act and Other Internal Security Laws of the Committee on the Judiciary,* United States Senate, 83rd Congress (First Session), November 17, 1953, 1130–1139.

62. "Freedom and Espionage," *Wall Street Journal*, November 19, 1953, 12.

63. "Freedom and Espionage."

64. "Freedom and Espionage."

65. "Freedom and Espionage."

66. "Brownell on Wiretapping," *Washington Post*, November 24, 1953, 24.

67. Minutes of Cabinet Meeting, December 15, 1953, 2. DDEL, Papers as President, 1953–1961 (Ann Whitman File), Cabinet Series, Box 2.

68. Minutes of Cabinet Meeting, December 15, 1953, 1.

69. "Memorandum for the National Security Council, Review of Internal Security Legislation," December 28, 1953, 3. DDEL, White House Office, Office of the Special Assistant for National Security Affairs: Records, 1952–61. NSC Series, Policy Papers Subseries, Box 11.

"IS THIS IDOLATRY OF SECURITY?" 343

70. "Memorandum for the National Security Council, Review of Internal Security Legislation," 3–10.
71. "Memorandum for the National Security Council, Review of Internal Security Legislation," 11.
72. S. 3229, offered by Senator Pat McCarran on March 31, 1954, 83rd Congress (Second Session).
73. H.R. 8649, offered by Rep Kenneth Keating, March 31, 1954, 2–4, 83rd Congress (Second Session).
74. *Congressional Record*, April 8, 1954, 4913–4914.
75. EO 10491, October 13, 1953. Accessed via the American Presidency Project website, https://www.presidency.ucsb.edu/documents/executive-order-10491-amendment-executive-order-no-10450-april-27-1953-relating-security.
76. See David A. Nichols, *Ike and McCarthy: Dwight Eisenhower's Secret Campaign against Joseph McCarthy* (New York: Simon and Schuster, 2017), 79–81.
77. Nichols, *Ike and McCarthy*, 117–121.
78. Nichols, *Ike and McCarthy*, 121–123.
79. Presidential Directive of March 13, 1948, *Confidential Status of Employee Loyalty Records*, 13 Fed. Reg. 1359, published March 16, 1948.
80. *Communist Infiltration in the Army, Part 3. Hearings before the Permanent Subcommittee on Investigations of the Committee on Government Operations.* United States Senate, 83rd Congress (Second Session), February 18, 1954, 147–148.
81. *Communist Infiltration in the Army, Part 3*, 153.
82. "Stevens vs. McCarthy," *The Washington Post*, February 22, 1954, 8.
83. Nichols, *Ike and McCarthy*, 150–151.
84. Nichols, *Ike and McCarthy*, 150–151.
85. Arthur Krock, "Senate to Investigate Investigating Methods," *New York Times*, February 28, 1954, E3.
86. Nichols, *Ike and McCarthy*, 194–200.
87. Nichols, *Ike and McCarthy*, 201.
88. Hitchcock, *The Age of Eisenhower*, 143.
89. Hitchcock, *The Age of Eisenhower*, 144.
90. Hitchcock, *The Age of Eisenhower*, 144–145.
91. Nichols, *Ike and McCarthy*, 296.
92. C. Trussell, "Congress Passes Softened Version of Communist Ban," *New York Times*, August 20, 1954, 6.
93. Senate Report No. 1709, 82nd Congress (2nd Session), *Amending the Subversive Activities Control Act of 1950*, Report to Accompany S. 3706, 5.
94. C. Trussell, "Congress Passes Softened Version of Communist Ban," *New York Times*, August 20, 1954, 6.
95. Statement by the President upon Signing the Communist Control Act of 1954, August 24, 1954. Accessed via the American Presidency Project at https://www.presidency.ucsb.edu/documents/statement-the-president-upon-signing-the-communist-control-act-1954.
96. Hamilton, *Adam Clayton Powell, Jr.*, 201–202.
97. *Congressional Record—Senate*, January 16, 1953, 408.
98. *Commission on Civil Rights. Hearings before a Subcommittee of the Committee on the Judiciary, United States Senate, on S. 1 and S. 535*, 83rd Congress (Second Session), January 26, 1954, 42.

344   CHAPTER 6

99. *Commission on Civil Rights.*, 45.

100. FBI HQ File 61-3176-769, July 19, 1954, 1. Available on the FBI's Vault website at vault.fbi.gov/.

101. FBI HQ File 61-3176-852, December 13, 1954, 8. Available on the FBI's Vault website at vault.fbi.gov/.

102. Smith, *Raising Cain*, 213–217.

103. Smith, *Raising Cain*, 215.

104. Harry Cain, "Can Freedom Live with Internal Security?" Speech before the Fifth Congressional Republican District Committee, January 15, 1955, 1. DDEL, WHCF, OF-50, Subversive Activities Control Board, Box 193.

105. Cain, "Can Freedom Live with Internal Security?" 2.

106. Cain, "Can Freedom Live with Internal Security?" 8.

107. Cain, "Can Freedom Live with Internal Security?" 9–13.

108. Cain, "Can Freedom Live with Internal Security?" 13.

109. Cain, "Can Freedom Live with Internal Security?" 14.

110. Cain, "Can Freedom Live with Internal Security?" 15.

111. Cain, "Can Freedom Live with Internal Security?" 15–16.

112. Cain, "Can Freedom Live with Internal Security?" 17.

113. Cain, "Can Freedom Live with Internal Security?" 17.

114. Smith, *Raising Cain*, 220.

115. Public Law 83–176, 67 Stat. 307.

116. *Administration of the Federal Employees' Security Program. Hearings before a Subcommittee of the Committee on Post Office and Civil Service,* United States Senate, 84th Congress (First Session), June 2, 1955, Part 1, 46.

117. *Administration of the Federal Employees' Security Program.*

118. *Administration of the Federal Employees' Security Program.*

119. *Administration of the Federal Employees' Security Program*, 47.

120. *Administration of the Federal Employees' Security Program.*

121. *Administration of the Federal Employees' Security Program*, 49.

122. *Administration of the Federal Employees' Security Program*, 50.

123. *Administration of the Federal Employees' Security Program*, 55.

124. *Administration of the Federal Employees' Security Program*, 55.

125. *Administration of the Federal Employees' Security Program*, 58–71.

126. Smith, *Raising Cain*, 223.

127. *Cole v. Young*, 351 U.S. 536 (1956).

128. *Wiretapping. Hearings before Subcommittee No. 5 of the Committee on the Judiciary,* House of Representatives, 84th Congress (First Session), Testimony of Irvin Ferman, April 26, 1955, 158.

129. *Wiretapping. Hearings before Subcommittee No. 5 of the Committee on the Judiciary,* 159.

130. *Wiretapping. Hearings before Subcommittee No. 5 of the Committee on the Judiciary,* 160.

131. *Wiretapping. Hearings before Subcommittee No. 5 of the Committee on the Judiciary,* 161–163.

132. *Wiretapping. Hearings before Subcommittee No. 5 of the Committee on the Judiciary,* House of Representatives, 84th Congress (First Session), Testimony of Assistant Attorney General Warren Olney, March 23, 1955, 29–33.

133. Memo of J. Edgar Hoover to National Security Advisor Dillon Anderson, July 19, 1955, 1. DDEL, Records as President, WHCF, CF, 1953–1961, Subject Series, Box 34.

"IS THIS IDOLATRY OF SECURITY?" 345

134. Memo of J. Edgar Hoover to National Security Advisor Dillon Anderson, July 19, 1955, 1–2.
135. Memo of J. Edgar Hoover to National Security Advisor Dillon Anderson, July 19, 1955, 2.
136. Hitchcock, *The Age of Eisenhower*, 234–235.
137. Memo of J. Edgar Hoover to National Security Advisor Dillon Anderson, September 6, 1955. DDEL, Records as President, White House Office, Office of the Special Assistant for National Security Affairs: Records, 1952–61, FBI Series, Box 3.
138. FBI file 61-HQ-3176, Serial 1077, October 21, 1955. Available on the FBI Vault website at vault.fbi.gov/.
139. See the full FBI file 61-HQ-3176 for details on NAACP chapters. Available on the FBI Vault website at vault.fbi.gov/.
140. *Civil Rights Proposals. Hearings before the Committee on the Judiciary*, United States Senate, 84th Congress (Second Session), on S. 900; S. 902; S. 903; H.R. 5205; S. J. Res. 29; S. Con. Res. 8; S. 904; S. 905; S. 906; S. 907; S. 1089; S. 3604; S. 3605; S. 3415; S. 3717; S. 3718. April 24, May 16, 25, June 1, 12, 25, 26, 27, and July 6 and 13, 1956.
141. *Communist Party v. SACB*, 351 U.S. 115 (1956).
142. *Supplementary Detailed Staff Reports on Intelligence Activities and the Rights of Americans, Book III. Final Report of the Select Committee to Study Governmental Operations with respect to Intelligence Activities*, United States Senate Report No. 94–755, 94th Congress (Second Session), April 23, 1976, 449.
143. FBI New York filed office file 100-NY-113352, June 7, 1955, 9, 13. LOC, Anthony Lewis Papers, Part II, Box 150.
144. FBI New York filed office file 100-NY-1352386, May 20, 1959. LOC, Anthony Lewis Papers, Part II, Box 150. The information on Markel in the report dates from 1955.
145. DeLoach, *Hoover's FBI*, 270.
146. Sullivan and Brown, *The Bureau*, 128.
147. *Intelligence Activities, Senate Resolution 21. Hearings before the Select Committee to Study Governmental Operations with Respect to Intelligence Activities of the United States Senate, Volume 6: Federal Bureau of Investigation*, 94th Congress (First Session), November 18, 19, December 2, 3, 9, 10, and 11, 1975, 372–376. Hereinafter cited as Church Committee, Vol. 6.
148. *Intelligence Activities, Senate Resolution 21*.
149. See the MFSA's historical timeline on their website, available at https://www.mfsaweb .org/history-timeline.
150. See FBI file 61-HQ-3615. FBI records collection on MFSA is located at the United Methodist Archives and History Center in Madison, NJ. Online catalogue at http:// catalog.gcah.org/publicdata/gcah2402.htm#g2402.05.
151. *Hearings Regarding Jack R. McMichael. Hearings before the Committee on Un-American Activities*, House of Representatives, 83rd Congress (First Session), July 30, 1953, 2615–2760.
152. *Hearings Regarding Jack R. McMichael*, 2760.
153. *Hearings Regarding Jack R. McMichael*, 2761–2762.
154. *The Communist Party of the United States: What It Is, How It Works: A Handbook for Americans*, Senate Document 117, 84th Congress (Second Session), Subcommittee to Investigate the Administration of the Internal Security Act and Other Internal Security Laws of the Committee on the Judiciary, United States Senate, April 23, 1956, 91.

346   CHAPTER 6

155. Howard L. Dutkin, "3-Judge Panel Will Rule on Handbook Row," *Washington Star*, May 5, 1956, A2. Retrieved via LOCCA.

156. *Methodist Federation for Social Action v. Eastland*, 141 F. Su 729 (D.D.C. 1956) at 731.

157. *Gayle v Browder*, 352 US 903 (1956).

158. Letter from J. Edgar Hoover to Maxwell Rabb, January 25, 1957, 1. DDEL, WHCF, CF—Subject Series, Box 34.

159. Letter from J. Edgar Hoover to Maxwell Rabb, January 25, 1957, 2–4.

160. *Civil Rights—1957. Hearings before the Subcommittee on Constitutional Rights of the Committee on the Judiciary*, United States Senate, 85th Congress (First Session), February 14, 1957, 1–50.

161. Memo from J. Edgar Hoover to Robert Cutler, Special Assistant to the President, April 26, 1957, 1. DDEL, Office of the Special Assistant for National Security Affairs, Records: 1952–61, FBI Series, Box 2.

162. H.R. 6127, 85th Congress (First Session).

163. H.R. 6127, 85th Congress (First Session).

164. H.R. 6127, 85th Congress (First Session), 2.

165. H.R. 6127, 85th Congress (First Session).

166. See for example *Investigation of Communist Activities in the New Haven, Conn. Area—Part 3. Hearings before the Committee on Un-American Activities*, House of Representatives, 85th Congress (First Session), February 26–27, 1957.

167. *Congressional Record*, June 18, 1957, D364 and August 7, 1957, D501.

168. Letter from Martin Luther King, Jr. to Vice President Richard Nixon, August 30, 1957, 1. DDEL, William Rogers Papers, Box 50.

169. Trezz Anderson, "New Rights Group Launched in Dixie!," *Pittsburgh Courier*, August 17, 1957, 2.

170. J. Edgar Hoover memo to Special Agent in Charge, Atlanta Field Office, "Southern Christian Leadership Conference, Information Concerning (Internal Security)," September 20, 1957. FBI file 100-HQ-438794X1. Available on the FBI's Vault website at vault.fbi.gov/.

171. See Michael R. Lemov, *People's Warrior: John Moss and the Fight for Freedom of Information and Consumer Rights* (Madison: Farleigh Dickinson University Press, 2011), 48.

172. Lemov, *People's Warrior*, 50.

173. Lemov, *People's Warrior*, 51.

174. *Availability of Information from Federal Departments and Agencies, Part 5—Department of Defense, First Section. Hearings before a Subcommittee of the Committee on Government Operations*, House of Representatives, 84th Congress (Second Session), July 9, 1956, 935–936.

175. Public Law 85–618, August 12, 1958.

176. Eisenhower signing statement on H.R. 2767, August 12, 1958. Accessed via The American Presidency Project at https://www.presidency.ucsb.edu/documents/statement-the-president-upon-signing-bill-relating-the-authority-federal-agencies-withhold.

177. *Benanti v. United States*, 355 U.S. 96 (1957).

178. *Wiretapping, Eavesdropping, and The Bill of Rights. Hearing before the Subcommittee on Constitutional Rights of the Committee on the Judiciary*, United States Senate, 86th Congress (First Session), Part 3, July 9, 1959, 540.

179. NSCID 9, *Communications Intelligence*, October 24, 1952. Declassified by NSA on June 14, 2012, pursuant to Executive Order 13526.

"IS THIS IDOLATRY OF SECURITY?" 347

180. NSCID 9, *Communications Intelligence*, October 24, 1952, 8.

181. NSCID 9, *Communications Intelligence*, October 24, 1952, 5.

182. *Intelligence Activities—Senate Resolution 21. Hearings before the Select Committee to Study Governmental Operations with respect to Intelligence Activities*, United States Senate, 94th Congress (First Session), Vol. 5: The National Security Agency and Fourth Amendment Rights, November 6, 1975, 57–58.

183. *Intelligence Activities—Senate Resolution 21*, Vol. 5, 58–60.

184. Letter and attachments from Secretary of Defense Charles Wilson to Bureau of the Budget Director Percival Brundage, July 23, 1957. DDEL, Office of the Special Assistant for National Security Affairs, Records, 1952–61, Special Assistant Series—Subject Subseries, Box 6.

185. Public Law 86–36, Section 6.

186. *See Secrecy and Science. Hearing before the Subcommittee on Constitutional Rights, Committee on the Judiciary.* United States Senate, 86th Congress (First Session), Part 1, April 28, 1959, and *Security and Constitutional Rights. Hearings before the Subcommittee on Constitutional Rights, Committee on the Judiciary,* United States Senate, 86th Congress (First Session), Part 3, July 2, 1959

187. *Wiretapping, Eavesdropping, and the Bill of Rights. Hearings before the Subcommittee on Constitutional Rights, Committee on the Judiciary, United States Senate,* 86th Congress (First Session), Part 3, July 9, 1959, and Part 5, December 15–16, 1959.

188. Richard Criley, *The FBI v The First Amendment* (Los Angeles: First Amendment Foundation, 1990). 32–33.

189. Criley, *The FBI v The First Amendment*, 33–34.

190. Criley, *The FBI v The First Amendment*, 34–36.

191. Kim Murphy, "Wilkinson vs. the FBI: Surveillance Case Sheds Light on McCarthy Era," *Los Angeles Times*, October 18, 1987 (digital edition).

192. Criley, *The FBI v The First Amendment*, 37–38.

193. *Communist Political Subversion—Part 1. Hearings before the Committee on Un-American Activities*, House of Representatives, 84th Congress (Second Session), December 7, 1956, 6747–6754.

194. Criley, *The FBI v The First Amendment*, 40–41.

195. Criley, *The FBI v The First Amendment*, 31–32.

196. Criley, *The FBI v The First Amendment*, 31–32.

197. Austin C. Wehrwein, "ACLU Asks End to House Inquiry," *New York Times*, April 25, 1960, 19.

198. *Congressional Record—House*, April 25, 1960, 8647.

199. *Congressional Record—House*, April 25, 1960, 8647.

200. *Congressional Record—House*, April 25, 1960, 8647. The *Daily Worker* was the principal publication of the CP USA.

201. *Congressional Record—House*, April 25, 1960, 8648.

202. *Congressional Record—House*, April 25, 1960, 8648.

203. "Scherer Hits Speech. James Roosevelt Accused of Taking Communist Line," *Associated Press* via the *New York Times*, June 3, 1960, 8.

204. "James Roosevelt Hanged in Effigy," *New York Times*, August 17, 1960, 15.

205. Rep James Roosevelt "Dear Colleague" letter, December 31, 1960, 1. Chicago History Museum, Records of the Chicago Committee to Defense the Bill of Rights, 1947–1998, Box 25.

348   CHAPTER 6

206. Rep James Roosevelt "Dear Colleague" letter, December 31, 1960, 3–4.
207. Letter from Deputy Attorney General William Rogers to J. Edgar Hoover, December 21, 1953. DDEL, Papers of William Rogers, Box 47.
208. Letter from Deputy Attorney General William Rogers to J. Edgar Hoover, December 21, 1953.
209. Letter from President Eisenhower to J. Edgar Hoover, January 19, 1961. DDEL, WHCF, OF 5-F, FBI, Box 106.
210. *Intelligence Activities: Senate Resolution 21. Hearings before the Select Committee to Study Governmental Operations with Respect to Intelligence Activities,* United States Senate, 94th Congress (First Session), Volume 6, Federal Bureau of Investigation, November 18, 19, December 2, 3, 9, 10 and 11, 1975, 993.

CONCLUSION

At the dawn of the twentieth century, the only two executive branch agencies routinely involved in domestic surveillance and related political repression were the Secret Service and the Postal Service, and the former—despite the relatively limited number of Secret Service agents—was far more active than the latter, which acted as a partner with the Treasury Department's investigative arm when needed. Three related events changed that and put the United States on the path to creating a domestic surveillance and political repression apparatus that in time would rival those of its European neighbors.

The first event was the growth of the popularity of anarchist, socialist, and communist ideals among major segments of American labor and left-leaning political elites.

As noted in Chapter 1, at least as early as 1898, the Secret Service was monitoring anarchist political activists and labor organizers in places like Patterson, New Jersey, at the time a major hub of both immigrant labor and textile mills with generally deplorable working conditions. In the period between the Spanish American War and President McKinley's assassination, federal authorities had generally been content to keep an eye on key anarchist groups and leaders while leaving it to state and local authorities to deal with anarchist-inspired or led strikes and labor–business disputes, even when violent incidents occurred.

The second key event was McKinley's assassination by the (likely mentally disturbed) recent anarchist convert Leon Czolgosz, which transformed the political and domestic security landscape.

Officials at the federal, state, and local levels went after known or suspected anarchists in communities across the country. During Roosevelt's first abbreviated term as McKinley's successor, the Secret Service intensified its surveillance of those deemed political radicals, and Congress passed the Anarchist Exclusion Act, which barred legal entry into the United States of anyone professing a belief in anarchism. Those measures failed to stamp out the appeal of anarchism, and its rival political philosophy, socialism, gained even more adherents during Roosevelt's two terms in office.

350   CONCLUSION

Roosevelt's subsequent efforts to employ the Secret Service and Postal Service against Socialist Party presidential candidate Eugene V. Debs and the socialist newspaper *Appeal to Reason* set additional, dangerous precedents that threatened the Bill of Rights. But it was the Roosevelt administration's more widespread misuse of the Secret Service to engage in politically related investigations, and even prying into the marital affairs of a junior US Navy officer, that would trigger a confrontation with Congress that sparked Roosevelt's unilateral expansion of federal domestic surveillance and the potential for widespread political repression in the decades that followed through the creation of the Bureau of Investigation.

The Navy Department's use of a Secret Service agent to uncover Ensign Earl Pritchard's extramarital affair in late 1907 generated a national uproar and a legislative backlash from Congress, which in April 1908 barred Secret Service agents from being used for anything other than presidential protection and capturing counterfeiters. When Roosevelt responded by instructing Attorney General Charles Bonaparte to create a cadre of investigators within the Justice Department itself, he did so despite the lack of any authorizing legislation allowing it. A precedent of presidential circumvention of a congressional ban on a surveillance activity or authority had been set, and it would be repeated by Roosevelt's successors or their subordinates over the balance of the twentieth century.

The episode also marked one of the last times Congress would take decisive action to rein in presidential overreach on surveillance activities during the twentieth century. The decline of true, probing congressional oversight actions targeting the executive branch was the third key development that accelerated the rise and growth of the American surveillance state.

With the outbreak of World War I and America's subsequent entry into the war in April 1917, Congress largely jettisoned its role as an overseer of executive branch actions in the areas of security policy and surveillance, instead becoming a full partner in expanding the legal framework that enabled widescale, pervasive domestic surveillance and political repression, particularly in connection with the First Amendment, free speech, and the press.

The enactment during the war of the Espionage Act, the Trading with the Enemy Act, the Food and Fuel Control Act, and the Sedition Act represented a radical expansion of federal surveillance and prosecutorial powers that harmed thousands of innocent Americans and the press while doing little, if anything, to help defeat the Central Powers. The subsequent Harding administration engaged in a limited rollback of those wartime authorities, persuading Congress to repeal the Sedition Act and Food and Fuel Control Act. But the Espionage Act and Trading with the Enemy Act were left in place, and

CONCLUSION 351

the broad language of the former would be used decades after the Great War to prosecute intelligence community whistleblowers like Edward Snowden. While it is true that the Army and Navy intelligence bureaucracies and the FBI shrank substantially after the war, the FBI's profile did not, largely supplanting the Secret Service as the premier domestic surveillance agency in the federal government, with the number of its field offices spreading to every state and territory well before the outbreak of World War II in Europe.

In his landmark work *Crisis and Leviathan*, historian Robert Higgs noted this "ratchet effect" on government power in the aftermath of a major crisis. "Without the powerful ideological and constitutional restraints that operated for over a century after the birth of the United States—restraints destroyed during the national emergencies of 1916–1945—modern governmental authorities may," Higgs wrote, "drink deeply and often from the heady wellsprings of political power and social control."[1] In the context of domestic surveillance and political repression, this proved true time and again between 1919 and 1961.

The victory of Soviet forces in the Russian civil war had a further galvanizing effect on American political elites and the emerging national security establishment. A political and economic philosophy totally at odds with the American and western European model had captured the largest (in geographic terms) country on the planet, and the leadership of the new Union of Soviet Socialist Republics was intent on exporting their philosophy and governing model around the world. In the United States, this triggered the first Red Scare and a related push by both the Congress and executive branch law enforcement and intelligence elements to identify, expose, and where possible prosecute or deport those openly sympathetic to the Soviet cause.

In the congressional context, it would lead first to the House creating the infamous Fish Committee, then the McCormack–Dickstein Committee, and later the Select Committee on Un-American Activities—with the latter conducting unconstitutional raids on civil society organizations and even engaging in wiretapping during FDR's presidency. Well before the end of World War II, the renamed House Committee on Un-American Activities would effectively be made permanent, going on to become among the most feared and loathed institutions in American history. During Truman's tenure, HUAC got a Senate counterpart—the Senate Internal Security Subcommittee.

Over the course of several decades, HUAC's and SISS's public show trial–style hearings would destroy the professional and personal lives of thousands of Americans who had no connection to Soviet espionage efforts. Even those who would confess to having been CP USA members or had

352   CONCLUSION

otherwise dabbled in radical politics would never be proven to be active Soviet espionage agents. Their "crime" was that they had explored, then in most cases abandoned, a political and economic philosophy that was vehemently opposed by their own government and the overwhelming majority of their fellow citizens but that never posed a realistic threat to the survival of the Republic.

The interwar period also saw the executive branch engage in vastly expanded domestic surveillance targeting known or suspected communists, with the FBI, MID, and ONI all heavily involved in the effort. Wiretapping controversies also grabbed the spotlight, especially after the Supreme Court effectively sanctioned it via its 1928 *Olmstead* decision. The congressional backlash against the decision led to the 1934 passage of the Communications Act, which banned the practice outright. In the six years that followed, FDR and his senior law enforcement and intelligence officials periodically debated whether or not to seek to change the law to allow wiretapping in specific circumstances. By the late spring of 1940, FDR decided to go it alone, ignoring the most recent Supreme Court decision affirming the Communications Act's ban on wiretapping (the *Nardone* case) and telling his then-Attorney General Robert Jackson in May 1940 to proceed with wiretapping in national security cases, particularly espionage. Like his late cousin and predecessor Theodore Roosevelt, FDR was comfortable circumventing Congress and the federal courts in matters involving domestic surveillance activities. It was yet another anti–Bill of Rights precedent, one that every one of his successors would follow for nearly thirty years.

Less than three months after the Japanese Navy's surprise attack on Pearl Harbor, FDR ordered the long-laid plans for the round-up and incarceration of Japanese Americans to be put in motion, via his now-infamous Executive Order 9066. Roosevelt took the action despite multiple reports from ONI and his taxpayer-funded private spymaster, John Franklin Carter, that the overwhelming majority of Japanese Americans were clearly loyal to the United States. Intense political pressure from West Coast House and Senate members, not the facts concerning Japanese American loyalty, is what ultimately moved FDR to order the Army to forcibly evacuate those American citizens from their homes to places in the interior of the United States. Subsequent Supreme Court rulings against Japanese Americans who challenged their evacuation and internment gave FDR's order a veneer of legality. Cabinet members like Interior Secretary Harold Ickes and even Attorney General Francis Biddle recognized the fundamentally discriminatory, unconstitutional nature of the act, yet they elected to stay in office

CONCLUSION   353

rather than resign in protest over the policy. Fear-driven racism, not legitimate national security concerns, would keep more than 100,000 Japanese Americans in concentration camps for nearly the entire war. Not until more than seven decades after the last Japanese American was released from War Relocation Authority custody would a different Supreme Court rule that "The forcible relocation of U.S. citizens to concentration camps, solely and explicitly on the basis of race, is objectively unlawful and outside the scope of Presidential authority."[2]

Other domestic surveillance structures and practices created during World War II—the systematic monitoring of federal employee loyalty, the FBI's creation of a massive informant network in the defense industry and elsewhere among civil society organizations, and the increased use of wiretapping and the collection of telegram traffic—became permanent fixtures during the Cold War. And while Army and Navy intelligence components continued to play a major role in all these areas, the FBI under J. Edgar Hoover's leadership solidified its position as the dominant player.

Hoover's long and close relationship with FDR stood in marked contrast with his relatively cool and distant one with Truman. Even so, as noted in Chapter 5, neither Truman or his senior White House advisors hesitated to employ Hoover and his agents to surveil political rivals like Tommy Corcoran and Ed Pritchard, despite the absence of any evidence either man had committed a federal crime at the time. Hoover himself utilized his agents to surveil those who dared to criticize him or the FBI. Interior Department official Jebby Davidson, who publicly criticized Hoover for the Bureau's tactics in federal employee and other investigations, would suspect as much at the time but was only able to confirm it decades later via a Freedom of Information Act request, as noted in Chapter 5.

The change of administrations from Eisenhower to John F. Kennedy coincided with an emerging social and political revolution in American society—changes that would drive the FBI, NSA, and military intelligence organizations to new extremes in their search for subversives and others challenging long-standing political, economic, and social paradigms.

By the time of Kennedy's assassination in November 1963, Students for a Democratic Society (SDS) was becoming a major force for social change and drawing Hoover's attention. As the decade of the 1960s progressed, opposition to the Vietnam War by multiple segments of American society paralleled the splintering of the civil rights movement into nonviolent (read King and SCLC) and militant (the new Black Panther Party) factions. The FBI, Army Intelligence, and ONI would all be involved in surveilling and trying to disrupt the groups seeking to stop the war in Southeast Asia,

354   CONCLUSION

end racial discrimination, advance the rights of women, and address long-standing grievances of the Native American community.

Yet the usual veil of secrecy over federal surveillance practices was occasionally, and tellingly, pierced in the years after Kennedy's death. A key player in the drama would be the late Missouri Senator Thomas Henning, Jr.'s replacement, Edward V. Long.

Between 1964 and 1967 Long would use his position as chairman of the Senate Subcommittee on Administrative Practice and Procedure to conduct a number of oversight actions and hearings designed to ferret out details of domestic surveillance operations by the IRS, Post Office, and other federal agencies.[3] Long's activities coincided with the emergence of the modern right-to-privacy movement, popularized by the publication of Alan Westin's *Privacy and Freedom* in 1967.[4] But neither Long nor Westin would surface the most damaging federal surveillance and political repression activities, and Long's efforts to get federal privacy legislation enacted fizzled when two key Supreme Court cases had the effect of limiting federal agencies use of wiretaps as well as creating "an expectation of privacy" in certain settings.[5] The passage in 1968 of the Omnibus Crime Control and Safe Streets Act, with its explicit probable cause–based warrant requirement for any federal criminal wiretap operation, also had the effect of blunting momentum toward more sweeping privacy-centric legislation.

Instead, a new phenomenon—the emergence of the government whistleblower—would, starting in early 1971, spell the beginning of the end of many secret federal surveillance and political repression programs described in this book.

A series of hearings in the House and Senate spanning 1971–1975, building off of those whistleblower revelations, would expose multiple COINTELPRO activities, along with other Army, Navy, CIA, and NSA domestic spying operations. Those hearings, televised to the nation, permanently altered how Americans viewed their government. The most famous of those congressional bodies, led by Senator Frank Church (D-ID), produced a series of recommendations that led to the passage of the Foreign Intelligence Surveillance Act (FISA), the Inspector General Act, and the creation of permanent House and Senate committees to oversee federal surveillance activities and monitor the intelligence operations of the FBI, CIA, NSA, and America's other intelligence components.

Yet over forty years after the enactment of these measures, it is clear that despite the best intentions of Church and his colleagues, their efforts to prevent a repeat of the surveillance and political repression abuses of the first half of the twentieth century failed. In the decades since the Church

CONCLUSION   355

Committee completed its work, multiple additional incidents of NSA, CIA, FBI, and other federal agency and department domestic surveillance scandals have surfaced with considerable regularity.[6]

Within a year of Ronald Reagan taking office, the FBI was back in the business of spying on domestic civil society organizations in the absence of a valid criminal predicate, in this case groups opposed to Reagan's Central America foreign policy.[7] In the waning days of George H.W. Bush's administration, then-Attorney General William Barr authorized the Drug Enforcement Agency to engage in a vast, warrantless telephone metadata collection program that did not allegedly end until 2013 and did not come to light until 2015.[8] And during at least the last term of the Clinton administration, the CIA ran an electronic mass surveillance program against the global telecommunications network backbone, according to a 2002 CIA Inspector General report only uncovered in 2023 via Freedom of Information Act litigation against the Privacy and Civil Liberties Oversight Board by the Cato Institute.[9] Indeed, the number of such episodes is lengthy enough to fill another entire book on the subject.

The pace and scope of those revelations have not been similarly matched by renewed congressional reform efforts, and absent such a new, in-depth reckoning, America's descent into a permanent domestic surveillance state will continue apace.

NOTES

1. Robert Higgs, *Crisis and Leviathan: Critical Episodes in the Growth of American Government* (Oakland: The Independent Institute, 2012), 257.
2. *Trump v. Hawaii*, 585 U.S. ____ (2018), at 38.
3. A brief but highly informative account of Long's activities can be found in Brian Hochman's, *The Listeners: A History of Wiretapping in the United States* (Cambridge: Harvard University Press, 2022), 179–192.
4. Alan Westin, *Privacy and Freedom* (New York: Simon and Schuster, 1967).
5. Hochman, *The Listeners*, 188–194.
6. The reader can get a sense of the scope and duration of these programs and episodes by visiting Cato's "American Big Brother" surveillance timeline at https://www.cato.org/american-big-brother.
7. See *The FBI and CISPES: Report of the Select Committee on Intelligence, United States Senate together with Additional Views*, July 1989, S. Rpt 101–46, 101st Congress (1st Session).
8. Brad Heath, "U.S. Secretly Tracked Billions of Calls for Decades," *USA Today*, April 8, 2015 (digital edition).
9. Patrick Eddington, "Is the CIA Still Secretly Capturing Americans' Communications?" *Orange County Register*, November 26, 2023 (digital edition).

BIBLIOGRAPHY

ARCHIVAL SOURCES

Library of Congress, Manuscript Division
  ADM Claude Charles Bloch Papers
  Charles J. Bonaparte Papers
  Calvin Coolidge Papers
  Emanuel Celler Papers
  Rudolph Forster Papers
  Frank Knox Papers
  Warren G. Harding Papers
  Harlan Fiske Stone Papers
  Robert Lansing Papers
  William McKinley Papers
  Robert H. Jackson Papers
  Josephus Daniels Papers
  William G. McAdoo Papers
  Newton Baker Papers
  Theodore Roosevelt Papers
  Joseph Tumulty Papers
  William H. Taft Papers
  Woodrow Wilson Papers
Library of Congress, Online Archival Resources
  Chronicling America website
National Archives
  RG 2, War Labor Board
  RG 4, Food Administration
  RG 21, US District Courts
  RG 28, Postmaster General
  RG 29, Bureau of the Census
  RG 38, Chief of Naval Operations
  RG 40, Department of Commerce
  RG 48, Department of the Interior
  RG 56, Department of the Treasury
  RG 59, Department of State
  RG 60, Department of Justice
  RG 65, FBI
  RG 67 Fuel Administration
  RG 80, Pearl Harbor Liaison Office
  RG 87, Secret Service Division
  RG 107, Secretary of War
  RG 111, Army Signal Corps

358 BIBLIOGRAPHY

RG 118, US Attorney's Office
RG 130, White House Records
RG 165, Military Intelligence Division
RG 181, Naval Districts-Shore Establishments
RG 182, War Trade Board
RG 204, Records of the Pardon Attorney
RG 220, Boards and Commissions
RG 389, Provost Marshal General
RG 407, Army Adjutant General
RG 494, Records of Army Forces Mid-Pacific 1942–46

Presidential Libraries
Herbert Hoover Library
Franklin D. Roosevelt Library
Harry S. Truman Library
Dwight D. Eisenhower Library

University Archives
Georgetown University
New York University
University of Mississippi
University of Virginia

State and Local Archives
Chicago History Museum

Periodicals
Indiana Journal of Global Legal Studies
Pacific Historical Review
Stanford Law Review
World Politics

Newspapers
Albuquerque Morning Journal
Appeal to Reason
Condon Globe
East Oregonian
New York Daily Mirror
New York Sun
New York Times
New York Tribune
Pacific Commercial Advertiser
Pensacola Journal
San Francisco Call
The Key West Citizen
The People's Voice
The World
Wall Street Journal
Washington Evening Star
Washington Herald
Washington Post
Washington Times
Wilmington Morning Star

Websites
Densho Encyclopedia
FBI Vault

BIBLIOGRAPHY 359

Department of Defense
Department of Justice
National Archives
The American Presidency Project
Library of Congress Chronicling America

BOOKS

Ackerman, Kenneth D. *Young J. Edgar: Hoover, the Red Scare, and the Assault on Civil Liberties.* New York: Carroll & Graf Publishers, 2007.

Austin, Norman J. E., and N. Boris Rankov. *Exploratio: Military and Political Intelligence in the Roman World from the Second Punic War to the Battle of Adrianople.* London: Routledge, 1995.

Beekman, Scott. *William Dudley Pelley: A Life in Right-Wing Extremism and the Occult.* Syracuse: Syracuse University Press, 2005.

Bernstein, Arnie. *Swastika Nation: Fritz Kuhn and the Rise and Fall of the German-American Bund.* New York: St. Martin's Press, 2013.

Bird, Kai, and Martin J. Sherwin. *American Prometheus: The Triumph and Tragedy of J. Robert Oppenheimer.* New York: Alfred A. Knopf, 2005.

Blum, Howard. *Dark Invasion 1915: Germany's Secret War and the Hunt for the First Terrorist Cell in America.* New York: HarperCollins, 2014.

Brissaud, André. *Canaris: The Biography of Admiral Canaris, Chief of German Military Intelligence in the Second World War.* New York: Grosset & Dunlap, 1974.

Burns, James MacGregor. *Roosevelt: Soldier of Freedom.* New York: Open Road Media, 2012.

Campbell, Tracy. *Short of the Glory: The Fall and Redemption of Edward F. Pritchard.* Lexington: University Press of Kentucky, 1998.

Catterall, Peter. *Labour and the Free Churches, 1918–1939: Radicalism, Righteousness and Religion.* London: Bloomsbury Academic, 2016.

Ceplair, Larry, and Steven Englund. *The Inquisition in Hollywood: Politics in the Film Community, 1930–1960.* Chicago: University of Illinois Press, 2003.

Cervini, Eric. *The Deviant's War: The Homosexual vs. The United States of America.* New York: Farrar, Strauss and Giroux, 2020.

Charles, Douglas M. *Hoover's War on Gays: Exposing the FBI's "Sex Deviates" Program.* Lawrence: University Press of Kansas, 2015.

Charles, Douglas M. *J. Edgar Hoover and the Anti-Interventionists: FBI Political Surveillance and the Rise of the Domestic Security State, 1939–1945.* Columbus: Ohio State University Press, 2007.

Chopas, Mary Elizabeth Basile. *Searching for Subversives: The Story of Italian Internment in Wartime America.* Chapel Hill: University of North Carolina Press, 2017.

Clifford, Clark, and Richard Holbrooke. *Counsel to the President: A Memoir.* New York: Random House, 1991.

Cole, Wayne S. *Roosevelt and the Isolationists, 1932–45.* Lincoln: University of Nebraska Press, 1983.

Cottrell, Robert C. *Roger Nash Baldwin and the American Civil Liberties Union.* New York: Columbia University Press, 2000.

Criley, Richard. *The FBI v The First Amendment.* Los Angeles: First Amendment Foundation, 1990.

DeLoach, Cartha D. *Hoover's FBI: The Inside Story by Hoover's Trusted Lieutenant.* Washington, DC: Regnery, 1995.

Donovan, Robert J. *Conflict and Crisis: The Presidency of Harry S. Truman, 1945–1948.* New York: W.W. Norton & Company, 1977.

Donovan, Robert J. *Tumultuous Years: The Presidency of Harry S. Truman, 1949–1953.* New York: W. W. Norton & Company, 1982.

Downs, Anthony. *Inside Bureaucracy.* Boston: Little, Brown and Company, 1967.

360   BIBLIOGRAPHY

Dupuy, R. Ernest, and Trevor N. Dupuy. *The Encyclopedia of Military History*. New York: Harper & Row, 1977.

Easton, Eric B. *Defending the Masses: A Progressive Lawyer's Battles for Free Speech*. Madison: University of Wisconsin Press, 2018.

Farrell, John A. *Richard Nixon: The Life*. New York: Vintage Books, 2017.

Frank, Richard B. *Tower of Skulls: A History of the Asia-Pacific War, July 1937–May 1942*. New York: W.W. Norton & Company, 2020.

Fraser, General Sir David. *And We Shall Shock Them: The British Army in the Second World War*. London: Sceptre, 1988.

Gage, Beverly. *G-Man: J. Edgar Hoover and the Making of the American Century*. New York: Viking, 2022

Gellman, Erik S. *Death Blow to Jim Crow: The National Negro Congress and the Rise of Militant Civil Rights*. Chapel Hill: University of North Carolina Press, 2012.

Gentry, Curt. *J. Edgar Hoover: The Man and the Secrets*. New York: W. W. Norton & Company, 1991.

Goldstein, Robert Justin. *Political Repression in Modern America: From 1870 to 1976*. Chicago: University of Illinois Press, 2001.

Goldstein, Robert Justin. *American Blacklist: The Attorney Generals' List of Subversive Organizations*. Lawrence: University of Kansas Press, 2008.

Gornick, Vivian. *Emma Goldman: Revolution as a Way of Life*. New Haven and London: Yale University Press, 2011.

Green, James. *Death in the Haymarket*. New York: Anchor Books, 2007.

Hamilton, Charles V. *Adam Clayton Powell, Jr.: The Political Biography of an American Dilemma*. New York: Atheneum, 1991.

Hayden, Sterling. *Wanderer*. Kindle Edition. Auckland: Pickle Partners Publishing, 2014.

Haynes, John Earl, and Harvey Klehr. *Venona: Decoding Soviet Espionage in America*. New Haven: Yale University Press, 1999.

Higgs, Edward. *The Information State in England*. New York: Palgrave MacMillan, 2004.

Higgs, Robert. *Crisis and Leviathan: Critical Episodes in the Growth of American Government*. Oxford: Oxford University Press, 1987.

Hitchcock, William I. *The Age of Eisenhower: America and the World in the 1950s*. New York: Simon & Schuster, 2018.

Hochman, Brian. *The Listeners: A History of Wiretapping in the United States*. Cambridge: Harvard University Press, 2022.

Ickes, Harold L., Sr. *The Lowering Clouds: The Secret Diary of Harold L. Ickes, Vol. III, 1939–41*. New York: Simon and Schuster, 1954.

Irons, Peter. *Justice at War: The Story of Japanese American Internment Cases*. New York: Oxford University Press, 1983.

Irwin, Lew. *Deadly Times: The 1910 Bombing of the Los Angeles Times and America's Forgotten Decade of Terror*. Guilford: Lyons Press, 2013.

Jacobs, Arthur D. *The Prison Called Hohenasperg: An American Boy Betrayed by His Government during World War II*. Boca Raton: Universal Publishers, 1999.

Jensen, Joan. *The Price of Vigilance*. New York: Rand McNally & Company, 1968.

Jensen, Joan. *Army Surveillance in America, 1775–1980*. New Haven: Yale University Press, 1991.

Johnson, David K. *The Lavender Scare: The Cold War Persecution of Gays and Lesbians in the Federal Government*. Chicago: University of Chicago Press, 2006.

Kennedy, David M. *Over Here: The First World War and American Society*. Oxford: Oxford University Press, 2004.

Kornweibel, Theodore, Jr. *Seeing Red: Federal Campaigns against Black Militancy*. Bloomington: Indiana University Press, 1998.

Lane, Charles. *Freedom's Detective: The Secret Service, the Ku Klux Klan, and the Man Who Masterminded America's First War on Terror*. New York: Hanover Square Press, 2019.

Lattimore, Owen. *Ordeal by Slander*. New York: Carol & Graf Publishers, 2004.

Layton, Edwin T., Roger Pineau, and John Costello. *And I Was There: Pearl Harbor and Midway— Breaking the Secrets*. New York: William Morrow and Company, 1985.

BIBLIOGRAPHY 361

Lemov, Michael R. *People's Warrior: John Moss and the Fight for Freedom of Information and Consumer Rights.* Madison: Farleigh Dickinson University Press, 2011.

Maraniss, David. *A Good American Family: The Red Scare and My Father.* New York: Simon & Schuster, 2019.

Marshall, Peter. *Demanding the Impossible: A History of Anarchism.* Oakland: PM Press, 2010, iBookstore version.

McCoy, Alfred W. *Policing America's Empire: The United States, the Philippines, and the Rise of the Surveillance State.* Madison: University of Wisconsin Press, 2009.

McCullough, David. *Truman.* New York: Simon and Schuster, 1992.

Meijer, Hendrik. *Arthur Vandenberg: The Man in the Middle of the American Century.* Chicago: University of Chicago Press, 2017.

Miller, Scott. *The President and the Assassin: McKinley, Terror, and Empire at the Dawn of the American Century.* New York: Random House, 2011.

Morison, Samuel Eliot. *The Two-Ocean War: A Short History of the United States Navy in the Second World War.* Boston: Little, Brown & Company, 1963.

Neely, Mark E. Jr. *The Fate of Liberty: Abraham Lincoln and Civil Liberties.* New York: Oxford University Press, 1991.

Nichols, David A. *Ike and McCarthy: Dwight Eisenhower's Secret Campaign against Joseph McCarthy.* New York: Simon and Schuster, 2017.

Nightingale, Robert V. *Camp Letters: 1942–1945.* Scotts Valley: CreateSpace Publishing, 2011.

Personal Justice Denied: Report of the Commission on Wartime Relocation and Internment of Civilians. Seattle: University of Washington Press, 2000.

Rossiter, Clinton, and Charles R. Kesler, eds. *The Federalist Papers.* New York: Signet Classic, 1999.

Sakamoto, Pamela Rotner. *Midnight in Broad Daylight: A Japanese American Family Caught between Two Worlds.* New York: HarperCollins, 2016.

Sarles, Ruth. *A Story of America First: The Men and Women Who Opposed U.S. Intervention in World War II.* Westport: Praeger, 2003.

Smith, Bradley F. *The Shadow Warriors.* New York: Basic Books Publishing, 1983.

Smith, C. Mark. *Raising Cain: The Life and Politics of Senator Harry P. Cain.* Bothel: Book Publishers Network, 2011.

Smith, Jean Edward. *FDR.* New York: Random House, 2007.

Stone, Geoffrey R. *Perilous Times: Free Speech in Wartime, from the Sedition Act of 1798 to the War on Terrorism.* New York: W.W. Norton & Company, 2004.

Sullivan, William C., and Bill Brown. *The Bureau: My Thirty Years in Hoover's FBI.* New York: W.W. Norton & Company, 1979.

Talbert, Roy, Jr. *Negative Intelligence: The Army and the American Left, 1917–1941.* Jackson: University Press of Mississippi, 1991.

Theoharis, Athan. *Chasing Spies: How the FBI Failed in Counterintelligence but Promoted the Politics of McCarthyism in the Cold War Years.* Chicago: Ivan R. Dee, 2002.

Theoharis, Athan, and John Stuart Cox. *The Boss: J. Edgar Hoover and the Great American Inquisition.* New York: Bantam Books, 1990.

Theoharis, Athan, and John Stuart Cox. *The FBI and American Democracy: A Brief Critical History.* Lawrence: University of Kansas Press, 2004.

Unger, Nancy. *Fighting Bob La Follette: The Righteous Reformer.* Chapel Hill: University of North Carolina Press, 2000.

Von Der Porten, Edward P. *The German Navy in World War Two.* New York: Ballantine Books, 1974.

Walker, Samuel. *In Defense of American Liberties: A History of the ACLU.* Carbondale: Southern Illinois University Press, 1990.

Weinstein, Allen, and Alexander Vassiliev. *The Haunted Wood: Soviet Espionage in America—The Stalin Era.* New York City: Random House, 1999.

Willett, Robert M. *Russian Sideshow: America's Undeclared War, 1918–1920.* London: Brassey's, 2003.

Zegart, Amy. *Flawed by Design: The Evolution of the CIA, JCS, and NSC.* Stanford: Stanford University Press, 1999.

INDEX

Page numbers in *italics* refer to figures.

Abbott, Robert, 74

Abraham Lincoln Brigade, American veterans of, 122–23; FBI raids on, 128; Eleanor Roosevelt's outrage at treatment of veterans of, 186; AGLOSO target, 294

Acheson, Secretary of State Dean, and Hiss spy scandal, 256–57, 260

ACLU (American Civil Liberties Union): conflict with FDR over ONI surveillance, 100–101; Dies Committee attacks, 118; opposition to HUAC, 336; opposition to wiretapping proposals, 79–82, 317–18; relationship with Nixon, 246; urges FDR to uphold the Bill of Rights, 173

Adams, John, and Army-McCarthy hearings, 306

Adams, Sherman, confrontation with Harry Cain over employee loyalty program, 313

Addams, Jane, and Army surveillance of WILPF, 75

Adee, Secretary of State Alvey, and surveillance of Nathan Boyd, 14

Albert, Heinrich, and Imperial German espionage in the US, 49

Alexander, Ralph, 98

Alien Registration Act (Public Law 76–670), 130

Alsop, Joe, 232

Alsop, Stewart, 232, 276

Amerasia, FBI investigation of, 228, 258

America First Committee (AFC): activities, monitoring by Bureau, 149–50, 179–81; anti-interventionist group formed, 131; Carter group monitoring of, 166–67; opposition to Lend-Lease, 145

American Peace Mobilization, FBI surveillance of, 155, 156, 159

American Protective League (APL), as BoI adjunct investigators, 54, 70, 84

American Union Against Militarism (AUAM), opposition to US military buildup, 52; as BoI surveillance target, 66

anarchism, 3, 8–12, 39–40

Anarchist Exclusion Act, 11, 72, 349

Anderson, Judge Albert B., 64

Anderson, Dillon, 318, 320

Anheir, Harry, 224

Anti-Defamation League (ADL), surveillance of alleged Nazis, 95

Appeal to Reason: article, Roosevelt on, 16–19; political harassment of, 39, 350

Arimoto, Hoshi, pleads with FDR for father's release from internment, 176

Army Ordnance Corps, and National Negro Congress, 155

Army Ordnance Department, 120

Army Service Forces (ASF), and domestic surveillance, 198, 201, 224

Arnold, Acting Attorney General Thurman, and Dies Committee, 109

Ashurst, Senator Henry, 99

Astor, Vincent, FDR intelligence operative, 164

Atomic Energy Commission (AEC), 296, 300

Attorney General's List of Subversive Organizations (AGLOSO), formalized under Truman, 234; Hatch Act as progenitor of, 118; Senator Cain critical of, 315–16; successes and failures, 294–95, 311

Baer, Elizabeth, convicted for obstructing conscription, 68

Baker, Ella, 327

Baker, Secretary of War Newton, and labor unrest, 66

Baldwin, Roger, complains to FDR about ONI surveillance, 100; confrontation with Fish Committee, 79–81; convicted for violating Selective Service Act, 66

Baldwin, William, National Urban League president, 195

Battle of Midway, 182

Belgian troops, 128

363

364 INDEX

Bell, William Y., FBI claims is communist, 196

Benanti v. United States, state wiretapping evidence bar in federal courts, 331

Bentley, Elizabeth Terrill, Soviet spy, 248–51

Berger, Rep. Victor, Espionage Act indictment, 59, 64, 68

Berkman, Sascha, 5, 72

Berle, A.A., 52

Berle, Assistant Secretary of State Adolph: and Carter spy network, 164; and Hiss spy scandal, 249; and Japanese government conscription rumors, 147; Sperry Gyroscope hiring controversy, 154

Bernstein, Carl, 233

The Best Years of Our Lives, Soviet propaganda allegations by HUAC, 238

Biddle, Attorney General Francis, *121*; and Detroit race riots, 193–96; and response to Pearl Harbor attack, 172, 176, 180; federal employee loyalty program originator, 185, 187; Japanese American internment as a political problem, 192–93, 352

Bielaski, Bruce, 38, 54

Bill of Rights, 10, 29, 34, 106–8, 128, 153–54, 173, 183–84, 202, 237, 240, 242, 247, 269, 302–3, 309, 317, 350, 352

Blackburn, Rep. Spencer, Secret Service investigative target, 23

Black people, as targets of surveillance and repression, 93–95, 116, 145, 155, 168, 193–96, 198, 203, 224, 242, 310, 319–22, 326, 328, 353

Blanton, Tom, 108

Bolsheviks, 69–70, 74

Bonaparte, Attorney General Charles, land frauds investigations, 23–24; creation of BoI, 28–34, *30*, 40

Bonneaud, L.E., Secret Service surveillance target, 15–16

Bonus Expeditionary Force (BEF), Bonus Marchers, 83–84

Borah, Senator William, Secret Service surveillance target, 24–25; and La Follette presidential campaign, 78–79

Boston Better Business Bureau (BBB), 98

Boston Post, 31

Boyd, Nathan, federal surveillance target, 12–16, 28

Boy-Ed, Karl, and Imperial German espionage in US, 50, 110

Bresci, Gaetano, 3–4

Briggs, Albert, creation of APL, 54

British Expeditionary Force (BEF), 128–30

Brooks, Senator Charles "Curly," 196

Brownell, Attorney General Herbert, and Civil Rights Act of 1957, 327; communist denaturalization program, 288; concerns over federal employee loyalty program, 289; loyalty program reforms, 316; and SACB, 294; and wiretapping, 301–5, 318–19

Brown v. Board of Education, 310, 328

Bryan, Secretary of State William Jennings, counterespionage support request to Treasury Department, 48–49

Buffalo, McKinley murder investigation, 2, 5

Buffington, District Court Judge Joseph, 58

Burdick, Rep. Usher, vote against Communist Control Act, 309

Bureau of Investigation (BoI), 1, 47, 50, 66, 70, 84; activities monitoring of AFC, 149; birth of, 28–35, 40, 350; augmentation by APL, 54; and Marcus Garvey case, 74

Burke, Frank, 49

Burleson, Albert, 56; reply to Wilson, 57; ban of IWW, other labor publications from the mails, 58; ban of *Milwaukee Leader* from the mails, 59

Burns, William, ousted as BoI director, 76

Butler, Senator John, Communist Control Act sponsor, 308

Byrns, House Speaker Joseph, 100

Cain, Harry Pulliam, federal employee loyalty program critic, 293–94, 311–17, 321; vs. Eisenhower, 311–17

Camp McCoy, 178

Canadian Pacific Railway bridge bombing, 48

Canaris, Admiral Wilhelm, head of Nazi intelligence, 107

Cannon, House Speaker Joe, 26

Capehart, Senator Homer, attacks FCC member Durr, 242

Carnegie, Andrew, 5, 35

Carnegie Endowment for International Peace, 249

Carpenter, Fred, 37

Carter, John Franklin: estimates on Japanese American loyalty, 169–72, 174, 352; political espionage for FDR, 163–67, 181, 196–97, 202

Cash, B.F., 24

Cathcart, R. Harry, 25

Celler, Rep. Emanuel: and wiretapping bills, 317–18; and Civil Rights Act of 1957, 327–28; no hearings on NSA Act of 1959, 334

INDEX 365

censorship: in WWI, 18, 60; and internment in WWII, 172–74

Chambers, Whittaker, and Hiss spy scandal, 248–51, 256

Charlie Chaplin, 239

Chicago Defender, 74

Chicago Tribune, 166, 179

Church Committee, 340

Church, Senator Frank, 354

Churchill, Brigadier General Marlborough, establishment of MID Japanese male tracking program, 102

Churchill, Prime Minister Winston, 129, 131, 164, 179

civil liberties: pre-WWI agitation for, 47, 52; 128–30; Franklin Delano Roosevelt and, 99–107, 118; Justice Department attitude toward, 128

Civil Rights Act of 1957, 287, 328

Civil Service Commission (CSC), federal employee loyalty program controversy, 229–31, 233, 242–43, 257, 259–61, 265, 273, 304

Clark, Attorney General Tom: and AGLOSO, 234; Coplon spy case, 254; defense of First Amendment, 246; and indefinite detention proposal, 263; post-WWII surveillance legality issues, 220–21; surveillance of Wallace presidential campaign, 245

Clifford, Clark, 233, 242–44, 250

Cobb, Frank, 49

Cochran, W.E., 8

Coffee, Rep. John, Dies Committee critic, 119

Coggins, Commander C.H., and Japanese Undercover Organization, 168

Cole, Lester, "Hollywood Ten" screenwriter, 241

Cole v Young, 317

COMINFIL (FBI surveillance program), 319–22

Commission on Wartime Relocation and Internment of Civilians (CWRIC), 102

Commission to Revise the Laws of the United States, 8–9

Committee on Public Information (CPI), 55

Communications Act of 1934: and NSA SHAMROCK telegram surveillance program, 332; statutory prohibition on wiretapping, 128, 152–53, 219, 302, 318

"Communist-affiliated and Communist-aiding organizations" (ONI memo), 100

Communist Labor Party, 72, 74

Communist Party of America, 72, 74

Communist Party of the United States (CPUSA), 83, 119, 229, 234–35; actor Sterling Hayden as member of, 267; allegations of J. Robert Oppenheimer membership in, 295–97; banned by Communist Control Act, 307–8; Eisenhower administration attempt to denaturalize members of, 288; false allegations of membership by Owen Lattimore, 259; as initial FBI COINTELPRO target, 322–23; Justice Department employee Judith Coplon as member of and Soviet agent, 253; Nixon and Mundt target, 245–49, 300–302

Communist Party v. SACB, 321

communists, 69–73, 106–7

Condon, Edward U., falsely accused of being Soviet spy, 250, 272

Conference on Civil Rights of the Washington Committee for Democratic Action, 124, 128

Congress, 11, 29, 32, 33; and passage of the Alien Registration Act, 130; and passage of the Communications Act of 1934, 125, 150–51; and Congressional "witch hunt" committee phenomenon, 135–36; and concerns over Japanese American loyalty, 146; and declaration of war against Germany, 53; FBI political surveillance of House and Senate members during Lend-Lease debate, 150; Wilson's message to, 50

Congressional Record, 119, 123, 167

Connorton, Lt (JG) John, and sweeping post-war surveillance proposals, 218–19

Coolidge, President Calvin: and FBI targeting of Wheeler presidential campaign, 76–77, 79; veto of veterans bonus bill, 83

Cooper, Eddie, 165

Corcoran, Tommy, Democratic political consultant and lawyer, 245, 353; FBI wiretapping of, 223–24

Cortelyou, George, 8, 21

counterintelligence (CI), 115–17; domestic surveillance and, 101–6; Hoover's industrial plant "surveys" for, 121–22

Counterintelligence program (COINTELPRO), FBI domestic surveillance and disruption program, 285, 322–23, 340, 354

Coyne, J. Patrick, NSC internal security staffer, 251–53, 266, 269, 273, 300

Creel, George, 55, 59

Creswell, Major Harry, surveillance of Alexander Sharton, 115

Criminal Anarchy Act, 1902, 10

366 INDEX

Crisis and Leviathan, 351, 355

Crist, CPT W. E., seeks mail cover authority, 123

Crowder, General Enoch, 66

Cummings, Attorney General Homer: FDR directs surveillance against subversives, 106; Japanese government espionage concerns, 103, 115–16; tax records and Dies Committee, 109

Currie, Lauchlin, 248, 249

Custodial Detention Program, 156–57, 170–71

Cutler, Robert, 327–28

Czolgosz, Leon, McKinley assassin, 2–5, 39

Daily Worker, 77, 269, 297, 311, 336

Daniels, Navy Secretary Josephus, 64

Darrow, Clarence, 11, 38

Daugherty, Attorney General Harry, and WILPF investigation, 75–76

Daughters of the American Revolution (DAR), 75, 176

Davidson, Jebby, federal employee loyalty program opponent, 241–44, 251, 271, 353

Davis, Benjamin J., 246

Davis, Elmer, 195

Dawson, William, 328

DeBelle, Kirk, 29, 31

Debs, Eugene V., 1; Canton, Ohio, speech triggers Espionage Act charge, 68; Theodore Roosevelt seeks prosecution of, 16–18, 350; loses 1908 election to Taft, 34–35; sentence commuted by Harding, 73

Department of Justice (DoJ), 18, 24, 29, 33, 53, 84, 111, 113, 117, 127, 151, 154, 157, 221, 228, 236, 255, 264, 301, 303

Dern, Secretary of War George, 103–4

Detroit race riots, 193–96

Detroit report of BoI on German American loyalty, 51

Dewey, Thomas, 244

DeWitt, Lieutenant General John, and Japanese American internment, 176, 193

DeWoody, Charles, 30–31

Dickstein, Rep. Samuel: and McCormack-Dickstein Committee, 95–96, 99–100, 107–8; as Soviet espionage agent, 112–13; 135, 227, 256, 351

Dies, Rep. Martin: creation of HUAC and early confrontations with FDR, 108–13, 116; confrontations with Hoover, 130–32, 157–59; exit from Congress, 225; federal employee loyalty investigation, 186–88; 239, 256; targeting of civil society groups, 118–19, 124, 136, 162

Diggs, Charles, Jr., 328

DiMaggio, Joe, 178

Dirksen, Senator Everett, 307, 310

District Intelligence Officer (DIO), 169, 197

Dodd, William E., Jr., bill of attainder victim, 187

domestic surveillance: antiwar movement and, 52–54; bureaucratic turf wars, 117–18; and counterintelligence, 101–6; "Plant Protection" and, 55

Downey, Senator Sheridan, 231

Downs, Anthony, 28

Drum, Lieutenant General Hugh, eastern seaboard "military area" scheme angers FDR, 177

Duquesne, Fredrick Joubert, Nazi spy, 107–8, 134

Durr, Clifford, opposition to federal employee loyalty program, 241–42, 244, 254–56, 317

Eastman, Max, 56–57

Eberstein, Marshall, 35–36

Eisenhower, President Dwight: Cain as SACB nominee, 293–94; Cain opposition to federal loyalty program, 311–17; COINTELPRO surveillance and disruption program, 323; counterattacks McCarthy, 305–8; embraces Communist Control Act, 308–9; and Hoover's misleading reports on civil rights protests, 320; intensification of internal security policies, 285–87; internal security legacy, 339–40; makes invoking Fifth Amendment a loyalty investigation trigger, 287, 304–5; NSA Act of 1959, 331–34; opposition to Rep. Moss's government transparency push, 329–31; pressure for civil rights legislation, 309–10, 327–28; revised federal employee loyalty program, 289, 291; urged to crack down on McCarthy, 299–300; *Wall Street Journal* criticizes violations of rights by, 301–2; warm relationship with FBI's Hoover, 338–39

Eisenhower, Milton, 190

Eliot, Tom, 151

Emergency Civil Liberties Committee, 289

Emergency Civil Rights Committee (ECRC), 269, 271

Emerson, Edwin, 162

Emmons, Lieutenant General Delos, and Nisei infantry unit push, 177, 182

Enemy Alien Control Program, 172

Espionage Act, 47, 52–53, 55–61, 63, 65, 67–68, 73, 84, 104–5, 114, 173, 218, 254, 256, 303, 350

ethnic bias, surveillance in WWI, 63–68

INDEX 367

ethnic and racial surveillance in WWII, 181–83
ex parte Endo decision, 253, 291

fascism, 80, 97, 106–8, 110, 112, 116, 122, 130, 133, 227, 233, 295, 309
FBI, 145; and alleged Axis "Negro subversion" operations, 154–56; and COINTELPRO surveillance and subversion program, 322–23; and COMINFIL, 321–22; confrontation with Dies Committee over surveillance and raids, 151–53; and Coplon wiretapping episode, 253–56; and Custodial Detention Program planning, 156–57; defense plant "surveys" and informant recruitment, 55, 121–22, 181, 185, 266–67, 270, 300, 353; and election of 1924, 76–79; J. Edgar Hoover and, 103; and espionage missteps, 107–8; labor union "subversives" card index system, 124; as national counterintelligence lead agency, 120; pre-war surveillance of Japanese Americans, 133–35, 147; raid on Abraham Lincoln Brigade members, 128; surveillance of AFC, 149–50; surveillance cooperation agreement with MID, ONI, 117; and targeting of federal homosexual employees, 288–90; and wartime censorship and internment implementation, 172–78; vs. John Franklin Carter over Japanese American loyalty estimates, 169–72; vs. MLK Jr., 326–29
FBI, Army, and Navy, as political intelligence collectors, 124–25, 129–30, 161–63, 179–81
Federal courts: administration officials withholding exculpatory evidence in Japanese American internment cases, 191–93; challenges to Japanese American interment, 184–85, 200; Espionage Act and *Masses* case, 57–58; *Kilbourn v Thompson* case and limits on Congressional subpoena powers, 98; *Olmstead v US* case on wiretapping and the Fourth Amendment, 125; *Nardone v US* and Communications Act ban on wiretapping, 125; *Schenck v US* draft protest case, 68–69; *US v Reynolds* and creation of the "state secrets" privilege, 292–93; *US v Wheeler* and constitutional right to freedom of movement, 195; *Weeks v US*, 50
Federal employee loyalty program: addition of homosexuality as federal employment disqualifier, 289–91; under FDR, 185, 200; under Eisenhower, 285–91; Senator Harry Cain opposition to, 293–95, 311–17; under Truman, 228–34, 237–39, 241–45, 250–51, 255, 258–60, 271 73
Feller, Abraham, 298–99
Ferenz, F. K., 97

Ferguson, Senator Homer, 196, 248, 250, 252, 262, 270, 307, 308
Ferman, Irving, 317, 318
Finch, Stanley W.: appointed first BoI director, 29; career fallout from managerial missteps, 38–39; confidential memo to Eberstein Russian Jewish emigre, 36; directs investigations of socialists, 35–36; proclivity for keeping sensitive investigations off-books, 29–31; reprisal investigation against Attorney General critic, 37
First Amendment, 19, 32, 56–59, 69, 129, 158, 167, 180, 219, 237, 246, 269, 301, 316, 335, 337, 350
Fish, Hamilton, 79, 81, 256
Fish, Hamilton, II, 15–16
Fish Committee, 79–82, 135, 237, 351
Fisk, James, 226
Flanders, Senator Ralph, censure resolution against McCarthy, 308
Flaxer, Abram, 231
Flynn, William, 53, 62
Food Administration, 62, 70
Food and Fuel Control Act (FCA), 47, 62–63, 67, 84, 350
Ford, Henry, 149
Foreign Intelligence Surveillance Act (FISA), 354
Forrestal, Navy Secretary James, post-war surveillance authority debate, 219–21
Fortas, Abe, 241–42, 259
Fortune magazine, 166
Frank, Richard B., 175, 176
Frankfurter, Supreme Court Justice Felix, 222
Freedom of Information Act, 113, 243, 353, 355
Free Speech League, 11, 57
French First Army, 128
Frick, Henry, 5
Fukuhara, Harry, 171, 172

Gage, Beverly, 70–71
Gallagher, H.M., 146
Garvey, Marcus, 74, 94
Gatch, Rear Admiral Thomas Leigh, post-war surveillance authority debate, 219–20
Gausebeck, August, 124
General Intelligence Survey, 133–34, 183
George, James Z., 225
German American Bund, 107–10, 151, 162, 234
German and Italian American WWII internment experience, 177–78

368 INDEX

Germanophobia in WWI era, 48–53
Germany: congressional end of war resolution, 73; Dickstein Committee investigation of, 95–99; espionage and sabotage on US and Canadian soil, 48–51; German immigrants as alleged security risks in defense plants, 120, 162–63; pre-WWII espionage in US, 107–8; sinking of *Lusitania*, 48; submarine warfare by in WWI, 52; US declaration of war against in WWI, 54
"Gilded Age" tycoons, 11
Gillan, Jim, 181
Gillette, Senator Guy, 146–47
Gold, Harry, 263
Goldman, Emma, 4–5, 11
Goldwater, Senator Barry, 308
Goldwyn, Sam, 239
Golos, Jacob, Soviet spy ringleader, 248
Gorham, Ensign Don, 188–89
Green, Theodore, 168
Greene, Thornton, 182–83
Greenglass, David, Soviet nuclear spy ring member, 263
Gregory, Thomas: authorization of American Protective League investigators, 54; response to Wilson regarding election eligibility of Michigan City German immigrant mayor, 64–65; Wilson's letter to regarding election eligibility of Michigan City German immigrant mayor, 64
Grew, Undersecretary of State Joseph, and 1924 election, 76–77
Griffin, D. J., 169–70
Gubitchev, Valentin, Soviet spy, 254, 256
Guhman, Josephine, 63
Gutstadt, Richard, 95

Haan, Kilsoo, 147
Haase, Horace, 180–81
Haegar Coffee Co., 62
Hagerty, James, 291, 307
Hammond, General Tom, AFC member, 179
Hand, Judge Learned, 57–58
Hankow Tea Company, 62
Harding, President Warren G., 73, 76, 84, 350
Harlem: as Adam Clayton Powell Jr.'s political power base, 198, 224; and Army Major Joseph Quittner's "Negro Survey" project, 93–94; and Secret Service surveillance of anarchists, socialists, 28
Hartley, Rep. Fred, Jr., 238
Hassett, William, 196

Hatch, Senator Carl, and Hatch Act, 117–18, 224, 233
Hawaii Hochi, 175
Hawkes, Senator Albert, 196
Hayden, Sterling, and HUAC appearance, 267
Haymarket Affair, 3–4
Hays, Arthur Garfield, 100, 246
Haywood, William "Big Bill," 16–17, 23–24, 28, 39
Hearns, 1Lt Alford T., 166
Henning, Arthur Sears, 179
Hennings, Senator Thomas, 329–31, 333–34, 354
Hermann, Rep. Binger, 23
Herrington, Clayton, 36
Hess, Jerry, 242
Hickenlooper, Senator Bourke, 261
Hill, Milton, 286
Hirabayashi, Gordon Kiyoshi, legal challenge to internment, 184–85, 191, 203
Hirth, Max, 163, 208
Hiss, Alger, Soviet espionage agent allegations, 249–51, 256–58
Hitler, Adolph, 93, 95–97, 107, 110, 119, 130–31, 148, 161, 163, 179, 225, 249, 296, 308
Hobbs, Rep. Samuel, 150–51, 262–63
Hoey, Senator Clyde, 290
Holman, Senator Rufus, 179–80
Holmes, John Haynes, 173, 210
Holmes, Justice Oliver Wendell, 68–69
Holt, Senator Rush, 149–50
Homestead Strike (1892), 5
Hoover, President Herbert, 62, 79, 83
Hoover, J. Edgar: air travel surveillance program focused on Japan, 118; alleges Soviet involvement in Detroit race riots, 193–96; assumes leadership of BoI, 76; battle with Congress over wiretapping authority, 317–19; blundering in Frankford Arsenal episode, 120; and COMINFIL, 319–22; and Communist Party-USA ban, 235–36; confrontations with Dies and HUAC, 130–33, 151–53; Coplon wiretapping, 253–56; counterattacks against critics, 124; criticism of over raids on Abraham Lincoln Brigade veterans, 122–23; Eisenhower personally briefed on COINTELPRO, 340; exposure and investigation of by the Church Committee, 354; as head of "Radicals Division" at BoI, 47, 70–74, 71; initial reaction to MLK Jr. and creation of Southern Christian Leadership Conference, 326–29; initiation of COINTELPRO domestic

INDEX 369

surveillance, infiltration, and disruption program, 322–23; letter to Lane alleging Soviet support for La Follette presidential bid, 78; memo to Edwin A. "Pa" Watson regarding leftist groups' anti-FBI campaign, 124; obsession with homosexuals in government, 288–90; obsession with "Negro subversion" by Soviets, 154–56, 159–61, 309–11; planning for wartime detention of German, Japanese, Italian aliens and communists, 120–21, 146, 156–57; political intelligence collection on Robert La Follette Sr., 76–79; relationship with Eisenhower, 338–39; relationship with FDR, 353; relationship with Truman, 221–22; scandal over Palmer Raids, 73; seeks expanded spy hunting powers, 103–4; success of defense plant informant penetration program, 266–67; surveillance on citizen opponents of FDR's rearmament, wartime policies, 128–30, 179–81; surveillance of AFC, 149–50; surveillance of Jebby Davidson, 243–44; White House leak investigation, 222–24; wiretapping at FDR's direction, 125

Hopkins, Harry, 164, 223

Hormel, Jay, 149

Horne, Admiral F. J., 219, 220

Horner, Garnett, 232

The Hour, 180

Hourwich, Isaac, 36

House, Edward, 49

House Joint Resolution 382 and repeal of Food Control, Sedition Acts, 73

House Resolution 220 (Fish Committee), 79

House Resolution 282 (Select Un-American Activities Committee), 108–9

House Resolution 293, creating Select Un-American Activities Committee, 79

House Un-American Activities Committee (HUAC): attacks on Methodist Federation for Social Action, 324–26; created as a special select committee 108–13; Eleanor Roosevelt critical of, 186; false allegations against Edward Condon, 250; field hearings across the country, 297–98; hearings and attacks on actors, screenwriters, 237–41; hearings on alleged communist control of labor unions, 234–37; Hoover vs. Dies Committee, 130–32; initial confrontation with FDR, 110–12; initial targeting of civil society groups, 118–19, 286; made a standing committee by Congress, 226–28; opposition to inside and outside

of Congress, 334–38; persecution of Hazel Scott Powell, 265; persecution of J. Robert Oppenheimer, 295–96; proposed communist registration legislation, 246–48; SISS "show trial" hearings, 267–69; targeting of federal employees with bills of attainder, 186–88

Hughes, Charles Evans, 52, 125

Hull, Secretary of State Cordell, 106, 147

Humphrey, Senator Hubert, 309, 310, 321

Hymans, Maurits, and surveillance of anarchists, 28

Ickes, Secretary of Interior Harold: confrontation with HUAC Chairman Martin Dies, 186; opposition to Japanese American internment, 189–91, 193, 198–201; opposition to Select Un-American Activities Committee proposal, 100; rails against Senator Burton Wheeler, 165; targeted by Truman for domestic intelligence collection, 223–24, 245, 352

Imbrie, James, 269

Immigration Act of 1903, 10

Immigration and Naturalization Service (INS), 172, 263

Imperial Japanese Navy (IJN), 104

Internal Security Act, 217, 262–65. *See also* McCarran Act

Jackson, Rep. Donald L., 324

Jackson, Attorney General (and later Justice) Robert, *121*; advocates wartime gun confiscation, 157; approves American Legion Contact program, 133; confrontation with Dies Committee over raids, 131–32; conflict with Hoover over wiretapping, 125; dismisses charges against former Abraham Lincoln Brigade members, 123; failure to stop Dies Committee wiretapping, 151–53, 202; FDR's order to engage in wiretapping in defiance of the Supreme Court, 219, 253, 318, 352; "Internal Defense Unit" memo, 126, *127*; opposition to War Department unconstitutional search and seizure proposals, 153–54

Jacobs, Lambert, 178

Japanese American Citizens League (JACL), 102, 114, 169–70, 184

Japanese American internment: administration officials withhold from federal courts exculpatory Japanese American loyalty estimates, 191–93; Harry Cain's opposition to, 294; initial preparations, 104, 120–21, 135;

370 INDEX

resolution and consequences, 198–202, 352; EO 9066, 174–77; *ex parte Endo* case, 253, 291; *Hirabayashi* case, 184, 185, 191, 203, *Korematsu* case, 184–85, 191, 200, 203, 291

Japanese Americans: alleged threat posed by, 146–48; loyalty of, 169–72; surveillance of, 101–6, 113–15

Japanese Navy's surprise attack on Pearl Harbor, 352

"Japanese Undercover Organization," 168, 209

Jenks, J.W., 21, 23

Johnston, Eric, 236–39

Johnston, Senator Olin, 262

Kahn, Albert E., 180

Kai-shek, Chiang, 257–58

Kamp, Joseph, 158

Kane, Michael J., 32

Keating, Rep. Kenneth, 302, 304, 317

Keep, Col. C. H., 15

Kelly, Governor Harry, 194

Kerr, Rep. John Hosea, 186–87

Keyserling, Leon, 241, 244

Kilbourn v. Thompson (103 U.S. 168), 98

Kim, Richard, 147

Kimball, Penn Townsend, 322

Kimmel, Admiral Husband E., 175

King, Admiral Ernest J., 219

King, Martin Luther, Jr., 321, 326–29

Kirk, Captain Alan, 159, 160, 165, 168

Kirkpatrick, Judge William H., 292

Knissel, Paulina, 178

Knowland, Senator William, 258–59

Knox, Secretary of the Navy Frank, 152, 174; negotiation with George Ray, 10

Knox, Secretary of the Treasury Philander Chase, 7–10

Korematsu, Fred, legal challenge to internment, 184–85, 191, 200, 203, 291

Kornweibel, Theodore, Jr., 74

Kramer, Rep. Charles, 98

Krenning, Henry, 65

Krock, Arthur, 307

Krueger, F.K., 64

Krug, Julius, 241

Kuhn, Fritz, 107

Kunzig, Robert, 324–25

Kurtz, Anna Marie, 180

La Follette, Senator Robert M., Sr.: allegations of Soviet support for 1924 presidential campaign, 76–79; opposition to US involvement in WWI, 52, 55; Senate colleagues' attempts to silence his anti-war speeches, 60–61

la Franier, De, 18–19, 43

La Guardia, Mayor Fiorello, 160

Lamar, L.Q.C., 225

Lamar, William, 56–58

Landry, Robert, 264

Lane, Arthur Bliss, 76–79

Lansing, Robert, 49

Lattimore, Owen: publicly vilified by Senators Knowland and McCarthy, 258–61; Senate Internal Security Subcommittee focus on, 268, 270–72

Laughland, Rev. J. Vint, 157

Lawson, John Howard, 240

Leche, Governor Richard, 106

Lehlbach, Rep. Fredrick, 96

Lend-Lease proposal, 135,145, 148–50, 181

Lenin, Vladimir, 69–70

Levison, Stanley, 327

Lewis, John, 181

Libby, Fredrick J., 75, 90

Lie, UN Secretary General Trygve, 299

Lincoln, President Abraham, 10

Lindbergh, Charles A., 131, 179

Lindsey, Richard, 51

Llewellyn, W.H.H., 14

Lodge, Senator Henry Cabot, Jr., 258, 302

Loeb, William, 19–21, 23–24

Long, Senator Edward V., 354

Longworth, Alice Roosevelt, 131, 149

Los Angeles Times, 38, 174

Lovett, Robert Morss, bill of attainder victim, 187–18

Lowenthal, Max, 123

Loyalty Review Board (LRB), 230, 232, 257, 261

Lucas, Senator Scott, 258

Lucero, J.R., 14

Lucitt, William, 97

Lusitania (passenger liner), sinking of, 48, 52, 85

MacQueen, William "Billy," anarchist activities in US, 19–21

Markel, Lester, 322

Marshall, George, as Army Chief of Staff, 165; as Secretary of State, 232, 286

Marshall, Chief Justice John, 187

Mason, Col. C.H., 147

The Masses, 56–58

May, Sam, 51

INDEX 371

Mayer, Louis, 239

McAdoo, Secretary of the Treasury William: and Secretary of State Bryan's request for Secret Service agents for intelligence work, 48–49; protest letter to Wilson regarding American Protective League, 54

McCabe, Col. E. R. Warner, 120

McCarran, Senator Pat: as author of Internal Security Act of 1950, 217; federal employee loyalty program, 231–32; Internal Security Act debate and enactment, 264–68; and Owen Lattimore, 270; resignation of UN Secretary General Trygve Lie, 299; wiretapping proposal, 303; supports censure of McCarthy, 308

McCarran Act, 217; and Internal Security Act debate and enactment, 264–68; Harry Cain's support of, 294

McCarthy, Senator Joseph Raymond: Army-McCarthy hearings and his political demise, 304–8; attacks on alleged communists in the federal workforce, 256–59; attacks on Owen Lattimore, and Lattimore's response, 259–61; Eisenhower's views on, 299–300; public attacks on George Marshall, 286; Tydings committee rebuke of, 261–62

McCauley, Commander Edward, Jr., 92

McCloy, Assistant Secretary of War John J.: blocks efforts to end Japanese American internment prior to 1944 presidential election, 200; concedes loyalty of Japanese Americans, 192; unconstitutional search and seizure proposal opposed by Attorney General Jackson, 153–54

McCormack, Rep. John W., as chairman of the Select Un-American Activities Committee, 97–99, 256

McCormack–Dickstein Committee, 95–99

McCormick, Robert, 179

McCullough, David, 222

McDonough, Rep. Gordon, 246

McDowell, Rep. John, and HUAC field hearings on alleged communists in the entertainment industry, 237–38

McDowell, Mary, 65

McGrath, Attorney General J. Howard: cautions Truman regarding potential civil liberties impacts of internal security bills, 263; confrontation with Senate over federal employee personnel and investigative files, 259–60

McIntyre, Marvin, 99, 117, 160, 194

McKinley, President William, assassination and aftermath, 2, 4–10, 20, 39–40, 349

McMichael, Rev. Jack, 324–25

McNamara, James, subpoenaed by HUAC, 298

McNamara, J.B., and *Los Angeles Times* bombing, 38

McNamara, J.J., and *Los Angeles Times* bombing, 38

McNarney, Lieutenant General Joseph, 192

Meitzenfeld, Otto, 64

Metcalfe, John, 109–10

Metcalfe, Secretary of the Navy Victor, 25

Miles, Brigadier General Sherman: March on Washington Movement, 159; monitoring of Senator Burton Wheeler's correspondence, 166–67; wartime detention planning, 156–57

Military Intelligence Division (MID), 48; alleged disloyal German American weekly "Suspect List" reports, 64–65; concerns over and surveillance of Black civil rights political activities, 155–56, 159–61, 203; domestic investigative workload, 70, 72; domestic mail surveillance, 123; intelligence collection on Bonus March participants, 83; FBI incompetence in Frankford Arsenal investigation, 120; investigations of German American workers, 162–63; Japanese American internment and censorship, 174–75; Japanese male tracking project, 101–2; investigation of alleged Japanese government conscription on US soil, 147; investigation of fencing clubs, 162; Pan American Clipper passenger surveillance, 114; participation in weekly WWI interagency surveillance conferences, 55; surveillance of Pete Seeger's mail, 189; surveillance of Black people in New York City, 93–94; surveillance of *New York Journal of Commerce* editor, 115; unhappiness with wiretapping limitations, 125, 303; use of DAR against National Council for Prevention of War, 75; wartime detention planning, 157; WWI Plant Protection Section, 55

Miller, Fred C., 64; citizenship status, 65

Mills, General Anson, in Nathan Boyd episode, 12–13

Milmore, J. Lewis, 32

Milwaukee Leader, 59

Mitchell, Clarence, 310

Mitchell, Senator John, 23

Moody, Attorney General William Henry, 16–17

Moore, Major F. M., 94

372 INDEX

Moran, William, 8, 53

Morgenthau, Secretary of the Treasury Henry, 109, 116, 125, 197

Moss, Rep. John, 286, 329–30

Multer, Rep. Abraham J., vote against Communist Control Act, 309

Mundt, Rep. (and later Senator) Karl: Alger Hiss episode, 257; Army-McCarthy hearings, 307–8, 316; concerns about Soviet subversion efforts in the US, 252; hearings on alleged communists in the entertainment industry, 239–41; Internal Security Act debate, 262–65; support for creation of HUAC, 227; work with Nixon to target CP USA, 245–47

Munson, Curtis, reports on Japanese American loyalty, 170–71, 174

Murphy, Charles, 262, 263

Murphy, Michael, 6

Murray, Phil, 181, 231

Muschinske, Alice, 178

Mussolini, Benito, 130, 225

Myer, Dillon, as WRA director, 200, 201

Myers, James, 99

Nardone v. United States: ACLU opposition to FDR's interpretation of, 317–18; Attorney General Jackson ignores Dies Committee violation of, 153; FBI wiretaps in Coplon case a violation of, 254; FDR orders Attorney General Robert Jackson to conduct wiretaps in violation of Supreme Court decision in, 125; Navy Judge Advocate General claims case does not apply to national security matters, 219–20; Supreme Court ruling affirming a statutory ban on wiretapping, 125, 180, 219, 253, 302; 352

National Association for the Advancement of Colored People (NAACP), 94; 1957 Civil Rights Act, 327–28; Detroit race riots of 1943, 194; 289; FBI interest in alleged Soviet influence or subversion of, 145, 156, 310–11, 320–21; federal surveillance of March on Washington Movement, 159–60, 203

National Civil Liberties Bureau (NCLB), 66, 89

National Committee to Defeat the Mundt Act, 265

National Negro Congress (NNC): formed to fight racism, 155; FBI and Army surveillance of, 155–56; and March on Washington Movement, 159–60

National Security Act of 1947, 251

National Security Agency Act (NSA Act) of 1959, 331–33

National Urban League, 94; FDR snubs over FBI allegations of CP USA links, 195–96; and March on Washington Movement, 159–60

Nazi/Nazism: allegations by FBI of support for March on Washington Movement, 159; allegations of America First Committee acting as propaganda arm of, 131; allegations of Virginia fencing club's ties to, 161–62; concerns over espionage threat presented by, 92, 106–8; creation of Axis Powers, 133–35; Dies Committee, 109–10; 112–13, 116; false allegations against and deportation of German American Jacobs family, 178; FBI and August Gausebeck episode, 124–25; 129; FBI's bungled Frankford Arsenal investigation, 119–20, 122; focus of McCormack-Dickstein Committee, 95–99; Foreign Agents Registration Act and, 242, 252; impact of allegations of Nazi sympathies on German American workers, 162–63; German immigrants in Milwaukee and, 172; proposed national gun confiscation scheme to combat, 157; Rep. Adolph Sabath demands FBI intern Nazis, 227; surveillance of German Americans for links to, 145, 148, 154

Nelson, Rep. John Edward, and minority views opposed to Fish Committee, 81–82

New, Senator Harry, and attempts to keep German immigrant from being seated as mayor of Michigan City, Indiana, 64

New York Sun, 33

New York Times: coverage of Emma Goldman's arrest post-McKinley assassination, 5; coverage of Nixon's attacks on CP USA, 246; coverage of Rep. James Roosevelt's attacks on HUAC, 337; coverage of Theodore Roosevelt's confrontation with Congress over Secret Service spying, 33; FBI informants in its newsroom, 322

New York World, 49

Nichols, FBI Assistant Director Louis, and confrontation with Jebby Davidson over FBI loyalty investigations of federal employees, 242–43

Niehbur, Reinhold, 327

Nippu Jiji, 174–75

Nixon, Rep. (and later Senator) Richard: as Eisenhower's VP and champion of outlawing CP USA, 300–303; encouragement from Hoover to investigate entertainment industry for communist subversion, 236; Hollywood-communist infiltration hearings, 237–41; as HUAC member investigating alleged communists in unions, 234–35; investigation of Alger Hiss as Society spy, 248–51; role in passage of the Civil Rights Act of 1957, 328; support for the Internal Security Act, 262–65; works with Mundt to target CP USA, 245–48

NKVD, 112–13, 116

Norris, Senator George, 123

Nye, Senator Gerald, and FBI surveillance of, 149–50, 180–81

Oahu, Hawaii, 104–5, 134, 175

O'Brian, John Lord, 55

O'Connell, Jerry J., 247

O'Conner, T.V., 78

O'Conor, Senator Herbert, 270

Office of Naval Intelligence (ONI), bureaucratic rivalries with FBI, MID, 117; characterization of the ACLU as a Communist-affiliated and Communist-aiding organization, 100–101; concern over alleged Japanese government conscription efforts on US soil, 147; domestic surveillance of Japanese regardless of nationality, 102–3, 167–70; domestic surveillance of allegedly subversive or foreign-connected domestic groups, 162–63; estimates on Japanese American loyalty, 167–69; FDR's use of during WWI, 92; investigation of alleged Japanese government attempts to foment racial unrest, 94; personnel turnover at, 115; Japanese American loyalty reports withheld from Supreme Court, 192; mail cover authority delegated to by FBI, 123; March on Washington Movement, 159; opposition to Bill Donovan as Coordinator of Information, 165; Niihau incident and Japanese American loyalty concerns, 173–74; role in Custodial Detention Program, 157; role in Pearl Harbor disaster, 332; Sperry Gyroscope anti-German American employment activities, 63; support for Palmer raids, 72; surveillance and informant penetration of Black civil rights groups, 203; surveillance and disruption operations aimed at Vietnam War protesters, 353–54; wartime domestic intelligence summaries, 183–85, 197–98; weekly interagency intelligence conferences during WWI, 55; wiretapping controversies, 125, 152–53, 266, 303, 352

Office of Personnel Management (OPM), 290

Office of Strategic Services (OSS), 228, 252

Office of War Mobilization and Reconversion (OWMR), 222

Ohta, Toshi Aline, 189

Olmstead v United States, 125, 352

Olney, Assistant Attorney General Warren, and wiretapping debate, 318

Oppenheimer, J. Robert, wiretapping target, 295–97

Ottenberg, Miriam, 250

Overman, Senator Lee, 52–53, 256

Pacific Citizen, 102, 170

Pacific Commercial Advertiser, 22, 44

Page, Charles Albert, 297

Palmer, Attorney General A. Mitchell, 70; and immigration raids controversy, 72–74, 76, 103, 154

Papen, Allen, and Post Office surveillance of Nathan Boyd, 14

Park, Clarence, and Secret Service surveillance of Nathan Boyd, 13–14

Parks, Rosa, 321, 326

Patterson, Undersecretary of War Robert, 153–54

Pauley, Edwin, 223

Pearl Harbor: attack as initial trigger for Japanese American internment plans, 352; Curtis Munson's Japanese American loyalty reports to FDR, 171–72, 191–92; failure of ONI to analyze Japanese consulate pre-attack intelligence tasking messages, 332–34; IJN agents' pre-attack surveillance of, 104; 117, 131; ONI Japanese American counterintelligence unit formed after attack on, 169; and Niihau incident, 173–74; effects on AFC, 179; post-attack success of Station Hypo codebreakers, 182, 199, 227, 294; wiretapping and microphone use domestically prior to attack on, 153

Pearson, Drew, and White House leak investigation, 222–23, 274

Pelley, William Dudley, and pro-fascist Silver Shirt movement as FBI and congressional target, 97–98, 110, 157

Pensacola Journal, 52

People's Voice: Adam Clayton Powell Jr. co-founder of, 198; as FBI surveillance target, 224–25

People's Voice (Montana), editorializes against HUAC entertainment industry communist witch hunt, 238

374 INDEX

Peress, Major Irving, and Army-McCarthy hearings, 305–8
Perkins, Secretary of Labor Frances, 158
Persons, General Wilton "Jerry," 286, 288
Pettigrew, Senator Richard Franklin, Wilson administration targeting of over anti-war, anti-surveillance views, 59–60
Pinchot, Amos, 56–57, 87
political radicals, as surveillance and political repression targets, 1, 12, 36–37, 55, 70, 72, 80, 83–84, 349
Polk, Frank, as State Department spymaster during WWI, 49
Post, Assistant Secretary of Labor Louis, and Palmer raids controversy, 72
Potter, Irvin L., 98
Powell, Rep. Adam Clayton, Jr.: as FBI surveillance target, 198, 224–28, 319; attacks Eisenhower over federally financed segregation policies, 309; pushes for passage of 1957 Civil Rights Act, 328; wife Hazel as HUAC target, 264–65
Powell, Hazel Scott, 225; as HUAC target, 264–65
Pritchard, Ensign Earl W., as Secret Service surveillance target, 25–26, 28–29, 40, 350
Pritchard, Ed, as Truman administration wiretap target, 222–23, 228, 245, 353
Provost Marshal General's Office (PMGO), 188
Purcell, James, 185
Purdin, W.H.P., 182

Quittner, Major Joseph, and MID surveillance project targeting Black population in New York City, 93–94

Rabb, Max: disputes with Senator Harry Cain over federal employee loyalty program, 311, 314; Hoover allegations of communist influence over MLK Jr., 327
race-based and ethnic surveillance and political repression, 93–95, 114, 135, 169, 172–79, 181–85, 191–92, 194, 198–200, 202–3; 224–28, 294, 353
Randolph, A. Philip: head of National Negro Congress, 145; leads March on Washington Movement, 159–61
Randolph, Rep. Jennings, and federal employee loyalty program, 229–30
Rankin, Rep. John E., and Hollywood communists witch hunt, 237–38, 241;

confrontation with Adam Clayton Powell Jr., 225–26, 226; saves HUAC, 217, 226–28
Ray, Rep. George, anarchist prohibition bill, 10
Reagan, Ronald, and Hollywood communist witch hunt, 239; and domestic surveillance, 355
Redman, Vice Admiral Joseph, and wiretapping controversy, 221
"Red Scare," 47, 69–73
Reed, John, opposition to Espionage Act, 56–57
Reilly, Michael, Truman rebuffs FBI agent, 224
Remington, William, alleged Soviet spy, 248
Reynolds, Pat, US v. Reynolds plaintiff, 292
Rhetts, C.E., Detroit race riot report, 194–95
Richards, J.K., McKinley assassination response speech, 9
Richardson, Seth, federal employee loyalty program controversy, 243–44, 260
Rickenbacker, Eddie, AFC co-founder, 149
Ringle, Lieutenant Commander Kenneth, Japanese American loyalty reports, 169–70, 174, 192
Robb, Assistant Attorney General Charles H., legality of mailing privilege exclusions, 17
Roberts, Justice Owen, Pearl Harbor attack report, 175
Roe, Gilbert, First Amendment lawyer, 57–58
Rogers, Attorney General William: internal security legislative proposals, 300, 302–3; praise for FBI's Hoover, 338, 341
Rogge, Assistant Attorney General O. John, guidance on civil liberties, 128
Rollins, Richard, undercover Congressional investigator, 97
Roosevelt, Eleanor: criticizes Truman's civil liberties record, 232; decries FBI's Gestapo-like tactics, 186; smeared by anti-communist group, 158
Roosevelt, Franklin Delano (FDR): abrogation of civil liberties, 99–101, 135–36; ascension to the presidency, 85, 92–93, 126; authorizes wiretapping in defiance of Supreme Court, 125; and communists, 106–7; firearms confiscation proposal, 157; interest in intelligence matters, 92–93, 117–18; and Japanese American internment, 174–77; 198–202; March on Washington Movement, 159–61; orders planning for concentration camps in Hawaii, 104; relationship with J. Edgar Hoover, 93, 106, 130, 180; use of private spymaster John Franklin Carter, 163–67,

181, 196–97, 202; vs. anti-interventionists, 129–30, 148–51; vs. Dies Committee, 108–13, 118–19, 157–59; wartime domestic political surveillance, 122–27, 129–30, 179–81

Roosevelt, Rep. James, opposition to HUAC, 334–38

Roosevelt, Theodore: anti-anarchism campaign, 8–12, 27; and creation of Bureau of Investigation, 28–29; interference in land frauds investigations, 23–25; Loeb's concerns over threats to, 19, 23; message to Congress on McKinley assassination, 9; orders investigation of De la Franier, 18–19; public criticism over Secret Service spying, 26–28, 32–34; rage over *Appeal to Reason* article, 16–19; and Secret Service investigation of California congressional delegation, 22; and surveillance of Nathan Boyd, 12–15; surveillance precedents set by, 1, 34

Rosenbergs, Ethel and Julius, and atomic spy ring, 263, 282, 295, 310, 304, 313, 332

Ross, Edward, wartime civil liberties concerns, 173

Ross, Lillian, *New Yorker* piece on Hollywood communists witch hunt, 241

Rothberg, Irwin, congressional investigator, 97

Rowe, James, wiretapping legislation controversy, 151

Ruick, Norman, surveillance of Senator Borah, 24–25

Russian revolution (1917), 69–70

Rustin, Bayard, FBI surveillance of, 327

Sabath, Rep. Adolph, opposition to HUAC's continuance, 227

Schenck, Charles, in *Schenck v. US*, 68

Schine, David, 305

Schofield, Lemuel, *121*

Schultze, Heinz, and MID German American bias, 162–63

Schwartz, Sidney, 35

Screen Writers Guild (SWG), and Hollywood "blacklist," 238–39

Secret Service Division (SSD), conflict with APL, 54; counterespionage operations prior to WWI, 48–53; during Spanish–American War, 50; Food and Fuel Control Act investigations, 62–63; surveillance of anarchists, 4, 20–22; surveillance of Earl Pritchard, 25–28; surveillance of German Americans, 48–53; surveillance of L.E. Bonneaud, 15–16;

surveillance of Nathan Boyd, 13–16, 28; surveillance of Senator William Borah, 23–25; War Trade Board investigations, 62–64; Western Union cooperation with, 53

Sedition Act of 1918, 47, 73

Senate Foreign Relations Committee, 168, 258–59

Senate Internal Security Subcommittee (SISS): anti-UN hearings, 298–300; impact of on Americans, 351–52; persecution of Owen Lattimore, 268–72; Senate companion to HUAC created, 265; targeting of Methodist Federation for Social Action, 324–26

Sexton, E.D., 65

SHAMROCK, NSA telegram surveillance program, 285, 332–33

Sharton, Alexander R., MID surveillance of, 115

Sherer, Rep. Gordon: and attacks on Methodist pastor, 325; as HUAC chairman, 337

Shirley, Rep. Joseph, opposition to SSD political surveillance, 26

Silberstein, Robert, 255

Silver, Edward, 331

Sino-Korean Peoples League, 146–47

Slack, Alfred Dean, and Soviet nuclear spy ring, 263

Slayden, 1Lt William, unpredicated interrogation of Heinz Schultze, 162–63

Smith, Senator Margaret Chase, moves against McCarthy, 261

Smith, Senator Willis, attacks Owen Lattimore, 270

socialists/socialism, 3, 68–69

Spanish–American War, 50

Spanish Civil War (1937–39), and Abraham Lincoln Brigade, 122, 186, 232, 240

Special Committee to Investigate Communist Activities (Fish Committee), United States, 79–82, 135, 237, 351

Sperry, Elmer, German American workers fired, 63–64

Sperry Gyroscope Company, 63–64; picketed for racial discrimination, 155

Spingarn, Stephen, White House aide, 262–64

Spruance, Admiral Raymond, 182

Stalin, Joseph, 223

Stettinius, Acting Secretary of State Edward, Jr., and Japanese American internment, 199

Steunenberg, Governor Frank, and alleged Idaho land frauds, 17, 23–24

376 INDEX

Stevens, Army Secretary Robert, and Army-McCarthy hearings, 305

Stiller, Bruno Victor, 178

Stimson, Secretary of War Henry: and Japanese American internment planning, 146–47; March on Washington Movement, 160–61; orders surveillance of Senator Wheeler's mail, 166–67; post-war wiretapping authority impasse, 220; support for wartime censorship, 162

Stokes, Isaac N.P., 242

Stokes, Rose Pastor, arrested for political speech, 65

Stone, Geoffrey, 10

String, Joe, murdered for political speech, 65

Stripling, Robert, HUAC chief of staff, 158–59, 248, 251

Stuart, Robert, AFC member, 179

Stuart, R. Douglas, Jr., AFC founder, 131

Subversive Activities Control Board (SACB): and AGLOSO, 294–95; and CP USA, 302, 308, 312, 321; created via McCarran Act, 265; Senator Cain and, 293–94

Sullivan, FBI Assistant Director William: and German Americans, 172; on Truman and Hoover, 221–22; and COINTELPRO, 322–23

Sumners, Hatton, 151

surveillance (domestic), 52–54, 101–6; ethnic, 93–95; and ethnic bias, 63–68; executive branch, 15–16; federal, 22–25; and infiltration, 19–22; and internment preparations, 133–35; racial, 93–95

Suspect List (MID), in WWI, 64–65

Swanson, Navy Secretary Claude, Japanese espionage concerns, 104–5

Sylvester, Major Richard, DC police and anarchists, 8

Taft, President William Howard, continuity with Roosevelt's surveillance policies, 34, 37–40

Talbert, Roy, Jr., 66

Taliaferro, S., anti-anarchist campaign recommendations, 6–7

Tamm, FBI Deputy Director Edward: authorizes military mail covers, 123; and internment policy, 120

Taylor, Robert, 239

Tavenner, Frank, as HUAC chief counsel, 267, 297

Tawney, Rep. Roger, 34

Teapot Dome scandal, 76, 149, 223

Tenth Amendment, 65, 111

Thomas, Rep. J. Parnell, as HUAC chairman, 234, 236, 256

Till, Emmett, murder of and protest aftermath, 320

Tomkins, 1Lt Floyd, Jr., and sweeping post-war surveillance proposals, 218–19

Trading with the Enemy Act (TWEA), 58–59, 73

Truman, President Harry: assumes the presidency, 217–18; Coplon wiretapping scandal, 254–56; McCarran Act and veto override, 262–64; confrontation with McCarthy over State Department employee loyalty, 256–62; distrust of FBI's Hoover, 221–22; expansion of domestic security state under, 271–73; and federal employee loyalty program, 228–34; internal opposition to loyalty program, 241–45; Silvermaster spy ring scandal, 249–50; veto of Taft-Hartley Act overridden, 238–39; wiretapping of Pritchard and Corcoran, 222–23

Turner, John, British trade union activist jailed, 11

Tydings, Senator Millard, and federal employee loyalty program, 259–62

Uniform Code of Military Justice (UCMJ), 288

United Mine Workers (UMW), 181

United Nations Human Rights Commission, 232

United Nations Technical Assistance Mission, 259

Urban League, 94; alleged communist connections, 195–96; and March on Washington Movement, 159

USS Texas battleship, grounding of, 92

Vail, Rep. Richard, CP USA ban bill, 236, 246

van Deman, Major Ralph, and revitalization of Army intelligence, 55, 86

Vann, J.W., 35

Vaughn, Harry, relationship with FBI's Hoover, 222–24, 229

Veterans of Foreign Wars (VFW): and Bonus March, 82; support for banning CP USA, 246

Viereck, George, 49

Vinson, Chief Justice Fredrick Moore, and "state secrets" decision, 292–93

Voice of America (VOA), 288–89

von Haake Cathcart, Hazel, 25

von Horn, Werner, 48

von Papen, Franz, expelled from US for espionage, 50, 110

INDEX 377

von Rintelen, Franz, German espionage agent, 49–50, 73

Voorhis, Rep. Jerry, as HUAC dissenter, 119

Wald, Lillian, co-founder of Anti-Militarism Committee, 52

Wallace, Vice President Henry, FBI surveillance of, 245, 247

Wall Street Journal, editorializes against wiretapping, 301

Walsh, Robert K., 271

Walz, William, 64

War Assets Administration, 224

Ward, Harry F.: criticizes FDR over ONI surveillance, 100; Dies Committee target, 118–19

War Department: Bonus March surveillance, 82; conflict over creation of Nisei military units, 182, 189; domestic surveillance of anti-military groups, 75; domestic unrest contingency War Plan WHITE, 160–61; internment operations transferred to Interior Department, 198–200; and Japanese internment, 156–57, 176–77; post-war surveillance legality impasse, 220–21; proposal to bar Japanese American employment in, 105; surveillance of Senator Wheeler's mail, 166–67, 181; unconstitutional search and seizure proposals, 153–54

Warner, Jack, 239–40

War Relocation Authority (WRA): created to oversee Japanese American internment, 176; internee unrest and violence, 193, 199; operations of, 190, 193

War Trade Board (WTB), 62–63

War Trade Intelligence (WTI), "blacklist" of allegedly disloyal firms, 63

Washington Evening Star: CP USA ban bill coverage, 247; FBI wiretapping allegations, 123; federal employee loyalty program coverage, 232, 236; Niihau Japanese American loyalty incident, 173; Secret Service spying scandal, 26; Silvermaster spy ring coverage, 248, 250, 263, 271

Watanabe, Faye, ONI surveillance of, 103

Watson, Edwin A. "Pa," FDR senior White House aide, 124, 158, 160, 161, 170, 173, 179, 181, 196

Watson, Goodwin B., Bill of Attainder target, 187

Watson, Senator James, 64

Weeks, Secretary of War John, seeks prosecution of WILPF, 75

Weeks vs. United States (232 U.S. 383 (1914)), as Fourth Amendment bypass, 50

Welker, Senator Herman, Communist Control Act cosponsor, 308

Wendelin, Eric, 168

Werner, John, illegal search and seizure victim, 71–72

Western Defense Command (WDC), and Japanese American internment, 183, 193, 200–201

Western Federation of Miners (WFM), Secret Service surveillance target, 16–17, 23, 28

Western Union Telegraph Company, covert cooperation with Secret Service, 53

Wheeler, Senator Burton K.: FDR targets with surveillance, 145, 148–50, 165–67, 181; target of BoI investigation, 76

White, Harry Dexter, member of Silvermaster spy ring, 248, 249

White, Walter, and NAACP as surveillance target, 145, 159–60, 194

White, Staff Sergeant William L., Wheeler anti-war post card recipient, 166

Wickersham, Attorney General George, 37

Wilkie, John, as Secret Service director, 8, 13, 14–15, 19–21, 23, 33–34

Wilkin, Judge Robert, and MFSA lawsuit against SISS, 325–26

Wilkinson, Frank, anti-HUAC activist, 334–36

Williamson, Senator John, land fraud investigation target, 23

Wilmington Morning Star, report on Army East Coast surveillance plans, 177

Wilson, Secretary of Labor William, opposition to Palmer raids, 72

Wilson, President Woodrow, 39; anti-German American rhetoric, 48–56, 67; attempted unconstitutional interference in local election, 64–65; and declaration of war against Germany, 53; refusal to pardon Debs, 73; signs Espionage Act into law, 55; and TWEA and FCA investigations, 62

wiretapping: Communications Act ban on, 125; Coplon episode scandal, 253–56; Dies Committee's unconstitutional use of, 151–53; fallout from Brownell's testimony on before SISS, 301–4; of German diplomats by Secret Service, 49; Hoover's opposition to judicial oversight of, 317–19; legislation to permit considered, 150–51; of Oppenheimer, 296; Senator Hennings hearings on, 330–31; violations of Communications Act involving, 125, 135, 202

378   INDEX

Wise, Rabbi Stephen, 52
Wishart, Alfred, 19–20
Women's International League for Peace and
  Freedom (WILPF), 75
Wood, Rep. John, as HUAC chairman, 268
Wood, General Robert, and AFC as FBI
  surveillance targets, 150, 179
Wood, Rep. William R., and Werner illegal search
  and seizure case, 72
Woodring, Secretary of War Harry: concerns
  over Imperial Japanese Navy espionage, 105;
  orders surveillance of people of "oriental" race,
  114–16
Works Progress Administration, 155
World War I: and Espionage Act, 47, 52–53,
  55–61, 63; and Food and Fuel Control Act,

47, 61–63, 67, 70, 73, 84, 350; German
  government espionage in America during,
  109–10; monitoring counterintelligence
  threats during, 120; political repression of
  German Americans, 50–51, 65–66, 70, 96,
  135; and Sedition Act, 65, 67, 73, 84,
  101, 350

Yasui, Minoru, Japanese internment victim and
  litigant, 184, 185, 191, 203
Young, Evan, State Department role in 1924
  election, 77

Zedong, Mao, 257
Zwicker, Brigadier General Ralph, and Army-
  McCarthy hearings, 305–7

ABOUT THE AUTHOR

Patrick G. Eddington is a senior fellow in homeland security and civil liberties at the Cato Institute. Eddington's opinion pieces have appeared in the *Washington Post, Los Angeles Times, Washington Times*, and elsewhere, and he has appeared on MSNBC, SKY News, CNN, and Fox News. **Eddington was a military analyst at the Central Intelligence Agency between 1988 and 1996**. From 2004 to 2014, he served as communications director and later as senior policy adviser to Rep. Rush Holt (D-NJ).

www.ingramcontent.com/pod-product-compliance
Ingram Content Group UK Ltd.
Pitfield, Milton Keynes, MK11 3LW, UK
UKHW011514100625
459515UK00004B/16